HISTORY OF THE CHURCH
THROUGH THE AGES

HISTORY OF THE CHURCH THROUGH THE AGES

From the Apostolic Age, through the Apostasies, the Dark Ages, the Reformation, and the Restoration

By ROBERT H. BRUMBACK

Wipf & Stock
PUBLISHERS
Eugene, Oregon

Wipf and Stock Publishers
199 W 8th Ave, Suite 3
Eugene, OR 97401

History of the Church through the Ages (Pricing is Net)
From the Apostolic Age, through the Apostasies, the Dark Ages,
the Reformation, and the Restoration
By Brumback, Robert H.
ISBN 13: 978-1-55635-196-9
ISBN 10: 1-55635-196-8
Publication date 2/21/2007
Previously published by Mission Messenger, 1957

DEDICATION

To Louise, my wife, whose love, help, and encouragement, have sustained me, this volume is affectionately dedicated.

THE AUTHOR

PREFACE

It is with a heart filled with admiration and thanksgiving that I present the author of this book. From the first time I heard the lectures on Church History it was my conviction they should be in print. Because many who avail themselves of the privilege of studying this course in Church History will not have the joy of face-to-face contact with the teacher, it is my joy to present him to you.

Robert H. Brumback, the son of John W. and Emma Goode Brumback, was born at Mystic, Iowa, May 31, 1892. The father was an evangelist of the church of Christ for almost forty-five years. It was he who first created in the son a desire to know something of the origin of the various denominations, a study which he has pursued for over forty years.

His evangelistic labors have been in the states of Iowa, Illinois, Indiana, Missouri, Oklahoma, Pennsylvania, Connecticut, Nebraska, Arizona, Arkansas, Colorado and California.

He possibly has one of the most complete libraries on Church History in the brotherhood, which includes some works that are very rare.

Brumback has had the opportunity of visiting some of the countries of Europe, Asia and Africa, devoting most of his time on the tour to countries that are directly connected with Bible History. His association with the people of those countries has given him a better understanding of their problems, their culture and customs.

I would like for you to know the author as I do. He is a kindly gentleman and always starts his remarks by saying, "Now I have no unkind feeling toward those who are present that might disagree with me." He is always able to distinguish between a system and those who profess it, between a creed, and the people, thus his war is against principles and not men.

The author has extracted material from hundreds of volumes and thousands of pages to bring you this documented work which he trusts all may have the means to purchase, the leisure to read and the disposition of mind to accept its truth.

May God bless all who peruse the pages of this book with a better knowledge of the one church of the Lord as revealed in the Book of Books, the Bible.

John L. Fleener

INTRODUCTION

The purpose of this volume is to tell in a simple and concise way the history of the greatest institution the world has ever known, the church of the Lord.

When first the writer prepared a general outline of the history of the church, it was for his own benefit. At the request of members of his home congregation the information was presented for their consideration. The interest created by the lessons brought requests from other congregations that they be presented there. Since that time they have been presented before congregations from coast to coast.

Brethren in various congregations suggested that the material which had been gathered over a period of years be put in book form and thus made available to the brotherhood.

The work of proclaiming the gospel and conducting Bible studies required so much of his time each year that the writer lacked opportunity to prepare the material for publication.

At the insistence of his fellow-laborer, Brother John Fleener, the writer agreed to undertake the work after he returned from his tour of the Bible Lands. As a student of church history for more than forty years, and a teacher of it for a third of that time, the author accepted the task cheerfully. He now admits that it has not been easy to search out the source of all the material he has presented in the lessons and document the information.

Confronting the author was the problem of what should be included and what should be excluded in a work of this kind. The reader may frequently be disappointed in failing to find the information for which he seeks, and may sometimes find information which he believes could have been left out.

So far as possible, proper credit has been given to all authorities and sources, ancient and modern. Some of the material, however, has been gathered from many works, over a period of years, and then edited, and it has not been possible to give proper credit since the author does not recall its source.

Indebtedness to many books and their authors is acknowledged, all of which are included in the bibliographical note.

This history is not designed to replace any other history of the church. The public has been well supplied with extensive works upon this subject, but in the study of them, the elementary student may become confused with the great amount of material presented, and lose interest. There are, too, numerous church histories which are so limited in the material presented that the very information desired is not available. The author trusts that this work shall find a place between the two types mentioned.

Church history is not identical with world history since a large part of the world was never subject to the church. Neither is it the same as religious history, for many religions exist separate and apart from the church established by Christ.

It is necessary, of course, to separate church history from secular history. This the author has endeavored to do, however, it has sometimes been necessary to relate incidents of secular history because of their relationship to the history of the church. As it is true that every American should have a knowledge of the history of America, so is it also true that every Christian should have a working knowledge of the history of the church. Next to the Bible every Christian should be interested in the history of the church.

As the reader studies the pages of this book he will be able to see the church for which our Lord died and will be able to distinguish it from those that have been established by men.

Jesus prayed that those who believed on him through the apostles' teaching might all be one.

The apostle Paul condemned division among those who professed to be the people of God, saying—

"And I brethren, could not speak unto you as unto spiritual, but as unto carnal, even as unto babes in Christ. I have fed you with milk, and not with meat; for hitherto ye were not able to bear it, neither yet now are ye able. For ye are yet carnal: for whereas there is among you envying, and strife, and divisions, are ye not carnal, and walk as men?" (1 Corinthians 3: 1-3).

The divisions that exist in the religious world are the result of following men instead of following Christ. May all who see the division and strife that exists among men be prompted to begin the study of God's word and led by its truth to obey the gospel of Christ and be added to the one body of Christ.

The Author

CHAPTER CONTENTS PAGE

ix

CHAPTER 1

ESTABLISHMENT OF CHRIST'S CHURCH

Church history deals with the establishment of Christ's church, its progress, its apostasy, its place during the dark ages, the Reformation and the Restoration. In pursuing the study of this subject, the structure, the worship and the doctrine of the NEW TESTAMENT church will be considered, as well as the heresies that swept the church into a midnight of darkness where it remained for twelve hundred and sixty years. It will be necessary also to give attention to the formation of some of the present day religious bodies.

Church history is not identical with world history since a large part of the world was never subject to the church. Neither is church history the same as religious history for many religions exist separate and apart from the church established by Christ.

In the period of time that preceded the coming of Christ, a large part of the then known world was pagan. Some nations worshipped the sun, moon, and stars. Other people bowed before idols and statues formed by their own hands. The Greeks and Romans had a deity for every purpose and in addition they worshipped the statue of the reigning ruler. Immoral practices also played a part in their religious service. The Jewish people, the chosen of God, sometimes followed the sins and the idolatry of the pagans until the punishment of God brought them back to the worship of Jehovah. Though the Jews were a despised nation, their religious services made a deep impression on the minds of the pagans, causing many of them to embrace the worship of God and accept the ceremonies set forth in the law of Moses.

The Old Testament reveals that the Jewish people often made alliances with the heathen nations around them and engaged in idol worship. The prophets of God warned them that God's judgment would come upon them for their disobedience. When they failed to return to the way of the Lord they became an oppressed and hated people. As the time approached for the long awaited Messiah of the prophets the sceptre of power had passed into the hands of the Romans. By the year 167 B.C. the Jews had established an independent monarchy, which continued until 63 B.C., when Pompey entered Jerusalem and established control over Palestine. All nations had been subdued and made a part of this far flung empire by the conquests of her victorious generals.

The struggles for power within the empire had ceased and peace and unity prevailed. Augustus Caesar was master of the world and his word and will were imposed upon all people. The Greek language was the universal language of the world. The splendid system of Roman roads, beginning at the milestone in the Forum, brought all parts of the empire within reach of the capital city.

This age was one in which culture, arts, and learning were given an important place, but morality and religion were at a low ebb. There was no sense of sin among the people. Immoral rites were part of the worship in many of the pagan temples. Under these conditions the long awaited Messiah was born into the world. Amid the darkness of that age he was the one ray of hope for mankind.

At the age of thirty years he entered upon his personal ministry, coming to John the Baptist to be baptized of him in the River Jordan. As Christ approached John said, "I have need to be baptized of thee, and comest thou to me?" Jesus said, "Suffer it to be so now to fulfill all righteousness."

Returning to Nazareth, he entered into the synagogue on the Sabbath and stood up to read. When he was handed the scroll of the law, he unrolled the parchment and found the place where it was written, "The Spirit of the Lord is upon me, because he hath anointed me to preach the gospel to the poor, he hath sent me to heal the broken hearted, to preach deliverance to the captives, and recovering of sight to the blind, to set at liberty them that are bruised, to preach the acceptable year of the Lord."[1]

Because of the searching nature of his teaching those present in the synagogue sought to put him to death by casting him headlong from a high cliff, but Christ passed through their midst and escaped out of their hands. From this time Christ made his home in Capernaum on the sea of Galilee. Here he called some of his disciples to follow after him. For three years he walked the paths of Judea, Samaria, and Galilee healing the infirm, opening the eyes of the blind, and preaching the gospel of the coming kingdom.

One day, near Caesarea Philippi, Christ asked his disciples, "Whom do men say that I, the Son of man, am?" And they answered, "Some say that thou art John the Baptist; some Elias; and others, Jeremiah or one of the prophets." Which answer was right they did not profess to know. Christ again asked, "Whom say ye that I am?" Quickly Peter answers, "Thou art the Christ, the Son of the living God." After pronouncing a blessing upon Peter, Christ added that upon this rock, the truth that he was the Christ,

1. Luke 4: 18, 19

he would build his church and all the forces of hell would not prevent him doing so. When he came to Jerusalem for the last time near the close of his ministry, the chief priests conspired to put him to death. Then followed the betrayal, the mock trial, after which Christ was led away to the agony and death of crucifixion. There on Calvary's cross he shed his blood, drank the cup of wrath to its bitter dregs and died the death of condemnation, paying the price of man's redemption.

His disciples tenderly removed his body from the cross and placed it in Joseph's new tomb. Three days later he arose from the dead and for forty days he taught his disciples the things that pertained to the kingdom of God. At the end of this time he led his disciples out to the Mount of Olives and while they looked on Him, he was caught up into the air and a cloud received him out of their sight. In obedience to his command his disciples continued in Jerusalem, waiting for the promise of the Holy Spirit which was to guide them into all truth. On the day of Pentecost the Holy Spirit came and endued them with power from on high and they proclaimed the first gospel sermon and three thousand were by the Lord added to the church and from that time henceforth we have the church of Christ in existence.

There is much confusion in the world concerning the establishment of the church. Some have contended that it has existed since the days of Abraham; others say that it was established by John during his ministry; while others contend that it was not established until after the death of Christ and his ascension into heaven.

33 A. D. THE ESTABLISHMENT OF THE CHURCH AT JERUSALEM

Shortly before Christ went to Jerusalem for the last time he said, "Upon this rock I will build my church and the gates of hell shall not prevail against it."[2] This definitely establishes the fact that the church of Christ was not established prior to that time. In the book of Zechariah we have a prophetic statement concerning the time when Christ would build the temple of the Lord and when he would begin his reign, "Speak unto him saying, 'Thus speaketh the Lord of hosts, saying, Behold the man whose name is The BRANCH; and he shall grow up out of his place, and he shall build the temple of the Lord; even he shall build the temple of the Lord; and he shall bear the glory, and shall sit and rule upon his throne; and he shall be a priest upon his throne; and the counsel of peace shall be between them both.' "[3]

This is a prophetic statement concerning Christ. It teaches that

2. Matthew 16 : 18
3. Zechariah 6 : 12, 13

THE CHURCH OF CHRIST IN PROPHECY

DANIEL 7:13	MARK 9:1	LUKE 22:30	DANIEL 2:31-45	ZECH. 6:12, 13
Son of man to receive dominion, glory and a Kingdom (Matt. 25:31)	Disciples to live to see kingdom come with power (Mark 9:1)	Lord's table to be in his kingdom—Apostles eat and drink at Lord's table (I Cor. 10:16-21)	Babylonian 604-536 B.C.	Church to be built when Christ is upon his throne, when he reigns as king and serves as high priest
Did Christ receive dominion and glory? (Rev. 1:6; Col. 1:13)	Power to come with Holy Spirit (Acts 1:8)	Christ reigns over his kingdom now (I Cor. 15:24; Isa. 2:2-4)	Medo-Persian 536-331	1. Acts 2:30
	Holy Spirit came in Jerusalem (Acts 2:4)		Greek 331-323	2. Rev. 11:15
	Church established (Acts 2:47)		Roman 146	3. Heb. 4:14; Heb. 7:22 I Cor. 3:16
			God's kingdom established (Dan. 2; Luke 3:1; Matt. 3:1)	

Christ shall sit and rule upon his throne. If we can learn when Christ began to sit, then we know when he began to rule, for he was to sit and rule when seated on this throne. Now when did Jesus begin to sit? "Therefore being a prophet and knowing that God had sworn with an oath to him, that of the fruit of his loins, according to the flesh, he would raise up Christ to sit on his throne."[4] Since Christ was to sit and rule on David's throne, he is now ruling. But at the same time that he rules he is to be a priest on his throne.

The writer of the book of Hebrews tells us that he is ascended into the heavens where he officiates as our great high priest. "Seeing then that we have a great high priest, that is passed into the heavens, Jesus the Son of God, let us hold fast our profession, For we have not an high priest which cannot be touched with the feeling of our infirmities; but was in all points tempted like as we are, yet without sin."[5]

Christ was to be a priest upon his throne at the same time that he rules. But when was the temple of the Lord to be built? At the same time that Christ sits upon his throne and reigns as king and serves as a priest. Peter, on the day of Pentecost, declared that Christ was seated upon his throne. Then this is the time when the temple of the Lord, his church, had its beginning. Why is the church spoken of as the temple of the Lord? Because it is in the church that we render worship and adoration to God. When Paul addressed the church in Corinth he said, "Ye are the temple of the living God; as God has said, I will dwell in them, and walk in them; and I will be their God, and they shall be my people."[6]

Isaiah foretold the establishment of the church in the city of Jerusalem. "And it shall come to pass in the last days, that the mountain of the Lord's house shall be established in the top of the mountains, and shall be exalted above the hills; and all nations shall flow unto it. And many people shall go and say, Come ye, and let us go up to the mountain of the Lord, to the house of the God of Jacob; and he will teach us of his ways and we will walk in his paths: for out of Zion shall go forth the law, and the word of the Lord from Jerusalem."[7] Isaiah speaks of the Lord's house as being established in the last days. He further states that all nations shall flow into it and that its beginning would be in Jerusalem. On the day of Pentecost the apostle Peter said the very time in which he spoke was the last days, "This is that which was spoken by the prophet Joel; and it shall come to pass in the last days saith God, I will pour out of my Spirit upon all flesh and your sons and your

4. Acts 2 : 30
5. Hebrews 4 : 14, 15
6. 2 Corinthians 6 : 16
7. Isaiah 2 : 2-3

daughters shall prophesy and your young men shall see visions and your old men shall dream dreams."[8]

All nations were to flow into it and the writer of the book of Acts tells us that men out of every nation were assembled in Jerusalem on Pentecost. "And there were dwelling at Jerusalem Jews, devout men, out of every nation under heaven."[9] The last verse of the second chapter of the book of Acts tells us, "And the Lord added to the church daily such as should be saved."[10] The house of God described by Isaiah is nothing other than the church, for Paul said, "These things write I unto thee, hoping to come unto thee shortly: but if I tarry long, that thou mayest know how thou oughtest to behave thyself in the house of God, which is the church of the living God, the pillar and ground of the truth."[11] The apostle Peter addressed his message to the people living in Jerusalem and they for the first time heard the message of salvation, the gospel of Christ, on the day of Pentecost. "Thus it is written, and thus it behooved Christ to suffer, and to rise from the dead the third day: And that repentance and remission of sins should be preached in his name among all nations, beginning at Jerusalem."[12] When was it that repentance and remission of sins was preached in the city of Jerusalem? It was on the day of Pentecost. "Therefore let all the house of Israel know assuredly, that God hath made that same Jesus, whom ye have crucified, both Lord and Christ. Now when they heard this, they were pricked in their heart, and said unto Peter and to the rest of the apostles, 'Men and brethren what shall we do?' Then Peter said unto them, 'Repent and be baptized everyone of you in the name of Jesus Christ for the remission of sins and ye shall receive the gift of the Holy Ghost.' "[13] This day, and this day alone, fills the divine requirements of the prophecy of Isaiah foretelling the establishment of Christ's church.

---

8. Acts 2 : 16, 17
9. Acts 2 :5
10. Acts 2 : 47
11. 1 Timothy 3 : 15
12. Luke 24 : 46, 47
13. Acts 2 : 36-38

CHAPTER 2

THE CHURCH IN THE APOSTOLIC AGE

The church of Christ was established by the apostles under the direction of the Holy Spirit. It was a divine institution built upon the foundation of the apostles and prophets, with Christ as the chief cornerstone. "Now therefore ye are no more strangers and foreigners, but fellow citizens with the saints, and of the household of God; and are built upon the foundation of the apostles and prophets, Jesus Christ himself being the chief corner stone."[1]

This was the only church established by the Lord as a means of saving the world. In the scriptures it is referred to as "the church." "And he is the head of the body, the church: who is the beginning, the first-born from the dead; that in all things he might have the preeminence."[2] It is sometimes called the church of God. "Take heed therefore unto yourselves, and to all the flock, over which the Holy Ghost hath made you overseers, to feed the church of God, which he has purchased with his own blood."[3] This, of course, refers to Christ. When Paul spoke of the church throughout the regions where he had traveled he said, "The churches of Christ salute you."[4] Any one of these terms may be used to designate the church.

The people who became disciples of Christ were called Christians. "And the disciples were called Christians first in Antioch."[5] This name showed they were followers of Christ. It was not given in derision as some have asserted, for it was recognized by the men who wrote by inspiration, as a divinely given name. "Yet if any man suffer as a Christian, let him not be ashamed; but let him glorify God on this behalf."[6] The church was a group of believers who were obedient to the commands of Christ as taught by the apostles. As the number of disciples increased, elders or bishops were appointed in each congregation. "And when they had ordained them elders in every church, and had prayed with fasting, they commended them to the Lord, on whom they believed."[7] The

---

1. Ephesians 2:19, 20
2. Colossians 1:18
3. Acts 20:28
4. Romans 16:16
5. Acts 11:26
6. 1 Peter 4:16
7. Acts 14:23

THE STRUCTURE, WORSHIP AND WORK OF THE APOSTOLIC CHURCH

1. CHRIST THE HEAD — No conferences, no associations

2. ELDERS, DEACONS, EVANGELISTS, MEMBERS — No presiding elders, no archbishops

3. GUIDED BY APOSTLES' DOCTRINE — No creeds, no church manuals

4. THE CHURCH SELF-EDIFYING — No clergy, no prelates

5. THE LORD'S SUPPER EVERY LORD'S DAY — No yearly or quarterly observances

6. THE CHURCH GAVE AS PROSPERED — No pledges, no assessments

7. PSALMS, HYMNS, SPIRITUAL SONGS — No mechanical music

8. PRAYERS AND THANKSGIVING — No vain repetitions, no liturgy

9. ALL TEACHING SUPPLIED THROUGH THE CHURCH — No theological schools

10. ALL AID GIVEN BY THE CHURCH — No institutions to supplement the church

word "elder" signified one who was older, a man of age and experience. The elders' work was to oversee the congregation, hence they were also called "bishops." When the apostle Paul spoke to the elders from Ephesus, he said, "Take heed therefore unto yourselves, and to all the flock over which the Holy Ghost hath made you overseers, to feed the church of God, which he hath purchased with his own blood."[8]

When Paul wrote to Titus, an evangelist of the church, he said "For this cause left I thee in Crete, that thou shouldest set in order the things that are wanting, and ordain elders in every city, as I had appointed thee: If any be blameless, the husband of one wife, having faithful children not accused of riot or unruly. For a bishop must be blameless, as the steward of God—"[9] These scriptures show that the words "elder" and "bishop" are used to describe the same official in the church. We notice also that these officers were over individual congregations. Deacons, selected by the congregation, were also appointed by the evangelists. They looked after temporal affairs of the church, seeing that the needs of those who were in distress were supplied. Attention is also called to the work of an evangelist. He was to set in order things that were lacking and to ordain elders in every church who were to feed the flock and to admonish those under their oversight.

No teaching of the scripture instructs evangelists to become a permanent integral part of the congregation to take over the work of the elders. The elders or bishops, the deacons, and the evangelists were the only officers of the church. An ecclesiastical hierarchy within the church was unknown. This may seem strange when one considers the multiplicity of church officials in the various religious organizations, denominations, and groups that exist in the world today, but in the New Testament these men are the only officials authorized.

> "There was no complex constitution, no studied distribution of powers, no sharp distinction of ranks. Each congregation, like a patriarchal tribe, like a Hebrew village, like a synagogue had its elders. Some were to preside in the assembly, leading and feeding the flock, others to serve in the communion of the saints, almoners for the church to the needy, comforters of the afflicted. Bishops or deacons—they were the servants of the community, not lords over it. In a brotherhood where all were kings and priests unto God, no elder was king over his brethren or stood as a priest between them and the Father of their Lord Jesus Christ."*

---

8. Acts 20 : 28
9. Titus 1 : 5-7
* *Genesis of the New England Churches*—Bacon.
Chapter 1, Pages 32, 33.

In discussing the structure of the church of the New Testament, an accepted authority said this,

> "To aid them in their work or to supply their places in their absence, the apostles ordained rulers in every church, who bore the common name of elders—presbuteroi, from their dignity, and of bishops—episkopoi, from the nature of their office.
>
> That originally the presbuteroi were the same as the episkopoi we gather with absolute certainty from the statements of the New Testament and of Clement of Rome, a disciple of the apostles. (See his First Corinthian Epistle—Chapters 42, 44, 57. The elders are expressly called episkopoi—Titus 1: 5-7.) Similarly the elders are represented as those to whom alone the rule, the teaching, and the care of the church is entrusted. In the face of such indisputable evidence, it is difficult to see how the Romish and Anglican theologians insist that these two offices had from the first been different in name and function."*
>
> "Irenaeus often uses the two terms presbyteri and episcopi as exactly equivalent; he argues in the same way with respect to the successiones of the presybteri and the successiones of the episcopi; he even calls the bishops of Rome presbyteri and unhesitatingly gives the office of the presbyters the name episcopatus. In agreement with this we find that no strict line of demarcation subsisted as yet between the functions exercised by the bishop and those of the presbyters; on the one hand, nothing might be done in the congregation against the will of the bishop; baptisms and ordinations could not be performed without his sanction. But, on the other hand, the presbyters also had power to perform both rites, which could scarcely have been the case if any essential distinction between their office and that of the bishop had been conceived to exist. Such appears the relation of the two orders in a canon of the synod of Ancyra in the year 314. There is reference to the same state of matters in a resolution of the Fourth Council of Carthage in 398, which commands that, at the ordination of a presbyter, all the presbyters and the bishop shall together lay their hands on the head of the candidate. This can only have been an ancient custom, derived from the time when presbyters and bishops were on an equality."†

In the beginning the church was guided by the apostles teaching personally such things as were necessary for the well being of the body of Christ. Later the apostles wrote letters to the various congregations and admonished them to give heed to the written word. "And they continued steadfastly in the apostles' doctrine and fellowship, and in breaking of bread, and in prayers."[10] When Paul wrote to the church in Thessalonica he said, "Therefore, brethren stand fast, and hold the traditions which ye have been taught, whether by word, or our epistle."[11] In the days of the apostles there

* *Text Book of Church History*—Kurtz. Section—The Primitive Church, Pages 67, 68.
† *The Church History of the First Three Centuries*—Baur. Volume 2, Chapter 1, Page 24.
10. Acts 2 : 42
11. 2 Thessalonians 2 : 15

was no such thing as a written creed or confession of faith. Indeed they were not needed for the Savior had promised the apostles the Holy Spirit to guide them into all truth. "Howbeit when he, the Spirit of truth, is come, he will guide you into all truth; for he shall not speak of himself; but whatsoever he shall hear, that shall he speak; and he will show you things to come."[12] The promise was fulfilled for the apostle Peter said that all things that pertain to life and godliness had been given unto us. "According as his divine power hath given unto us all things that pertain unto life and godliness, through the knowledge of him that hath called us to glory and virtue."[13] The apostle Paul confirmed what Peter had stated by calling attention to the purpose of the inspired writings, "All scripture is given by inspiration of God, and is profitable for doctrine, for reproof, for correction, for instruction in righteousness; that the man of God may be perfect, throughly furnished unto all good works."[14] Thus it is evident that the church was guided by the apostles' teaching while they were on earth, but the Lord knowing they would not always be here, inspired them to put into writing the things that were profitable for doctrine and that pertained to life and godliness. No church of the New Testament had a human creed or confession of faith for its guidance. They had the apostles' doctrine. When the church assembled they were able to admonish and to edify one another. "And I myself also am persuaded of you, my brethren, that ye also are full of goodness, filled with all knowledge, able also to admonish one another."[15]

This was not done by proxy. The body was able to edify itself. "But speaking the truth in love, may grow up into him in all things, which is the head even Christ; From whom the whole body fitly joined together and compacted by that which every joint supplieth, according to the effectual working in the measure of every part, maketh increase of the body unto the edifying of itself in love."[16] The church of the days of the apostles was able to function without the assistance of a one man pastor to supply the spiritual food.

The members were able to attend to all of the work of the Lord's house. They are revealed as being able to edify themselves, to exhort and to admonish one another to faithfulness and to do all of the work of the church without the aid of a preacher.

The purpose for which they came together was to remember the life, death, and resurrection of the Redeemer of mankind. To enable them to keep in remembrance these facts Christ instituted

---

12. John 16:13
13. 2 Peter 1:3
14. 2 Timothy 3:16
15. Romans 15:14
16. Ephesians 4:15, 16

a simple memorial, saying, "This do in remembrance of me." The early church carried out his instruction, for "upon the first day of the week the disciples came together to break bread." There is no mention in the scriptures of a quarterly communion, of a ritualistic service in connection with this simple institution.

There is no apostolic example that it was ever observed on Thursday, Friday, or Saturday. Some religious groups observe this memorial once a month, others observe it every three months, and others once a year, asserting that the scriptures do not say they observed it upon the first day of EVERY week. No religious group thinks of questioning the propriety of taking up a collection on the first day of every week, yet the same Bible that authorizes the collection on the first day of every week, authorizes the Lord's supper upon the first day of every week, for they were observed together by the church under the guidance of the apostles' doctrine.

The singing of the church was a part of its teaching and admonishing, for Paul said, "Teaching and admonishing one another in psalms, and hymns and spiritual songs, singing with grace in your hearts to the Lord."[17] In the worship of the church the use of such songs and of such melody is as old as the church; but the use of mechanical music is not, for there is no example or teaching in the New Testament that authorizes its use. Here is the picture of the church as revealed in the scriptures.

From the beginning the church continued to grow and prosper. "And the word of God increased; and the number of the disciples multiplied in Jerusalem greatly; and a great company of the priests were obedient to the faith."[18] The religious fervor of the apostles amazed the Jewish nation. Cities of commercial importance and centers of pagan worship heard the gospel of Christ proclaimed in its purity and simplicity.

The religion of Christ opposed the carnality of paganism. It was in open conflict with the human philosophy of that age. It demanded complete separation from all things of a worldly nature and complete devotion to the cause of the Lord Jesus. By these things it aroused bitter hatred among the people of that age, yet it continued to grow and spread until eventually it controlled the thoughts and actions of the world of mankind.

---

17. Colossians 3:16
18. Acts 6:7

64 A.D. THE BEGINNING OF THE PERSECUTION OF CHRISTIANS BY THE ROMAN EMPERORS

Because the church recognized that the authority of Christ was above all other authority, the emperors of the Roman empire and the pagan priests began a series of persecutions against the followers of Christ.

The pagan priests had appealed to the Roman rulers to stop the spread of Christianity. They called it a strange superstition which had fastened itself upon the cities and the open country as well.

The first persecutions directed against the church were brought against it by the Jews, but from the year 64 A.D. the Roman authorities began to persecute the Christians, putting them to death in every way their cruelty could devise.

> "And in their deaths they were made the subjects of sport; for they were covered with skins of wild beasts and worried to death by dogs, or nailed to crosses, or set fire to, and, when day declined, burned to serve for nocturnal lights."*

The blood of the martyrs was the seed of the kingdom. The more severe the persecution, the more willing the Christians were to die for their faith in Christ, the Son of God.

The prejudice and fury of the pagans was directed against the Christians. They had become alarmed at the progress of Christianity and employed the sword, wild beasts and imprisonment in an effort to blot from the face of the earth the Christian religion.

70 A.D. THE DESTRUCTION OF JERUSALEM BY TITUS

While the persecution of Christians and internal strife occupied the attention of the emperors in Rome the Jews in Palestine revolted. Vespasian raised an army to deal with the insurrection. He laid siege to the city of Jerusalem hoping to be able to take the city in a short time. Learning of the hatred of the people of Rome against Vitellius, the emperor, he sent an army under two of his ablest generals to assist in the overthrow of that ruler. A fierce battle was fought outside of the walls of the city. Vespasian's army was victorious and he was immediately proclaimed emperor. Vitellius was beaten to death by the clubs of the soldiers and his body was dragged through the streets of the city and then thrown into the Tiber River. When this information was conveyed to Vespasian he transferred the leadership of the army to his son Titus, and he hastened to Rome to assume his duties as ruler of the empire. When the engines of war had battered down the walls of Jerusalem on the west and the north Titus gave command to his soldiers to

* *History of Christianity*—Abbott—Chapter 9. Page 220.

grant no quarter but to go from house to house and from street
to street putting all to death.

When the city was completely taken and the Roman soldiers
began to seek for plunder they came upon such scenes of suffering
that they turned away from looting the homes of the dead.

"When they were come to the houses to plunder them, they found
in them entire families of dead men, and the upper rooms full of
corpses, that is, of such as died by the famine, that they stood in
a horror of this sight and went out without touching anything."*

Thousands of the captives were put to death by crucifixion in
fulfillment of the imprecation they placed upon themselves when
they said to Pilate, as they sought the death of Christ, "His blood
be on us, and on our children." Others were sold into captivity
to fulfill the words of Moses, "There ye shall be sold unto your
enemies for bondmen and bondwomen, and no man shall buy you."[19]
In the destruction of Jerusalem no Christians perished. The Savior
said, "When ye shall see Jerusalem compassed with armies, then
know that the desolation thereof is nigh. Then let them which are
in Judea flee to the mountains; and let them which are in the
midst of it depart out; and let not them that are in the countries
enter thereinto."[20] After the Roman armies surrounded Jerusalem
they met with such strong resistance that they withdrew to the
west and thus the Christians were given an opportunity to escape.
They then fled to Pella beyond Jordan and thus escaped the suffering that was inflicted upon the Jewish populace in the fall of the
city of Jerusalem.

Titus, laden with the spoils of war returned to Rome, bringing
with him eighty thousand Jewish captives whom he compelled to
build the Colosseum. His great victory strengthened the throne
of his father, Vespasian. To commemorate his success in bringing
all Judea again under the control of Rome a great triumphal arch
was erected.

This arch, built nineteen hundred years ago, still stands. It is
one of the chief attractions for tourists in the city of Rome.

Under the reign of Vespasian there was very little persecution
of the Christians, but when his son Domitian came to the throne
following the death of Titus, a bitter persecution was launched
against Christians.

The hatred of the emperor brought about the arrest of thousands.
Many of these were put to death by torture. Others were sacrificed
to wild beasts in the arena of the Colosseum. In this persecution
the aged apostle John was banished to the isle of Patmos.

* The Wars of The Jews—Josephus. Book 6, Chapter 8, Section 5, Page 685.
    19. Deuteronomy 28:68
    20. Luke 21:20, 21

96 A.D. NERVA BECAME EMPEROR
FOLLOWING THE DEATH OF DOMITIAN

Nerva ended the persecution of Christians. The prisons which had been filled with those who were to be put to death were emptied. All who had been exiled were invited to return. Nerva issued a decree prohibiting the persecution of any one on account of his religious faith.

The government of Rome under Domitian was despotic in form. Nerva changed it to a constitutional monarchy which lessened taxes, recalled political exiles, and provided for the support of poor children in Roman cities at public cost. He adopted Trajan, the commander of legions in Germany, as his son, who succeeded him.

With the ascension of Trajan, persecutions were renewed against the Christians and continued from that time, with little interruption, to the reign of Diocletian.

The followers of Christ opposed all worship except that which was offered to God and Christ. The pagan priests were willing to place a statue of Christ in the Pantheon at Rome by the side of the most important gods. The Christians rejected the offer, refusing to have Christ thought of as only another god.

Idol worship was a part of the very life of Rome. Every home had their household gods before whom sacrifices were offered daily. All feasts and festivals called for the citizens to bow in worship before the statues of the gods. This the Christians refused to do. This caused them to be considered as atheists who rejected all gods. To bow in worship before the statues of the emperor was considered an indication of one's loyalty to the reigning sovereign. The refusal of the Christians to bow in adoration to an idol resulted in them being considered as unfaithful subjects.

> "Under Trajan, too, we hear the ominous cry, 'The Christians to the lions.' There was no security against the rage of Jews or heathen. The aged Symeon, bishop of Jerusalem, is said to have been crucified to gratify the former; the fury of the populace at Antioch caused Ignatius to be torn by lions in the coliseum as a spectacle for the latter."[*]

In the face of such persecution Christianity grew and flourished. Persons of wealth and position turned from paganism to embrace Christianity. Those who came from paganism sought to bring into the church the images, the oblations, and ritualism that had been connected with the old system of religion. During the lifetime of the apostles they kept the church pure. Warnings had been given against departing from the faith once delivered to the saints. "Now the Spirit speaketh expressly, that in the latter times some shall

---

[*] *History of the Christian Church*—Cheetham—Chapter 3, Page 40.

depart from the faith, giving heed to seducing spirits, and doctrines
of devils; speaking lies in hypocrisy; having their conscience seared
with a hot iron."[21] The faithfulness of the church to the teaching
of Christ, as delivered by the apostles, was unchanged until near
the close of the apostolic age. As the apostles approached the time
when they would leave the world, they warned of the false teachers
who would attempt to destroy the faith once delivered to the saints.
"For I know this, that after my departing shall grievous wolves
enter in among you, not sparing the flock. Also of your own selves
shall men arise, speaking perverse things, to draw away disciples
after them."[22] "But there were false prophets also among the people,
even as there shall be false teachers among you, who privily shall
bring in damnable heresies, even denying the Lord that bought
them, and bring upon themselves swift destruction."[23] As this
apostasy developed, human philosophy and paganism crept into the
church and it became difficult for the church to preserve the simplicity of the gospel, the purity of the worship and the form of
government that existed in the church in the beginning.

Practices that were unauthorized by God's word began to be
added to the worship. The Lord's supper became the object of a
ritualistic ceremony that included with it the teaching that Christ's
sacrifice was enacted with every observance of this institution.

The first change in the government of the church was an easy
one to make. When difficulties arose in the small congregations the
older congregations were called upon to assist in correcting such
matters. Groups of elders would come together in solemn assembly
to render a decision. One elder would be selected to preside over
the meeting. He was called the bishop. His voice would be the
deciding one in matters of discipline.

Special honors were conferred upon the bishops. They were
exalted above their fellow servants. Soon men were seeking for this
place of preeminence and authority. The bishops began to assume
powers that were not vested in them by the scriptures.

"That the name "episkopoi" or bishops was altogether synony-
mous with that of presbyters, is clearly evident from those passages
of scripture, where both appellations are used interchangeably. Acts
20: compare verse 17 with verse 28, Titus 1: 5 compare with verse
7, and from those where the office of deacon is named immediately
after that of bishop, so that between these two church offices there
could not still be a third intervening one."*

"The societies which were instituted in the cities of the Roman
Empire were united only by the ties of faith and charity. Indepen-

21. 1 Timothy 4:1, 2
22. Acts 20:29, 30
23. 2 Peter 2:1
* *History of The Christian Religion and Church*—Neander—Section 2, Page 185.

GOVERNMENT OF CHRIST'S CHURCH

ELDERS TO RULE
DEACONS TO SERVE

APOSTASY STARTED WHEN ONE
ELDER WAS CALLED "THE BISHOP"

THIS DESTROYED THE DIVINE
PLAN OF CHURCH GOVERNMENT
AND LED TO CORRUPTION OF

1. Doctrine
2. Worship
3. Work

THIS CONDITION WAS CAUSED BY

1. Lack of knowledge
2. Desire for pre-eminence
3. Plans for a new worship

GOVERNMENT OF APOSTATE CHURCH

ELDERS, LATER CALLED PRIESTS
RULED OVER LOCAL CONGREGATIONS

BISHOPS PLACED OVER ELDERS
1. Country bishops over rural congregations
2. Metropolitan bishops over city congregations

METROPOLITANS BECAME ARCHBISHOPS
OVER DIOCESAN CONGREGATIONS

BECAME PATRIARCHS IN
Antioch
Ephesus
Alexandria
Constantinople
Rome

UNIVERSAL BISHOP OVER ALL
CHURCHES—LATER BECAME POPE

dence and equality formed the basis of their internal constitution. The want of discipline and human learning was supplied by the occasional assistance of the prophets who were called to that function without distinction of age, of sex, or of natural abilities . . . The public functions of religion were solely intrusted to the established ministers of the church, the bishops, and the presbyters; two appellations which, in their first origin, appear to have distinguished the same office and the same order of persons. The name 'presbyter' was expressive of their age or rather of their gravity and wisdom. The title of 'bishop' denoted their inspection over the faith and manners of the Christians who were committed to their pastoral care. In proportion to the respective numbers of the faithful a larger or smaller number of these episcopal presbyters guided each infant congregation with equal authority and united counsels."*

Apostasy developed, the authority of the Word of God was rejected, an ecclesiastical hierarchy began to form by which the church was swept into a midnight of darkness where it remained for twelve hundred years. This change in the government of the church began shortly after the death of the apostles. As the influence of the gospel began to be felt in the surrounding communities, other congregations were formed in the country. It became the practice of the bishops of the parent congregation to select an elder from the city church to look after the spiritual welfare of several of these rural churches.

These elders were designated as the country bishops, while those who had charge of the city churches came to be known as the Metropolitans.

Following this the bishops in each of the centers of religious influence thought they should be held in higher esteem than the Metropolitans, so the bishops in Alexandria, Antioch, Jerusalem, Constantinople and Rome were called Patriarchs. That this practice was a departure from the divine plan is evident, for Polycarp, a disciple of the apostle John, writing to the church at Philippi about the mutual duties of office bearers and people, refers only to presbyters and deacons, indicating that there was no bishop (separate from the elders) in the church at Philippi. This change in the government of the church brought about changes in the doctrines of the church.

---

* *The Decline and Fall of The Roman Empire*—Gibbon—Chapter 15, Pages 565, 566.

CHAPTER 3

BEGINNING OF APOSTASY

The church of our Lord was established in Jerusalem on the first Pentecost after the resurrection of Christ. In it practices that are common in the religious world today were not found. Before the death of the apostles they gave such admonitions and exhortations as were necessary to keep the church pure. This information was supplied under the inspiration of the Holy Spirit. "Therefore, brethren, stand fast, and hold the traditions which ye have been taught, whether by word, or our epistle."[1] "According as his divine power hath given unto us all things that pertain unto life and godliness, through the knowledge of him that hath called us to glory and virtue."[2] "All scripture is given by inspiration of God, and is profitable for doctrine, for reproof, for correction, for instruction in righteousness, that the man of God may be perfect, throughly furnished unto all good works."[3] Thus the word of God was to be the guide for the church. The failure of those who professed to be the people of God, to accept the scriptures as the only safe guide, allowed pagan ceremonies and Jewish practices to be brought into the worship of the church.

120 A.D. HOLY WATER FIRST USED

The use of holy water was introduced into the church by Alexander, a bishop of the church. He taught that the water for baptism must first be blessed and thus consecrated for religious purposes. This grew out of the practice of the heathen's custom of dipping their hands in water and sprinkling it upon themselves as they entered the pagan temples. As paganistic ideas were introduced into the church, it became a custom to provide holy water for the use of the worshippers. The purpose for the introduction of holy water is not made clear by those who originated the custom, however at a later age its use is connected with superstition. Marsilius Columna, the Archbishop of Salerno, attributed to holy water "the power to frighten away devils, to remit venial sins, to cure distraction, to elevate the mind and to dispose it to devotion." This innovation was followed by others that were just as unscriptural.

---

1. 2 Thessalonians 2 : 15
2. 2 Peter 1 : 3
3. 2 Timothy 3 : 16-17

140 A.D. THE INTRODUCTION OF LENT AND EASTER

The observance of Lent was first taught by Telsephorus, a bishop at Rome. Forty days were set apart between Ash Wednesday and Easter as a period of fasting.

Such information as is given of the origin of the observance of Lent at this time shows that it was not universally accepted until almost two hundred years later.

The first mention of ecclesiastical law concerning fasting is in 312 A.D.

> "Originally the fast was forty hours long between the afternoon of Good Friday and the morning of Easter. Of the Lenten fast the first mention of it is in the fifth canon of the council of Nicea, and from this time it is frequently referred to."[*]

Many religious groups attach much importance to the observance of Lent. Their members are called upon to surrender the eating of meat, to abstain from strong drink, to give up certain foods, and to refrain from worldly pleasure.

How could any habit or practice be declared wrong at one time and not at another time? Why would it be wrong for a disciple of Christ to go to a theatre or dance during the forty days of Lent and not be wrong the remainder of the year?

The word "Lent" is derived from the old English word "Lencten" which means spring. It was connected with a pagan feast that was celebrated in honor of the goddess "Ostra," the goddess of the east. The sacrifices to this deity were offered just about the time of the passover and in this way it became associated with the resurrection of Christ which followed the Jewish passover.

Not until the Council of Nice (325 A.D.) decreed that Easter should be kept on the Sunday next after the first full moon on or after the vernal equinox, was there a definite day for the observance of Easter. Here is the evidence that it has a human origin, as it was not known until after the fourth century just when Easter would be.

> "Many of our religious ideas, festivals and ceremonies, as witness Easter, and Christmas may be traced back to an origin in the practice and belief of our heathen ancestors."[†]

True, the word "Easter" is found in the twelfth chapter of Acts of Apostles. A better translation renders it "passover." The word "pascha" that is there translated "Easter" is found twenty-two times in the New Testament. Every time it is rendered "passover" except in this one place. Why the translators of the King James Version ignored its real meaning and called it Easter here no one

---

[*] *Encyclopedia Britannica*—Volume 13, Page 928.
[†] *Medieval and Modern History*—Meyers—Page 42.

seems to know. Certainly no such day is authorized by the teaching of the Apostles.

Socrates, a prominent church historian said, "The aim of the apostles was not to appoint festival days, but to teach a righteous life and piety." What brought these changes about? Why did disciples submit to having these days set apart as special days for the church? The answer is found in the failure of those who were the people of the Lord to know what God's word taught. Lack of this knowledge made it possible to introduce new doctrines and new practices into the teaching and worship of the church. The apostasy of the church and the corruption of the gospel resulted from neglect of the church to study God's word.

The false teachers who introduced these new doctrines were called "heretics" and what they taught was called "heresy." Heresy is from a Greek word which means choice. For one to be a follower of heresy implies that instead of believing what the scriptures teach he chooses for himself what he wants to believe. In this period of time following the apostolic age heretics were called Gnostics, a word which signifies knowledge.

These men professed to know more than those who accepted the scriptures as the only safe guide. Even at the close of the apostolic age the Gnostics were beginning to be influential in the Christian communities. Their teaching was often a combination of Jewish and pagan ideas, combined with the faith of Christ.

With the change in the government of the church and the development of the clergy, the scriptures were taken out of the hands of the members and the church sank deeper and deeper into the mists of superstition.

The pagan idols of Rome were replaced by statues and paintings of the saints. Before these the converted pagans began to prostrate themselves and to offer gifts.

Angels began to be adored and prayers were offered to them. Here, too, was the beginning of the adoration of Mary, the mother of Christ, who was thought to have great influence with God in obtaining an answer to prayer.

Pagans were accustomed to observe a feast to Proserpine with the burning of candles. To make the transition from pagan worship to Christian worship easy, the church in apostasy instituted on the same day a feast to the virgin Mary and burned tapers in her honor. Lactantius, a historian of the church, spoke of this practice as superstition, ridiculing those who lighted candles for God, as if He lived in the dark. Here were changes that appeared in the teaching and worship of the church as it developed into an apostate institution. Holy water, the burning of incense, the observance of Lent, and Easter, the worshipping of angels and the lighting of candles were connected with paganism. When the church dropped the guidance of God's word pagan ceremonies found their way into the church and they are today a part of that system of worship which grew out of the apostasy.

155 A.D. THE DEATH OF POLYCARP

Shortly after the ascension of Antoninus Pius as emperor of Rome a severe persecution was inaugurated against the Christians. The emperor in the beginning of the persecution remained silent while the followers of Christ were subjected to scourging, consigned to the flames, or sacrificed to the wild beasts in the arena.

During this time the empire suffered great calamities. There was constant warfare, earthquakes, floods, famine, and pestilence. These misfortunes were charged to the Christians. The persecution spread to Asia Minor and centered about Smyrna, the home of the aged Polycarp, a disciple of the apostle John.

"Through the urgency of friends he was induced to leave the city, to seek a retreat in the country . . . A band of soldiers thoroughly armed hastened to seize him. It was late on Friday night and the bishop was calmly sleeping in his chamber. Aroused by the noise of their entrance he descended to meet them, greeted them kindly, and ordered refreshments to be set before them. He asked of them the favor to grant him one hour for prayer. The soldiers, impressed by his venerable appearance and kindly spirit, could not refuse his request. At the close of this season of devotion they conducted him to the city. . . .

Many of the pagans who had long known Polycarp and who appreciated the nobleness of his character, entreated him to simply say, 'Lord Caesar,' to offer sacrifice to the idols and thus be saved. He merely replied, 'I can not follow your advice.' He was brought before the tribunal of the procounsul, Philip, who seemed to wish to save the venerable old man. He said to Polycarp, "If you will only swear by Caesar and reproach Christ, I will immediately release you." Polycarp replied, "Eighty and six years have I served Christ and he hath never wronged me. How can I blaspheme my king, who hath saved me. I am a Christian, if you desire to learn the Christian doctrine, assign me a day and I will declare it to you."*

When Polycarp refused to comply with the proconsul's request, he was first threatened with being exposed to the wild beasts, and then threatened with death by being burned at the stake. When he steadfastly refused to renounce Christ he was thrust through with a sword and his body consigned to the flames.

At the death of Antoninus Pius, his son Marcus Aurelius came to the throne and the persecution of Christians continued. Among

* *History of Christianity*—Abbott. Chapter 11, Pages 259, 260.

the other church leaders who lived after Polycarp, mention should be made of Irenaeus, Tertullian, Origen, and Cyprian, all of whom lived prior to the time in which the church was wholly given over to apostasy.

Irenaeus was born in Asia Minor and came under the influence of Polycarp while yet a young man. After the martyrdom of Polycarp, Irenaeus became a resident of Lyons. Here he assisted in the spread of the gospel to the regions beyond the Alps, into northern Gaul and into Britain.

When Pothinus, an elder in the church at Lyons, died of the wounds inflicted by his persecutors, Irenaeus, was appointed an elder in the church there. While he wrote much against the heresies, which were developing in the church, yet he was one of the first to exalt the office of bishop above that of the presbyter. He became the acknowledged leader in western Gaul because of his great zeal and piety.

Tertullian, who lived in the same period, was born about 130 A.D., the son of a Roman centurion who was stationed at Carthage. In his younger days his life was wholly given over to vice. Little is known of the beginning of his spiritual life. He suddenly appears upon the scene as a bold defender of the Christian religion. He became a bishop of the church and addressed himself to the emperors of Rome in the following language, "Rulers of the Roman Empire, you surely cannot forbid the truth to reach you by the secret pathway of a noiseless book. She knows she is but a sojourner on the earth, and as a stranger finds enemies, and more, her origin, her dwelling place, her hope, her rewards, her honors, are above one thing, meanwhile, she anxiously desires of earthly rulers, not to be condemned unknown. What harm can it do to give her a hearing? The outcry is that the state is filled with Christians; that they are in the fields, in the citadels, in the islands. The lament is, as for some calamity, that both sexes, every age and condition, even high rank, are passing over to the Christian faith."

Tertullian regarded those who fled from persecution as being worse than those who denied Christ. He believed that to seek martyrdom was a virtue, while those who forsook Christianity to escape persecution could not escape condemnation. Tertullian believed that the waters of baptism literally washed away sins. He overlooked the teaching of God's word that we receive the remission of our sins by our obedience to baptism.

> He stated in his treatise on baptism, "Blessed is our sacrament of water, in that by washing away the sins of our early blindness, we are liberated into eternal life." Again he stated, "But we, little fishes, after the example of our Jesus Christ are born in water,"

to which he added, "All waters, therefore, in virtue of the pristine privilege of their origin do, after invocation of God, attain the sacramental power of sanctification."*

Tertullian was much opposed to the baptism of children and of those who did not fully understand what was enjoined upon them by their obedience to the gospel. He believed that sins committed after baptism could not be pardoned and taught that no one should be baptized unless they were sure they could live without sinning again. He failed to recognize the provision of God for the forgiveness of sins committed after baptism. "And if any man sin, we have an advocate with the Father, Jesus Christ the righteous."[4]

Tertullian had much to do with the spread of Christianity over all of northern Africa. By the end of the second century Christians were numbered by the thousands in Carthage and the surrounding territory.

Contemporary with Tertullian, but living in a different district, was Clement, who was born about 160 at Athens. His early training was by various teachers in various systems of philosophy. Eventually he came to Alexandria and placed himself under the instruction of Pantaenus, giving full attention to the study of Christianity. He became a teacher in the theological school at Alexandria where he taught until he was forced to leave by persecution. After he left the school Origen became a teacher there. This man was well versed in the scriptures, having committed to memory large parts of them while he was yet a child. He became a student of philosophy and is said to have been more speculative than his teacher.

Origen believed children were born into the world polluted by sin and therefore they needed baptism for the remission of sins. He was much given to the allegorical method of interpreting the scriptures and often allowed his speculations to carry him beyond the bounds of inspiration. He held to the newly developed teaching that a difference existed between presbyters and bishops.

Alexander Severus, the Roman emperor, was brought under the influence of the gospel by this great teacher. Though the laws against the Christians were not repealed, they were ignored; and Christianity enjoyed a period of prosperity and growth. The emperor inscribed the golden rule upon public buildings, employed Christians in his household and, permitted bishops also to appear at his court. When the emperor met death at the hands of the agents of Maximin, persecution was once again directed against the Christians especially against servants of the church. Origen

---

* *A Manual of Church History*—Newman—Chapter 3, Pages 262, 263. (Published 1933, by Judson Press.)
4. 1 John 2:1

was compelled to flee into Cappadocia. Later he went to Tyre where he died and on his tomb was the single word Origen. He was the superior of any man of that age in scholarship and the most loved of all of the early church teachers.

Following the reign of Maximinus, Gordian, and Philip, the emperor Decius set out to restore the pagan religion. All Christians were to appear before a magistrate, abjure their religion, and offer a sacrifice to the pagan gods. Many refused to do so, though some in fear either joined in such sacrifice or obtained a statement from the magistrates that they had complied with the law. Decius was followed by Valerian (253-260) who continued the persecution.

Cyprian was apprehended and accused of being the enemy of the gods at Rome. Gibbon tells us of his last days, saying, "Two officers of rank, who were intrusted with that commission, placed Cyprian between them in a chariot; and as the proconsul was not then at leisure, they conducted him not to a prison, but to a private house in Carthage, which belonged to one of them. An elegant supper was there provided for the bishop. His Christian friends were permitted for the last time to enjoy his society, while the streets were filled with a multitude of the faithful, who were anxious and alarmed, fearful of what might be done to their spiritual leader.

In the morning he appeared before the tribunal of the proconsul, who, after informing himself of the name and situation of Cyprian, commanded him to offer sacrifice and pressed him to reflect on the consequences of disobedience.

The refusal of Cyprian was firm and decisive, and the magistrate, when he had taken the opinion of the council, pronounced with some reluctance the sentence of death. It was conceived in the following terms,—"That Thascius Cyprianus should be immediately beheaded, as the enemy of the gods of Rome, and as the chief and ringleader of a criminal association, which he had seduced into an impious resistance against the laws of the most holy emperors, Valerian and Gallienus." He was led away under a guard of tribunes and centurions, without resistance and without insult, to the place of his execution, a spacious and level plain near the city, which was already filled with great numbers of spectators. The martyr then covered his face with his hands, and at one blow his head was separated from his body." Thus died one who had devoted his entire life to the spread of the gospel and to upholding the church's unity and greatness. While some of his teachings were without a doubt based upon a wrong understanding of the scriptures yet his thoughts upon the church as the one place of salvation are worthy of the record here.

He believed to be a Christian one must be in the church. "Whosoever he is and whatsoever his character, he is not a Christian who is not in the church of Christ." "There is no salvation outside of the church." Furthermore, "It is not possible that one should have God for his father, who would not have the church for mother."

157 A.D. THE DOCTRINE OF PENANCE

The doctrine of penance was first advocated at this time, but not until the year 411 was the doctrine fully developed, nor was it fully accepted by the apostate church until 1022.

Under the fear of persecution, weak Christians sometimes left the church. At a later time they often expressed a desire to return but this was not so easy. Sometimes a special act was imposed upon them to prove they had truly repented. Those who showed signs of contrition were called penitents.

> "They had a special seat in the meetings for worship and had to go through a course of public humiliation, the duration and severity of which were appointed by the clergy."*

Four groups of penitents were formed of those who had sinned and then came back to the church. Some could not enter the place where services were conducted but must remain without and beg others to pray for them. Others could hear the lesson, but had to leave before the conclusion of the services. Another group could have others to pray for them in the assembly but could have no part in the worship. From these practices developed the idea of the mourners bench. This course of public humiliation was designed to prove they were truly repentant. This prescribed penance was supposed to remit sins.

> "Penance is a sacrament in which sin committed is forgiven. Penance remits the eternal hell and some of the temporal purgatory."†

Where is the scripture that teaches that a person can be justified by obeying the commands of some person just as human as he is?

The apostle Paul said, "For there is one God and one mediator between God and men, the man Christ Jesus."[5]

The teaching that a human intercessor has the power to forgive sins developed from the imposition of acts of penance upon those guilty of sin. The clergy were soon saying, "I absolve thee from thy sins, in the name of the Father and of the Son and of the Holy Ghost."

* *History of The Christian Church*—Fisher—Chapter 2, Page 58.
† *Baltimore Catechism*—Page 52.
5. 1 Timothy 2:5

161 A.D. MARCUS AURELIUS BECAME THE EMPEROR OF ROME

He persecuted the Christians and caused many to be put to death by beheading or by being thrown to the wild beasts in the amphitheatre. After the death of Marcus Aurelius a number of weak and worthless emperors ruled over the affairs of the empire.

166 A.D. THE DEATH OF JUSTIN MARTYR

Justin Martyr was one of the foremost men of his time. He was a native of Neapolis, near Sychar in Samaria. When young he obeyed the gospel of Christ and traveled about, intent upon winning some one to Christ. He was put to death for no greater crime than being a Christian.

190 A.D. THE APOSTLES' CREED DOES NOT GO BACK OF THIS DATE

In this year we have the first mention of the Apostles' Creed in history. By the fourth century the theory that each of the apostles contributed to it had been developed.

The reading and the statements of the creed have been changed materially through the years yet it is still referred to as the Apostles' Creed and is used by many Protestant churches in the liturgical services and is regarded by some as a confession of Christian faith.

"The simple confession of faith in Christ made at baptism, gradually expanded itself, until in process of time, it grew, in the western church into what was known as the Apostle's Creed. This however, differed somewhat in form in the different churches, as Rufinus found to be the case when late in the fourth century, he entered into the study of the subject."*

"Laurentius Valla went from classic to Christian Greek. He wrote notes upon the New Testament. Erasmus edited them. He pointed out errors in the Latin Vulgate. He exposed such frauds as 'the donation of Constantine.' He denied that the "Apostles' Creed" was written by the apostles."†

The Apostles' Creed—190 A.D.

"I believe in God, the Father Almighty and in Jesus Christ, His Son, who was born of Mary, the virgin, was crucified under Pontius Pilate and buried, on the third day rose from the dead, ascended into heaven, sitteth on the right hand of the Father, from whence he cometh to judge the quick and the dead, and in the Holy Ghost, and in the resurrection of the body."

The Apostles' Creed—Today

"I believe in God, the Father Almighty, maker of heaven and earth, and Jesus Christ, His only Son, our Lord, who was conceived by the Holy Ghost, born of the Virgin Mary, suffered under Pontius

---

* *History of The Christian Church*—Fisher—Chapter 3, Page 67.
† *History of The Christian Church*—Blackburn—Chaper 15, Page 365.

Pilate, was crucified, dead and buried. He descended into Hell;
the third day he arose again from the dead. He ascended into
Heaven and sitteth on the right hand of God, the Father Almighty,
from thence he shall come to judge the quick and the dead. I believe in the Holy Ghost, the Holy Catholic Church, the communion
of the saints, the forgiveness of sins, the resurrection of the body
and the life everlasting—Amen."

This creed has been changed sixteen times through the centuries,
yet those who use it today still call it the Apostles' Creed.

One proof that it did not come from the apostles is the fact that
it is found in different forms.

If one simply believes all that is recorded in God's word, what
more is there to believe and where is it to be found? There is no
divine authority for the formation of a human creed by which
people are to be guided religiously. None of the apostles delegated
to any man, or set of men, the right to produce a human creed.

Had it been necessary to form an outline of those things which
were to be believed the Lord would have selected some of his
divinely inspired apostles for that purpose. This he did not do.
Why? Because everything that is necessary has been supplied in
the written word. "According as his divine power hath given unto
us all things that pertain unto life and godliness, through the
knowledge of him that hath called us to glory and virtue."[6]

---

6. 2 Peter 1: 3

CHAPTER 4

APOSTASY AND PERSECUTION

One of the most important periods of Church history is that which immediately follows the apostolic age. Within a few years after the death of the apostles the church came into conflict with civil authority and with the paganism of that age. Here was the beginning of the sufferings of the Christians, for while they endured some persecution during the lifetime of the apostles, yet it was sporadic and not to be compared with the persecution launched against the Christians in the second century; which continued into the fourth century.

In this same period we shall see the influence of the Christians upon those who opposed their religion and the development of the heresies which swept the church into the great apostasy.

The power of the Roman government was directed against Chr s-tianity in an effort to overcome a religion which undermined and destroyed the ancient religions. Much information that might have come down to us concerning the church in this period has been lost. The works of the ante-Nicean fathers consist largely of attacks on heathenism, Judaism, and apostasy. They contain some information on the church but much of it is so obscure and so scattered that it is difficult to gather facts that would throw light upon the activities of the church in this age. The secular historians considered Christianity one of the many varieties of superstition, a delusion that called first for pity, then sarcasm, and ultimately persecution.

The Romans were inclined to reject a religion that taught virtue rather than license, that proclaimed doctrines that were in opposition to the philosophy of that age, and whose followers were ready to receive the slaves and the unlearned with the same degree of love with which the noble and the wise were received.

In the face of much opposition Christianity grew rapidly. The writers of that age inform us that the teachings of Christ were to be found among the barbarian nations.

Justin Martyr spoke of the growth of the religion of Christ saying, "There is no race of men, whether barbarian or Greek or by whatsoever appellation they may be designated, whether they wander in wagons, or dwell in tents, among whom prayers and thanksgivings are not offered up to the Father and Creator of all things in the name of the crucified Jesus."

With the growth of Christianity those who once rejoiced in sin, now found delight in obedience to Christ; those who were devotees of the heathen gods now served the one true God. Those who once had no association with the people of other nations now were willing to dwell with men of any tribe.

Paganism had nothing to offer mankind when compared with Christianity. The religion of Christ alone offered a better way of life and it was not surprising therefore that it was accepted above paganism. True, paganism, with its mysteries, its temples, its priests and its ritualism had a strong hold upon the people, but these things were only external and supplied no spiritual strength to the worshipper. The worship of the Christians was simple indeed.

> Justin, a native of Neapolis, near the old Sychar in Samaria said, "On the day called Sunday all who live in the cities, or in the country, gather in one place and the memoirs of the apostles or the writings of the prophets are read, as long as time permits, then the president (the elder) verbally instructs and exhorts to the imitation of these good things. Then we all rise together and pray; (singing is elsewhere mentioned) then bread and wine are brought and the president offers prayers and thanksgivings according to his ability and the people say, 'Amen.' There is a distribution to each and a partaking of that over which thanks have been given . . . The wealthy among us help the needy; each gives what he thinks fit; and what is collected is laid aside by the president who relieves the orphans and the widows and those who are sick or in want from any cause."*

Christianity was considered as a proselyting sect which refused joint participation in worship with other religions. The followers of Christ spared no efforts to show their contempt for all other gods, for the temples, and for the ceremonies of idolatry. These things brought Christianity into open conflict with paganism and launched against it a persecution that continued until 313 A.D.

During this time the lives of all Christians were in jeopardy. The Roman authorities were very tolerant toward all other religions, yet they singled out the Christian religion as one that should be persecuted. This was because the Christians were unwilling to burn incense upon the emperor's altar. They were willing to suffer punishment as rebellious citizens rather than to be guilty of idol worship.

The spread of the gospel planted congregations in almost every city. Each of these congregations was separate from all others,

---

* *History of The Christian Church*—Blackburn—Chapter 2, Page 35.

being bound together only by the ties of faith and love. Every congregation selected men for the office of presbyters or elders, and for that of the deacons, the servants of the church.

The elders were also called "bishops" or "overseers" signifying the work they were appointed to do, that of seeing to the spiritual needs of the congregation. They were men qualified to teach, who knew how to defend the doctrine of the church against her enemies. The deacons, acting under the elders, supplied the needs of those in distress.

In the beginning the church was pure. The divine plan of the church as revealed in the New Testament was followed. Now the apostasy of which the apostles warned, began to develop. The teaching of the Scriptures called for a plurality of elders in every congregation, each of whom had just as much authority as his fellow elders. Now congregations began to select an elder who was designated the bishop. He soon became the most important man in the local congregation. This distinction gave him a position of prominence and he gradually assumed control of all congregations within a given district.

> "The public functions of religion were solely intrusted to the established ministers of the church, the bishops and the presbyters, two appellations which in their first origin, appear to have distinguished the same office and the same order of persons. The name of Presbyter was expressive of their age or rather of their gravity and wisdom. The title of 'Bishop' denoted their inspection over the faith and manners of Christians who were committed to their pastoral care. In proportion to the respective numbers of the faithful, a larger or smaller number of these episcopal presbyters guided each infant congregation with equal authority and with united counsel."*

The "bishops" in each of the centers of religious influence, Jerusalem, Antioch, Ephesus, Constantinople, and Rome occupied a position of honor and power for they were regarded as spiritual representatives of the authority of Christ. In later years they received the title of Patriarch as a mark of distinction and were considered as the successors of the apostles.

When a difficulty arose within a congregation, a council of elders and the bishop would be called to render a decision. In this the "bishop" had the deciding vote. Out of this practice developed the teaching that the bishop could legislate for the churches in his district.

Much of the teaching in the early church was by members who had no official status.

"And I myself also am persuaded of you, my brethren, that ye

---

* *Decline and Fall of The Roman Empire—Gibbon.* Volume 1, Chapter 15, Pages 565, 566.

also are full of goodness, filled with all knowledge, able also to admonish one another."[1] "Wherefore comfort yourselves together, and edify one another, even as ye also do."[2] Now a change was made. The admonishing, the exhorting, and the public work of the church was taken out of the hands of the individual members of the church and vested in the eldership.

The preaching of the word, the prayers, and the administration of the Lord's supper became their official work also. This marks the beginning of the division between the "clergy" and the "laity."

192 A.D. SEPTIMIUS SEVERUS CAME TO THE THRONE IN ROME

He at first persecuted the Christians but when a Christian physician saved the life of his child he appointed another Christian as an instructor for the son. When the fury of the Roman people was directed against the Christians, Severus sought to shield them.

In the distant parts of the empire where the power of the emperor was weak, the persecution was very severe. The father of Eusebius, the historian, was beheaded and his property appropriated, leaving his family in want. Eusebius was restrained from following his father to martyrdom only by the entreaties of his mother.

200 A.D. ELDERS IN THE CHURCHES
NOW BEGAN TO ASSUME THE TITLE OF PRIESTS

Prior to this time there were none who wore this title. The word which is translated "elder" comes from an original word which signifies only an older man. In the New Testament there is no mention of a priesthood only in the sense that every Christian is a priest unto God.

211 A.D. CARACALLA BECAME EMPEROR AT ROME

He conferred citizenship upon all who were not slaves. This was a great benefit to the Christians. They could no longer be thrown to the wild beasts or crucified unless they were slaves.

220 A.D. ORIGEN ADVOCATED PURGATORY

"Purgatory, where literal fire was conceived to be the instrument of punishment, was the abode of souls guilty of no mortal sins, but burdened with imperfections which needed to be removed, and with dues of "temporal punishment," or satisfaction, for sins from the guilt of which they have been absolved."[*]

---

1. Romans 15:14
2. 1 Thessalonians 5:11
* *History of The Christian Church*—Fisher. Chapter 5, Page 226.

Another authority states, "This doctrine was well defined by the beginning of the sixth century, but was condemned by the Council of Constantinople in 533. By 1070 it had become a part of the doctrine of the apostate church." God never commanded such teaching, Christ never authorized it, but the clergy persuaded by the gifts of anxious friends said masses for the benefit of the departed that their souls might be delivered from the fires of purgatory.

249 A.D. PERSECUTION BROKE OUT ANEW UNDER DECIUS BEGINNING AT ALEXANDRIA

"Decius published a bloody edict against the Christians and sent it to the governors of all the provinces. They were ordered vigilantly to search out Christians and to punish them with the utmost severity, by scourging, by burning at the stake, by beheading, by tossing them to wild beasts, by the dungeon, by seating them in iron chairs heated red hot, by tearing out the eyes with burning irons, by tearing the flesh from the bones with steel pincers."[*]

Prior to the time of Decius the church had a period of rest from persecution. Though the Christians were hated the Romans were beginning to drop their opposition to them and to accept their presence as something to be endured. When Decius became emperor he determined to put an end to Christianity. All Christians were to give up their religion or suffer the penalty provided for disobedience.

In the years when there was no persecution the church grew rapidly, but it was not the growth of the church that brought about the resolution to destroy Christianity, but rather the declining strength of the empire.

The Roman senate, believing the gods had been offended by the great number who had forsaken paganism, decided that all must return to the ancient religion of Rome. Christians were required to bow before the statue of the emperor and there offer incense. Many Christians refused to do this, though some outwardly denied Christ to save their lives. Others purchased from dishonest officials letters stating that the bearer had offered his sacrifice to the pagan gods.

A small part of the Christians refused to resort to trickery to save their lives. These were first imprisoned, then deprived of their property, and if they then refused to renounce Christianity, they were put to death.

The persecution ended with the death of Decius in 251. Those who had forsaken Christianity now pleaded to be restored to the fellowship of the church.

* *History of Christianity*—Abbott. Chapter 13, Page 287.

250 A.D. SPRINKLING FIRST PRACTICED

Novation was the first person, so far as history records, to have water sprinkled upon him as a substitute for baptism. Eusebius, in speaking of Novation said,

> "Who aided by the exorcists when attacked by an obstinate disease and being supposed at the point of death was baptized by aspersion, in the bed on which he lay; if, indeed, it be proper to say one like him did receive baptism."*

The great historian, Neander, remarks,

> "In respect to the form of baptism, it was in conformity with the original institution and the original import of the symbol, performed by immersion, as a sign of entire baptism into the Holy Spirit, of being entirely penetrated by the same. It was only with the sick, when the exigency required it, that any exception was made; and in this case baptism was administered by sprinkling. Many superstitious persons, clinging to the outward form imagined that such baptism by sprinkling was not fully valid; and hence they distinguished those who had thus been baptized by denominating them the clinici."†

Sprinkling thus originated in the baptism of the sick but did not come into general use until after the eighth century when it was legalized by Pope Stephen.

> "The first law for sprinkling was obtained in the following manner: Pope Stephen III, being driven from Rome by Astulphus, king of the Lombards, in 753, fled to Pepin, who, a short time before had usurped the crown of France. Whilst he remained there the monks of Cressy in Brittany consulted him, whether, in a case of necessity, baptism, performed by pouring water on the head of the infant, would be lawful. Stephen replied that it would. But though the truth of this fact should be allowed, which some Catholics deny, yet pouring or sprinkling was only admitted in case of necessity. It was not till 1311, that the legislature, in a council held at Ravenna, declared immersion or sprinkling to be indifferent."‡

The teaching of the apostles shows that New Testament baptism was a burial in water. "Therefore we are buried with him by baptism into death: that like as Christ was raised up from the dead by the glory of the Father, even so we also should walk in newness of life."[3] "Buried with him in baptism, wherein also ye are risen with him through the faith of the operation of God, who hath raised him from the dead."[4] In his comments upon these scriptures, Adam Clarke, a profound Bible scholar, said.

> "We are buried with him by baptism into death. It is probable that the apostle alludes to the mode of administering baptism by immersion, the whole body being put under water."§

---

  * *Ecclesiastical History*—Eusebius. Chapter 43, Page 266.
  † *History of The Christian Religion and Church*—Neander. Volume 1, Page 310.
  ‡ *Edinburg Encyclopedia*—Volume 3, Page 236.
  3. Romans 6 : 4
  4. Colossians 2 : 12
  § *Clarke's Commentary*—Volume 4, Page 78.

And again in discussing the second chapter of Colossians he said,

"Alluding to the immersion practiced in the case of adults, wherein the person appeared to be buried under water as Christ was buried in the heart of the earth."*

This change from baptism to sprinkling did not take place in a day or even in a year. It came slowly and not within all churches. Some of the churches rejected it and declared that no fellowship existed between them and the churches which accepted and practiced these departures from the truth. Only when the church left the word of God and went into apostasy was it possible for this change to be made.

253 A.D. CONFIRMATION FIRST ADVOCATED

The apostles confirmed the disciples by exhorting them to continue in the faith but there was no ceremony connected with their teaching nor do the Scriptures enjoin such upon Christians. In this same period it became a common practice for the clergy to make the sign of the cross in religious services. There is nothing in God's word that authorizes such a practice. Priests' vestments first make their appearance at this time. Originally they were the garb of the century past and as changes were made in the apparel of men the clergy retained the old styles, lengthening the Roman toga into a robe.

Altar clothes make their first appearance at this time. The use of these was forbidden by the council of Trulla.

296 A.D. THE TITLE OF POPE FIRST APPLIED TO THE BISHOP OF ROME

It was also used as a title by Siricius, the bishop of Rome in 384 and by Leo, bishop of Rome in 440.

When John the Faster, the Patriarch of Constantinople, assumed the title of Universal Bishop, Gregory the Great, Patriarch of Rome, wrote to him a letter of reproof for assuming a title which would give offence to all, saying, "You know it, my brother, hath not the venerable council of Chalcedon conferred the honorary title of Universal upon the bishops of this Apostolic See, whereof I am, by God's will, the servant. And yet no one of us hath permitted this title to be given to him, none has assumed this bold title, lest by assuming a special distinction in the episcopate, we should seem to refuse it to all brethren. The Lord said to his disciples, 'Be ye not called Rabbi, for one is your Master, and ye are brethren, neither be ye called Father, for ye have but one Father, 'What then could you answer, beloved brother in the terrible judgement to

* *Clarke's Commentary*—Volume 4, Page 78.

come, who desire not only to be called Father, but universal Father of the world." This change like many others, to which attention has been called, did not take place overnight. It required a long period of time for these changes to fully develop and be bound upon the church.

303 A.D. THE COUNCIL OF ELVIRA

The Council of Elvira opposed the painting of religious subjects on the walls of the buildings used for the services of the church. Church buildings had their beginning at about this time. They were built with a raised platform for the clergy, who were thus elevated above the laity. Decorations were first looked upon as an innovation. They first appeared in the form of pictures of the saints. This practice of decorating the buildings used for the services of the church did not come from the clergy but from those who had been lately converted from paganism and from those who encouraged the practice by gifts of paintings, statues, and other insignia.

The use of images was foreign to the worship of the New Testament church. They first were used by the families who had been converted from paganism to Christianity and later found their way into the church, along with miniature crosses and other religious emblems.

In a later period, Agobard, of Lyons, moved by the exaggerated veneration paid to the images of saints, wrote against them. He was assured that no one believed that any thing divine dwelt in the images themselves, for the adoration was not paid to the image but to the object represented by them. To which he replies,

> "That we have no authority for paying even to the saints that worship, which is due to God alone, and which they were ever found to decline. It was a cunning device of Satan to bring back idolatry, and under pretext of showing honor to the saints, to draw men away from that which is spiritual and to degrade them to that which is sensual."*

The council of Elvira also prohibited the marriage of the clergy. Yet one of the qualifications of an elder in the church established by Christ through the apostles was that an elder was to be a married man.

"If any be blameless, the husband of one wife, having faithful children not accused or riot or unruly."[5] Celibacy, refraining from marriage, is not bound upon the servants of the church. "Now the spirit speaketh expressly, that in the latter times some shall depart from the faith, giving heed to seducing spirits, and doctrines of

---

* *History of The Christian Religion and Church*—Neander. Volume 3. Section 3. Pages 428, 429.
  5. Titus 1 : 6

devils; speaking lies in hypocrisy; having their conscience seared with a hot iron; forbidding to marry, and commanding to abstain from meats, which God hath created to be received with thanksgiving of them which believe and know the truth."[6] Where then did the doctrine originate that marriage was forbidden to those who were public servants of the church? It originated with men, not with God!

303 A.D. THE PERSECUTION UNDER DIOCLETIAN

Diocletian, who had been a slave, became Emperor of Rome by his genius and force of will. He chose as a fellow emperor Maximian, an able general. The empire was divided between them, Diocletian ruling in the east and Maximian in the west. At a later time two Caesars were appointed who were to rule outlying provinces of the empire, Galerius, the son-in-law of Diocletian, being assigned to the district bordering the Danube and Constantius to the countries of Gaul and Britain.

Diocletian resolved that paganism should be the religion of the empire and that Christianity should be destroyed. To accomplish this end all church buildings were to be demolished and all copies of the sacred writings of the Christians were to be burned. All who failed to renounce Christianity were to lose their citizenship and be without the protection of the laws of the land. A decree was issued ordering every soldier in the army to join in idolatrous worship. The penalty for refusing was a scourging and dismissal from military service.

Christians of every age and rank were punished by torture in an effort to make them surrender their religion. They were assembled in their church buildings, the doors were locked and then the buildings set on fire and burned with the worshippers.

> "Imperial edicts were everywhere published, to tear down the churches to their foundations, and to destroy the sacred Scriptures by fire, and which commanded, also, that those who were in honorable stations, should be degraded, but those who were freedmen, should be deprived of their liberty, if they persevered in their adherence to Christianity."*

In the midst of this persecution Diocletian resigned as emperor and compelled Maximian to do the same. Galerius and Constantius then became the emperors and they continued the persecution against the Christians. One effect of these trials through which the church passed was that the church was kept pure. No one identified himself with the church for popularity or worldly show.

6. 1 Timothy 4:1-3
* *Ecclesiastical History*—Eusebius. Book 8, Chapter 2, Page 320.

The half converted and weak left it and only those who were willing
to suffer for Christ remained. Despite the persecutions that were
endured by the Christians, the church continued to grow, and when
Galerius saw that Christianity could not be destroyed by persecution he granted religious tolerance to its subjects.

His fellow emperor Constantius had long since ceased to persecute
Christians, so now the church enjoyed peace. At the death of
Constantius, his son, Constantine, who had married the daughter
of Maximian, became ruler of Gaul and Britain.

Maximian caused a report to be circulated while Constantine
was fighting the Franks, that he had been killed in battle and so
he proclaimed himself emperor. Constantine returned and defeated
his father-in-law in battle, put him to death, then turned his attention to Maxentius who disputed his claim to the crown.

As the two armies met for battle Constantine claimed to have
seen in the sky a cross formed by the clouds. He considered this
an omen from God and promised that if he was victorious he would
become a Christian.

308 A.D. CONSTANTINE GAINED A DECISIVE VICTORY OVER MAXENTIUS AT MILVAN BRIDGE

Although the army of Maxentius was superior in numbers to
that of Constantine and was strongly entrenched, the battle terminated in favor of the soldiers of Constantine. Maxentius was
routed with a terrible slaughter and while trying to escape across
the Tiber River, he was crowded from the bridge by the fleeing
soldiers. The weight of his armor caused him to sink beneath the
water and it was not until the next day that his body was recovered.

Constantine entered Rome in triumph and was proclaimed co-
ruler of the empire with Licinius who ruled in the east. A magnificent arch of triumph was erected in honor of Constantine
which remains with its ornamentation and its flattering words
unto this day. Outwardly Constantine became a Christian and his
subjects followed his example though they had but little conception
of the nature and purpose of Christianity.

As the influence of Christianity grew the people of the provinces
began to look to the elders or bishops of that province or city for
guidance. Constantine was quick to see the advantage that might
be gained by the support of the church. He placed Christians in
positions of prominence and power and sought in every way possible to advance the cause of Christianity.

Here began the union of church and state which eventually
brought the church into complete subjection to the state.

CHURCH OF THE NEW TESTAMENT

Jerusalem
33 A.D.—325 A.D.

Christ, the Head	Col. 1:18
Apostles Foundation	Eph. 2:20
New Test. Scriptures	1 Pet. 4:11
Faith	Heb. 11:6
Repentance	Acts 17:30
Confession	Rom. 10:9
Baptism	Col. 2:12
Lord's Day	Acts 20:7
Pray	Phil. 4:6
Teach-Admonish	Rom. 14:19
Sing	Eph. 5:19
Lord's Supper	1 Cor. 11:23
Contribution	1 Cor. 16:2
Elders-Deacons	
Members	

THE APOSTATE CHURCH

Rome
325 A.D.—1074 A.D.

120	Holy Water
140	Lent, Special Days, Fasts
157	Penance, Mourners' Bench
200	Prelates, Clergy, Doctors, Reverends
220	Purgatory, Second Chance
251	Sprinkling, Immersion Not Essential
313	Celibacy, Free Love, Immorality
325	Creeds, Prayer Books, Manuals
361	Auricular Confession
428	Idolatry, Praying To Statues
588	Extreme Unction, Death Bed Repentance
	Cardinals, Archbishops, Bishops, Patriarchs, Metropolitans

313 A.D. THE COUNCIL OF NEO-CAESAREA
DECREED THAT ELDERS COULD NOT MARRY

The doctrine of celibacy for the eldership grew out of the supposition that if they were unmarried they could better care for the work of the Lord. The idea that marriage implied imperfect sanctity developed within the church, and as an imperfect sanctity was considered unbecoming to those who served at the Lord's table, the celibacy of the elders was first recommended, and later bound on them.

> "In the West the prejudice in favor of a celibate clergy was carried to a further extreme than in the East. The more the clergy were exalted above the laity, the higher rose the demands for a peculiar sanctity which were made upon them by the popular feeling."*

Watch the work of the councils. New doctrines were being advocated by those who were seeking for prominence. When a council would later be called the matter would be placed before the council and a vote taken and thus a doctrine foreign to God's word would be bound upon the church. Had there been no councils, no conferences, and if people had been content to take God's word as their guide there would have been no apostasy. A fearful responsibility rests on those who made the changes in the worship of the one church for which Christ died.

Weak-minded people might have made changes through ignorance, but responsibility for these changes rests upon the ecclesiastical dignitaries, upon the clergy who forced these things upon the people.

In this same year (313) the Edict of Toleration was issued by Constantine and Licinius. This edict granted freedom of worship to Christians. No longer could they be persecuted because of their religious belief. This edict was issued at Milan and read in part as follows—

> "Wherefore, as I, Constantine Augustus and I, Licinius Augustus, came under favorable auspices to Milan, and took under consideration all affairs that pertained to the public benefit and welfare, these things among the rest appeared to us to be the most advantageous and profitable to all. We have resolved among the first things to ordain, these matters by which reverence and worship to the Deity might be exhibited. That is how we may grant likewise to the Christians, and to all, the free choice to follow that mode of worship which they may wish. That what so ever divinity and celestial power may exist, may be propitious to us and to all that live under our government.
>
> Therefore, we have decreed the following ordinance, as our will, with a salutary and most correct intention, that no freedom at all

---

* *History of The Christian Church*—Fisher. Chapter 3, Page 62.

shall be refused to Christians, to follow or keep their observance of worship. But to each one power be granted to devote his mind to that worship which he may think adapted to himself. . . . That you may know we have granted liberty and full freedom to the Christians to observe their own mode of worship, which as your fidelity understands absolutely granted to them by us, the privilege is also granted to others also to worship whatsoever divinity he pleases."*

This decree also restored church property which had been taken from Christians. The sword of persecution was sheathed and buried. Church buildings were restored and reopened everywhere. Cities reimbursed Christians for those structures which had been destroyed. New buildings were erected everywhere. In design they followed the plan of the Roman basilica or courtroom. They were usually rectangular in form, with a raised dais at the end for the elders.

324 A.D. LICINIUS, CO-EMPEROR WITH CONSTANTINE, TURNED AGAIN TO PAGANISM

Licinius befriended Sinicus, who had plotted against the life of Constantine in 314. These acts brought Licinius into open conflict with Constantine. Gathering an army of one hundred twenty thousand foot soldiers and ten thousand horsemen he marched against Licinius. The forces of the two generals met near Adrianople. It was a contest between two emperors, a battle between two religions, between Christianity and paganism. The battle continued throughout the day. Licinius fled under the cover of darkness leaving twenty thousand dead upon the field. He rallied his forces and fought a second battle upon the plains of Thrace where his army and almost annihilated. Licinius fled to the mountains of Macedonia and sued for peace.

Constantine, out of regard for his sister, the wife of Licinius, spared his life. For several years peace prevailed between the rival emperors, ending when they again took up arms against each other. Licinius, though aged and infirm, showed surprising ability in assembling a hundred and fifty thousand soldiers and a great number of armed galleys. Constantine was victorious, taking possession of the Bosphorus and the Hellespont.

He changed the name of Adrianople to Constantinople in honor of himself and moved the capital from Rome to Constantinople. Again the Roman world was at peace and under the rule of one emperor.

The Arian controversy developed within the church at about this same time. Arius was a presbyter of Alexandria. He intro-

* *Ecclesiastical History*—Eusebius. Book 10, Chapter 5, Pages 426, 427.

duced the doctrine that Christ was a created being, the first of all of God's creation, and the being by whom all other beings were created. He was deposed by his bishop at Alexandria, but was befriended by other ecclesiastics. The controversy spread and threatened to destroy the peace of the church.

325 A.D. CONSTANTINE CONVENES THE COUNCIL OF NICEA

A council of three hundred eighteen bishops assembled from all parts of the world to consider the doctrine of Arius and other controversial matters. The city of Nice in Bythinia was the seat of their deliberations for sixty-seven days. Their decision was to govern the church upon the subject of the nature of Christ. Here was legislation where God had not legislated, a procedure for which there was no authority.

The council was presided over by Constantine, who bore the expense of all who assembled. The deliberations of the council were directed to the doctrine of Arius, that Christ was not equal to the Father, or of the same substance.

Athanasius, a deacon of the church led the discussion against the doctrine of Arius and his party eventually prevailed.

By the findings of the council, Arius and two of his friends were banished to Illyria, while others were deposed. The decision of the council was given in the Nicean Creed which was a stinging rebuke to Arianism.

The Nicean Creed

"We believe in one God the Father almighty, maker of all things both visible and invisible, and in one Lord, Jesus Christ, the son of God, begotten by the Father, begotten—that is to say of the substance of the Father, God of God, light of light, very God of very God, begotten not made, being of one substance with the Father, by whom all things were made, both things in heaven and things on earth, who for us men and our salvation, came down and was made flesh, made man, suffered and rose again on the third day and went into the heavens and is to come again to judge both the quick and the dead, and in the Holy Ghost."

The peace that was thus made was not permanent, for Constantine later accepted the doctrine of Arius, turning against Athanasius, who was banished from his diocese. The Nicean Creed failed to unite all believers for at a later date a second council was convened at Constantinople. This council changed the creed to conform to later beliefs.

God gave to no man nor to any set of men the right to form a creed, to legislate concerning things divine, or to intrude into those things which are not revealed. Some have mistakenly affirmed that a creed is only a comprehensive statement to make clear the teaching of God's word. If man has the ability to clarify the teaching of God, to make it more understandable then he would be wiser than God.

Are uninspired men able to present the doctrine of the Bible better than the holy men of God who spoke as the Holy Spirit gave them utterance? To affirm that creeds and confessions of faith are more easily understood than the Bible is to impeach the wisdom of God.

The Nicean Creed did not unite those who claimed to be the people of God. In the gospel age, when only the apostles' doctrine was the guide, the church stood united, but with the formation of creeds, division began among the believers and has continued to the present time.

The council of Nice also fixed the date for the observance of Easter. The name "Easter" comes from Ostra, goddess of the morning light or of the return of the sun in the spring. The eastern church and the western church differed upon the observance of the date of this festival. It was first observed in the East on the 14th of Nisan, the day on which the passover fell. Many of the churches observed it on the Sunday after that day. The Council of Nicea settled the matter by fixing the day to be observed as the first Sunday after the first full moon which appears next after March 21. The very fact that no day was observed as Easter by the apostles shows that it is of later origin.

The Nicean council was the first of six general councils which were held to deal with speculative heresies concerning the nature of God, of Christ and of the Holy Spirit.

The Second Council, held at Constantinople in 381, was called to deal with the heresy of Apollinaris, a bishop of Laodicea, who denied the humanity of Jesus Christ. This council also changed the Nicean Creed by adding the words which define the divinity of the Holy Spirit.

The Third Council was held at Ephesus in 431. The purpose for which it was called was to settle the controversy which had developed over the nature of Mary, the mother of Christ.

The clergy of that age had begun to use the term—"Mary, the Mother of God." Nestorius, the Bishop of Constantinople said God could not have a human parent. Cyril held there was a unification of the two natures. He received the endorsement of the Roman bishop. To end this controversy Emperor Theodosius II called the council to assemble at Ephesus.

There Cyril gathered his followers together and without waiting for the arrival of the Oriental bishops condemned Nestorius.

Later the Oriental bishops met together and condemned Cyril.

Theodosius opposed Nestorius who was driven into exile where he died.

He held that God and Christ were two different beings. The Egyptians who opposed this doctrine, and who taught that the human and divine natures of Christ were blended into one, were called Monophysites.

Eutyches confused the person of Christ with that of God and went so far as to deny that Christ had a human body the same as ours.

The Fourth Council which assembled at Chalcedon in 451, prepared a new creed which affirmed the two natures of Christ, united together with the characteristics of each nature being preserved. The Monophysites broke away from the church at Chalcedon and formed groups in Egypt, Armenia, Syria, and Ethiopia which were known as Coptic, Jacobite, and Ethiopic churches which continue to the present time.

Justinian sought to end the controversy by an edict called The Three Chapters which only created more trouble and which was unacceptable to the churches of the West.

The Fifth Council was held at Constantinople in 553. This council was called to bring to an end the opposition to the Chalcedon creed. A new controversy developed over the theory that there were two separate wills in Christ. This teaching brought about the Monothelite controversy and the conflicting parties were driven farther apart.

The Sixth Council was called by Constantine Pogonatus and was convened at Constantinople in 681. This council decided that those who held that two wills were possessed by Christ were right. Honorius, the bishop of Rome was condemned by the council as a heretic for contending that Christ had only one nature. The Monothelite theory continued to be held by the Maronites, a group who had separated from the apostate church. They were united to the Church of Rome by the Council of Florence in 1445 but still retained their identity.

Both the Greek Catholic and the Roman Catholic churches accepted the findings of the Seventh Council which was held at Nicea in 787. Church historians reveal that some of these councils lacked the dignity and decorum which one would expect to find in a religious assembly. Nazeanzus, who presided over the council held at Constantinople in 381, affirmed that the evils they were called to remedy were only aggravated by the councils.

Christianity made its converts chiefly from the common people, from the slaves, the tradesmen, and the merchants. True, persons of noble birth would be found here and there in the congregations, but this was the exception rather than the rule. It was said of the Savior that the "common people heard him gladly." His message appealed to those in bondage, to those who were oppressed, and to those in distress.

Other religions, too, found converts among the citizens of the empire. Prior to the coming of Christianity the religions of Asia and Africa shared with Judaism the attention that was being given to new religions.

While Christianity was opposed to paganism which was falling into disrepute, there were other doctrines that were opposed to the religion of the Savior. The philosophy developed by the Greeks came into conflict with the doctrine developed by the apostles under the guidance of the Holy Spirit.

The converts to Christianity came from Judaism and Paganism, and although these systems of religion were antagonistic to each other, yet each exerted a direct influence upon Christianity and contributed to the formation of many heretical groups, some of which demand attention.

The book of Acts of Apostles and the epistle of Paul to the churches of Galatia reveal that Judaizing teachers were attempting to influence Jewish Christians before the end of the apostolic period. Certain Jews came to Antioch and endeavored to bind circumcision and the law of Moses upon the disciples. The decision of the apostles at Jerusalem shows that no such obligation was bound upon the Christians. Such teachers traversed many parts of the empire attempting to influence Christians to accept certain parts of the law and its rites.

Ebionism developed from those Jews who had been converted to Christianity, but who refused to give up the ceremonial observances of the Old Testament. The Ebionites taught that Jesus was a prophet, but denied his miraculous birth and counted his sufferings and death of little value. They believed they were the chosen people of God.

Gnosticism developed from attempting to blend paganism and philosophy with Christianity. The Gnostics were the knowing ones who sought to answer every question concerning the origin of the world, of man, and of good and evil. They rejected most of the New Testament, except Paul's letters and part of the gospels. While professing themselves to be Christians they gathered their doctrines from all available sources.

"The questions that busied the Gnostics were such as were raised by the Graeco-Roman and Graeco-Jewish philosophy: How did the world of matter originate? What is the nature and destiny of man? Men were divided by them into three classes, the spiritual, the psychic, and the carnal. The liberation of physical natures, children of light, from their entanglement in matter, was the process of redemption. The historical Christ was a mere man, but he was the mask or vehicle of a higher aeon, the heavenly Christ, who acted in him and through him, but without being really incarnate."*

The Manichaeans were followers of Mani, an eloquent and learned man who believed that he was an apostle of Christ and the promised Paraclete. His doctrine emphasized the contrast between the kingdom of light and the kingdom of darkness, between good and evil, right and wrong. The Manichaeans rejected the Old Testament and those portions of the New Testament which contradicted their doctrines. They claimed to be the only true Christians, practiced celibacy, believed that their ministers were intercessors between God and man, from which the doctrine of indulgences was later developed.

The Monarchian heresy rejected the idea of the sonship of Christ, teaching that he was only an ordinary man until he was baptized, at which time he received the Holy Spirit and his divine characteristics. They also taught that the Father, the Son and the Holy Spirit were the same person. This doctrine still exists among the denominations of this day.

In addition to the above heresies attention should be called to Montanism, so called because the tenets of this doctrine were developed by Montanus of Phrygia. He taught the continuance of miracles, a new order of prophets with new revelations. The Montanists were opposed to the changes that were being made in the church. They condemned the neglect of discipline, the low morals of those who professed to be Christians. In their condemnation of the desires of the flesh they were much like the Gnostics. Montanus claimed to be the Paraclete and to have been selected as the one to establish the kingdom of Christ.

Tertullian accepted the views of Montanism and became one of its greatest teachers.

"About the middle of the second century, Montanus, a native of Ardaban, appeared at Pepuza, in Phrygia, as a prophet and reformer of Christianity, to which he had only lately become a convert. He had visions and while in a state of unconsciousness and ecstasy, prophesied of the near advent of Christ and inveighed against corruption in the church. . . . Montanus felt convinced that in him was fulfilled the promise of Christ concerning the Paraclete who was to guide the church into all truth."†

Some of these heresies were brought into existence by those who sought to reform practices they believed contrary to the Scriptures. The methods used by these reformers only led to further strife and schism.

---

* *History of The Christian Church*—Fisher. Chapter 4, Page 76.
† *Text Book of Church History*—Kurtz. Section 1, Paragraph 37, Pages 131, 132.

The Novatianists came into being as the result of the controversy over those who had left the church when persecution was directed against it. Later, when the persecution ended they wanted to be restored to the fellowship of the church, but some of the bishops would not receive them though they gave evidence of repentance.

The Donatists had their beginning in Carthage very soon after the persecution of Diocletian. They believed that those who gave up their sacred writings became guilty of a mortal sin. They were called traditores. When Caecilian was consecrated as a bishop the ceremonies were performed by Felix of Aptunga, who was declared to be a traditor. This, it was claimed, rendered all of his official acts void. Later a group of bishops elected Majorinus as bishop instead of Caecilian. At the death of Majorinus, Donatus became the bishop and from him this group took its name. The contention that the acts of a bishop were void if his character was called in question troubled the church for years. One council after another declared the Donatists in error and their doctrines died out in the invasion of the Vandals into northern Africa.

A large part of the errors which corrupted the church grew out of the heresies developed in the three centuries after the death of the apostles. Great changes were made in the government, the structure, and the doctrine of the church established by Christ through the apostles. No longer did elders rule the local congregations. The bishops, who have been elevated above their fellow elders, now decided matters for the local church.

The Bishops in the cities became Metropolitans. Those in the five centers of religious influence, Alexandria, Jerusalem, Antioch, Constantinople, and Rome were now called Patriarchs. New doctrines were formed by combining human philosophy and paganism with Christianity. With these changes the church became an apostate organization wholly unlike the church of the Jew Testament age.

> "The state of Christianity might, on the whole, be sound and vigorous; but morbid humours had corrupted many of its parts, and paralyzed much of its influence. Faith is represented as having grown languid, the works of charity had fallen into neglect; the fervour of devotion had been quenched; the simplicity which marked the primitive disciple had been sacrificed on the altar of vanity; insatiable thirst for gain seized men who were devoted to the profession of holiness, and bishops forgot the duties of their sacred charge and the wants of poorer brethren, in their anxiety to promote their own private benefit."*

* *Church History of The Second and Third Centuries*—Jeremie. Chapter 3, Page 50.

326 A.D. CONSTANTINE MOVES CAPITAL TO CONSTANTINOPLE

Constantine issued a general exhortation to all of his subjects to embrace Christianity. The capital was moved to Byzantium and the name changed to Constantinople in honor of the emperor. Here he filled public offices with Christians, exempted the public servants of the church from taxes, built churches, and prohibited all ordinary work on the Lord's Day.

> "In the process of time he acquired more extensive views of the excellence and importance of the Christian religion and gradually arrived at an entire persuasion of its bearing alone the marks of celestial truth and of a divine origin. He was convinced of the falsehood and impiety of all other religious institutions, and, acting in consequence of this conviction, he exhorted earnestly all his subjects to embrace the gospel; and at length employed all the force of his authority in the abolition of the ancient superstition . . . His designs however with respect to the abolition of the ancient religion of the Romans, and the toleration of no other forms of worship but the Christian, were only made known toward the latter part of his life by the edicts he issued out for destroying the heathen temples, and prohibiting sacrifices."[*]

330 A.D. CONSTANTINE HAS SCRIPTURES COPIED

Constantine ordered fifty copies of the scriptures to be prepared under the direction of Eusebius. The three oldest manuscripts, the Vatican, the Sinai and the Alexandrian are supposed to be three of the original manuscripts prepared under the direction of Eusebius, or copies of the originals.

The Vatican manuscript is in the Vatican Library at Rome. It was brought to Rome by Pope Nicholas in 1448. Where he obtained it no one knows. It contains seven hundred, fifty-nine leaves, measuring twelve by twelve inches. In 1889 a photographic copy was made of each page and thus it became available to all the world.

The Sinai manuscript was discovered in a monastery at Mount Sinai by Tischendorf in 1868. He had previously visited this monastery and on his second visit one of the monks informed Tischendorf that he had a copy of the Septuagint translation of the Scriptures. Tischendorf accompanied the monk to his room, where he took from a chest a roll of cloth and from it produced an ancient copy of the scriptures written in the Greek language. Tischendorf was allowed to take it to Cairo, Egypt, where he and two other scholars copied the hundred and ten thousand lines by hand.

The Alexandrian Manuscript was presented to the King of England, Charles I, in 1628 by the Patriarch of Constantinople. It contains seven hundred, seventy-six leaves of vellum, is bound in four volumes and is kept in the British Museum.

---

[*] *Ecclesiastical History*—Mosheim. Volume 1, Book 2, Part 1, Chapter 1, Page 16.

331 A.D. PAGANISM ABOLISHED BY CONSTANTINE

The hierarchy being developed under Constantine was growing. The union of the church and state under Constantine debased the church and destroyed its purity. An outward show of religion was sufficient to secure the favor of those in positions of authority. The morals of those who claimed to be Christians were often at variance with the word of truth. The disputes of the clergy over the heretical doctrines they had developed only revealed their unconverted state. This sad state of affairs caused many to plead for the old religion as a system of worship that brought about no enmity of one worshipper against another. The persecution of the pagans, allowed by the government and carried out by the clergy, caused many to sympathize with the persecuted. The church had joined itself to a temporal government and was no longer concerned with executing the laws of the New Testament. From this time forward the apostasy developed rapidly, with the church legislating against, nullifying, or amending the teaching of the New Testament.

337 A.D. DEATH OF CONSTANTINE AT THE AGE OF SIXTY-FOUR

He received baptism the day before he died at the hands of Eusebius, bishop of Nicomedia. Constantine had three sons, Constantine, Constantius, and Constans, all of whom had given themselves over to dissipation. In the division of the empire, the East fell to Constantius, but later after the death of his two brothers the whole empire was united under his rule.

Constantius favored Christianity for political reasons. He regarded the pagans as adversaries who desired his ruin. The persecutions of the Christians by the pagans had indeed been severe, now the pagans were to be tortured by the same weapons they had used against the Christians. The true disciples of the Lord protested against this persecution of the pagans by one who was a Christian in name only. Constantius ordered the destruction of the pagan temples and sentenced the idolators to death by fire and sword.

Christianity had become the established religion of the empire by the end of the fourth century. The pagan temples were fast disappearing, and great numbers of people were entering the church as a means of securing political advancement. They were little concerned with spiritual things but sought only to make of the religion of Christ a system that was replete with ritualistic ceremonies and human doctrines.

> "Lured by hopes of court favor and preferment, many who were still in heart pagans had hypocritically professed Christianity. Corruption thus crept into the church. To conciliate the ignorant,

idolatrous populace, and to lure them into the Christian churches,
the pomp and pageantry of pagan rites were introduced to supplant
the unostentatious and simple ordinances of the gospel."*

350 A.D. THE BEGINNING OF MASS IN THE CHURCHES

When the sermon ended those who were not allowed to remain
for the Lord's supper were to leave at the words of the deacon, "Ite
Missa Est"—You are dismissed. This was a signal that they could
depart without disturbing the services. It originally had nothing
to do with the services which followed. Later the phrase was short-
ened to "the mass" and was applied to the Lord's supper.

An eminent authority, Polydore Virgil said, "When the Mass is
ended, the deacon turning to the people sayeth, "Ite Missa Est,"
which words are borrowed from the rites of the pagans, and sig-
nifieth that the company may be dismissed. It was used in the
sacrifice of Isis, that when the observances were duly and fully performed and accomplished, then the minister of religion should give
warning or a watchword what time they should lawfully depart.
And of this springs our custom of singing "Ite Missa Est" for a
certain signification that the full service was finished." This practice was not bound upon the apostate church until 394.

354 A.D. THE BIRTH OF AUGUSTINE

Augustine was the son of Patricus, a pagan freeman and Monica,
a Christian mother. In his youth he was sent to Carthage to study
and there, surrounded by the opulence of the pagan city, her great
temples and stately buildings, he began to live a dissolute and
wicked life. He finished two years of study in Cathage, then taught
at Tagaste for a year after which he taught for a period of years in
Carthage and Rome. Later he became a teacher at Milan where he
became associated with people of prominence. Among these was
Ambrose, the bishop of Milan, who was instrumental in converting
him to Christianity in the year 386. He later became the founder of
a school at Tagaste, where he taught theology and philosophy.

He was later appointed Bishop of Hippo, an office which he held
for life. Hippo was not a place of importance but the fame of
Augustine spread to all provinces of the Roman Empire by the
many treatises he produced in defense of Christianity. Christianity had been the official religion of the empire for almost a
century, but when the barbarians came against Rome and captured
it the pagans contended that the gods had brought the calamity
upon the city because the public had forsaken the deities who had
before protected the city from her enemies.

---

* *History of Christianity*—Abbott. Chapter 17, Page 330.

Augustine began his thesis, defending Christianity, in 412. In the work he called attention to the calamities Rome suffered when she worshipped the pagan gods. Augustine held paganism up to ridicule, turning aside the insults and the mockery of the heathens by his caustic ridicule. This voluminous work he called "The City of God" and today it is held by the Roman Catholic Church to be second only to the Bible.

360 A.D. THE FIRST OBSERVANCE OF CHRISTMAS

This was based on a festival of Roman origin, taking the place of the heathen festival in honor of the sun, which was celebrated at the winter solstice on the twenty-fifth day of December, the day erroneously assigned for the solstice in the Julian calendar.

> We account for the late introduction of this festival (Christmas) by the circumstance that the ancient church failed to set any value on the day of Christ's birth and placed it rather in the background as compared with the day of his death."*
>
> "When the first efforts were made to fix the period of the year when Christ's birth took place, there were, as we learn from Clement of Alexandria, advocates for the twentieth of May and for the twentieth or twenty-first of April. The Oriental Christians were of the opinion that both the birth and the baptism of Jesus took place on the sixth of January. Julian I, Bishop of Rome from 337 to 352 contended for the twenty-fifth of December, a view to which the Eastern church came round, while the Western church adopted the Eastern church's view that the baptism was on January sixth. When the festival was at length placed in December, it afforded a substitute to the various nations who had observed a festival of rejoicing that the shortest day of the year had passed."†

The harder the world has tried to justify this date as the day upon which Christ was born, the more hopelessly they become lost in the misty haze of ancient history.

The apostle Paul condemned the Galatian brethren for observing days and months and times and years religiously. Christmas stands in a class with Ash Wednesday, Good Friday, and Easter. All originated with the apostate church and were fully developed by the church of Rome.

The word "Christmas" is derived from "Christes Masse," meaning the mass of Christ. It was not celebrated by the church in the first, second, or third centuries. In the fourth century the apostate church began to honor the birthday of Christ and in the fifth century, as the Roman Catholic Church developed, it became a part of their practice to celebrate the feast day of the pagan god Sol and call it Christ's mass.

---

* *Text Book of Church History*—Kurtz. Volume 2, Paragraph 55.
† *Standard Encyclopedia*—Article—"Christmas."

There is no information as to the day on which Christ was born.
God's word is silent upon the subject. The logical conclusion is that
if the Lord had desired that the birthday of his Son be celebrated,
he would have revealed it. It can not pertain to our spiritual life
for we have been supplied with all things that pertain to life and
godliness.

If we celebrate Christmas we have to borrow it from the church
of Rome. This day has been made a day of festivity and carousing,
which is out of harmony with the spirit of Christ and his teaching.
It is based on tradition and not on God's word. In reality no Christian should observe Ash Wednesday, Good Friday, Easter, or Christmas, for all originated with the church of Rome.

361 A.D. JULIAN BECOMES EMPEROR

Constantius died at Tarsus in Cilicia and Julian, a cousin, who
had been named as heir to the throne became emperor. Julian had
been a pupil of Libanius and had secretly embraced paganism. He
prohibited Christians from teaching rhetoric or the classics, hoping
in this way to prevent the spread of knowledge among the children
of followers of Christ. Christians were deprived of the offices to
which they had been appointed.

Julian favored the Jewish people and endeavored to assist them
in the restoration of their religion. Jesus had said of the temple
that not one stone should be left upon another that should not be
thrown down. Julian wanted to rebuild the temple in Jerusalem
to prove that Christ was a false prophet. His attempt met with
failure. The fact stands forth in history that Julian did not succeed
though all the power of the empire and thousands of workmen were
at his command. The workmen were driven away by earthquakes
which shook the foundations, by the bolts of lightning which accompanied the downpour of rain, and by the fire that appeared along
the walls. These facts are records by many eminent historians.

The Roman historian, Ammianus Marcellinus said, "While
Alphius, assisted by the governor of the province, urged with vigor
and diligence the execution of the work, horrible balls of fire breaking out near the foundations, with frequent and reiterated attacks,
rendered the place from time to time inaccessible to the scorched
and blasted workmen; and the victorious element continuing in this
manner, absolutely and resolutely bent, as it were, to drive them
to a distance, the work was abandoned."

361 A.D. THE PURITY OF THE CHURCH WAS CORRUPTED BY ITS ALLIANCE WITH THE STATE

The Roman emperor, by the office of Pontifex Maximus, directed all religious affairs. When Christianity became the state religion, Constantine assumed all of the authority in the church, which he had exercised as supreme director of paganism. The Christian emperors who followed him claimed the same right, and no one called their claims in question. When decisions were to be made on matters of worship or doctrine they would convene a council, accept its findings, and by the imperial endorsement, bind them upon the church. The theologians of the court tried to justify this course, by investing the emperor with the office of a priest, asserting that Melchisedec was a type of both. The emperors finally decided what could be taught and what could not be taught in the empire. They sold ecclesiastical offices, used the church for political purposes, and allowed intrigue and vice to flourish within her borders.

363 A.D. JULIAN, THE APOSTATE DIED

He was followed by Jovian, Valentinian, Gratian, and Theodosius, all of whom were Christian emperors.

370 A.D. THE FIRST CASE OF INFANT BAPTISM

Christian baptism was immersion of believers in water for the remission or forgiveness of sins. It was a burial signifying the death of the old man of sin and the resurrection to a new life. The meaning of the word, the statements of the scriptures that it is a burial, the fact that a New Testament example shows the candidate went down into the water show the ordinance to be immersion.

> "Baptism probably always took place through immersion in flowing water. . . . That in the New Testament is found no direct case of infant baptism must be regarded as firmly established; attempts to prove its necessity from the manner of its institution, its practice from such passages as Acts 2: 38, I Cor. 1: 16, suffer from the defect that the thing to be proved is presupposed."[*]

379 A.D. THEODOSIUS ASCENDED THE THRONE AS EMPEROR

He attempted to blot paganism from the earth, ordering all pagan temples to be destroyed, including the temple of Serapis at Alexandria. The pagans of Alexandria were from ancient times very fanatical. When the temple of Bacchus was converted into a meet-

---

[*] *A Manual of Church History*—Newman. Volume 1, Chapter 3, Page 136. (Published 1933, by Judson Press.)

ing place for Christians the pagans became so enraged that they killed a large number of Christians and then fled to the temple of Serapis. When Theodosius received the report of their conduct he ordered that the guilty pagans should be pardoned for their crime but that the temple should be destroyed.

A great throng assembled about the temple but no one was willing to destroy the image of their god until a believing soldier seized an axe and cut asunder the head of the idol.

The tradition existed that when the idol fell heaven and earth would fall apart. When this did not happen the whole image was demolished and consigned to the flames. The disillusioned pagans flocked into the church in great number to the detriment of its purity. At this same time Theodosius made Christianity the state religion and compelled his subjects to become Christians. Up to this time conversion was entirely voluntary. Church membership was dependent upon a change of heart and life.

Forced church membership filled the church with unregenerated people. The military spirit of Imperial Rome now entered the church; and its nature was changed. It now began to concern itself with politics and affairs of the state, influencing government officials and endeavoring to mould the minds of men as it desired.

So deeply did the apostate church imprint her mark upon the world that men today are still influenced in religious matters by the things she taught.

CHAPTER 5

CORRUPTION AND FALSE ALLIANCE

We have observed that the first persecution brought against the church was by Judaism. As this opposition to the church began to decline, Christianity came into conflict with paganism, and persecution after persecution was brought against the church. Ultimately Christianity overcame paganism and thousands of those who had once opposed the church now became identified with it, without understanding that such a step called for the reformation of life, separation from the world, and devotion to the cause of Christ. Christianity in its purity was thus destroyed by paganism.

381 A.D. THE FIRST UNBAPTIZED BISHOP, NECTARIUS PLACED IN OFFICE

This was at the request of the Bishop of Tarsus. The primitive idea of the bishop or elder was forgotten and the requirements of the New Testament rejected.

This was repeated over and over again. The people of Milan selected Ambrose to be their bishop. He had not yet been baptized, yet in eight days he was elevated to the episcopal throne. It now becomes evident that when men begin to drift away from the divine guide, the word of God, they lose respect for it and begin to substitute human doctrines to make the gospel attractive to the world. Attention has been called to the changes in government, in doctrine, and in worship. Did God authorize these changes to be made or did he intend for the church to be just as it was when first founded by Christ through the apostles? Paul said, "But though we, or an angel from heaven, preach any other gospel unto you than that which we have preached unto you, let him be accursed."[1]

In this same year a second church council was called by Theodosius at Constantinople. It was attended by one hundred fifty Oriental bishops. This council slightly changed the Nicean creed and affirmed their belief in the personality of the Holy Spirit.

Theodosius issued a decree which prohibited the Arians and the Manichaeans from holding meetings of any kind. If a person turned

---

1. Galatians 1 : 8

from Christianity to paganism, he could not will his property to anyone. The only means by which one could be sure of his life and liberty was to subscribe to the creed of the emperor. Pagan worship was not to be allowed anywhere. Some of the temples had been changed into places of Christian worship but in many of them the priests carried on the pagan rites in secrecy. This was to cease. The priests were to be deprived of their salary, the images of their gods destroyed and their doors closed forever. The Christians marched from city to city. They battered down a stately temple at Palmyra, the ruins of which are still a wonder today.

382 A.D. AN ASSEMBLY FIXED THE LIMIT OF THE BOOKS OF THE NEW TESTAMENT

The collecting of the sacred writings had been going on for a number of years. but there was no agreement among the congregations as to the books that were accepted as being inspired. From the very first the various congregations exchanged their letters with one another. Nearly all of the congregations were in possession of the letters written by the apostles before the close of the first century. As the years passed each congregation decided for itself what books were inspired and what were not. Early church fathers, as they were sometimes called, addressed many letters to the churches in the century after the death of the last apostle. Among them may be mentioned Clement, Barnabas, Papias, Origen and Tertullian. While these men wrote many letters to the churches they were not inspired. These of course found no place in the lists that were prepared by various congregations.

> "There was no central head, no united organization and therefore no possibility of securing a general vote in which all churches should join, or an authoritative edict to which all would submit. Granting that there was no formal settlement at all, but that under the guidance of the Spirit of God the question should settle itself; is there not something sublime in the thought, that works so casually written as many of the books and letters were, should be slowly collected by churches scattered over all the world, until at length they all possessed, in the very same form, that perfect work, which our New Testament unquestionably is. It adds to the certainty, and does not by any means diminish it, to know that there was no restraint upon the fullest inquiry and the freest expression of opinion, and that after two or three hundred years of careful discussion, without general consultation, without collusion, and without any authoritative decision, the churches, with marvelous unanimity, adopted the same collection, and thus the canon was closed."*

---

* *The Origin and History of the New Testament*—Martin. Part 2, Chapter 1, Pages 151, 152.

385 A.D. SIRICIUS, BISHOP OF ROME, DECREED THAT PEOPLE COULD ONLY BE BAPTIZED AT EASTER AND PENTECOST

Here again is legislation where God has not legislated. The great commission of the Savior placed no limit on the time when one could obey the gospel. "Go ye therefore, and teach all nations, baptizing them in the name of the Father, and of the Son, and of the Holy Ghost."[2]

> "The narrow spirit of the Roman church, on the other hand, was here again the first to lay a restraint on Christian liberty. The Roman bishop Siricius, in his decretal addressed to Himerius, bishop of Tarrace, in Spain, A.D. 385, styled it arrogant presumption in the Spanish priests that they should baptize multitudes of people at Christmas, at the feast of Epiphany, and at the festivals of the apostles and martyrs, as well as at other regular times."[*]

The power of the bishop of Rome was extended to other districts, the hierarchy developed, which soon sought to control all religious thought and action.

390 A.D. THE BEGINNING OF AURICULAR CONFESSION

Following the return of those who left the church under persecution, a penitentiary presbyter was appointed to hear their confession of wrongs privately. If they were of such a nature as to render the confession unsuitable for modest ears no public confession was made. Out of this practice came the doctrine that a private confession to a priest was compulsory upon every member of the apostate church. Auricular confession thus became a practice of the church in the fourth century but not until 1215 did it become a universal custom. Later Pope Innocent III made it a fixed part of the doctrine held by the church. This teaching is in direct conflict with Paul's teaching. "For there is one God, and one mediator between God and men, the man Christ Jesus."[3]

395 A.D. DEATH OF THEODOSIUS

His sons, Arcadius and Honorius were proclaimed emperors of the Eastern and the Western part of the empire. There was but one empire but it was to have two emperors. Here was one of the events that eventually led to a separation of the church in the East and the West.

The churches and the bishops of most of the religious world were now dominated by the Patriarchs in the five centers of religious influence, Antioch, Alexandria, Ephesus, Constantinople and Rome.

---

2. Matthew 28:19
* *History of The Christian Religion and Church*—Neander. Volume 2, Section 3, Page 324.
3. 1 Timothy 2:5

All of these patriarchs had equal authority with one another. With the division of the empire under two emperors, the Patriarchs of Antioch, Ephesus, and Alexandria gradually acknowledged the leadership of the Patriarch of Constantinople. This was contested by the Patriarch at Rome and eventually contributed to the break between the church in the Eastern part of the empire and that in the West.

397 A.D. CHRYSOSTUM BECAME BISHOP OF ANTIOCH

This learned man was one of the few who tried to stay the march of the church toward ecclesiastical corruption. He was born in Antioch in 347 and educated under Libanius, a pagan philosopher, but was converted to Christianity by his mother, Anthusa. When he was elevated to the office of bishop, he began to preach against the practice of simony and the immorality of the ecclesiastics. This resulted in accusations being brought against him by Theophilus, Arch-bishop of Alexandria, who called a council of bishops to sit in judgment on Chrysostum. He refused to attend the council and was banished to Nicea in Bithynia. Later he was exiled to Putyos, on the northeast shore of the Black Sea, and compelled to make the journey on foot, bareheaded. The hardships of the journey terminated his life.

400 A.D. PELAGIUS DENIED THE DOCTRINE OF ORIGINAL SIN

Pelagius, a native of Britain, came to Rome near the close of the fourth century. He was well educated in Greek, though the place of his education is not known. He was a man of deep learning and great piety. He was offended by the conduct of the ecclesiastics in Rome. His doctrines were at variance with the accepted teaching of that day. Briefly summed up they were as follows as listed by Augustine, his greatest opponent:

1. Adam was created so he would have died whether he sinned or not.
2. Adam's sin affected only himself and not the human race.
3. New born infants are in the same condition they would have been in if there had been no fall.
4. The human race dies neither in consequence of Adam's death nor his transgression—nor does it rise from dead in consequence of Christ's resurrection.
5. Unbaptized infants will obtain eternal life.
6. The law is as good a means of grace as the gospel.
7. There were some men even before the appearance of Christ who did not commit sin.

Leaving Rome, Pelagius and his disciple, Celestius, came to Africa, where his doctrines came into conflict with the teaching of Augustine. Against these doctrines Augustine brought his teaching that no person could do anything to save himself, but God must do it all. The doctrines of Pelagius were condemned by the council of Ephesus in 431. Long after the death of Augustine the Pelagian doctrine was still taught in the church.

404 A.D. THE ALLIANCE BETWEEN THE CHURCH AND STATE BECAME MORE EVIDENT

Everyone sought membership in the church and nearly everyone was received. Those who were evil and those who wanted to be righteous were alike received into the assemblies. Ambitious and worldly minded men sought office in the church for personal honor and political influence. The real spiritual power of Christianity was far below that of the persecution period. The worship increased in splendor and ritualism but it lost in spirituality. Forms and ceremonies of paganism were introduced into the worship. Some of the old heathen feasts became church festivals with a change in name. Images of saints and martyrs began to appear in church buildings, first as memorials, then as objects of adoration, and eventually as something to be worshipped. As the result of these things the church did not transform the world to her ideals, but the world began to dominate the church.

405 A.D. JEROME COMPLETED THE LATIN TRANSLATION OF THE BIBLE CALLED THE VULGATE

The Old Testament was completed and in general use for several hundred years before the coming of Christ. The epistles to the churches had been carefully collected by various congregations. They exchanged such epistles as they had received until virtually all congregations had complete copies of the inspired writings.

Several translations were made prior to the time of Jerome, among them the Peshito Translation for the Syrians and the translation of Ulphilas for the Teutonic people.

Jerome translated from the Greek into the Latin at Bethlehem where he resided for several years. This Latin translation was made the official translation of the Roman church by the council of Trent. In 1587 Pope Sixtus V appointed a number of scholars to revise the Vulgate pronouncing a papal bull against anyone who would change it in the least way. Pope Clement, in 1590, ordered further revision of the text because of the many errors it contained. More than two thousand changes were made in the text, many of them of a serious nature.

The edition published in 1593 became the official text for the Roman Catholic Church. The English translation of the Vulgate is called the Douay version because it was first published at Douay, in northern France.

410 A.D. THE CAPTURE OF ROME BY ALARIC, THE GOTH

Honorius, Emperor of the western part of the empire, removed his capital to Milan. When he learned that the soldiers of Alaric had occupied northern Italy he fled to Ravenna and there set up his court. Starvation eventually caused the city to surrender. Alaric demanded all the gold and silver and hundreds of silken robes and even after these were paid his soldiers plundered the city, loading their carts with such trophies as appealed to them. Thus eleven hundred sixty-three years after the founding of Rome the proud city became the prey of the Barbarians from the north. After they had sacked the city they moved south along the Appian Way, overrunning all of Southern Italy. Alaric died soon after the capture of Rome and his body was buried in the bed of a river.

411 A.D. THE STEPS OF PENANCE ARRANGED FOR THOSE
WHO LEFT THE CHURCH

For various causes people sometimes left the church and later wanted to be restored to its fellowship. The confession of their sins was accepted as evidence of their repentance but certain acts of penance were imposed upon those who were restored. This might be repeating a certain number of prayers, or singing a definite number of songs. Those who left the church and did not soon return were excommunicated from the fellowship of the believers. The ones who showed signs of repentance were assigned to special seats in the assembly and had to submit to a period of public humiliation, the time and severity of which was determined by the presbyters. When these requirements had been met this was accepted as an indication of their sincerity and they were again allowed to partake of the Lord's Supper.

> "The steps in the process of penance were systematically arranged. The confession of private sins was not required, and therefore, when made it was regarded as a hopeful token of repentance, and was rewarded with the mitigation of the ordinary punishment. Those penitents whose lives had been notoriously sinful were to follow the directions of the bishop or the penitentiary presbyter, if there was one, as was frequently the case in the large Eastern cities."*

In this same period of time the worship of images became more prevalent. The half-converted heathen substituted paintings and

---

* *History of The Christian Church*—Fisher. Chapter 2, Page 109.

images of Christ in the place of the artistic decorations of the temples. People now began to prostrate themselves before them. The defenders of the practice said they were showing their reverence for the absent Lord and his saints. Miraculous cures began to be ascribed to these statues and images. Churches began to be called after the statues, such as, Saint Stephen's, Saint Paul's, Saint Peter's. Relics began to be placed in the churches and to be sold by one church to another.

Along with these changes the primitive idea of the elders as shepherds of the flock, as taught in the New Testament, rapidly passed from view. The bishops presided over the churches and next below them were the presbyters. In many places the deacons tried to assume a position over the presbyters, because they were the ones who were called on by the bishops to read portions of the gospels and to offer prayer. There is a continual growth of the hierarchy that is developing in the apostate church.

Various officials were added to the ranks of the clergy. They increased so rapidly that eventually a law had to be passed limiting their number. No longer were the elders the highest officials in the congregation—they were supplanted by the bishops and above them were the archbishops. No longer was the proclamation of the gospel essential for obedience to Christ, for now church membership was compulsory upon all citizens of the empire. No longer was a burial in baptism necessary as a part of the divine plan, for now sprinkling or pouring water upon the candidate was accepted instead of baptism.

No longer were the oracles of God accepted as the sole guide for the church, for creeds enacted by human legislation had taken the place of the teaching of God's word.

No longer was the church solely concerned with the salvation of souls, it was gradually becoming a religio-political organization.

No longer was purity of life and separation from the world conditions of church membership, for impurity had become so common that no one was shocked by the corruption that existed in the body.

No longer did all Christians have the right of pouring out their spirits before the brethren and speaking for their edification in the public assembly, for now it had become necessary to have a clergyman present to supply the spiritual food for the congregation.

The church thus became an entirely different institution than it was when established by Christ and the apostles. It had forgotten the simplicity of the gospel and the worship had assumed all of the splendor of the temples of the pagans.

416 A.D. INFANT BAPTISM BECAME COMPULSORY

Faithful churches rejected this practice of infant baptism, not only refusing to baptize their children but contending for the baptism of believers only.

> "Baptism was administered at first only to adults, as men were accustomed to conceive baptism and faith as strictly connected. We have all reason for not deriving infant baptism from apostolic institution, and the recognition of it which followed somewhat later, as an apostolical tradition serves to confirm this hypothesis. Irenaeus is the first teacher in whom we find any allusion to infant baptism."*

431 A.D. THE COUNCIL AT EPHESUS

This council composed of two hundred bishops was called to condemn Nestorius. Many of those who attended came with an armed escort. Nestorius believed that Christ was not God, the Father, reasoning that God could not have a human parent. He eventually was driven into exile where he died. About this same time it was decreed that bishops could not be appointed in small towns as the presbyters were sufficient. Later the country congregations were denied permanent elders. Visiting elders were sent to the country churches to look after their spiritual welfare. Thus the country churches in a district became affiliated with the city churches in a district and this came to be known as a parish.

The Roman empire has now become Christianized, slavery has decreased, gladiatorial combats were prohibited, crucifixion was abolished. In turn Christianity had become paganized. It became the state religion and all other religions were suppressed. Heathen temples were destroyed. Worshippers of idols were ordered put to death and their property delivered to the state.

Church membership became compulsory, thousands of persons who had no change of heart and who did not purpose to change their lives were thus brought into the church. The church became an entirely different institution than it was in the beginning. Its government had been changed, the simplicity of the worship had been destroyed by the introduction of pagan practices and ceremonies. The doctrine of Christ and the apostles was forgotten and the church was swept into apostasy. When the teaching of the New Testament was rejected the church was like a ship at sea without chart or compass. The scriptures had virtually been taken from the people and Christianity had been buried beneath human affairs. The church in its purity was fast disappearing from the face of the earth and in its place rose an ecclesiastical hierarchy that directed both civil and religious affairs.

---

* *History of The Christian Religion and Church*—Neander. Section 3, Page 311.

434 A.D. LEO I BECAME BISHOP OF ROME

He is called the first pope by some historians. He issued notice to the priests that they could no longer marry. Following his ascension he assumed all authority over the churches of the West.

The events which followed were steps in the development of the doctrine of the Primacy of Peter. Leo I asserted the claim that Peter was the chief of the apostles and the first bishop of Rome with such vigor that he is often called "the first pope."

He eventually secured from Valentinian an edict that required all churches of the West to submit all questions of dispute to him and the decision he made was to be final. About this same time the title of "papa" or "pope" began to be applied to the bishops and later it became the exclusive title of the Roman bishops.

The teaching that Peter was the first pope was of slow growth. The conclusion that Peter was selected by the Lord to be the head of the visible church was drawn from a wrong understanding of the words of our Savior to the apostle Peter at Caesarea Philippi. In response to the question of the Savior, "Whom do ye say that I am," Peter replied, "Thou art the Christ the Son of the living God." Jesus said, "Blessed art thou Simon, son of Jonas, for flesh and blood hath not revealed this unto thee, but my Father which is in heaven, and I say unto thee, That thou art Peter, and upon this rock I will build my church and the gates of hell shall not prevail against it. And I will give unto thee the keys of the kingdom of heaven and whatsoever thou shalt bind on earth shall be bound in heaven and whatsoever thou shalt loose on earth shall be loosed in heaven." The word "Petros" means a stone—while the word that our Savior used was "Petra" which means a great rock—it was the great rock—the truth that He was the Christ the Son of God upon which He purposed to build his church and not upon Peter.

After the resurrection of Christ he met his disciples on the shore of the sea of Galilee after they had returned to their former vocation. Jesus asked Peter, "Lovest thou me more than these?" When Peter professed his love for Jesus, the Savior said, "Feed my lambs." Again he asked the same question and again Peter assured the Savior of his love and received the admonition to feed his sheep. When the Lord asked the question the third time the apostle Peter said, "Lord, thou knowest all things, thou knowest that I love thee." And again Peter received the instruction to "Feed my sheep." This has been regarded by some people as the appointment of Peter to be the chief shepherd of the flock of God.

The tradition developed that Peter became the first bishop of Rome and that his ministry as bishop passed to the bishops who were appointed after his death.

Thus the teaching was developed that the successors of Peter, the bishops of Rome, hold the keys of the kingdom and exercise all spiritual authority as head of the church.

The development of the papacy is not based upon the teaching of the scriptures. It is revealed upon the pages of history as something that was of slow growth, resulting from the elevation of one elder above his fellow elders.

The study of the scriptures and of the history of the early church reveal that there was no distinction between the elders and the bishops in the New Testament times. The word "elder" signified that they were men of age and experience, while the word "bishop" signified the work they were to do in overseeing the flock and looking after its spiritual welfare. No elder or bishop exercised authority over more than one congregation in the New Testament times. "And when they had ordained them elders in every church, and had prayed with fasting, they commended them to the Lord on whom they believed."[4] "And from Miletus he sent to Ephesus and called the elders of the church."[5] Attention has before been called to the elevation of one elder to a position of authority or prominence over his fellow elders. The one thus elevated was to have the deciding voice in matters of judgment. Gradually a line of separation was drawn between the elders and the bishops. Here is the beginning of a system of church government that was contrary to the New Testament.

Because of the tradition that Peter was the founder of the church in Rome, a certain honor was conceded to the bishop in that place, though no special power was exercised or claimed by him in the beginning.

440 A.D. ATTILA AND HIS HUNS INVADE ROME

This followed the defeat of Attila at Chalons by the Romans and the Visigoths. The cities of Aquileia, Padua, Vicenza, and Bergamo and the plains of Lombardy were laid waste. As he drew near Rome, Leo I, the Bishop of Rome went to his camp and persuaded him to spare the city, and thus the bishop was elevated in the minds of the people and the way was made easy for him to assume more power.

> "When Attila declared his resolution of carrying his victorious arms to the gates of Rome, he was admonished by his friends, as well as by his enemies, that Alaric had not long survived the conquest of the eternal city. His mind, superior to real danger, was assaulted by imaginary terrors, nor could he escape the influence of superstition which had so often been subservient to his designs.

4. Acts 14 : 23
5. Acts 20 : 17

The pressing eloquence of Leo, his majestic aspect and sacerdotal robes, excited the veneration of Attila for the spiritual father of the Christians. The apparition of the two apostles, St. Peter and St. Paul, who menaced the Barbarian with instant death, if he rejected the prayer of their successor, is one of the legends of ecclesiastical history."*

451 A.D. THE COUNCIL OF CHALCEDON

Five hundred bishops were present at this council called by Emperor Marian. This council advocated the worship of Mary, the mother of Jesus. Here is another step in apostasy, for the clergy taught that prayers should be addressed to Mary and that she would convey them to Christ.

Mary was given a position of prominence because she was the mother of Christ and because the angel had said, "Blessed art thou among women."

The adoration of Mary grew rapidly and the tradition that Mary remained a virgin after the birth of Christ became a doctrine of the apostate church.

The controversies over the doctrines concerning the nature of Christ increased the respect for Mary to a place where it surpassed the respect that was paid to the martyrs. Mary was called the "mother of God" and the tradition grew that when Mary died she was taken to heaven by the angels where she became queen of heaven. This developed into the doctrine of the Assumption of Mary.

As Mary came to be regarded as the ruler of heaven the prayers of the people began to be addressed to her rather than to God, through Jesus Christ. The pagans of all lands had a female deity whom they worshipped, who was called "The Great Mother." From this pagan idea developed the adoration of Mary.

Religious festivals also began to be observed in honor of Mary, such as The Feast of The Annunciation, The Feast of Purification, The Feast of The Ascension of Mary, and The Feast of The Birth of Mary.

The Council of Chalcedon voted that the Patriarch of Constantinople should be the chief bishop for the church. The protests of the Roman bishop and his delegates fell on deaf ears. The struggle for power between these two rivals was to have a deep and lasting influence upon the church.

The foundation was being laid for the differences which ult n-ately would divide the apostate church into the Roman Catholic Church in the West and the Greek Catholic Church in the East.

---

* *Decline and Fall of The Roman Empire*—Gibbon. Chapter 25, Page 407.

476 A.D. ROME CAPTURED BY ODOACER WITH THE HERULI

Odoacer deposed the boy emperor Romulus Augustus and took the title of King of Italy and the empire of the west went down. The eastern empire, with Constantinople as the capital continued until 1453.

500 A.D. THE FIRST CODE OF ECCLESIASTICAL LAWS
COMPILED BY EXIQUICES

This code of laws contained all of the decrees of the bishops from Siricius and the findings and rules of all ecumenical councils and provincial synods. Here we have the introduction of something more that is new in religion, something that is entirely unlike that which is revealed in the New Testament. Here is the substitution of human ideas for the Word of God.

If God approved these changes, how may we know that he did? At what place and at what time was man authorized to make such changes? One departure from the truth will bring about another departure from the Word of God.

One thing is evident from God's word and that is the fact that Christ gave to the church no legislative power, and to take from or to add to the Word of God is to bring oneself under the anathema of heaven.

Paul said, "But though we or an angel from heaven preach any other gospel unto you than that which we have preached unto you, let him be accursed."

During the lifetime of the apostles, the church looked to them for spiritual guidance. Knowing that the time would come when the apostles would no longer be here to supply that guidance the Holy Spirit gave this message by inspiration, "Therefore, brethren, stand fast, and hold the traditions which ye have been taught, whether by word, or our epistle."[6] Through the years these admonitions have been forgotten. Religious leaders left the simplicity of the apostles' doctrine, producing a new religious organization that was wholly unlike the church established by Christ.

In order to prevent the spread of views opposed to the apostate church those accused of teaching heresy were cruelly persecuted. Those who refused to depart from the faith by giving up the teaching of the New Testament were condemned as heretics. As the apostate church continued to grow, it became apparent that it had within it more of the practices and customs of paganism and Judaism than of Christianity.

---

6. 2 Thessalonians 2:15

CHAPTER 6

A UNIVERSAL BISHOP

514 A.D. THE BISHOPS OF ROME ASSUMED THE POWER OF RULING OVER MORE CITIES THAN THE CITY OF ROME

The Patriarchs in the centers of religious influence; Antioch, Alexandria, Ephesus, and Constantinople refused to surrender all authority to the Bishop in the city of Rome, though he pleaded that Rome was recognized as the capital of the world, although the seat of government was at Constantinople. The position of prominence that the Bishop of Rome demanded for himself was bitterly contested every step of the way.

533 A.D. THE BEGINNING OF THE PAPACY

Justinian, emperor of the eastern part of the empire decreed that Boniface, the Bishop of Rome, should be called "Rector Ecclesiae," Lord of the Church.

When Justinian came to the throne of the eastern empire in 525, he planned to conquer the lands occupied by the barbarian emperors, to revive the empire, and to bring about a uniform doctrine in the church.

He succeeded in bringing most of Italy and part of northern Africa under control. To bring about uniformity of doctrine in the church he gave supreme authority to Boniface as the Universal Bishop of a universal church. Here is the real beginning of the papacy.

The formation of the apostate church was now complete. The doctrines and practices of this organization are not found in the New Testament. Nowhere within that record will you find mention of a Universal Bishop, of Patriarchs, Metropolitans, Arch-bishops, Arch-deacons, Monks, or Abbots.

Neither is there any mention of the mass, Lent, holy water, purgatory, compulsory celibacy, abstaining from meats, or indulgences, and yet these things are part of the system of religion set forth by the Roman Catholic Church.

According to Roman Catholic teaching Christ intended that the powers he conferred upon his apostles should pass on to their successors.

CHANGES WHICH PRODUCED THE APOSTATE CHURCH

1. The study of God's word neglected
2. The government of the church changed
3. The office of elder disappeared
4. The plan of redemption altered
5. Simplicity of worship changed by ritualism
6. Christianity became paganized
7. Church membership made compulsory
8. Tradition accepted as authority equal to Scriptures
9. Councils determined doctrine of the church
10. Obedience to Christ as the means of Salvation forgotten

They believe that Peter, by appointment, was invested with special power and became the first pope. This is denied by the non-Catholic world. Christ and not Peter is called "the head of the church." "And he is the head of the body, the Church: who is the beginning, the first born from the dead; that in all things he might have the preeminence."[1] The New Testament and history fail to support the authority of Peter as the first bishop of Rome. The tradition that Peter was the first bishop of Rome and that he became the first pope is without foundation. It is true that the church in Rome had bishops or elders, but for five hundred years after the establishment of the church those bishops were not popes.

It was Leo I, bishop of Rome, who first emphasized the doctrine of the supremacy of Peter. He was able to elevate himself, as bishop of Rome, in the minds of the people by persuading the barbarian invaders to spare the city when they came against it. This caused the populace to look to him as leader rather than to the emperor.

"Leo I, (A.D. 450) seems to have been the first bishop of Rome who interfered with the election of bishops in other dioceses. He is reported to have interposed in the institution of Anatolius, 'by the favor of whose assent he obtained the bishopric of Constantinople'; and he is stated to have confirmed Maximus, of Antioch, and Donatus, an African bishop. But on the other hand, other

---

1. Colossians 1 : 18

bishops arrogated the same privileges—for instance, Lucifer, a Sardinian bishop, ordained Paulinus, bishop of Antioch; Theophilus, of Alexandria, ordained Chrysostum; Eustathius, of Antioch, ordained Evagrius, bishop of Constantinopole, etc.; and Acacius and Patrophilus expelled Maximus, and instituted Cyril, bishop of Jerusalem in his stead. All these acts, and many more might be cited, were done without any reference to the bishop of Rome. Here we have the battle of the bishops—the raging battle for supremacy. Is it not remarkable that we read of no such functionaries, and of no such ungodly stratagems, in the apostolic age? We are still in the mystical regions of the fifth century, tracing out the successive innovations which corrupted the primitive church, and which, by degrees, led the church into the wilderness, where its identity was entirely lost to view."*

Apostacy develops slowly and fixing a definite date for the beginning of any certain apostasy is often difficult and sometimes impossible. It is certain that the apostasy seen by Paul began when the man of sin developed.

The basic departure was exalting one elder or bishop above his fellow elders, or bishops, and giving him the title of "The Bishop." His authority soon extended to other congregations. At a later time special honor was conferred upon the bishops having authority in prominent cities. They received the title of "Metropolitans" as spiritual leaders in a metropolis. Those in the centers of religious influence, Alexandria, Antioch, Ephesus, and Constantinople were called Patriarchs.

The contest for supremacy among the patriarchs narrows down to a contest between Constantinople and Rome, with Rome eventually gaining the victory. From this time forward the church in its purity gradually disappeared under the persecution of the apostate church.

Pagan Rome had been the ruling power down to the time of Constantine, now as the apostate church began to assume the characteristics of papalism the true church was compelled to flee away into the wilderness where she was nourished for twelve hundred and sixty years. John said the serpent cast out a flood after her that she might be destroyed.

A flood of false teaching was launched against the church in its purity in an effort to destroy her, but the destruction of the pure church could not be accomplished as long as the gospel was accepted as the means of salvation and Christ remained as the head of the church. Though the true church was compelled to flee into the wilderness, she was to re-appear in all of her purity at the end of the twelve hundred and sixty years.

---

* *History of Reformatory Movements*—Rowe. Second Part, Pages 290, 291.

568 A.D. LOMBARDS CONQUER THE NORTHERN PART OF ITALY

Under their King Alboin, the Lombards who came from the lower Elbe in Germany, invaded and conquered the northern part of Italy, which still bears the name Lombardy. They were converted to the faith and Pope Gregory bestowed upon their king the "Iron Crown," so called because tradition said it was made in part from one of the nails of the cross on which Christ was crucified. The Lombards ruled in northern Italy for two hundred years during which time the papacy grew unopposed. Gregory occupied the papal throne for fourteen years and in this time he became the leading man in Rome. His greatest problem in this time was to prevent the Lombards from encroaching on his territory.

To prevent this he raised armies, fought the Lombard kings, and signed treaties of peace with them when it was to his advantage to do so. The Roman church had endowments of land from which she derived a large income that was used for the benefit of the church. It became the responsibility of Gregory to prevent the Lombards from extending their rule over the territory which later came to be known as the Papal States. The landowners of these districts supported him in his efforts to defend their interests and the power of the papacy continued to grow. In his contacts within the church Gregory professed to have all the authority which Leo I had claimed as the successor of the apostle Peter. He sternly rebuked the Patriarch of Constantinople for using the title of "Universal Bishop," which Gregory contended belonged alone to the Patriarch in the city of Rome. While occupied with these affairs Gregory continued to labor for the spread of the doctrines of the Catholic church among the barbarian nations. He put forth a strong effort to end the heresies and the contentions which found their way into the church. In his own district he severely punished those guilty of selling offices in the church. Though he was a nominal subject of the eastern emperors, he received no protection from them against the Lombards, who from time to time threatened the papacy and the city of Rome.

By refusing to be submissive to either the Lombard kings or to the eastern emperors, the popes came to be acknowledged as the real rulers of Rome and the surrounding provinces. The relationship of the popes and the eastern emperors was never friendly and eventually their relation was ended by the refusal of the popes to obey the edict of the emperor prohibiting the use of images in the church. The Lombard king sustained the popes and since the emperor had no troops to send to enforce his decrees, his imperial power shortly came to an end. This break between the pope and the emperor contributed to the break between the church in the

East and the church in the West which later resulted in the formation of the Roman Catholic Church in the West and the Greek
Catholic Church in the East.

588 A.D. JOHN, THE PATRIARCH OF CONSTANTINOPLE ASSUMED THE TITLE OF UNIVERSAL BISHOP

Gregory, the Bishop of Rome denounces the act in a letter to the
emperor, saying that whosoever assumed the title was the fore-
runner of the antichrist. This date marks the beginning of the
doctrine of Extreme Unction for the dying.

590 A.D. ASCENSION OF GREGORY TO THE PAPAL CHAIR

Gregory was the first monk to occupy the papal chair. He sought
the seclusion of the cloister in preference to the position which his
high birth conferred upon him. He was a man of deep piety and
was much opposed to the heresies and disorders which had developed within the Roman church. He was very active in punishing
those guilty of simony.

> "This remarkable man had a great diversity of gifts. He was fiery,
> zealous, charitable, quick to discern the tendencies of his times and
> use them. He had, besides, administrative ability of a high order.
> Through this splendid combination of gifts and qualifications he
> gathered up into himself the lines of history and determined the
> future course of papacy. Consciously or unconsciously, he was con-
> trolled by the idea that the authority of Peter was universal. He
> was the successor of Peter, and he was consequently the source of
> all authority."*

593 A.D. THE DEVELOPMENT OF THE DOCTRINE OF PURGATORY

This doctrine was first advocated in 220. Now it was advocated
by Augustine, though it had been condemned by the council of
Constantinople in 553.

> "The introduction of the doctrine of purgatory was due to the
> influence of Augustine, who suggested that imperfect Christians
> may be purified in the intermediate state, by purgatorial fire, from
> their remaining sin. His conjecture was converted into a fixed
> belief. Thus the intermediate state was transmitted into a purga-
> tory. All perfected saints, it was now believed, and not alone
> martyrs, with others of exceptional sanctity, as had been formerly
> assumed, go at once to heaven."†
>
> "We shall not here enter into a particular account of the public
> supplications, the holy pilgrimages, the superstitious services, paid
> to departed souls, the multiplication of temples, altars, penitentine
> garments, and a multitude of other circumstances, that showed the
> decline of genuine piety, and the corrupt darkness that was eclipsing

---

* *History of The Christian Church*—Moncrief. Chapter 2, Page 176.
† *History of The Christian Church*—Fisher. Chapter 4, Page 142.

the lustre of primitive Christianity. As there were none in these times to hinder the Christians from retaining the opinions of their pagan ancestors concerning departed souls, heroes, demons, temples and such like matters, and even transferring them into their religious services; and as, instead of entirely abolishing the rites and institutions of ancient times, these institutions were still observed, with some slight alterations. All this swelled of necessity the torrent of superstition and deformed the beauty of the Christian religion and worship with those corrupt remains of paganism which still subsist in a certain church. It will not be improper to observe here, that the famous pagan doctrine, concerning the purification of departed souls, by means of a certain kind of fire, was more amply explained and confirmed now than it had formerly been. Everybody knows, that this doctrine proved an inexhaustible source of riches to the clergy through the succeeding ages, and that it still enriches the Romish Church with its nutritious streams."[*]

Lowet gave this description of purgatory—"At the center of the earth is the place of the damned, above it lies purgatory, divided into three regions. The lowest division is largely tenanted by the souls of the priests, bishops and monks. The bishops with mitres of fire on their heads and a burning cross in their hands are clad in chasubles of flame. The average time of a Christian of more than usual sanctity, (in purgatory) one who has never committed a mortal sin, is a hundred and twenty-three years, three months, and fifteen days."

In the writings of Michael Muller, we find this information: "From the smallest spark of this purgatorial fire, souls suffer more intense pain, than all the fires of the world put together could produce. In these fires they suffer more than all the pains of disasters and the most violent diseases. They suffer more than all the most cruel torments undergone by malefactors or invented by the most barbarous tyrants. They suffer more than all the torture of the martyrs summed up together. Our terrestrial fire was not created to torment man, but the fire in purgatory was created by God for no other purpose than to be the instrument of his justice."

The doctrine of purgatory had been condemned by the council of Constantinople in 533, but by the year 1070 it became a part of the teaching of the apostate church. The clergy persuaded by the gifts of anxious friends, said masses for the deliverance of the souls of the departed from purgatory. This proved to be a profitable source of income for the prelates.

Search your Bible through and you will not find this doctrine taught by Christ or any of the apostles. Since the word of God does not supply such information, it can only be based upon the traditions of men.

---

[*] *Ecclesiastical History*—Mosheim. Volume 1, Part 2, Chapter 3, Page 126.

607—FURTHER GROWTH OF THE PAPACY

Phocas became the emperor by the murder of Mauricius, the rightful emperor, his wife and five children. Phocas, a general, led a revolt against Mauricius, who fled to Chalcedon where he was put to death. Boniface, the bishop of Rome, recognized Phocas as the rightful emperor and Phocas recognized Boniface as the Universal Bishop, head of all the churches. The development of the papacy had been of slow growth. Paul's warning to the church of Thessalonica foretold of the falling away that made it possible for the man of sin to destroy the purity of the Lord's church and to develop a hierarchy that dominated the world. "Let no man deceive you by any means: for that day shall not come, except there come a falling away first, and that man of sin be revealed, the son of perdition; Who opposeth and exalteth himself above all that is called God, or that is worshipped; so that he as God sitteth in the temple of God, showing himself that he is God."[2]

When Paul wrote to Timothy he gave him information concerning the coming apostasy, stating as a part of the teaching of that dark age, the doctrine of "forbidding to marry, and commanding to abstain from meats which God hath created to be received with thanksgiving—." These prophetic warnings have been fulfilled in the development of the doctrines of the papacy.

The era of the Dark Ages now swept over the church. Human heads now directed the affairs of the papal institution which had driven the church of Christ into obscurity.

Bribery, corruption, immorality and bloodshed marked the course of the papal church among the children of men. Kings habitually sold church offices to the highest bidders, regardless of their qualifications. The corruption of the clergy brought about the corruption of the doctrine also. Men drifted away from the word of God, forgot its warnings, ignored its teaching, and substituted human ideas to make a religion that was attractive to the world.

Councils legislated for the churches, bound upon them human doctrines, formed rituals to be used in church services, introduced new ceremonies and created offices unknown to the word of God. In the church of Christ there was no legislating by uninspired men, but with the creation of church councils this was changed.

Questions would arise on some point of doctrine that were unanswered by the Scriptures, but instead of accepting the teaching that "the secret things belong unto God," a council would be called to decide what should be the teaching of the church on the matter. With a great display of dignity and piety the presiding bishop would state a proposed change in doctrine. Discussion and debate

2. 2 Thessalonians 2 : 3-4

would follow and at the end of the session a vote would be taken, the ballots counted and the doctrine or practice accepted by the majority would become the teaching of the church. What had happened? Uninspired men had fastened upon the religious world a doctrine, a practice or a ceremony unknown to the word of God.

632—THE RISE OF MOHAMMED

The only religion tolerated within the Roman Empire at this time was their form of Christianity. Now a new religion began to take the place of Christianity in the East. Its founder was Mohammed, who was born in the city of Mecca. He was brought up by his relatives, who were heathens, without an education. He was first a shepherd and later a merchant. His travels brought him into contact with Juadism and certain of the heresies developed by the Greek philosophers within the Church. Later a journey through Syria brought Christianity to his attention. From a corrupted form of Christianity, from Judaism, and from heathenism, Mohammed developed a system of religion called Islam, which means submission to God.

Prominent points of the religion of Mohammed are the belief that Allah or God is one; that all events, whether good or evil, are ordained and must be borne without murmuring; that God's revelation to man is found in the sayings of Mohammed.

The followers of Mohammed believe that God sent his prophets Adam, Abraham, Moses, and Jesus into the world to reveal his will to men, but the greatest prophet of them all was Mohammed, the Comforter promised by Jesus. Man, they believe, will be able to gain Paradise by his own good works, his prayers, his fastings, his alms, and by his pilgrimages to Mecca.

When Mohammed's friends and relatives were aroused by his teaching he was forced to flee to Medina, where he established a government in which he was the prophet, the lawgiver, and the supreme ruler. After the death of Mohammed his followers launched their holy war for the spread of Islam.

They first fell upon Persia and spread their religion over a large part of Asia. Turning to the West they brought Egypt, Palestine, and Syria under their control. People were forced to accept the religion of Mohammed or be put to death. As the forces of Islam approached the borders of the Eastern empire they met with stout resistance so they turned to the northern part of Africa, where they planted their religion all the way to Gibraltar. Here they crossed the strait and extended their influence to Spain. In a period of less than one hundred years they had conquered most of the eastern and southern provinces of the empire of Rome.

"According to the prophet, heathen, apostates and schismatics were to be exterminated, while Jews and Christians were given the choice of Koran, tribute, or death. The Arabian armies were full of unquenchable fanaticism, and a thirst for plunder and dominion. They were terrible in attack, but mild in victory. The favorite battle-cry of one of their great leaders was; "Fight—fight—Paradise—Paradise." To the victor and the slain alike the delights of heaven were promised. The successors of Mohammed united all Arabs under their banners. The Eastern provinces of the empire, poorly supported by the emperor, fell an easy prey to the invaders. By 637 Damascus and Jerusalem were in the hands of the infidel. Africa, weakened by doctrinal dissension, was next invaded and conquered. The enemies of Christianity did not fare any better. Persia shared the fate of Syria and Africa. At the beginning of the eighth century the Saracens passed over into Spain and in eight years completed the conquest of that country. Then they crossed the Pyrenees and occupied the south of Gaul. The Mohammedan power seemed to be encircling Christendom, and threatening to destroy the church and Christianity itself."*

The influence of the church was hurt by these conquests. The church had lost the power and zeal that it possessed when it was the subject of persecution. For years it had depended upon the influence of the state to bring others into the fold of believers. When that support was removed the church was helpless. It could not change the religion of the invaders and by them it was almost destroyed. The churches founded by Paul, the churches which had occupied a position of prominence and influence, the churches of northern Africa, where Origen, Athanasius, Tertullian and Augustine had been leaders of religious thought and activity, were all brought under the control of the Moslems and their work stifled.

The Moslem religion had some points that are worthy of mention. They destroyed all pictures and images that they found in churches, regarding them as idols. None of their subjects could partake of strong drink, and all of them were required to pray five times each day.

666—POPE VITALIAN AUTHORIZED THE USE OF INSTRUMENTAL MUSIC IN THE WORSHIP

Pope Vitalian sanctioned the use of an organ in the worship of the Roman church in this year, but many years elapsed before they were received with favor by the Catholic churches. There is just as much authority for the mass, for the worship of images, for purgatory, and for the adoration of Mary as there is for instrumental music in church worship. Not until the apostasy developed and the papacy was formed did mechanical music find its way into

---

* *History of The Christian Church*—Fisher. Period 4, Chapter 1, Page 154.

the church worship. There is no mention of its use in the New Testament church nor any mention of it by the apostles.

For hundreds of years after the death of the apostles there is no mention of its use. Ambrose, Chrysostum, Eusebius and Basil wrote much about the worship of the church but they do not make mention of, mechanical aids to the worship. Basil expressly condemns its use as ministering only to the base appetites of men. No one who is guided by the scriptures can be led to believe that instrumental music was connected with the worship of the early church.

> "The general introduction of instrumental music can certainly not be assigned to a date earlier than the fifth or sixth centuries, yea, even Gregory, The Great, who, toward the end of the sixth century, added greatly to the existing church music, absolutely prohibited the use of instruments."*

The use of instrumental music was abolished by Pope Gregory in 1074, and Thomas Aquinas writing two hundred years later, said, "The church does not use instrumental music, harps and psalteries to praise God that she may not seem to Judaize." The Bible does not authorize it, God never commanded it and those who use it have borrowed it from the practices of the apostate church. Here is another practice which the religious world needs to surrender to get back to the religion of Christ.

672—BEDE TRANSLATED THE BIBLE INTO ENGLISH

He also wrote the Ecclesiastical History of the British Nation. It is an authority on the period of time of which he wrote.

680—THE SIXTH COUNCIL CONVENED AT CONSTANTINOPLE

This council was called by Constantine Pegonator to condemn heresy. During this meeting Pope Honorius was deposed and excommunicated. The doctrine of the infallibility of the pope had not yet been advocated.

732—CHARLES MARTEL DEFEATED THE MOSLEMS AT THE BATTLE OF TOURS

This battle, fought one hundred thirty miles southwest of Paris broke the power of the Moslems and saved Christian civilization by preventing further spread of their religion.

---

*44 *History of Reformatory Movements*—Rowe. Part 2, Page 318.

753—POPE STEPHEN AUTHORIZED SPRINKLING WHEN NECESSARY

The first departure from apostolic teaching and practice was the case of Novatian who in the year 251 received clinic baptism at the hands of the elders of the church. Being, as he believed, about to die he requested that they pour or sprinkle water upon him for baptism and if recovery was made he would then be immersed.

Certainly this practice did not come into common use until after it received the endorsement of Pope Stephen in 753, of which the Edinburgh Encyclopedia said, "The first law of sprinkling was obtained in the following manner: Pope Stephen II being driven from Rome by Adolphus, King of the Lombards, in 753, fled to Pepin, who, a short time before had usurped the crown of France. Whilst he remained there, the monks of Cressy, in Britany, consulted him, whether, in case of necessity, baptism poured on the head of the infant would be lawful.

Stephen replied that it would. But though the truth of this fact be allowed—which, however, some Catholics deny,—yet pouring or sprinkling was admitted only in cases of necessity. It was not till the year 1311 that the legislature, in a council held at Ravenna, declared immersion or sprinkling to be indifferent. In Scotland, however, sprinkling was never practiced in ordinary cases till after the Reformation (about the middle of the sixteenth century). From Scotland it made its way into England in the reign of Elizabeth, but was not authorized in the Established Church." (Article on Baptism.)

Dr. Whitley, a distinguished preacher of the Church of England said, "Immersion was religiously observed by all Christians for thirteen centuries, and was approved by the Church of England. And since the change of it into sprinkling was made without any allowance from the author of the institution, or any license from any council of the Church (of England), being that which the Romanist still urgeth to justify his refusal of the cup to the laity, it were to be wished that this custom (immersion) might be again of general use." Indeed the writings of the apostles show the baptism of the New Testament to be a burial. "Buried with him in baptism, wherein also ye are risen with him through the faith of the operation of God, who hath raised him from the dead."[3] It cannot be shown either in the Old or the New Testament that the sprinkling or pouring of water alone upon a person was in any way connected with salvation.

The testimony is indisputable that for thirteen hundred years from the time of the apostles immersion was universally practiced until license was granted by the Pope to practice sprinkling by the

3. Colossians 2 : 12

authority of the Catholic church. It was bound upon the people against their wishes, though they later yielded to the ecclesiastical decree. Here, too, is a practice and doctrine that must be surrendered if the churches of Christendom are to get back to the Bible.

754—PEPIN DEPOSED CHILDERIC, KING OF THE FRANKS

Charles Martel, who had saved Christian civilization by defeating the Saracens at the battle of Tours was only an officer of the court of Childeric though he exercised authority as the head of the nation of Franks. At the death of Martel, his son Pepin desiring to be king sent an embassy to Pope Stephen asking if he should not have the right to be king in name, since he was king in reality. Pope Stephen replied that it seemed only reasonable that such should be the case, so Pepin deposed Childeric and was himself crowned King of the Franks.

When the Lombards encroached upon the lands of the Pope, Stephen appealed to Pepin for assistance. Pepin entered Italy, defeated the Lombards and restored to the Pope the lands that were under dispute. These lands rightfully belonged to the emperor of the East, but his claims were ignored and these lands were added to the papal possessions.

764—LEO III CAME TO THE THRONE IN THE EAST

He immediately issued a decree condemning the use of images in the worship and the use of incense. When he had cleared the churches of the East of images he turned his attention to the churches of the West. He demanded that they cease the use of images. The pope not only opposed the execution of the edict but excommunicated the emperor and the churches of the East. The term "Iconoclasts" meaning "image breakers" was applied to those who destroyed the images in the churches of the East.

Here was another conflict between the Papacy in the West and the Empire in the East. This contributed to the separation of the church in the East and West, resulting in the formation of the Roman Catholic Church and the Greek Catholic Church. Watch for the final break which brought these institutions into existence.

774—CHARLEMAGNE SENT BACK TO DESIDERIUS HIS DAUGHTER WHOM HE HAD DIVORCED

Desiderius, King of the Lombards, declared war on Charlemagne. Desiderius was defeated and Charlemagne placed on his own head the Iron Crown of the Lombards.

787—THE BEGINNING OF THE CELEBRATION OF THE EUCHARIST

The word "eucharist" is a Greek word meaning "thanksgiving." Since we read in connection with the Lord's Supper—"and when he had given thanks," this term came to be applied to the Lord's Supper. In the observance of this institution a custom developed among those who believed they should not drink wine, of dipping the loaf into the fruit of the vine.

Gelasius, a bishop of Rome in 492 condemned this practice as a heresy. On the subject he said, "Certainly the sacrament of the body and blood of our Lord, which we receive, are a divine thing; because by these we are made partakers of the divine nature. Nevertheless, the substance or nature of the bread and wine cease not to exist, and, assuredly, the image and similitude of the body and blood of Christ are celebrated in the action of the mysteries."

Not until a much later date did the doctrine of Transubstantiation develop. This doctrine affirmed that the loaf and the cup, when blessed, became the actual body and blood of Christ. The decree of the council of Trent confirming this doctrine of transubstantiation was framed in these words, "By the consecration of the bread and wine, the whole substance of the bread is converted into the substance of the body of Christ, and the whole substance of the wine is converted into the substance of his blood. Which conversion is suitably and properly called by the Catholic Church, transubstantiation." Here is a contradiction between the statement of Pope Gelasius and the council of Trent that can not be explained.

Paschasus Radbertus first advocated this doctrine.

> "This wild enthusiast published it, not as falsehood generally gains ground, by little and little, but at once glaring in its full absurdity. He informed the world in plain language that the elements after consecration, are instantly changed into the body and blood of Christ; that very body, which was born of Mary, suffered on the cross, and rose from the dead. It is amazing, that an opinion so big with absurdity, and yet unaided by prejudice, could fasten upon the minds of men, however rude of science. Yet the improbable tale, we find, went down; as if the greater the improbability, the more venerable the mystery. It was found a doctrine well adapted to impress the people with that awful and superstitious horror, which is the necessary foundation of false religion; as such, the church of Rome with great zeal upheld it; and if any were staggered by the appearance of an impossibility, they were presently told, that, "The accidents, or forms of bread and wine, it was true, still remained after consecration; but by the omnipotence of God they remained without a subject." This was the argument of the clergy; and it was thought conclusive, for who could doubt the omnipotence of God? Wicliffe, after a thorough examination of this doctrine was entirely satisfied, that it had no scriptural foundation."*

* *The Life of Wicliffe*—Gilpin. Pages 41, 42.

Here is another point in which the churches became enslaved to a doctrine contrary to God's word, which robbed people of the real teaching of the scriptures.

789—THE NICEAN COUNCIL

This is the last council on which the Roman and the Greek church agreed.

This council was the first to sanction image worship. The pagan priests headed processions in honor of Bacchus, Ceres and Diana, whose images they carried and ere long the clergy of the papal church adopted this pagan custom, marching through the streets by night, carrying torches and singing hymns. The priests at the altar turned their faces to the east in conducting the services, a practice which was borrowed from the pagans also.

> "But elements of paganism had entered in the thought and manners of the Christian world. We can not ignore the fact that much of the apparent success of the church had been gained by her accommodation to heathen sentiments, customs and superstitions. She had compromised with the society which she sought to convert. Many rites of the pagan temple were brought into the Christian chapel. The process went on until she was described by Jerome as 'greater in riches, less in virtues, and he confesses the dangerous charms of pagan literature which then had a life that has since perished.' "*

795—POPE LEO ORDERED INCENSE TO BE USED IN WORSHIP

This, too, was a pagan custom. Pictures on pagan monuments show a boy with an incense box. Here was a practice that was eventually bound on religious people, although it was unauthorized by the law of Christ.

---

* *History of The Christian Church*—Blackburn. Chapter 6, Page 106.

CHAPTER 7

FROM CHARLEMAGNE TO THE CRUSADES

800—CHARLEMAGNE CROWNED AS KING OF THE HOLY ROMAN EMPIRE

Charlemagne, the King of the Franks, grandson of Charles Martel recognized the temporal power of the pope over the papal states and approved of the donation of certain lands made by his father, Pepin, to the pope.

Visiting Rome he attended the worship in St. Peter's Cathedral on Christmas day. While there he was crowned Emperor and Augustus with a gold crown by Pope Leo. This established the Holy Roman Empire which later came to include Holland, Germany, France, Belgium, Switzerland, Hungary and Italy. Out of the ruins of the Western empire arose the papal empire and again Rome dominated a large part of the world.

The pope, backed by Charlemagne, had set up an independent church state, casting off all allegiance to the Eastern Empire. This had been prompted in part by the acts of Irene, the Empress of the Eastern Empire, who had deposed her son and assumed the throne as ruler. The pope affirmed that the crown of the Caesars could not be worn by a woman and declared that the empire in the West was forever separated from the empire in the East. This division of the empire contributed to the eventual division of the Catholic church into the Roman Catholic Church and the Greek Catholic Church.

813—THE CHURCH OF ROME CHANGED ITS TEACHING ON THE EPIPHANY

Originally the date, January sixth, commemorated the birth and baptism of Christ, but since the year 813 it has been celebrated as a special festival in honor of the manifestation of the child Jesus to the wise men of the east who were guided to Bethlehem by the star. This date is now accepted as the date of the baptism of Jesus and as such is observed by many Protestant denominations. There is no authority for such observance in the Bible.

814—THE FIRST SALE OF INDULGENCES BY POPE PASCAL I

The doctrine of indulgences did much to corrupt the practice of the church of Rome. Pope Pascal found it to be profitable to promise a shortening of the torments of purgatory upon the payment of a certain sum of money. Indulgences were a means of escaping some of the torment of purgatory. To obtain an indulgence one had to perform some good deed prescribed by the church, such as a visit to some sacred place, a prayer repeated a number of times, or a sum of money contributed to some worthy cause. These things would mitigate the penalties one would have to suffer in purgatory for his transgressions. It was affirmed that the church had at its disposal all of the good deeds of the saints and of the Savior himself and that the church could dispense these to those who had proved themselves worthy.

This gave the church a continuous source of revenue. Indulgences were freely granted on the condition that the recipient contribute to the church or some worthy cause. Eventually the goodness of Christ and the saints was bought and sold publicly as the doctrine developed.

> "An indulgence is, according to the Roman Catholic Church, a remission by the pope of the temporal punishment due to sin, which a sinner would otherwise be obliged to undergo, either in this world or in purgatory. Originally, it indicated remission, relaxation, or mitigation of some censure, penalty or penance prescribed by the church. In process of time, pilgrimages to certain places began to be substituted for the appointed penance. Of plenary indulgence —i.e., remission of all penalties—we have no mention before the Crusades. Toward the close of the eleventh century, plenary indulgences were proclaimed by Urban II, as a recompense to those who went in person upon the Crusades.
>
> They were afterward granted to those who hired a soldier for that purpose, or sent a sum of money, instead of fulfilling the vow they had taken of going on that service themselves. Hence originated the sale of them. The progress of evil is rapid, and it was not long before every sin had its price."*

The sale of indulgences became a source of papal revenue. It ultimately developed into the practice of offering pardon for all sins. By the year 1190 it had become very much a part of the doctrine of the Roman church. Upon what Scripture was it based? You may read the Bible from Genesis to Revelation but you will not find it taught there. Where then did it originate? It came from men and not from God.

---

* *History of the Christian Church*—Blackburn. Chapter 12, Page 271.

842—THE COUNCIL OF CONSTANTINOPLE RESTORED THE USE OF IMAGES TO THE CHURCHES

"Upon the death of Theophilus, which happened in the year 842, the regency was entrusted with the Empress Theodora during the son's minority. This superstitious princess, fatigued with the importunate solicitations of the monks, deluded by their forged miracles, and not a little influenced also by their insolent threats, assembled, in the year above mentioned, a council at Constantinople in which the decrees of the second Nicene council were reinstated in their lost authority, and the Greeks were indulged in their corrupt propensity to image worship by a law which encouraged that wretched idolatry. So that after a controversy which had been carried on during the space of a hundred and ten years, the cause of idolatry triumphed over the dictates of reason and Christianity; the whole east, the Armenians excepted, bowed down before the victorious images, nor did any of the succeeding Emperors attempt to cure the Greeks of this superstitious frenzy, or restrain them in the performance of this childish worship."*

Those who prostrated themselves before the images claimed they were only showing their reverence for the symbols of Christ and the departed saints.

Miraculous powers were said to dwell in the images. Stories of wonderful cures were reported by those who bowed and prayed before them. The adoration of the departed saints and martyrs became more common and churches began to be named for them also. This new form of idolatry was condemned by many of the church leaders.

863—THE POPE AND THE PATRIARCH EXCOMMUNICATED EACH OTHER

Photius, a scholar of repute was elevated to be patriarch by the emperor, Michael III, who had removed Ignatius for condemning the wicked conduct of the uncle of the emperor. Photius sought the endorsement of the pope. This he failed to secure, and was excommunicated by Nicholas I, the pope, at a synod at Rome.

Nicholas supported his claim as Universal Bishop with great effect by using the "Pseudo-Isidorian Decretals," a collection of documents, said to be letters and decrees of the bishops and the councils of the second and third centuries, all tending to exalt the power of the pope.

The decretals were supposed to have been collected by one Isidore Mercator, but it was believed that they were prepared by the clerics of Reims, under Archbishop Ebo and his successor, Hinkmar. These decretals emphasized papal supremacy, limited the power of the archbishops while adding prestige to the bishops and the lower

---

* *Ecclesiastical History*—Mosheim. Volume 1, Part 2, Chapter 3, Page 203.

clergy, affirming that none of the clergy could be summoned before a civil court.

They stated also that a layman could not accuse a priest and if a bishop was compelled to face a charge, it must be confirmed by the testimony of seventy-two witnesses.

Centuries later they were declared to be deliberate forgeries and corruptions of ancient historical documents. Whether or not Nicholas I knew them to be forgeries is not known. He did, however, represent that they had been in the archives of the Roman church from ancient times.

Though they were forgeries, they stamped the claims of the medieval priesthood with the authority of antiquity. The papacy, the growth of centuries, was made to appear as something that was complete from the beginning of the church. The decretals have been referred to by both Catholic and Protestant historians as the most colossal fraud in history, yet they were used to strengthen the claims of the papacy and to form the basis of some of the laws of the Roman church.

> "There existed in each of the national churches a collection of ecclesiastical laws or canons, which were made use of as circumstances required. One of these collections was in use in Spain as early as the sixth century and was subsequently attributed to Isadore, Bishop of Seville. Toward the middle of the ninth century, a new recension of these canons appeared in France, based upon the so called Isadorian collection, but into which many spurious fragments borrowed from private collections and bearing upon their face incontestable evidence of the ignorance of their authors had been introduced. This recension contained also a number of forged documents. These were altogether, above a hundred spurious decrees of popes, from Clement to Damasus, A.D. 384, not to mention some of other popes, and many false canons of councils. It also contained the forged deed of "Donation" ascribed to Constantine."*

Photius now sent out an encyclical letter in which he charged the Latin church with heresy for its rule on celibacy, for its ritual peculiarities and its interpretation of the Nicean Creed. The next year Photius had the Pope excommunicated by a synod at Constantinople. Thus the break grew wider between the church in the East and the church in the West.

869—THE LAST JOINT COUNCIL OF THE GREEK AND ROMAN CHURCHES

Up to this date the Scriptures alone were accepted as authority by the apostate church, though they were not followed by that institution. The council of Constantinople which convened in this

---

* *Manual of Universal Church History*—Alzog. Volume 2, Page 195.

year decreed that tradition was of equal authority with the scriptures. This was the foundation of a doctrine that denied to the human family the right to read and use the Bible.

In contradiction to this decree the apostle Paul in writing to Timothy said. "All scripture is given by inspiration of God, and is profitable for doctrine, for reproof, for correction, for instruction in righteousness: that the man of God may be perfect, throughly furnished unto all good works."[1]

Paul teaches that the Scripture given by inspiration of God supplies or furnishes a man unto all good works, that it instructs him in righteousness, and is profitable for doctrine.

John in the gospel record said, "And many other signs truly did Jesus in the presence of his disciples which are not written in this book: but these are written, that you might believe that Jesus is the Christ, the Son of God; and that believing ye might have life through his name."[2] Here the teaching of the Scriptures tells us that what was written was for the purpose of producing faith in Christ, that by obedience we might be saved.

In the conclusion of Paul's last letter to Timothy he said, "Reprove, rebuke, exhort with all long suffering and doctrine." What is doctrine? That which is taught in the Scriptures given by inspiration of God. Paul tells why the Scriptures are to be used for this purpose: "For the time will come when they will not endure sound doctrine."[3] What is sound doctrine? It is the divine revelation supplied in the Scriptures.

God inspired men to write his word for the guidance of the human family. The apostle Peter tells us that God has "given unto us all things that pertain unto life and godliness, through the knowledge of him that hath called us to glory and virtue."[4] This being true it could not be safe to reject a divine revelation for human traditions. The chief reason for the Bible being rejected by this council was because the doctrines that had become prominent in the church of Rome could not be found in the Bible. There is no priestly celibacy in the Bible. The worship of Mary is not there. Purgatory is not in the Bible. Here is the reason for the acceptance of traditions as of equal authority with the Bible.

904—THE BEGINNING OF THE PORNOCRACY

It is not the purpose of this volume to condemn unnecessarily the moral frailties and delinquencies of men but the cause of truth sometimes demands that this be done. The church that developed

---

1. 2 Timothy 3 : 16, 17
2. John 20 : 31
3. 2 Timothy 4 : 3
4. 2 Peter 1 : 3

from the apostasy sends forth the claim that she is the "only true church."

The heads of that institution have claimed that they have had the keys of the kingdom committed to them as the successors of the apostle Peter. If this is true then they should be able to show that all who have occupied the papal chair were very holy men. But that is not true. History shows that the heads of the Roman church have been some of the most unholy and immoral men the world has ever known—and it necessarily follows that the claims of the institution headed by them are based on deception.

Let it not be supposed that the material which is here presented has been assembled by dint of a long and diligent search for the most atrocious things that might be said against the papal church.

Indeed much more might have been presented from the pages of history revealing the low morality of the leaders of that institution and the great abuses within the church.

Baronius, a Roman Catholic cardinal said, "Evil desire, leaning on the arm of the state, raging with ambition and lust of power stretched out her hands to control all things." Milman affirmed that those who occupied the papal throne were loaded with every vice and enormity which can blacken the character of men. The things that are recorded herewith show that the papal church was doctrinally and morally corrupt for hundreds of years and that there was little or no attempt at reformation.

The tenth century is referred to as the midnight of the human mind. It is sometimes called the Pornocracy, the period of time when papal power reached its lowest depths.

Sergius III was the first of a long list of dissolute popes. He was placed in power by Marozia and Theodora her mother.

These licentious women filled the papal chair with their lovers and their illegitimate offspring.

Marozia lived as the wife of Adelbert, one of the powerful counts of Tuscany, and became the mother of his son Alberic.

Sergius, who was elevated to the papacy in 904, also lived with Marozia and to them was born a son who was named John, who later ascended the papal throne through the influence of his wicked mother. Baronius, a Roman Catholic historian, states that Sergius was the slave of every known vice and the most wicked of men.

Pope John X was only a deacon in the Catholic church at Ravenna when Theodora saw him and fell in love with him. She contrived to have him appointed Bishop of Ravenna and when Pope Lando died in 914 Theodora had enough influence in Rome to cause him to be raised to the papal throne.

"After the death of Lando, which happened in the year 914, Alberic, Marquis or Count of Tuscany, whose opulence was prodigious, and whose authority in Rome was despotic and unlimited, obtained the pontificate for John X, archbishop of Ravenna, in compliance with the solicitation of Theodora, his mother-in-law, whose lewdness was the principal that interested her in this promotion. This infamous election will not surprise such as know that the laws of Rome were at this time absolutely silent; that the dictates of justice and equity were overpowered and suspended; and that all things were carried on in that great city by interest or corruption, by violence or fraud."*

John XI, the son of Marozia and Sergius III, was placed upon the throne at the death of Pope Stephen in 931, as the successor of Peter.

Albert Barnes in his "Notes" said, "Pope Vagilius that waded to the pontifical throne through the blood of his predecessor, Pope Marcellinius, sacrificed to idols." Concerning Pope Honorius, the Council of Constantinople decreed: "We have caused Honorius, the late Pope of Old Rome, to be accursed; for that in all things he followed the mind of Sergius, the heretic, and confirmed his wicked doctrines."

The Council of Basil thus condemned Pope Eugenius: "We condemn and depose Pope Eugenius, a despiser of holy canons, a disturber of the peace and unity of the church of God, a notorious offender of the whole universal church; a Simonist, a perjurer; a man incorrigible; a schismatic; a man fallen from the faith, a willful heretic."

The Bishop of Orleans, referring to John XII, Leo VIII, and Boniface VII called them monsters of guilt reeking with blood and filth, antichrists sitting in the temple of God.

"At the close of the 9th century Stephen VI dragged the body of an obnoxious predecessor from the grave and after subjecting it to a mock trial, cut off its head and three fingers and threw it into the Tiber.

He himself was subsequently deposed and strangled in prison. In the years that followed, the power of electing to the popedom fell into the hands of the intriguing and licentious Theodora and her equally unprincipled daughters, Theodora, and Marozia. These women, members of a patrician family, by their arts and beauty, obtained an unbounded influence over the aristocratic tyrants of the city. One of the Theodoras advanced a lover, and Marozia a son, to the popedom.

The grandson of the latter, Octavian, succeeded to her power, as well as to the civil government of the city, elevated himself, on the death of the then pope, to the apostolic chair at the age of 18, under the title of John XII, A.D. 956.

His career was in keeping with such a commencement. The Lateran Palace was disgraced by becoming a receptacle for courte-

---

* *Ecclesiastical History*—Mosheim. Volume 1, Part 2, Chapter 2, Page 221.

sans, and decent females were terrified from pilgrimages to the
threshold of the Apostles by the reports which were spread abroad
of the lawless impurity and violence of their representative and
successor. At length he was carried off by a rapid illness, or by
the consequences of a blow received in the prosecution of his
intrigues.

Boniface VII in the space of a few weeks after his elevation,
plundered the treasury and basilica of St. Peter of all he could con-
veniently carry off, and fled to Constantinople.

John XVIII (A.D. 1003) expressed his readiness for a sum of
money from the Emperor Basil, to recognize the right of the
Greek Patriarch to the title of ecumenical or universal Bishop, and
the consequent degradation of his own see; and was only prevented
by the general indignation excited by the report of his intentions.

Benedict IX (A.D. 1033) was consecrated pope-according to
some authorities at the age of 10 or 12 years and became notorious
for adulteries and murders. At length he resolved on marrying his
first cousin; and, when her father would not assent, except on the
condition of his resigning the popedom, he sold it for a large sum
and consecrated the purchaser as his successor. Such are a few of
the most prominent features of the ecclesiastical history of these
dreadful times, when in the words of St. Bruno, "the world lay in
wickedness, holiness had disappeared, justice had perished, and
truth had been buried; Simon Magus lording it over the church,
whose bishops and priests were given to luxury and fornication."*

What a contrast is presented between the church established by
the Lord through the apostles and the apostate church that is
revealed to us upon the pages of history.

No one denies that Christ established but one church here upon
the earth. The history of that institution is revealed upon the pages
of the book of Acts and the epistles addressed to the churches. In
all of the epistles purity of life and righteous conduct is emphasized.
The writers exhorted the congregations to whom their letters were
addressed to hold fast the teaching that had been delivered unto
them. Paul warned that false teachers would endeavor to lead the
disciples away from the truth. "For the time will come when they
will not endure sound doctrine; but after their own lusts shall they
heap to themselves teachers, having itching ears; and they shall
turn away their ears from the truth, and shall be turned unto
fables."[5]

The pages of history reveal that the true church of Christ was
wholly lost to view at this time, its purity was forgotten and ultimately there came into view a human institution dominated by the
Pope of Rome. The changes that were made by the apostate church
reveal that when men leave the counsel of God's word they lose
their respect for things divine and substitute in their place doc-

* *History for Ready Reference*—Larned. Volume 4, Page 2485.
5. 2 Timothy 4:3, 4

trines that are designed to make religion attractive to the world. The hierarchy of the priesthood of the apostate church found it to their advantage to keep the people in darkness and superstition.

Over a long period of time the popes were the lovers, or the sons and grandsons, of the above mentioned wicked women. John XII, appealed to Otho I, the ruler of Germany, to aid him in his conflict against Berenger II, of Italy. Later he entered into a conspiracy to force the Germans to return to their own land. When Otho learned of this, he called a synod in St. Peter's which deposed John XII on the charge of being a murderer, a blasphemer and a libertine.

Otho had been crowned as emperor by John XII, now John was deposed by Otho and Leo VIII was appointed in his stead. The conflict of the rulers of the provinces of the Holy Roman Empire with the popes brought about the deposition of Arnulf, Archbishop of Rheims by a synod which showed no regard for papal authority. This synod was supported and directed by Gerbert, who desired to bring about reforms in the church.

Gerbert was deprived of his support by John XV, though he was unable to force Gerbert and the French king, Hugh Capet into complete submission.

The authority of Otho III had been established in Italy and when Pope John died, Otho's cousin, Bruno, was elevated to the papal chair as Gregory V. He threatened to put the French church under an interdict and Robert, the successor of Hugh Capet, restored Arnulf to the see of Rheims.

> "Twice at Rome Gerbert inspected affairs with eyes like those of Luther, five hundred years later, and wrote, similarly, to a friend; 'All of Italy appears to me a Rome, and the morals of the Romans are the horrors of the world.' He would not remain there as abbot of Bobbio. If he wrote a certain speech, he startled one synod by his bold words, when Arnulf, the Archbishop of Rheims, was tried, in 991, by a synod, for treason against Hugh Capet. The papal party defended Arnulf, and wished to have the pope decide the case. Opposed to him was the Bishop of Orleans, who said in a speech that Gerbert is said to have written, 'It is notorious that there is not one at Rome who knows enough of letters to be a door keeper.' As to the recent popes, 'are all the priests of God— men of learning and holy lives—to submit to such monsters, full of infamy, void of all knowledge, human and divine? Is not a pontiff, who refuses to hear the voice of counsel, the Man of Sin, Antichrist, the Mystery of Iniquity?' "*

Each of these popes held one of the large churches of Rome. This scandal so aroused the emperor, Henry III, that he came into Italy, called a council at Sutri in 1046 by which the three popes were set

---

* *History of The Christian Church*—Blackburn. Chapter 12, Page 254.

aside. A zealous reformer was then elected pope but he soon died; another had a shorter life and then the Emperor named his cousin, Bruno, the Bishop of Toul to be pope, who openly confessed that he was guilty of simony. He was persuaded by Hildebrand not to assume the office until elected at Rome. He made the journey to Rome garbed as a pilgrim, taking Hildebrand with him as a sub-deacon. Here he was installed as Leo IX and immediately he set about to institute some much needed reforms. He endeavored to abolish simony, to end the immorality among the priests and to enforce the ruling of the church on celibacy.

1053—THE PATRIARCH OF CONSTANTINOPLE, MICHAEL COERULARIUS, RENEWS THE CONTEST FOR SUPREMACY WITH ROME

The patriarch abolished the Latin liturgy in the churches and monasteries of the East and addressed a letter to the Bishop of Trani condemning the use of unleavened bread in the sacrament. The pope excommunicated the patriarch, who in turn expelled the pope. In this action he was supported by the patriarchs of Antioch, Alexandria, and Jerusalem.

1054—SEPARATION OF THE CHURCH IN THE EAST AND THE CHURCH IN THE WEST

The pope sent a messenger to Constantinople who laid upon the altar in St. Sophia's Cathedral the decree of excommunication, whereupon the patriarch issued his decree excommunicating the pope and all the churches that stood with him. Here is the forma-tion of the Greek Catholic Church and the Roman Catholic Church. Since this time the Greek and the Latin churches have continued to exist separately, neither recognizing the existence of the other.

Doctrinally the differences between the two are few, the principal difference being over the doctrine of the procession of the Holy Ghost. The Greek church holds that the Holy Ghost proceeds from the Father only, while the Latin church contends that it proceeds from both the Father and the Son.

In the ceremonies of the church usages became customs and cus-toms were formulated into laws. The marriage of the priests was ultimately forbidden in the Latin church but sanctioned in the Greek Church.

The Latin church uses images, while the Greek church uses only pictures.

In the services of the mass the Latin church uses unleavened bread while the Greek church uses common bread.

The Greek Catholic Church rejects the papacy, the doctrine of celibacy, the practice of sprinkling and refuses to consider the findings of any of the ecclesiastical councils after the year 869. They observe communion on the first day of every week, they immerse and have no instrumental music in the worship.

The series of events which contributed to the separation of the church in the East and the church in the West may be listed as follows—

395—Theodosius divided the rulership of the Roman empire between his two sons, Arcadius to be ruler in the East and Honorius in the West.

410—Rivalry between the rulers brought about the capture of Rome by Alaric.

451—The Bishop of Rome contends for the title of Universal Bishop.

514—The contest for supreme leadership narrows down to a contest between the Patriarch of Constantinople and the Bishop of Rome.

588—John, the Faster, assumes the title of Universal Bishop in Constantinople.

764—Emperor Leo III cleared the churches of the East of idols, then turned his attention to the churches of the West, for which he was excommunicated by the pope.

789—Nicean council endorsed image worship. The preeminence of the pope caused it to be restored.

869—The last ecumenical council of the church in the East and the church in the West.

1022—Separation of the church in the East and the church in the West. They were reconciled the same year.

1054—The complete separation of the Greek Catholic Church and the Roman Catholic Church. Caused by the pope excommunicating the churches of the East.

1070—ACCEPTANCE OF THE DOCTRINE OF PURGATORY

This doctrine was first advocated by Origen. He taught that the faithful, as well as the unrighteous, would pass through a fire which would consume the world on the last day. His theories were condemned by the Council of Constantinople in 553.

Augustine, the Bishop of Hippo, in Africa, developed his own doctrine of purgatory from the speculations that prevailed in Egypt. Through several centuries they grew into the doctrine of purgatory in the church of Rome.

This doctrine taught that imperfect Christians could be purified from their sins by fire. Purgatory was a place through which all would have to pass. Every soul at death was consigned to purgatory, there to remain until every sin which had been committed in this life was atoned for by the purgatorial fire. Where did this doctrine originate? You may read your Bibe through and you will not find it there. God never commanded it, Christ did not authorize it, and the apostles never taught it.

It originated in the minds of the clergy who used it to secure from anxious friends of the departed the payment of money for prayers to secure their deliverance from purgatory. In other days the sins of the living had been turned into profit, but now the clergy began to avail themselves of the sins of the dead. It was said the living, by making certain sacrifices, could shorten or even terminate the torments their loved ones were enduring in purgatory.

> "The pope by a bull annexed purgatory to his domain. In that place, he declared, men would have to expiate the sins that could not be expiated here on earth; but that indulgences would liberate their souls from that intermediate state in which their sins would detain them. Thomas Aquinas set forth this doctrine in his famous Summa Theologiae. No means were spared to fill the mind with terror. The priests depicted in horrible colours the torments inflicted by this purifying fire on all who became its prey. In many Roman Catholic countries we may still see paintings exhibited in the churches and public places, wherein poor souls, from the midst of glowing flames, invoke with anguish some alleviation of their pain. Who could refuse the ransom which falling into the treasury of Rome, would redeem the soul from such torments?"*

> "The fears of purgatory, of that fire that was to destroy the remaining impurities of the departed souls, were now carried to the greatest height, and exceeded by far the terrifying apprehensions of infernal torments; for they hoped to avoid the latter easily, by dying enriched by the prayers of the clergy, or covered with the merits and mediation of the saints; while from the pains of purgatory they knew there was no exemption. The clergy, therefore, finding these superstitious terrors admirably adapted to increase their authority and to promote their interest, used every method to augment them, and by the most pathetic discourses, accompanied with monstrous fables and fictitious miracles, they labored to establish the doctrine of purgatory, and also to make it appear that they had a mighty influence in that formidable region."†

1073—HILDEBRAND CROWNED AS POPE GREGORY VII

Hildebrand was counsellor and papal director for Leo IX. They set out to suppress the practice of simony. They went first to Rheims to assist in the consecration of the Abbey Church of

---

* *History of The Reformation*—D'Aubigne. Volume 1, Book 1, Chapter 2, Page 56.
† *Ecclesiastical History*—Mosheim. Volume 1, Part 2, Chapter 3, Pages 225, 226.

St. Remi. Here Leo called upon the priests to meet him in council. Many of them were afraid of an inquiry into their practices. This council was attended by twenty bishops and fifty abbots. At the opening of the council Leo said, "We are met for the reformation of disorders in the church and the correction of morals. The bishops and abbots will come forward and swear their innocence, if they have not been guilty of simony." All the bishops took the oath. Several of the abbots confessed their guilt. Greater sins were charged and proved on some of the bishops who were severely punished. After Leo's death Hildebrand controlled the election of the four succeeding popes, removing one whom the Italians had elected by night.

Hildebrand became a popular papal chancellor and with the aid of Cardinal Damian invented the plan by which the popes were to be elected by the college of cardinals.

The office of the cardinals was of slow growth. It started with the organization of seven bishops, living near Rome, into a college of cardinals. They played the chief role in the election of the popes, who in turn appointed the cardinals. When the number of the college of cardinals was increased to represent the various countries, they became the sole electors of the popes. Leo was followed by several other popes some of whom lived only a few months after their election, and two of them, Alexander and Honorius, were rival popes for six years. When Alexander died the cardinals assembled for the election of a new pope.

Hildebrand was chosen pope and crowned with great solemnity as Gregory VII. He decreed that there should be but one pope in the world and that should be himself.

He forced the priests to surrender their wives, making celibacy compulsory for all. He planned to make the hierarchy of Rome into a universal empire over all kingdoms, of which himself and his successors should be the head, whose laws and whose decrees were to be above all other laws and to whom all other kings and rulers should be submissive. He purposed to have a uniform ritual for all the churches and unity of practice for all the priesthood.

Other reforms of Gregory were the correction of simony, the practice of buying religious offices for money and the prohibition of instrumental music in the church services. Simony had been openly practiced for a period of years. Persons who were nominated for the office of bishop had to pay the king a stated sum when inducted into office. Vacancies were sold to the highest bidder. Gregory issued an order forbidding anyone to receive an office from a king. This order was to be enforced by excommunications and interdicts. A person who was excommunicated was cut off from his fellow men, if a king was excommunicated his subjects were released from their oath of allegiance. Interdicts were issued against cities to bring them to obedience to the papal throne.

Gregory foresaw the differences that would develop between himself and Henry IV of Germany and so purposed to humble the emperor and thus to teach all rulers that they were subject to him.

He assembled a synod at Rome and called upon Henry to appear under the penalty of excommunication.

Henry called a council of such prelates as would attend and ordered Gregory to vacate the papal throne. He styled Gregory a false monk, no longer pope and closed his letter with these words, "Let another ascend the papal throne who will not cloke violence with religion, for I, Henry, king by the grace of God, with all my bishops say "Get down, get down."

Henry was excommunicated by Gregory and his kingdom placed under an interdict which meant that all churches would be closed, all services and sacraments suspended, marriages prohibited, and those who died would be denied the rites of the Christian burial, and all his subjects released from their oath of allegiance.

Henry's subjects revolted and when he saw that his kingdom was on the point of going to pieces he set out in the depth of winter to obtain pardon from the pope at the castle of Canossa, the home of the Countess Matilda, with whom the pope was on such intimate terms that their morality stands in doubt. For three days Henry did penance outside the gate of the castle, standing in the snow barefooted and clothed only in sackcloth. On the fourth day the Countess Matilda pleaded that he be permitted to enter. When he came into the pope's presence, Henry was compelled to surrender his crown and promise that he would not seek revenge, and that until his case was heard that he would not use his kingly office, nor usurp the authority to govern, nor exact any oath of allegiance from his subjects. Henry agreed to the conditions and was released from excommunication.

1078—THE REVIVAL OF THE DISPUTE CONCERNING THE PRESENCE OF CHRIST'S BODY AND BLOOD IN THE LORD'S SUPPER

From time to time the dispute concerning the actual presence of the body and blood of the Lord in the Lord's Supper had been revived in the Roman church. No council had given a definite sentence upon this matter, neither had they set forth a rule of faith upon the subject, hence all felt free to openly discuss the doctrine of Paschasius Radbert. Berenger, principal of the public school of Tours and afterward Archbishop of Angers, maintained publicly that the bread and wine were not changed into the body and blood of Christ in the Eucharist, but that these elements preserved their natural qualities, being no more than figures or symbols of the body and the blood of the Lord.

Two councils, one at Rome and the other at Vercelli solemnly condemned the doctrine of Berenger and ordered the work of Johannes Scotus, from which his teaching had been drawn, to be burned. Berenger and his adherents were threatened with punishment.

These threats were carried out against Berenger who was deprived of all of his income. This treatment did not shake the firmness of his mind on these matters nor influence him to surrender the doctrine he had taught.

He was afterward summoned before two councils where, when he was threatened with severe punishment, he abjured the doctrine and made his peace with the Roman church. This was not an act of sincerity upon his part, for no sooner was he away from the council and back in his own territory than he began the proclamation of his doctrine again, but with more prudence and less boldness.

The controversy was prolonged until Gregory VII came to the papal throne at which time he purposed to end the dissension. With this in mind he called for Berenger to appear in Rome. His conduct toward the archbishop indicated that he had a high regard for him, for Gregory displayed all possible mildness toward this rebellious son of the Catholic church.

In the council that was held in the above year Berenger was allowed to draw up a confession of his faith, renouncing that which he had been compelled to sign twenty years before, which had been prepared by Humbert and confirmed by a council and approved by Pope Nicholas II and therefore rendered sacred by papal authority.

Berenger made a second declaration and confirmed it with an oath that henceforth he would adhere to the following proposition: 'The bread laid upon the altar, became after consecration, the true body of Christ, which was born of the virgin, suffered on the cross, and now sits at the right hand of the Father; and that the wine placed upon the altar became after consecration, the true blood, which flowed from the side of Christ."

The pope was satisfied with this declaration, but the opponents of Berenger were not. They insisted that he should be required to sign another statement that was less vague. To this the pope agreed and a council was called at Rome in 1079 which drew up a new confession of faith for Berenger which he signed in the presence of those assembled. He was also required to give his oath that the statement he signed was his conviction upon the disputed subject. By his statement he professed to believe, "That the bread and wine were, by the mysterious influence of the holy prayer, and the words of our Redeemer substantially changed into the true, proper, and vivifying body and blood of Jesus Christ."

The pope showed his esteem for the Archbishop of Angers by giving a testimony of his own friendship for him. When Berenger returned to France he retracted publicly the statement he had been compelled to sign in Rome, writing out a defense of the doctrine to which he held.

Gregory showed no signs of resentment against his apostate subject which caused many to believe that he had in part adopted the views of Berenger.

> "It now remains for us to give a more full and distinct explanation of the doctrine of Berenger. He contended not only against transubstantiation, but against every notion of a bodily presence of Christ in the Lord's Supper, drawing his arguments from reason, from the testimonies of the Scriptures and from the older church teachers. Considered from his own point of view, the intellectual apprehensions of a clear understanding, such a notion appears to him altogether absurd, worthy only of the ignorant populace. Paschasius Radbert and the populace he always conjoins. With intense indignation he noticed those legends of Paschasius Radbert about the sensible appearances of Christ after the consecration of the eucharist, which were immediately veiled again under the forms of the bread and wine. The words of the institution would involve a falsehood—Christ who is the truth, would not contradict himself, if the bread and wine, which he presupposes to be present, were no longer there. He constantly maintained, that the confessions which he had been forced to lay down, testified for him, rather than against him; for to predicate anything of bread and wine presupposed the present existence of these sensible objects. Subject and predicate must both alike be true, in order to the truth of the general proposition which they express. Now when it is predicated of one thing, that is something else, there would be a contradiction in terms, if predicate and subject must both be understood alike in the proper and literal sense. In such cases, we should rather understand the subject in the proper, the predicate in a figurative sense. He cites in illustration such expressions as those where Christ is called 'a rock,' 'a lamb,' 'a cornerstone'—. It were an unworthy trifling, could we suppose it true, to think that when the Lord's Supper is a million times distributed, from heaven, and returns back as often. A favorite maxim of Berenger often cited by him, was the passage from St. Paul, 'Though we have known Christ after the flesh, yet now henceforth know we him no more.' 2 Corinthians 5:16. He dwells upon the words in the Acts of the Apostles, that Christ glorified, was received up into heaven until the times of the restitution of all things.—Acts 3:21. Yet Berenger believed it might be said, in a certain, that is, as he himself explains, a figurative sense, that bread and wine are the body of Christ."*

---

* *History of The Christian Religion and Church*—Neander. Volume 3. Section 4. Chapter 1, Pages 521, 522, 523.

The opposition of Berenger to the doctrines of the Roman church was only the beginning of a greater opposition that was soon to develop within and against the church. That corrupt institution had within its organization those who would shortly seek to reform its doctrine and practice, to reject and renounce the teachings which brought about the departure from the purity and simplicity of the apostles' doctrine.

1080—THE GERMAN PRINCES SELECTED RUDOLPH OF SUABIA TO BE THEIR KING

Henry gathered his loyal subjects together and defeated the soldiers of Rudolph in a battle in which Rudolph was killed. Henry was then free to turn his attention to Gregory. He invaded Italy with an army and Gregory fled to Rome where he took refuge in the castle of San Angelo.

The emperor, the clergy and the nobles selected Gusbert, the Archbishop of Ravenna to the pontificate under the name of Clement III. Gregory fled to Salerno where he died in exile with these words upon his lips, "I loved justice and hated iniquity and therefore I die in exile."

Gregory was the first pope to attempt the reformation of the Roman church. His ban against instrumental music was the most outstanding of his reforms. The use of instrumental music was first sanctioned by Pope Vitalian in 666. He introduced the organ into church service but hundreds of years elapsed after the introduction before it came into general use.

Organs were never regarded with favor in the Eastern churches. The early reformers, Luther, Knox, Calvin, and others regarded them as monuments of idolatry. There is no warrant for the use of instruments of music in the New Testament. There is no example of their use by the apostles.

Not until the mystery of iniquity was at work did they come into general use. We have much information in the Scriptures upon the subject of singing, for we are told what to sing, how to sing, and where to sing, but we have no directions about singing with instrumental music. Singing in the worship is obeying a divine command of God. It is also a method of teaching in the worship. The words of a song, when sung or spoken so they may be understood, teach and admonish, but the very purpose of a song, so far as we are concerned, is defeated by the use of musical sounds that drown out the words.

1095—THE BEGINNING OF THE CRUSADES

The preaching of Peter the Hermit was largely responsible for the beginning of the Crusades. He went throughout Europe telling of the outrages inflicted upon the pilgrims who went to Jerusalem to view the places made sacred by the Savior and the apostles. The preaching of the monk produced a lasting impression upon the minds of the people without a doubt, but the real originator of the First Crusade was Pope Urban who called a council at Piacenza to consider the appeal of Emperor Alexis Comnenus for aid against the Turks who were threatening to take Constantinople. Nothing was accomplished at this meeting but the same year a second council was convened at Cleremont where fourteen archbishops, two hundred and twenty-five bishops, four hundred abbots and a vast multitude came together for the meeting. After considering minor matters the question of delivering the Holy Land from the hands of the unbelieving Mohammedans was brought before the council. Pope Urban was one of the principal speakers. In his eloquent speech he pictured the humiliation and misery of the provinces of Asia, the desecration of the places made sacred by the footsteps of the Son of God, when he called upon the multitude to be willing to leave father, mother, brother or sister for Christ's sake. The people with one voice cried out "Dieu le Volt"—"It is the will of God."

Thousands immediately pledged themselves as soldiers of the cross of Christ and this emblem became the badge of their warfare.

From the time that Christianity took root in Western Europe thousands of pilgrims had made their way to the Holy Land. The Saracen caliphs were very tolerant and treated the pilgrims kindly, but all of this was changed when Jerusalem was captured by the Seljuk Turks, a fanatical Tartar tribe.

From this time forward brutal treatment, persecution, and insults were the lot of the pilgrims.

The people of France, Italy, Germany and England were aroused to a high pitch of religious fervor. They were determined to deliver the city of David from the hands of the infidels. The pope issued an edict granting to all who would enlist in the army of the Lord the remission of their sins and promised that those who might be killed in battle would enter into life eternal if they were truly penitent. Love of adventure, desire for military glory, and personal ambition brought the princes and nobles, the rich and the poor, saints and sinners under the standard of the cross.

1096—THE FIRST CRUSADE

"An innumerable multitude composed of all ranks and orders offered themselves as volunteers in this sacred expedition. This numerous host was looked upon as formidable in the highest degree, and equal to the most glorious enterprises and exploits, while, in reality, it was no more than an unwieldy body without life and vigor, and was weak and contemptible in every respect. This will appear sufficiently evident, when we consider that this army was a motley assemblage of monks, prostitutes, artists, laborers, lazy tradesmen, merchants, boys, girls, slaves, malefactors, and profligate debauchees, and that it was principally composed of the lowest dregs of the multitude, who were animated solely by the prospect of spoil and plunder, and hoped to make their fortunes by this holy campaign. Every one will perceive how little either discipline, counsel or fortitude were to be expected from such a miserable rabble. This expedition was distinguished, in the French language, by the name of a 'croisade,' and all who embarked in it were called 'croises' or cross-bearers; not only because the end of this holy war was to wrest the cross of Christ out of the hands of the infidels, but also on account of the consecrated cross of various colors, which every soldier wore upon his right shoulder."*

Before the regular army of the Crusaders was ready to move, those who had been influenced by the preaching of Peter the Hermit, became impatient and asked Peter to place himself at their head and lead them to the Holy Land. He divided the command with a poor knight called Walter, the Penniless, and with an army of eighty thousand untrained and unequipped followers they set out for Constantinople by the overland route. Thousands of them perished from hunger and exposure on the way and those who crossed the Bosporus were surprised by the Turks and slaughtered.

Later in the same year several other armies which were well equipped set out for Constantinople. Prominent among their leaders were Godfrey de Bouillon, Raymond of Toulouse, Robert of Normandy and Robert of Flanders. They crossed over Germany, Hungary and passed through the Eastern Empire, crossed over the Bosporus, captured Nicea in Bithynia, won several battles over the Turks and stormed and captured the city of Antioch.

After a long delay they pushed on toward Jerusalem, passing through many of the coastal cities where the ruins of the castles they constructed may be seen today. When they came within sight of the Holy City a shout of rejoicing came from the lips of the Crusaders. Because they were treading on ground made sacred by the feet of the Messiah and the apostles and prophets they took off their shoes and marched with uncovered heads. The city of Jerusalem was taken by storm and a terrible slaughter of the Turks fol-

---

* *Ecclesiastical History*—Mosheim. Volume 1, Part 1, Chapter 1, Page 232.

lowed. One account of the battle states that on Mount Moriah in the court yard where Solomon's temple had stood the victors rode in the blood of the vanquished up to their horses' knees.

Here the Crusaders established the Kingdom of Jerusalem, with Godfrey de Bouillon as the head of the kingdom. He declined to wear a robe and a crown of gold in the city where his Lord had worn a crown of thorns. The only title he would wear was that of "Baron of the Holy Sepulchre."

1146—THE TURKS RE-CAPTURE THE CITY OF EDESSA

This city, the outlying bulwark to the east of the Kingdom of Jerusalem was taken by the Turks and the entire population was slaughtered or sold into slavery. This event aroused the people of central and southern Europe to a holy zeal and Bernard of Clairvaux began to preach another crusade to regain what had been lost.

1147—THE SECOND CRUSADE

Early the following year the second crusade, composed of two large armies, led by Louis VII of France and Conrad III of Germany, set out for Jerusalem. The greater part of these armies exhausted their strength in Asia Minor. Their siege of Damascus was unsuccessful and the Crusaders, broken in spirit and exhausted in strength had to return home.

1189—THE THIRD CRUSADE

The third crusade was led by Frederick Barbarossa of Germany, Philip Augustus of France, and Richard I of England. Frederick was drowned while crossing a stream in Syria and his soldiers joined the French and the English in the siege of Acre which surrendered after twenty-three months. Though Saladin was unable to relieve the defenders of Acre, he did inflict a crushing defeat upon the Crusaders upon the plain of Esdraelon where fourteen thousand Crusaders were slain in one battle.

Dissension between the English and the French caused the French to withdraw, leaving Richard as the leader of the expedition. He obtained from Saladin a treaty of peace which permitted the pilgrims to visit the Holy Sepulchre unmolested and left the entire sea coast from Tyre to Joppa in possession of the Crusaders. Richard now set out for home, but while crossing Germany in disguise he was arrested and placed in prison by the order of Henry VI, his political enemy. His release was secured by the payment of an enormous sum of money which was paid by the English people.

1201—THE FOURTH CRUSADE

This crusade was made up of unscrupulous adventurers and the marine forces of Venice. It was to move against Egypt and then Palestine, but the Venetians in an attempt to right wrongs that had been inflicted upon the imperial family in the Byzantine capital and in an effort to promote their interest in the region of the Black Sea took great pains to insure that the crusade was directed against Constantinople.

The city of Constantinople was captured and sacked and a Latin prince, Baldwin of Flanders, was proclaimed Emperor of the East. Most of the islands, which had belonged to Greece, and some of the shore lands were given to Venice as her share of the spoils.

The Children's Crusade was launched by a French lad named Stephen who was about twelve years of age. He was persuaded that Christ had commanded him to lead a crusade of children to the Holy Land. The children of France became wild with excitement and flocked in great numbers to the appointed gathering places. Some children declared that the crusade was inspired by the Holy Spirit, others were of the opinion that the whole procedure was prompted by the devil.

When the children found that the sea did not open up and give them a passage to the land of Palestine they became discouraged and part of the group returned home.

Others accepted the offers of two merchants of the city of Marseilles, who promised to take them to the Holy Land without cost. The young Crusaders were crowded into seven small ships which sailed for the Holy Land, but the merchants betrayed the trustful children and sailed to Alexandria where the children were sold as Mohammedans.

THE FIFTH CRUSADE

Three crusades are the only ones to which all authorities give the same numbers. The Fifth Crusade is the name generally given to one that was undertaken by Frederick II, the German Emperor. He proceeded to the Holy Land and concluded a treaty with the Mohammedans which secured possession of the Holy City. In making a treaty with the infidels he was severely censured by Pope Gregory IX. In 1244 Jerusalem was retaken by the Mohammedans.

THE SIXTH CRUSADE UNDER LOUIS IX OF FRANCE

Louis IX tried to enter Palestine through Egypt but was defeated and captured. His release was secured upon the payment of a large ransom by the people of France. When he returned to France he began making plans for the Seventh Crusade.

1270—THE SEVENTH CRUSADE

In 1270 Louis IX started on his second expedition, but died at Tunis on the way to Palestine. In this crusade he was associated with Edward Plantagenet, who was later Edward I of England, who landed an Army at Acre which accomplished nothing and after two years Edward returned home. This marked the end of the crusades. Though the crusades failed to accomplish the deliverance of Jerusalem, they had a great influence upon European history.

By promoting commerce between the East and the West they added much to the wealth of Europe. They also increased the power of the Roman church. In the absence of the kings and princes the bishops and the popes assumed control. The papacy was enriched by loaning money to the monarchs to enable them to carry on the crusades. The greed of the popes for power and their unlawful use of that power laid the foundation for the revolt brought against the church in the Reformation.

CHAPTER 8

RISE OF THE INQUISITION

It will not be neccessary to picture the corruption and wickedness of the Roman Catholic Church in the period of time immediately following the crusades, nor to deal at length with the sins of the rulers of the Roman church. It is sufficient to say that instead of being examples of righteousness they became examples of sinful conduct.

> "The people were sunk in the grossest superstition: and employed all their zeal in the worship of images, and relics, and in performance of a trifling round of ceremonies, which were imposed upon them by the tyranny of a despotic priesthood. The more learned, it is true, retained still some notions of the truth, which, however, they obscured and corrupted by a wretched mixture of opinions and precepts, some of which were ludicrous, others pernicious and the most of them equally destitute of truth and utility—Notwithstanding all this, we find, from the time of Gregory VII several proofs of the zealous efforts of those, who are generally called by the Protestants, the witnesses of the truth; by whom are meant, such pious and judicious Christians, as adhered to the pure religion of the gospel and remained uncorrupted amidst the growth of superstition; who deplored the miserable state to which Christianity was reduced, by the alteration of its divine doctrines, and the vices of its profligate ministers, who opposed with vigor, the tyrannic ambition, both of the lordly pontiff, and the aspiring bishop; and in some provinces privately, in others openly, attempted the reformation of a corrupt and idolatrous church, and of a barbarous and superstitious age. This was indeed bearing witness to the truth in the noblest manner and it was principally in Italy and France that the marks of this heroic piety were exhibited. Nor is it at all suprising that the reigning superstition of the times met with this opposition; it is astonishing, on the contrary, that this opposition was not much greater and more universal, and that millions of Christians suffered themselves to be hoodwinked with such a tame submission and closed their eyes upon the light with so little reluctance. For notwithstanding the darkness of the times and the general ignorance of the true religion, that prevailed in all ranks and orders, yet the very fragments of the gospel, (if we may use that term) which were still read and explained to the people were sufficient, at least, to convince the most stupid and illiterate, that the religion which was now imposed upon them, was not the true religion of Jesus."*

---

* *Ecclesiastical History*—Mosheim. Volume 1, Part 2, Chapter 3, Page 260.

1110—PETER DE BRUYS REJECTED THE MASS AND
THE DOCTRINE OF CELIBACY

Peter de Bruys had at one time been a priest but had been suspended because of his teaching. After his suspension he went through the valleys of France openly assailing the doctrine and practice of the Roman church.

He taught that God could be worshipped anywhere, that he did not need a chapel or require loud singing. The wooden crosses he found by the roadside he uprooted and burnt in the villages. He affirmed that no one ought to be baptized until they came to the age of reason, that the body and blood of Christ are not distributed in the sacred supper. He taught that the oblations and prayers of the living do not profit the dead. He denied the validity of baptism when administered by the clergy of the dominant church and re-baptized those who professed faith in Christ. He taught much that was in harmony with God's word, endeavoring to point men to the Christ and elevate their morals. The world was not yet ready to forsake the doctrines that had developed from following men and return to God's word so this man, too, was burned as a heretic and a disturber of the church in 1124.

1115—THE PERSECUTION OF THE ALBIGENSES

These people took their name from the town of Albi, near Toulouse, in France. They followed simplicity in dress and in their manner of living. In doctrine and in worship they had many things in common with the church established in Jerusalem, though in some points there was wide separation. They were primitive Christians or those who in many points followed the doctrine of the primitive church, who rejected the attempt of the church of Rome to evangelize them. They denied that they separated from the church of Rome but affirmed that the church of Rome had been a part of the new Testament church at one time but that it modified the teaching of the Scriptures, changed the worship and created a system of religion that was unknown in the days of the apostles.

The Albigenses carried on their worship, taught their doctrines and instructed their children in the tenets of their religion. The growth of Catholicism, with a worship that was contrary to God's word and a doctrine that was contrary to the apostles' teaching revealed the sharp contrast between the church of Rome and the simplicity of the Albigenses. With respect to their character and doctrine no one could doubt their sincerity and piety. Among the doctrines they advocated was their denial that church buildings were more adapted to worship than private homes. They disapproved of the use of incense and consecrated oil in services of a religious nature. They denied that the sins of departed spirits could in any way be atoned for by the celebration of masses, holding that the doctrine of purgatory was a ridiculous fable.

They declared the use of instrumental music in the churches and other religious assemblies superstitious and unlawful. They refused all acts of adoration rendered to images of Christ.

To compel them to become a part of the hierarchy of Rome monks were sent throughout their territory to dispute with them and to force them to end their opposition to the apostate church. When these efforts proved unsuccessful, armed troops were called in to exterminate them.

These troops were headed by Simon de Montfort, who ravaged their territory for a period of years in which more than one hundred thousand of them were put to death. The crusades against the Albigenses are a foul blot on the character and administration of Pope Innocent III.

The people against whom this crusade was directed were peaceful and prosperous. Although some of their doctrines were out of harmony with the Scriptures, yet much of their doctrine was based upon the Scriptures. They were noted for their industrious and orderly lives which were in sharp contrast with the lives of the licentious and mercenary clergy of the Roman church. The simplicity of their religion and their zeal in the work of the Lord led many away from the cold and unsatisfying ritualism of the papal church. Innocent III purposed to bring these people into conformity with the teachings and practice of the Roman Catholic Church and so launched against them all the strength of the church, backed by the power of the state, promising an indulgence to all who participated in the crusade against them.

Thus we have the picture of the man who proclaimed himself as the Vicegerent of God, the one who professed to be the personal representative of Christ, sweeping down upon the unoffending Albigenses and inflicting upon them all terrors of war, murder, and uncontrolled lust. Innocent confirmed the excommunication of Raymond VI of Toulouse who ruled over the provinces occupied by these people, because he had failed to convert these heretics, as they were called, to the established church. All who entered the war against them had their lands protected by the church during their absence, their creditors were compelled to postpone the debts of the crusaders without interest, and such lands as they were able to take from the Albigenses became the property of the crusaders.

1122—CONCORDAT AT WORMS

The successors of Henry IV continued their quarrel with the popes until this year. At this time an agreement was reached whereby those having the qualifications should receive their appointments, ring and staff, signifying their spiritual jurisdiction from the pope. The emperor was to exercise the right of inducting them into office by the touch of his scepter, signifying his temporal right and authority. This concordat or agreement brought about peace between the popes and the kings of the Holy Roman Empire.

1123—THE LATERAN COUNCIL BANNED THE MARRIAGE OF THE CLERGY

The Lateran Council, convened in the Lateran palace, a great structure once belonging to the Laterani family, but later given to the Roman bishops. Here in this building the popes carried on their business for a thousand years. This council decreed the end of the marriage of the clergy. This was opposed by Aeneas Sylvius. Afterward when Sylvius became Pope Pius II he affirmed in his "Commentary on The Council of Basil" that "as marriage was taken away for weighty reasons, upon more weighty reasons it ought to be restored." In 1667 this commentary was placed on the list of books prohibited to members of the Roman Catholic Church.

1134—ARNOLD OF BRESCIA ENTERED HIS PROTEST AGAINST THE CORRUPTIONS OF THE PAPACY

This man was well educated, but also of an impetuous disposition. He created much trouble for both the church and the state by the reforms he tried to institute. When the Lateran council met in Rome in 1139 he was condemned, Pope Innocent II affirming his condemnation. He fled to Switzerland to escape the death penalty and remained there till the death of the pope when he returned to Italy. His efforts to reform the Roman Catholic Church and her doctrines met with little success although he was able to create quite a following. His followers became known as Arnoldists and as often as opportunity presented they attempted to bring about a reformation of the church of Rome.

> "He fell at last a victim to the vengeance of his enemies; for, after various turns of fortune he was seized in the year 1155, by a prefect of the city, by whom he was crucified, and afterward burned to ashes. This unhappy man seems not to have adopted any doctrine inconsistent with the spirit of true religion; and the principles upon which he acted were chiefly reprehensible from their being carried too far, applied without discernment and discretion, and executed with a degree of vehemence which was as criminal as it was imprudent. Having perceived the discords and

animosities, the calamities and disorders that sprung from the overgrown opulence of the pontiffs and bishops, he was persuaded that the interests of the church, and the happiness of nations in general, required that the clergy should be divested of all their worldly possessions, of all their temporal rights and prerogatives. He, therefore, maintained publicly, that the treasures and revenues of popes, bishops, and monasteries, ought to be solemnly resigned and transferred to the supreme rulers of each state, and that nothing was to be left to the ministers of the gospel but a spiritual authority and a subsistence drawn from tithes and from voluntary oblations and contributions of the people."*

1170—THE PERSECUTION OF THE WALDENSES

The Waldenses, sometimes called "The Vaudois," were followers of Peter Waldo of Lyons, France. They were like the Albigenses in many respects. They were branded as heretics and were savagely persecuted. In Bohemia they were allied to the Hussites and in Switzerland they were associated with the Calvinists.

They pleaded for a purified Christianity. They claimed their group went back to the early church, before it became corrupted by the doctrines of the ecclesiastics.

The laymen among this group preached to the people independent of the clergy. These people made the Scriptures alone their only source of doctrine. They studied the Bible and sought edification from it. Of course, they often misinterpreted the Scriptures, but not more so than the priests. "They went abroad as peddlers and employed ingenious methods to introduce their doctrines or copies of scriptural books."

In the mountains, in the forests, and in the caves of the earth these people met for worship. Those who taught the Scriptures would suddenly appear in a village where a few souls met in secret to worship God. There they would admonish all to faithfulness, exhort them to continue to serve God in the face of all persecution, bidding them farewell they would hurry away to teach the word in another locality.

The Waldenses taught that oil was not to be mingled with the water of baptism, that prayers over inanimate things were superstitious, that meat could be eaten in Lent, that the clergy may marry, and auricular confession is unnecessary.

They boldly affirmed that confirmation was no sacrament, that no one was bound to pay obedience to the pope and that no dignity set one minister above another. They believed that images in the churches were absurd, that image worship was idolatry, the pope's indulgences ridiculous and the miracles pretended to be done by the

* *Ecclesiastical History*—Mosheim. Chapter 5, Part 2, 12th Century, Page 120.

church of Rome false. They believed also that purgatory was a fictitious plan to extort money from the friends of the deceased, that extreme unction was not a sacrament and that masses and prayers for the dead were of no service to them.

The Waldenses lived in the valleys of Piedmont as a united group separate from the church of Rome, claiming unbroken succession from the church of the early ages.

The Waldenses brought to the people of Metz copies of the Scripture in the French language. These were eagerly accepted by the people, who were hungry for the word of God. The clergy tried to stop the reading of the Scriptures but the people refused to surrender their books. They insisted that God meant for his word to be understood and that the Bible taught them truths that the priests had neglected to teach. The truth-seeking people had found out that the priests were often in error with the word of God. When the pope sent abbots among them to force them to give up their Bibles, they refused to obey the pope's orders to surrender the Scriptures. Force was applied to them, they were forced to flee to save their lives and so far as possible their copies of the Scriptures were burned. The desire to know more of God's word now increased among the laymen. To counteract this desire the church of Rome was soon forced to act.

> "When persecution brought them to the light of the world, they had the Bible, loved it, studied it, they had lay teachers, and ordained presbyters, they had no prelatic bishops; they had quite a definite creed, expressed in scriptural terms; they were strongly opposed to the entire system of Rome; they declared the pope to be antichrist, and the church ritual to be folly; they refused confession to priests, penances, the abuses connected with the only two divine sacraments, and nearly all the Roman rites, and it is hardly too much to say, 'that no candid reader of the creeds, confessions and other public documents which they have left, can hesitate to conclude that their leading opinions were very nearly the same with those which were afterward entertained by Luther, Calvin, and other Reformers, so that they fell in very readily with the church of Geneva in the sixteenth century.' "*

The Catholic church sent monks through all the southern part of France to dispute with them because of their violent opposition to the doctrines of the Roman church.

Finding that their efforts were unsuccessful, armed troops were called in to exterminate them. These troops fought against the Waldenses for twenty years during which time thousands were put to death.

---

* *History of The Christian Church*—Blackburn. Chapter 14, Section 3, Page 311.

1179—THE BEGINNING OF THE INQUISITION

The third Lateran council issued a decree of excommunication and punishment for all the heretics of Southern France, notably the Albigenses and the Waldenses. An indulgence was granted to anyone who would fight against them for two years and should he be killed in action he had the promise that his soul would go directly to God. Whoever concealed a heretic lost all of his property; if he was a landowner he incurred other penalties. The people of any community were afraid to shelter heretics and were always ready to turn over to the papal authorities those suspected of heresy. Heretics who recanted had to seek a new home and wear an emblem on their clothing showing they had been guilty of heresy. Whoever missed the Lord's Supper was suspected of heresy.

In the Inquisition more than thirty-one thousand were put to death. After the Reformation began, the Inquisition became the most powerful weapon of the Roman Catholic Church to undo the work of the reformers. Courts of Inquisition were opened in all towns in an effort to crush the work of the preachers who were teaching purity of life, separation from the papacy, and a return to the Bible.

The Dominican and Franciscan monks were invested by the pope with the right of managing the courts of Inquisition. Their power was almost unlimited. They were permitted to excommunicate or sentence to death any person suspected of heresy. Those believed to be guilty were often placed upon the rack, a contrivance for stretching the bones of their arms and limbs out of joint.

The Inquisitors were instructed to "draw him into confidential disclosures or utterances prompted by hopes and fears, repeatedly examine him so that he may contradict himself; when his answers are confused the doctors agree that you may put him to torture. This method is almost sure to succeed; and he must be clever indeed who does not fall into the snare."

People were punished in every conceivable manner that the ingenuity of wicked men could devise, some had their flesh cut in strips from their bodies, others were pushed over cliffs, burned at the stake, strangled or drowned—all in the name of religion.

Few people were willing to face the terrors of the Inquisition. Resistance to the inquisitors was of no avail and it was next to impossible to escape the torments of the papal representatives by flight. Thousands perished on the scaffold, in the dungeons, on the rack and by starvation. Still great numbers of those opposed to the papacy continued to live. The word "inquisition" signifies that it was a search, an investigation, an inquiry. It was a difficult matter to detect heresy. Some who outwardly were obedient to the church

of Rome were indeed "heretics." Many of the local prelates were
indifferent toward the heretics but when the bishop arrived in
a local province all of the people of the parish were compelled to
assemble before him. A number of men were selected who might
know of offenses which required attention. These witnesses became
an established institution for the detection of heresies and they
were required to swear that they would reveal anyone suspected of
heresy or those whose life did not conform to the established practice of the church. Later the responsibility for conducting the Inquisition was placed in the hands of the various orders of the
Roman church.

All rulers were to publicly place heretics under a ban. The person who detected a heretic could seize him and claim his estate for
his own. After a magistrate was placed in office, the bishop selected
those who were to constitute the inquiry court. Two officials were
appointed to arrest heretics, seize their possessions, and bring
them before the inquisition. The salary of the arresting officials
was paid by the state and their testimony was accepted without
oath. They received one-third of all the fines imposed on the heretics, also one-third of all the property taken from the heretics. No
laws could be passed limiting their action; the ruler of each district
was to aid in arrest of the offenders and to execute judgment
against them within fifteen days. The fines and property confiscated, were divided between Inquisitors, the city, and the bishops.

"In the Province, in Lombardy, in the Piedmont and Dauphine,
the so called Waldensians had preserved from earlier days a purer
faith. They possessed the Bible in the language of the people and
were untouched by many of the superstitions of the prevailing
religion.

These people, certainly the best representatives of the Christian
church in that age, became the object of the most ferocious
persecutions.

Thousands upon thousands of Waldensians were slain during
the riots which the Dominicans incited against them. It was a
common sport to harry a congregation of Waldensians out of their
village, and drive them into winter solitudes to perish in the mountains or to roast them alive in caves in which they had sought
refuge.

Such assistance on the part of a fanatic populace was demanded
by the spiritual courts entrusted with the eradication of heresy and
was regarded as highly meritorious work."*

"The state was bound to arrest all accused persons, to hold them
in prison, to deliver them to the bishop or inquisitor under safe
escort, and to execute within fifteen days all judgments pronounced
against them. The ruler was, moreover, required to inflict torture
on those who would not confess and betray all heretics of their
acquaintance."†

* The Dark Ages—Graebner. Chapter 6, Page 139.
† The Age of Hildebrand—Vincent. Chapter 36, Page 397.

Lea in his "History of The Inquisition of The Middle Ages" declares how the hands of a suspect would be tied behind his back with a stout rope which passed through a pulley near the ceiling, with which he was gradually lifted from the floor. This authority states that the elevating movement was slow, for if it was suddenly accomplished the pain would not be lasting. For a short time the patient was kept with his toes just touching the floor and then gradually lifted and repeatedly admonished to tell the truth. If he failed to do so, then he was lowered and weights were attached to his feet to increase the pain. After being suspended for a time the inquisitors would let him fall a short distance with a jerk and this was repeated as often and as long as was judged expedient.

Such punishment produced some kind of a confession whether the accused was guilty or not.

1190—INDULGENCES WERE AGAIN OFFERED FOR SALE

Here is the doctrine which did much to further corrupt the practices of the apostate church. The doctrine of indulgences was believed to have had its beginning in the days of Pope Pascal in 820. He is said to have found it profitable to promise a person freedom from the penalty of sin. Indulgences were farmed out to be sold for so much money. This became a source of papal revenue and eventually developed into offering pardon to all who sinned, without confession to, or absolution by a priest.

Bishop Fisher, in a work he wrote against Luther said, "Many persons are inclined to place but little reliance upon indulgences, because their use seems to have come in rather late in the church—. No orthodox doubts whether there is a purgatory, concerning which, nevertheless, there is no mention or the very rarest mention in ancient writers. To this day purgatory is not believed in by the Greek church. As long, then, as there was no anxiety concerning purgatory, no one looked for indulgences, for all the value of indulgences depends upon it. If you take away purgatory, what use will there be in indulgences? Indulgences, therefore, began when the people began to entertain fears about the torments of purgatory."

"An indulgence is defined in Roman Catholic theology as remission of that temporal punishment which, even after the sin is forgiven, we have yet to undergo, either here or in purgatory. The basis of the doctrine is found in the works of supererogation, that is, works in excess of the actual needs of individual redemption. According to Roman Catholic teaching, our Savior and the saints accomplished much more than was needed for salvation. This excess constitutes a spiritual treasure, of which the pope is trustee or guardian, and which he may draw on at will to meet the wants of individual believers. Or, to quote from Deharbe's Full Catechism: Indulgences derive their value and efficacy from the spiritual

> treasure of the church, which consists of the superabundant merits and satisfactions of Christ and the saints. This treasure is to be considered as the common property of the faithful, committed to the administration of the church, since, by virtue of the communion of saints, by which we are united as members of one body, the abundance of some supplies the want of others."*
>
> "Religious and secular clergy—gave absolution for money to those who did not even confess to have contrition. Cardinal Canisio was of the opinion that the facilities for absolution encouraged sinners and were an inducement to sin."†

The development of this doctrine violated every principle set forth in the Bible on the subject of repentance and the forgiveness of sin. "Forasmuch as ye know that ye were not redeemed with corruptible things, as silver and gold, from your vain conversation received by tradition from your fathers; but with the precious blood of Christ, as of a lamb without blemish and without spot."[1]

The doctrine of indulgences was one of the most corrupt doctrines that ever came out of Rome and without a doubt it contributed to the dismemberment of the papacy.

1215—THE ACCEPTANCE OF THE DOCTRINE OF AURICULAR CONFESSION

This doctrine grew out of the practice of penitents who returned to the church making a statement of their wrongs to the presbyter appointed for that purpose. The corruption of the priesthood was brought about to a large extent by the confessional. The Lateran Council in this year first bound upon all who had reached the years of discretion the obligation of confessing their sins. The doctrine had been taught in the fourth century and reintroduced in the year 763.

Now we see it converted into a doctrine of the papal church. It first appears as a heathen custom in the apostate church, a custom which originated in the religion of Babylon which required those who were introduced to the mysteries of that system of religion to make a confession of their thoughts and actions. Dr. David Patrick refers to the abuse of auricular confession in the pre-Reformation Church of Scotland saying,

> "Worst of all in the eyes of the historical student, anxious not to judge the church of the thirteenth century, or even of the first, is the distinct implication that bishops and priests, rectors and vicars, were not free from the guilt of abusing the solemn sacraments of the church, the church fabric, and the church yard by indecently and sacrilegiously dishonoring the women who came to

* *The Dark Ages*—Graebner. Chapter 7, Pages 147, 148.
† *The Dark Ages*—Graebner. Notes on Chapter 7, page 213.
1. 1 Peter 1:18, 19

them for confession and absolution. Our Scottish statutes make it painfully clear that Scottish mothers and aunts had the same strong reasons as St. Catherine of Siena had for urgently imploring the girls and women of their kith and kin to fly from their confessors the moment confession was ended."*

The private confession of sins to a priest for the forgiveness of those sins began to be practiced in the fourth century but not until the thirteenth century did it become a universal custom. This teaching, that the clergy had the power to absolve one from his sins was openly taught and that it was the continued practice of the Roman church is confirmed by the following form of confession from Dens' Theology.

"I confess to God, the Father Almighty, to his only begotten Son, Jesus Christ and to God, the Holy Ghost, before the whole company of heaven, and to you my Father, that I have sinned exceedingly in thought, word and deed, by my fault, my own fault, my most grievous fault." (Then follows a detailed account of the sins.) "For these sins I most humbly ask pardon of God, and of you my ghostly Father, penance, counsel and absolution."

Having heard the confession, and the necessary questions being finished, the priest will say—"May God Almighty have mercy upon thee, and having remitted thy sins, lead thee through to eternal life." Then raising his hands toward the penitent, let him say—"May the Almighty and Merciful Lord, give thee indulgence, absolution and remission of thy sins, Amen. May our Lord Jesus Christ absolve thee, and I by his authority loose from every bond of excommunication and interdict so far as I am able and thou hast need. I absolve thee from thy sins, in the name of the Father, the Son and the Holy Ghost, Amen."

This teaching that a human being can absolve one from his sins by acting as a mediator between God and the sinner is in conflict with Paul's teaching, "For there is one God and one mediator between God and men, the man Christ Jesus."[2]

The confessional proved to be a plague spot with which the synods and councils were unable to deal. In all of the legislation of the pre-reformation period the effort of local and national councils, pastoral epistles, statutes of churches reveal the ceaseless yet unavailing efforts to repress the abuses of the confessional.

"The abuse of the awful authority given by the altar and the confessional was a subject of sorrowful and indignant denunciation in too many synods for a reasonable doubt to be entertained of its frequency or of the corruption which it spread through innumerable parishes. The almost entire impunity with which these and

* *The Dark Ages*—Graebner. Chapter 3, Pages 74, 75.
2. 1 Timothy 2:5

similar scandals were perpetrated led to an undisguised and cynical profligacy which the severer churchmen themselves admitted to exercise a most deleterious influence on the morals of the laity, who thus found in their spiritual guides the exemplars of evil."*

Trevelyan says in his *History in The Age of Wyclif*: "In the earlier middle ages the secular clergy had wives. The Saxon priest had known no rule of celibacy. About the time of the Conquest, Hildebrand's dreaded decree began to find its way to England and by the fourteenth century it had long been an established rule that no priest should marry. But the old custom had never died out completely among the parish clergy, although their partners were now in the eyes of the law mere concubines. The church authorities were often bribed to neglect visitation and inquiry into such cases, and priests brought up their children without fear, if not without reproach. Sometimes indeed, the law of celibacy forced them into more irregular and less permanent unions; but in this age of vice and coarseness, when all writers agree that incontinence was the prevailing sin of the laity, it was the friars, and not the parish priests who were singled out as having a lower standard than even the laymen."

The Crusades against the Waldenses, the Albigenses, the continuance of the Inquisition, and the acceptance of the doctrine of auricular confession were outstanding events during the reign of Pope Innocent III. He proclaimed himself the earthly representative of Christ on earth and therefore the rightful ruler of the world, affirming that the claims of kings were valid only when approved by the papacy. King John of England was one of the first rulers to deny the claims of Innocent III. Following the death of Hubert, the papal representative, the king appointed John de Grey, the Bishop of Norwich, to the vacancy, but the pope declared the appointment null and void and the monks of Canterbury appointed Stephen de Langton to the archbishopric and the pope confirmed the appointment. The King refused to acknowledge Langton and expelled the monks from Canterbury and seized their possessions. The pope immediately placed the kingdom under an interdict. This meant that no churches were to be opened, no services held and the dead were either left unburied or buried in unconsecrated ground without religious ceremony. King John defied the pope and seized the revenue of all the clergy who sided with the pope. For this the king was excommunicated, by which he was deprived of the sacraments, of divine worship and forbidden the association of the faithful. The pope finally compelled King John to give up his whole realm and pay tribute to the pope for the return of his crown.

---

* *The Dark Ages*—Graebner. Chapter 3, Page 77.

One may see in the British Museum today the bull of Pope Innocent III accepting the grant by King John of the kingdoms of England and Ireland to the Roman Catholic Church.

In return the pope took the king, his heirs, and the two realms under the protection of St. Peter's and granted the realm in fee to John and his successors on the condition of oath of fealty at accession. Dated at St. Peter's, Rome, April 21, 1214.

This document is attested by the pope's signature and that of fourteen cardinals with the pope's leaden bulla appended by silk strings.

> "The king of England—assembled his forces, and was putting himself in a posture of defence, when Pandulf, the pope's legate, arrived at Dover, and proposed a conference in order to prevent the approaching rupture, and to conjure the storm. This artful legate terrified the king, who met him at that place, with an exaggerated account of the armament of Philip on one hand and the disaffection of the English on the other; and persuaded him that there was no possible way of saving his dominion from the formidable arms of the French king, but that of putting them under the protection of the Roman see.
>
> John finding himself in such a perplexing situation and full of diffidence both in the nobles of his court and in the officers of his army, complied with this dishonorable proposal, did homage to Innocent, resigned his crown to the legatee and received it again as a present from the see of Rome, to which he rendered his kingdoms tributary and swore fealty as a vassal and feudatory."*

These events reveal to us the power of the papacy at this time. The church had become a ruling institution exercising its authority over kings and their subjects. It controlled their thoughts and lives on temporal affairs as well as spiritual. Thus the papacy reached the height of its power in England.

1215—KING JOHN SIGNS THE "MAGNA CHARTA"

The barons and nobles of England, aided by Archbishop Langton of Canterbury met King John at Runnymead June 15, 1215 and there exacted of him a constitution which became known as the "Magna Charta."

This document formed the basis of English liberty. It proclaimed that "the Church of England shall be free and shall have her rights entire and her liberties uninjured."

Pope Innocent appealed to King John to stop such proclamations, but John in his wrath informed the pope that since his reconciliation with God and the pope that he had suffered from the intervention of twenty-four kings. Pope Innocent took issue with John and

---

* *Ecclesiastical History*—Mosheim. Volume 2, Part 2, Chapter 2, Page 818.

attempted to annul the "Magna Charta" by a papal bull, suspended the Archbishop, laid an interdict upon London and an anathema upon the barons. Pope Innocent died the next year without having brought England into complete subjection to the papacy again.

In this same year the Fourth Lateran Council gave the church its doctrine on the seven sacraments which they declared to be Baptism, Confirmation, Holy Communion, Penance, Extreme Unction, Holy Orders and Matrimony.

The doctrine of Transubstantiation was by this council declared to be a tenet of the Roman church. All the laity were ordered to confess their sins to a priest once a year; the Eucharist was to be received by all members of the church, at least once a year or they were to be excommunicated; heresy was to be ended by persecution. All rulers were called upon to exterminate all heretics in their provinces, for failing to do so their subjects were absolved from their oath of allegiance and their kingdom was to be given to those who would obey.

1229—THE COUNCIL OF TOULOUSE PROHIBITED THE READING OF THE BIBLE

"We forbid also the permitting of the laity the books of the Old and New Testament in the common tongue." The Bible, God's divine revelation was to be denied to all laymen of the Roman Catholic Church. Only priests or higher officials were permitted to read or possess a copy of the Bible.

The purpose of withholding the Bible from the laity was to prevent the private interpretation of it. Isn't it strange that God would give the human family a book that is "profitable for doctrine" and "instruction in righteousness" and then deny them the right of reading it? Why does the Roman Catholic Church oppose the reading of the Bible? If the Roman church has the truth why is the hierarchy afraid to let it come into competition with the Bible?

The following excerpt is from an address by the cardinals to Pope Pius III and is said to be preserved in the National Library at Paris—

> "Of all the advice we can offer your Holiness—we must open your eyes well and use all possible force in the matter—viz: To permit the reading of the gospel as little as possible in all the countries under your jurisdiction. Let the very part of the gospel suffice which is read in mass and let no one be permitted to read more. So long as people will be content with the small amount, your interests will prosper, but as soon as the people want to read more your interests will begin to fail.
> The Bible is the book, which more than any other has raised against us the tumults and tempests by which we have almost

THE CONTINUED GROWTH OF APOSTASY

THE CHANGE
- 120 A.D. Baptismal water consecrated
- 140 A.D. Observance of Lent
- 325 A.D. Easter adopted from pagan worship
  Adoration of angels
- 190 A.D. Burning of candles and incense
- 200 A.D. Elders assumed title of priests
- 303 A.D. Compulsory celibacy of eldership

THE CAUSE
- Neglect of study of God's word (2 Tim. 3: 16, 17)
- Change in government of the church (2 Ths. 2: 15)
- Members drawn away from the gospel (Acts 20: 28-32)
- Creeds accepted as a guide for faith (Rom. 10: 17)

THE RESULT
- Development of an ecclesiastical hierarchy
- Distinction between the clergy and laity
- Worship of the church combined with paganism
- Tradition placed upon equality with the Scriptures

perished, in fact if one compares the teachings of the Bible with
what takes place in our churches he will soon find discord, and
will realize that our teachings are often different from the Bible,
and oftener still contrary to it."*

When men are deprived of the guidance of God's word a moral
depression develops and there is nothing to restrain them from evil
conduct. History shows that the moral and spiritual condition of
the countries under the control of the Roman Catholic Church sank
to a low level.

True there was prosperity and freedom in the larger cities of
those countries resulting from the wealth and industry of the
artisans. Continual feuds and warfare prevailed in Europe and
roving bands of robbers placed the lives of travelers in jeopardy.

Scholasticism, a combination of Greek philosophy and the theology of the dark ages prevailed in the universities of this medieval
period. Speculation upon the nature of God and work of Christ
brought forth questions as to whether God was capable of knowing
more than he is aware of and whether the body of Christ arose with
its wounds or not, whether the dove in which the Holy Spirit appeared was a real being.

At the universities lewd women were kept in the fraternity
houses and houses of ill fame were alluded to as the "fifth department of college studies." Adultery was not regarded as a sin and
absolution for such required only the payment of a small sum. A
Benedictine monk from Gascony, Bernard Baptisatus, delivered an
invecture against the corruption of the clergy in which he said:

> "Among the prelates we find malice and iniquity, negligence,
> ignorance and vanity, pride, greed and love of pomp, and they who
> used to be shepherds of the sheep now are wolves and feed upon
> the sheep . . .
>
> Unless the greed and rapacity of the clergy is removed from the
> church there will in a short while occur such a persecution of the
> clergy as never has yet occurred. Why? Because these ecclesiastical
> gentlemen privately and publicly conceive lewdness, bring forth
> shame, nurse greed, gather pride, conduct feuds and wars and walk
> in deceit and fraud—to such an extent that almost the entire
> clergy is subject to the devil."†

In the years that followed the conduct of the medieval clergy was
one of the subjects of discussion by the church councils which convened to reform the Roman Catholic Church, but while there was
discussion the councils did not legislate in favor of chastity. In
writing of the condition of the clergy an accepted authority said,
"The priests are not ashamed to enter the taverns or even brothels,

---

* Folio No. 1068, Volume 2, Pages 650-651. Printed in the *Scripture Standard*,
Volume 20, No. 7.
† *Compendium of Ecclesiastical History*—Giesler. Volume 3, Page 135.

to corrupt married women and nuns, to keep concubines in public houses and to procreate with them. The bishops, however, because they live in the same vice, accept an annual fee from them, and permit things to remain in such awful condition."

> "They lay every day in taverns and houses of ill fame, feasted, drank and spent their time with gambling; when in their cups, they quarreled and shouted and would come to blows; from the embraces of their meretrices they went to the altar. Those who lived a chaste life were ridiculed as impotent or were suspected of worse crimes."*

These shocking conditions within the church upon the part of those who were regarded as spiritual guides called for a change.

1268—PAPAL CHAIR VACANT FOR THREE YEARS

When Gregory X was elected, he proclaimed a law by which cardinals in conclave were denied food until they had elected a new pope.

1274—A COUNCIL CALLED TO REUNITE THE GREEK CATHOLIC AND THE ROMAN CATHOLIC CHURCH

Other efforts prior to this time had only resulted in failure. Under the pontificate of Gregory proposals of peace were made by each group which were designed to end the controversy and bring reconciliation. The emperor of the eastern part of the old Roman Empire, in the face of opposition from the clergy of the Greek church, sent ambassadors to the council that had convened at Lyons. After much discussion the Roman pontiff set forth the plan upon which they could be reconciled which was accepted by John Veccus, Patriarch of Constantinople. This did not bring about peace for it was later declared null and void and Veccus was sent into exile.

1309—1376—THE PAPAL THRONE REMOVED TO AVIGNON, FRANCE

A quarrel developed between Boniface VIII and Philip the Fair, king of France, over the jurisdiction of the pope. Philip refused to acknowledge the right of the pope to dictate to temporal rulers in matters that did not affect the church. Boniface had contended that all kings and princes were obligated by a divine command to submit to the authority of the pope in civil matters as well as those of a religious nature. He informed Philip of his claim by letter and Philip replied to the pope in terms of contempt. The pope affirmed that Jesus Christ had placed all mankind under the author-

---

* *The Dark Ages*—Graebner. Chapter 2, Page 71.

ity of the pope and that whoever denied this was a heretic and had no hope of salvation.

Philip called an assembly and ordered William de Nogaret to draw up an accusation against the pope charging him with heresy, simony and other vices, demanding that an ecumenical council be convened and the pope deposed.

The pope replied by excommunicating Philip. Philip then sent Nogaret into Italy with a small army, which seized the pope, bringing him to Lyons where he was to face trial. As soon as Nogaret had the pope in his power he treated him with the utmost disrespect, striking him upon the head with his iron gauntlet.

He was rescued from Nogaret by the citizens of Anagni, taken back to Rome where he died from the insults and the wounds he had suffered at the hands of Nogaret.

When Benedict XI succeeded Boniface upon the throne he immediately repealed the excommunication of Philip but he did not absolve Nogaret of his crime against the head of the church. Nogaret insisted that Boniface be branded as an heretic but before this matter was settled Benedict died and Philip by promises and threats succeeded in having Bishop Bertrand de Got of Bordeaux appointed as pope by the conclave. He took the name Benedict V and removed the papal residence to Avignon where it remained for seventy years.

Benedict was followed by Clement V, John XXII, Benedict XII, Clement VI, Innocent VI, Gregory XI, Urban VI, Clement VII, Boniface IX, Benedict XIII, and finally by Pope Gregory who returned the papal chair to Rome, where he died.

The cardinals now chose a Roman to succeed him, but later held another election and chose a Frenchman, stating that they were forced to elect the Roman. Now there were two claimants to the papal throne, one at Rome and the other at Avignon, each of whom had his supporters. A council was called at Pisa which deposed both of the popes and elected a new pope. The findings of the council were not accepted and the result was that now there were three popes, each declaring himself the rightful pope and excommunicating the other two. This schism was ended by the German emperor displacing all three and electing Martin V who was accepted by all parties.

"The papal power was lessened by the Great Schism (1378—1429) not its first, but at least the twenty-second schism—which began when Urban VI sat at Rome as the choice of England, Ireland, Italy, and most countries east of the Rhine: while Clement VII sat at Avignon, supported by France, Spain, Scotland, Sicily, and Cyprus. The whole western church was rent in twain by the secularized papacy, which never recovered its former power. But

Romish theologians say that the faithful, thus divided in their view of a fact, were not at variance on the principle of a united and infallible primacy, that this fateful division should not be called a schism, because the number of obediences did not impair the principle of unity, since all the churches believed in but one Roman church and only one sovereign pontiff."*

By setting aside the popes the Council of Constance had rejected the doctrine that had been held by the popes for years that only God could correct a pope if he went astray. This council had placed itself above popes and from henceforth the papacy would be compelled to heed the voice of the rulers of Europe.

---

* *History of The Christian Church*—Blackburn. Chapter 14, Section 7, Pages 330, 331.

"Wycliffe, longing to bring home to the great body of the people the words of eternal life, encouraged many who believed and understood some important scriptural truths to go forth as 'poor preachers.' 'Barefoot, and clad in long russet garments of coarsest material, and, being unmarried, content with food and lodging, they passed two and two through the land, denouncing everywhere the sins of all sorts and conditions of men, but with an especial emphasis the sins, the luxury, the sloth, the ignorance of the clergy. They declared, with simplicity and earnestness, the plain truths of the gospel in the vernacular tongue. Not one in five hundred of the people could read; and their ministers did not preach to them. The naked truth of the Scriptures shook, thrilled, enthralled the souls of men so that the adversaries of Wycliffe soon complained the half of England was infected with Lollardy.' "

Church History—Cushing Biggs Hassell

CHAPTER 9

REFORMATION IN ENGLAND

A powerful movement had begun to develop in England for reforming the Roman Catholic Church, for ending monasticism, for telling the unlearned the way of salvation and pointing them to the teaching of the Holy Scriptures.

Robert Grosseteste, a man of sterling worth, and well educated, long had been a leader for reform. He became Bishop of Lincoln, a large diocese which had partly been reformed by Bishop Hugh, who was the foe of immorality and indolence among the monks. There was no other cleric in England who so zealously worked for reform. He took from the clergy their appointed powers because they were wicked, unlearned and lazy. This bishop opposed the collecting of tithes to be sent to the pope and the sending of countless numbers of monks and priests to be supported by the church in England. The nobility objected to the great number who were sent to England who drew from the church a greater sum than was paid to the king, in addition to what was given to Rome.

In a sermon he foretold of the coming break with the Roman Catholic Church, saying, "To follow a pope who rebels against the will of Christ is to separate from Christ; it is schism! If the time shall come when men follow an erring pontiff, then will be the great apostasy. Then will true Christians refuse to obey Rome." The pope, Innocent IV nominated his nephew, a mere child, to a high office in the cathedral of Lincoln. This caused the bishop to write to the pope protesting the appointment, saying, "Your orders are destitute of piety. Every faithful Christian should oppose them with all his might." This caused Pope Innocent to threaten to have the bishop thrown into prison. He was later excommunicated by the pope, but he did not submit to the sentence and refused to relinquish his office. Before his death he denounced the friars as hypocrites and the pope as antichrist. He died while in possession of his office, rejected by Rome, but accepted by his people.

The struggle for more civil and religious freedom in England was now well under way. Laws were enacted at the request of Edward III which revealed the increasing hatred of the English for the jurisdiction of Rome. Among the laws were those that prevented dying persons from being influenced to give their prop-

erty to the priests or to the church. This was to prevent the church
from getting more and more lands. Other laws rendered null all
ecclesiastical appointments that infringed on the rights of the king,
prohibiting papal interference, excommunications and appeals to
Rome, allowing England the right to sit in judgment and to punish
her subjects as she saw fit.

> "The spectacle of rival popes—Clement resting in inglorious
> ease at Avignon, Urban leading a partisan warfare in Italy—each
> imprecating curses on the other, stirred up Wyclif to declare that
> the very papal office was poisonous to the church. The English
> nation was so united in their resistance to ecclesiastical encroach-
> ments that this champion of civil and kingly authority against papal
> claims could utter such words without fear."*

Edward refused to pay tithes to the Roman church and was
called upon by Pope Urban V to acknowledge the pope as the lawful
and accepted ruler of England. The king invoked the vengeance
of God to rest upon the papacy.

1374—FROM OXFORD UNIVERSITY CAME THE AVENGER IN THE PERSON OF JOHN WYCLIF

Wyclif was born at Richmond, in Yorkshire. Graduating from
Oxford he became teacher of Divinity there. Here he expressed
his anti-Roman views, openly showing his hatred for the church
of Rome. His opposition against the papacy began in 1354. This
was directed against the practices and doctrines of the papal church.

Wyclif began his condemnation of the church of Rome at the
very time when the laity seemed determined to throw off the yoke
of papal influence, while the clergy seemed determined to hold to
it. His first attack against the church was a treatise titled "The
Last Age of The Church"; in which he condemned the avarice of
the papal church and the wickedness of the clergy. A vote of Parliament against the power of the Catholic Church, led to a petition
against the clergy being admitted to civil offices. Wyclif is believed
to have been the author of this petition, for soon after he was
named as one of a commission to Bruges to confer with the pope's
representatives concerning certain grievances against the church
relative to the English benefices.

During his stay of two years in Bruges he obtained much information concerning the profligacy of the Papal Court, which caused
him to denounce the pope as antichrist, reject his primacy, and
attack the teachings and practices of the church of Rome. He
declared that the Scriptures alone contained the things that were
essential to salvation.

---

* *History of The Christian Church*—Fisher. Period VII, Chapter 1, Page 2.

Wyclif publicly preached what he believed and appealed to the Scriptures for proof. Some of his teaching was not based upon the word of God, some was indeed contrary to it, but much of what he taught was sound.

He obtained many followers who came to be called Lollards, a name of uncertain origin, but thought to have been applied to his disciples because of their habit of going about singing. It was said that his "poor priests" became so numerous that if you met two people in the way, one of them was sure to be a Lollard. The monks of the Roman Catholic Church put forth every effort to stop the spread of his doctrines. He was accused of heresy on nineteen counts and ordered to be arrested by Pope Gregory XI for trial. A "bull" was also sent to the University of Oxford, requesting them to aid in his arrest. The university ignored the papal request and the delegates dared not arrest him. The university did send a number of theologians to cooperate with the delegates in a commission of inquiry to be held at Lambeth.

Later Wyclif appeared before a Papal Court at St. Paul's in London where the support of the Duke of Lancaster and Lord Percy prevented a decision being rendered against him.

Wyclif was accused of affirming among other opinions—

1. That Christ was not really present in the sacrament at the altar.
2. That no clergyman in mortal sin could exercise the ministerial function.
3. That true penitence is enough without outward confession to a priest.
4. That Christ never instituted the mass.
5. That it is contrary to the Scriptures for churchmen to have temporal possession.
6. That the secular power may deprive churchmen of their charge for delinquency.
7. That a man in mortal sin can not perform the magisterial function.
8. That tithes may be withheld from a wicked pastor.
9. That persons entering a monastery do not belong to the Christian religion.
10. That friars are bound to labor for their living and not beg.
11. That it is presumptuous to say that infants dying without baptism will not be saved.
12. That there are but two orders of the clergy: elders and deacons.

13. All things which happen absolutely, happen necessarily.
14. That subjects are not bound to obey kings or rulers while they are in a state of mortal sin.
15. That images or crosses ought not be worshipped.
16. That every person may preach the gospel.
17. That oblations ought not be made at the obsequies of the dead.
18. That confession to a priest is unnecessary.
19. That the pope is not supreme in authority.
20. That indulgences could not remit sins.

Because of this opposition to the Catholic church he was called "The Morning Star of the Reformation." The Catholic church had reasons for wanting to suppress his teaching, for he attacked both its life and structure. At the time of its greatest wealth Wyclif declared the way to reform the church was to take away its wealth.

> "While he was divinity professor at Oxford he published certain conclusions against transubstantiation, the infallibility of the pope, that Rome was not the head of all churches, that Peter had no more power of the keys than the other apostles, that there were only two degrees of church offices, presbyters and deacons, that human traditions are sinful, that mystical ceremonies in worship are unlawful and that to force men to conform to a prayer form is sinful and contrary to God's will."*

He denied that the bread and fruit of the vine of the Lord's table were changed into the actual body and blood of the Lord. He taught that auricular confession was unscriptural, that indulgences were of no value, and that purgatory did not exist. Wyclif found many who shared his view of reform and these teachers traveled about England teaching the people the Bible. Wyclif and two of his disciples, Nicholas Herford and Richard Purvey gave to the English speaking people a Bible in their own language. While making this translation Wyclif became seriously ill. When the friars of the Roman Catholic Church heard of his critical condition they came to visit him and called attention to the injury he had done to the church and to them by his writings. They exhorted him, as one near death, to repent and to recant.

When they had finished speaking he asked his servant to raise him to a sitting position. The friars, supposing that their purpose had been accomplished waited expectantly.

When Wyclif spoke it was in a stern voice. Pointing an accusing finger at them he said, "I shall not die but live to condemn the friars and all of their evil deeds." The friars left hurriedly and

---

* *History of the Puritans*—Neal. Volume 1, Page 30.

Wyclif lived to finish his translation. He became paralyzed the last Lord's day of 1384 and died a few days later.

After his burial his body was dug up and burned and his ashes were thrown in the Avon river.

Some have said that Wyclif was not the first translator of the Bible for the English people. Bede translated portions of the Bible into English, but Wyclif seems to be the first to translate the entire Bible into English. He collected such Latin Bibles as he could find, from these he made one correct copy of the scriptures and from this he translated into English. His works, of course had no tendency to reinstate him in the good graces of the Catholic clergy.

A universal clamor was raised against him when his translation was finished.

Knighton, a canon of Leicester, said,

> "Christ intrusted his gospel to the clergy and doctors of the church, to minister to its laity and weaker sort. But this, Master John Wyclif, by translating it has made it vulgar and has laid it more open to the laity, (and even to women who can read) than it used to be to the most learned of men."*

Against the doctrine of indulgences Wyclif was very severe. A mere trick, he called them, to rob men of their money.

> "The pope, says he, has the surplus merits of pious saints to dispose of. A profitable doctrine this, but where found? Certainly not in the scripture. For my own part, says he, I meet not, in the whole New Testament, one saint who has more merit than was necessary for his own salvation.
>
> And if Christ, who taught all that was needful and profitable, taught not this doctrine it may be fairly presumed that this doctrine is neither needful nor profitable. All men are partakers of the merits of Christ and no man can expect more. How absurd then is it for men to squander away their money on indulgences."†

The doctrines of Wyclif spread to Bohemia where they were eagerly accepted by John Huss, who was a professor at the University of Prague. Here it was that the work of Wyclif produced the greatest results. Bohemia was the land of the Czechs. They were of Slavic origin and had been ruled by Germany as a part of the German empire. Charles, the king of Bohemia, became king of the German people in 1347. His efforts were always directed toward strengthening the national spirit of his people. Under his reign the Bohemian church became a separate institution, eventually breaking away from the Papal church.

John Huss was the leader in this separation. He was a teacher and a preacher also. He had learned of Wyclif's writings through

---

* *The Lives of Wyclif and The Most Eminent of His Disciples*—Gilpin. Chapter 1, Pages 38, 39.
† *The Lives of Wyclif and The Most Eminent of His Disciples*—Gilpin. Page 69.

the students who had been taught at Oxford. While Huss taught at the university he also preached in Prague in Bethlehem chapel, one of the most influential pulpits in the city.

Here he attacked the abuses of the Roman Catholic Church, the sale of indulgences, the immorality of the priesthood. He declared the pope was the successor of Judas Iscariot. The reforms for which he contended caused him to be excommunicated by the Archbishop of Prague in 1410 but King Wenzel compelled the archbishop to restore him to the fellowship of the Roman Catholic Church.

The following year he was excommunicated by the pope. The reformation in Bohemia caused the Roman Catholic Church great concern. The entire nation became interested in the reformation of the church. Huss became a hero in the sight of the people and the efforts of the church to suppress his doctrines met with failure. The doctrines he advocated were such as would have changed the entire structure of the church.

1412 A.D. POPE JOHN STARTED THE SALE OF INDULGENCES

Huss condemned them as unchristian and wrote a book titled "On the Church" in which he called attention to the abuses of the papacy. The Roman Catholic Church by its many departures from the teaching of the Scriptures, its cruel laws, and low state of morals had become obnoxious and repulsive to its own members. Many of its priests attempted to reform it and lead it back to the Word of God.

1414 A.D. THE COUNCIL OF CONSTANCE CONVENED

This council was to decide who was the rightful pope. There were three claimants to the throne at this time: Gregory XII of Rome, Benedict XIII of Avignon, and Alexander V who was elected by the council of Pisa. These three contenders for the papal office were all deposed by the council which consisted of eighteen hundred bishops, cardinals and priests. They purposed to bring about a reformation within the Roman Catholic Church. After disposing of the charges against John Huss, all of the cardinals took an oath that whosoever among them was elected as the next pope, would not dissolve the council nor leave the city until the desired reforms were made. Cardinal Colonna was elected pope and he assumed the name of Martin V. As soon as the crown was placed upon his head he arose and shouted, "The council is ended" and the effort to correct the evils that beset the Roman Catholic Church came to nought.

The complaints against papal simony were loud and bitter. One of the reasons for the reformation of the church in head and members, urged at the Council of Constance, was the holding of the church benefices or offices. In England they were held by strangers who had no knowledge of the language. These offices were habitually sold by the pope. If ever an age called for reform, it was this period of time.

The pope sold absolution for the most horrible crimes and granted indulgences beforehand for the commission of crimes of lust and violence. Synods expressed their disapproval of the concubinage of the priests by assessing upon them an annual fine. In the course of time the protests ceased because the bishops found it a profitable business.

> "It was a common thing, says Nicholas de Clemanges, that the priests kept concubines publicly for a certain price agreed upon between them and their bishops. Even the grossest immorality was compounded for with the prelates by a similar arrangement.
>
> At the Council of Constance a complaint was read, "The priests are not ashamed to enter the taverns and even houses of ill fame, to corrupt maidens, married women and nuns—and then celebrate mass. The bishops, however, because they are infected with the same vice—receive an annual fee from them, and thus permit them all to remain in their wretched state.*

Little wonder that Huss condemned the papacy when such sins were openly practiced.

> "This eminent man, whose piety was truly fervent and sincere, though his zeal, perhaps, was rather too violent, and his prudence not always equally circumspect, was summoned to appear before the Council of Constance. Obedient to this order, and thinking himself secured from the rage of his enemies by the safe conduct which had been granted him by the Emperor Sigismund, both for his journey to Constance, his residence in the place, and his return to his own country, John Huss appeared before the council, to demonstrate his innocence, and to prove that the charge of his having deserted the church of Rome was entirely groundless. And it may be affirmed with truth that his religious opinions, at least in matters of moment and importance, were conformable to the established doctrine of the church in this age. He declaimed, indeed, with extra-ordinary vehemence against the Roman pontiffs, the bishops and monks, but this freedom was looked upon as lawful in these times, and it was used every day in the Council of Constance, where the tyranny of the popes of Rome, and the corruption of the sacerdotal and monastic orders were censured with the utmost severity. The enemies, however, of this good man, who were very numerous both in the kingdom of Bohemia and also in the Council of Constance, colored the accusation that was brought against him with such artifice and success, that by the most scandalous breach of public faith, he was cast into prison, declared

* *The Dark Ages*—Graebner. Chapter 7, Page 159.

a heretic, because he refused to obey the order of the Council,
which commanded him to plead guilty against the dictates of his
conscience, and was burnt alive the 6th of July 1415.*

When Huss was led out to the stake he said, "You are going to
burn a goose, but a hundred years from now you will have another
goose whom ye can neither burn nor boil and he will make you
sing a different song."

The bishops appointed by the council stripped him of his garments and put a paper miter on his head on which devils were
painted, with this reading: "A Ringleader of Heretics." His books
were burnt at the gate of the church and Huss was led to the
suburbs of the city to be burnt.

When the fagots had been lighted he lifted his voice to God in
a hymn and closed it by saying, "Jesus Christ, thou Son of God,
have mercy on me." When his body was consumed his ashes were
carefully gathered up and thrown into the Rhine. His only offence
was that he wanted people to be guided by the Bible in their
religious life.

Jerome of Prague, a disciple of Huss was also burned at the stake
the following year.

---

* *Ecclesiastical History*—Mosheim. Internal History of The Church, Part 2, Chapter
1, Page 381.

CHAPTER 10

REFORMS IN SWITZERLAND AND GERMANY

1450 A.D. THE RENAISSANCE

In approaching the pre-Reformation period we have learned that morality had declined, the spirit of faith had been crushed, and religion had become an outward show of ritualism and ceremony. The church had developed into a commercial organization occupied chiefly in making new laws and then freeing her subjects from transgressing them by paying so much money for each transgression. Absolution, pardons, and indulgences became a source of revenue for the Roman church. Now spiritual offices were offered to the highest bidder by the archbishops of a diocese or by the popes when a vacancy occurred.

They assumed the right of appointing the new official as a reward for services he had rendered to the papacy or if there was no one who deserved the reward, the office was sold for a designated sum of money. The one who secured the office from the pope now entered in upon his office, carried out its functions and received the revenues that were due to the incumbent.

Ofttimes the appointee did not leave his Italian villa, but simply drew his revenue from the German, French, or Belgian benefices. These offices were held for life and of course brought a vast income to the holder.

The Council of Constance urged a reform in head and in members because of this practice. Upon receiving the appointment to some well paying office, the prelate would pay the first year's revenues to the pope.

Cardinal Cibo held ten bishoprics. The bishop of Toul held three archbishoprics in addition to occupying the office of bishop in ten dioceses.

Peter de Alliaco in addressing the Council of Constance said, "It is highly necessary that a reformation be made with reference to the manner in which the Roman church grinds the parish churches and their priests. The monstrous number of benefices held by their cardinals must be reduced."

After nine hundred years of such abuses by the Roman Catholic Church the Renaissance dawned. Learning was reborn—brought

about largely by the invention of printing. The credit for this
discovery lies with John Gutenberg of Mayence, Germany. The
first book he printed with movable type was a Latin Bible and these
began to appear among the common people as well as in the centers
of learning. There followed an abundance of dictionaries, gram-
mars, and commentaries. The Bible studied by the laity, revealed
the vast difference between the simplicity of the gospel and the
doctrines of the hierarchy headed by the pope of Rome.

The human mind was freed from priestly rule and made ready
for the great work of restoring the Bible to the world.

Within twenty years after the invention of printing every important city in Europe had its own press. The world was thus
provided with a means for the spread of knowledge.

In the beginning of the Renaissance the language of Greece was
almost an unknown tongue in western Europe. When Constantinople fell to the Mohammedans in 1453, marking the end of the
eastern part of the Roman Empire, the scholars of Greece were
thus exiled from their country and sought new homes. They found
such homes in Rome and in Florence where they became teachers
of the ardent seekers for more knowledge.

Chalcondyles and Bessarion became Greek professors at Florence. In that school were several Englishmen who carried the
desire for more knowledge to England. The wealthy competed with
each other as patrons of the new learning. The monasteries were
searched for the writings of the ancient poets and philosophers.

The students brought them out of the dust of the garrets and
the man who found the oldest and rarest manuscript became the
most honored man in the seats of learning. Cosmo de Medici at
Florence sent out agents to collect the works of Homer, Herodotus
and Plato. Lorenzo de Medici made his palace an academy of art
and learning. Sixty universities were built in Europe; the scholasticism of the monasteries began to decline. A new field of learning
was opened up to mankind. Laurentius Valla turned from the
poetry and philosophy of classic Greek to New Testament Greek.
He prepared a brief commentary on the New Testament which was
edited by Erasmus who had come to Italy from Oxford where he
had been divinity professor.

Valla detected errors in the Latin Vulgate. Such frauds as the
Donation of Constantine were exposed. The Apostles' Creed, he
declared was not written by the apostles. He rebuked the ambition
of the popes. In some instances this revival of learning bred infidelity and hatred for the Scriptures which were now being restored
to the people, in others it produced a desire to know the truth upon
religious subjects. The writings of the early church historians were

brought to light and compared with the doctrines of the church. This revealed the wide difference between the gospel and the doctrines of the Roman Catholic Church.

Many young Englishmen who went to Italy to study brought back with them books on a variety of subjects in which they had before shown little interest. Some learned Italians also visited England and by their teaching created a love for classical learning.

When Grocyn, Linacre, and Colet returned from Italy laden with new learning, they found the university waiting for all they could offer. The growth of learning was marvelous. The increase of knowledge was closely related to the Bible.

This was due to John Colet, son of the Mayor of London, who had been a seeker after truth while in Italy and who was now the accepted leader of a group of distinguished students at the University of Oxford. His views of religion were much like those of Wyclif. He became familiar with the Greek language because it opened up the truths of the New Testament. Here, as he studied its pages, he found an abundance of the teaching of Christ and the apostles, but the traditions and errors of papal Rome were nowhere contained therein. At Oxford, Thomas More, the historian, came under the influence of Colet; as did Erasmus, the orphan boy, who had received his education at the University of Paris.

Erasmus, and his pupil Lord Montjoy, joined the Oxford group and set about to reform the Catholic church with knowledge, culture, and the word of God. "Reform without schism" became the plea of those who saw the necessity for a change. Colet became the dean of St. Paul's Cathedral at London and boldly preached his doctrines to the thousands who assembled there.

Erasmus went to Italy and later returned to become professor of Greek and theology at Cambridge University. Men in the humble walks of life were now on an equality with the churchmen in learning, and were unwilling to give to them a continuance of the wide powers they once held. A growing dislike for religious interference was now manifest in England.

A desire to settle English questions in England without foreign dictation grew into strong opposition against the papacy.

The English Parliament found fault with the excessive fees of church courts, the increase of church taxes, and the practice of the people of England in leaving their property to the church. These things laid the foundation for a reformation in England, bringing about a separation of the church from Rome, the abolishment of monasteries and the adoption of the ideas of the reformers.

Erasmus became the critic of the pope and popery, yet he believed the Catholic church could be reformed and preserved.

He hoped that the king and the pope would heed his protest against the sale of indulgences and wickedness within the church. He taught against the evil within the church, the corruption of the priesthood, the separation of morals from religion.

The degeneration of the papal office is revealed in the fact that those who were elevated to that position of honor became immoral and corrupt in their lives. Intrigue became the means by which one was elevated to the head of the Church of Rome. If his edicts and decrees were not acceptable to the cardinals, archbishops, bishops and kings, the pope was sometimes removed from his throne by violence.

The pope as the head of the Roman Catholic Church professed to have the keys of the kingdom of heaven, with the power to bind or loose the sin of those who transgressed the law of God. Those who questioned this were excommunicated and burned as heretics.

The high position occupied by the pope was used as a means of extorting money for the support of his corrupt court.

The sale of indulgences, church offices, and permission to violate the laws of the church upon the payment of a sum of money, to appoint officials to countries they never saw or visited, brought a constant flow of money into the coffers of the papacy, enabling them to build great palaces for themselves and their courtiers, maintain luxurious courts, and live lives that were unspeakably vile. Such conditions offended the whole church. The sins of her officials were winked at by those in authority over them. The leaders of the Renaissance ridiculed the claims of the church to spiritual authority because of the immorality of the clergy.

The promises of the Council of Constance for a reformation in head and members had not been forgotten by the people.

The council preached reform and the settlement of the schisms which now affected the church, corrupted by the world which it was obligated to save. But this council did not reform the church because the very men who sat in council were the ones who needed reformation.

John Wessel, a professor of theology, condemned the doctrine of the infallibility of the pope and called attention to the difference between the claims of the church and the actual performance of her beliefs. Another reformer of this period who made an attempt to purify the church was Jerome Savonarola.

1452 A.D. THE BIRTH OF SAVONAROLA AT FERRARA

His parents wanted him to take up the study of medicine when he became a young man but he became concerned over the wickedness that he saw everywhere about him and entered the Dominican order and began to travel about preaching purity of life.

He came to Florence in 1482 at the insistence of Lorenzo de Medici who wanted to bring every prominent teacher and philosopher to that city. Here he began to preach to the pleasure-loving inhabitants at the cathedral of St. Mark. His plainness of speech brought sharp criticism against his discourses. though the people enjoyed the depth of his wisdom and the warmth of his oratory. In Florence he was surrounded by scholars, philosophers, and poets. Here, too, was the center of all the arts. Amid all of this he stood like one of the prophets of old—he cried aloud and spared not, showing the people their sins. Wisdom was on the increase in the cities, but morality was on the decline. As Savonarola preached the need of reform, his crowds increased. The building became too small for his audiences, so he moved to the garden surrounding the structure and soon this was filled with the wealthy nobles of the city. Those who came to jeer bowed their heads and wept. The ones who came to display their fine attire returned home and donned plain clothing. When Savonarola was urged to use more tact in the presentation of his lessons he answered his critics by calling attention to the fact that he condemned only crime, frivolity and injustice.

His preaching had a great influence upon the Renaissance and the people of the city. The de Medicis gave up the control of the city, a new constitution was prepared by Savonarola and the republic was restored. Schools were established. The Bible was studied in the original tongue and the people were instructed in civil and religious duties. He taught even the children to shun bad companions, vile songs, wicked books, dances, and carnivals.

The poets and scholars brought their bad books and licentious poems and burned them before the door of the church.

The pope alarmed at the growing power of Savonarola, sent a fellow monk to visit him with a plea to be more careful in his condemnation of sin. There were days of earnest discussion between the two, with the monk at last saying "Cease your attacks on the clergy and your prophecies and I am authorized to say that you shall receive the red hat of a cardinal." Savonarola did not even consider the bribe, "God forbid that I should be unfaithful to the embassy of my Lord. But, be at the sermon tomorrow and you shall hear."

The pope's messenger was present to hear the sermon. Savonarola began as usual with sundry admonitions for purity of life but as he warmed to his subject, he hurled charges of grievous sins against the clergy, not sparing Pope Alexander, whom he accused of being devoid of honesty, shame, truth, and morality. He was accused as the most evil of popes, ruled by a courtesan who was the mother of his five children, one of whom was a cardinal; another, Lucretia, was the most evil of all women in crime. The last words of the sermon of the monk revealed the contempt he had for the papacy, "A red hat! I wish for no other red hat than that of martyrdom reddened with my own blood."

A conspiracy revealed that his foes were vicious. A new class gained power. He was excommunicated by Pope Alexander, but he pronounced it null and void because it was contrary to the word of God. The threat of an interdict caused Savonarola to be seized by a mob, charged with heresy and condemned by his bitterest enemies.

When he was about to be hanged the bishop said. "I separate thee from the church militant and triumphant." Savonarola said, "Militant, but not triumphant, that of yours is not." He was hanged, his body burned, and his ashes thrown into the Arno River.

The Renaissance is sometimes spoken of as a rejection of traditional ideas which had been blindly followed for generations. In reality it was an awakening, a search for new culture and new learning, as well as the acceptance of the culture of the ancient Greeks which had been forgotten. The period of time spoken of as "The Dark Ages" were days in which learning was largely confined to the clergy. Now men's minds were freed from the narrow limits that were before imposed by scholasticism. A new impetus was given to learning, a search was made for the knowledge of the ancient Greeks and Romans and men's minds were freed from the narrow channels in which they had been confined for ages.

This revival of learning gave men a new desire for knowledge, especially knowledge of the Bible, which was now made available to all and contributed materially to ushering in the Reformation.

1484 A.D. BIRTH OF ULRICH ZWINGLI

Zwingli became one of the early reformers of the Roman church in Switzerland. After studying at Basel and the University of Vienna he became a priest at Glarus, where he remained for a period of years. He first began to advocate ideas of reform at Einsiedeln. He was invited to come to Zurich as a priest of the people. Here he advocated the reformation of the church in doctrine and ceremony.

By the scriptures he tested the doctrines of the Roman Catholic Church and also that of the heretics. Those willing to take their stand on the word of God alone were few in number in Switzerland. At a meeting of all the deans of the clergy, it was revealed that only a few were at home in the Bible, while many admitted that they had never read the Bible through. The clergy of the apostate church had little time for the study of the scriptures, but plenty of time for luxurious living.

We are informed by history that Zwingli assailed the doctrine of the church of Rome on sixty-seven points and defended them so successfully before the Council of Zurich that they charged all the clergy of Zurich to preach the same things. Before eight hundred people, many of them priests, he attacked the doctrine of the mass and affirmed that the loaf and the fruit of the vine only represented Christ's body and blood. Under the preaching of Zwingli the churches of Zurich abolished the procession and Feast of Corpus Christi, removed the organs from the churches, and the loaf and the cup were both administered to the laity. Zwingli wanted to exclude from the church everything which could not be justified by the Scriptures, while Luther thought nothing should be excluded unless it was specifically forbidden by the Scriptures. The zeal and eloquence of Zwingli gave him the prestige and authority of a bishop. When Samson, the peddler of indulgences, came to Zurich, the gates of the city were closed against the sale of these papal pardons and Pope Leo X recalled his representative.

Zwingli purposed to purify the moral condition of Zurich, to prevent Swiss citizens from engaging in a mercenary service to other nations and to interpret the word of God, not by comparing a few texts together, but by searching out the real meaning by an intensive study of each book. Efforts to overthrow his work were unsuccessful for the citizens were strong in their support of this reformer. The Council of Zurich convened October 1523 in the town hall. Representatives from Zurich, St. Gall, and Schaffhausen were present but other cantons refused to send their priests or bishops to a meeting where that "heretic Zwingli and his followers" were to preside. All parish priests were ordered to follow his method of expounding the Scriptures.

Zwingli wanted to lead the church out of the bondage of the hierarchy and restore her rights and privileges. He claimed that the true church consisted of those who believed in Christ and obeyed his word and not the words of the clergy alone.

He taught against the mass and images in the worship and sustained his teaching with the Scriptures. The church in Zurich was freed from the control of the Bishop in Constance and the lay members declared to have equal rights with the clergy in a common priesthood.

This meeting was designed to restore the church as it was in the beginning. The clergy who were present agreed to drop their sacerdotal office and henceforth act only as presbyters.

In all discussions Zwingli appealed to the Word of God. This resulted in the images and frescoes being removed, paganistic ceremonies ceased, and rituals which had existed for a thousand years came to an end. Organs and bells were hushed and the public service of song restored to the service. The Lord's Supper, with bread and the fruit of the vine, was administered at a table instead of an altar, free from every sign of a mass.

Other cities of Switzerland followed the example of Zurich, but the city of Bern seemed determined to hold on to the customs and ceremonies of the Roman church. Others who assisted Zwingli in his efforts to reform the papal church were Haller, Meyer and Kolb.

The effort was made not to destroy the partisans of Romanism but to drive out their errors with the Sword of the Spirit.

1528 A.D. THE DISCUSSION AT BERN

In this Zwingli, Oecolampadius, Farel and Martin Bucer were the leaders. On the day of St. Vincent, who was the patron saint of the city, the priests were left free to say mass, but no worshippers attended the service. The organist found himself alone and after he left the cathedral, the radicals at the council entered the building and splintered the organ to pieces. The mass was abolished, images were removed from the church and twenty-five altars were destroyed.

1509 A.D. MARTIN LUTHER BECAME PROFESSOR AT WITTENBERG UNIVERSITY

Martin Luther was born at Eisleben, Saxony, on November 10, 1483. His parents were poor, but they were determined that Martin should have a good education. He was sent to school at Magdeburg and Eisenach where he supported himself by singing before the homes of the wealthy. He attended the University of Erfurt from which he obtained his Master's degree before entering the Monastery of the Augustine Monks at Erfurt. He was ordained a priest in 1507 and two years later he became an instructor in philosophy at Wittenberg University. In the year 1510 Luther went to Rome, partly to fulfill a vow and partly to attend to some affairs for the church. He went to Rome as an enthusiastic devotee, but he was greatly shocked by what he saw there, though the effects of it were not visible until much later.

Luther said—"I would not take 100,000 florins not to have seen Rome; although I do not yet thoroughly know its great and scandalous abominations. When I first saw it, I fell to the ground, lifted up my hands and said—'Hail, thou holy Rome, yea, truly holy, through the holy martyrs, and their blood that has been shed there.' " In Rome, Luther found the very opposite of what he expected. Instead of piety he found levity; instead of holiness, lasciviousness; instead of spirituality he found carnality. Of his visit there he said, "Nobody would believe, unless he saw with his own eyes the licentiousness, the vice and the shame that is in vogue in Rome."

Luther was shocked by the immorality he saw in Rome. His pilgrimage there was a disappointment. He said of that visit, "As was my case at Rome, where I too, was a mad saint, ran the round of all the churches and vaults, and believed every lie that was invented there."

He had imposed upon himself the task of climbing the sacred stairs in the Sancta Scala church while in the city of Rome. As he ascended these stairs upon his knees, for the sake of the indulgence granted to those who did so, he seemed to hear a voice shouting in his ears, "The just shall live by faith." He arose to his feet without completing the act of penance he had imposed upon himself. Out of this incident developed the doctrine of justification by faith only, after he separated from the church of Rome.

1517 A.D. JOHN TETZEL, A DOMINICAN MONK ENTERS GERMANY SELLING INDULGENCES

When Luther heard that the people were flocking to Tetzel in great crowds to secure indulgences he was greatly grieved, for he believed the methods of Tetzel were contrary to the teaching of the church.

> "Indulgences were nothing new. The sale of them had grown into a trade. The pardon of sins was offered in the market, as government bonds are now sold. The buyer purchased a pardon ticket, which guaranteed to him a release from all the penalties of the sin named on it (such as murder at seven ducats, simony at ten, robbing at twelve, and blacker crimes at cheaper rates), or the release of a soul from purgatory. The Germans had never liked this business. They had said, at the Council of Constance, "It is the most abominable that popes put a price upon sins, as shopkeepers upon wares."[*]

While Luther was zealously fulfilling his pastoral and professional duties, he was suddenly met face to face by an evil which struck at the root of all godliness in the flock committed to his charge.

---

[*] *History of The Christian Church*—Blackburn. Chapter 16, Page 388.

Pope Leo X, ostensibly to raise money for the building of St. Peter's, but really in order to maintain his corrupt court, had instituted a general sale of indulgences; which were, as their name imports, a remission of the penances and good works enjoined as conditions of forgiveness, or a license to receive absolution upon bare confession, unaccompanied by satisfaction. The sale of these indulgences in Germany was committed to the Dominican monk, Tetzel; a man of loose life, unconcerned with religion and good morals, so long as he scraped together money enough to please his masters and gratify himself, and who scrupled not at the most blasphemous inventions, to exalt the value of his wares. When this man was preaching a few miles from Wittenberg, as we learn from Myconius, some of Luther's congregation came to him to confess, having bought these letters of indulgence. "And when they disclosed heinous crimes, and gave him to understand that they would not cease from their adultery, usury, fraud, and the like, the doctor would not absolve them; whereupon they pleaded their papal indulgence received from Tetzel. But Luther was not moved by this but appealed to that Scripture, "Except ye repent, ye shall all likewise perish." (Luke 13:3.)

Luther thus related the beginning of the contest in the tract against Hans Wurst.

> "At that time I was a preacher in the convent here, and a young doctor fresh from the anvil, hot and ready in the Holy Scriptures. Now, when much people of Wittenberg were running after these indulgences to Juterbock and I (as truly as I hope to be redeemed) did not even know what the indulgence was, I began to preach with great moderation that they might do something better and more certain than buying pardons. I had before preached such a sermon against indulgences in the parish church, and earned little favor thereby with Duke Frederick, who was very fond of that church of his founding.—Meanwhile, it came to my ears how Tetzel had preached shocking, frightful doctrines; to wit, that the red cross of the indulgence, with the pope's arms set up in the churches, has as much virtue as the cross of Christ; that he would not change places with St. Peter in heaven, for he had saved more souls with his indulgences than St. Peter with his preaching; that when one dropped a penny into the box for a soul in purgatory, so soon as the money clinked in the chest the soul flew up into heaven;—that repentance or sorrow or atonement for sin was needless for one who had bought an indulgence, which would hold good equally for *future* sins."*

When Leo X came to the papal throne he was without money to finish St. Peter's cathedral and to maintain his court, which was said to be the most corrupt in Europe. He appointed cardinals as young as seven years of age, sold church offices, and was utterly

---

* *The Life of Luther*—Winkworth. Chapter 16, Page 56, 57.

indifferent to the welfare of the church. To obtain money for his needs he sent sellers of indulgences through the various countries under his jurisdiction. Tetzel came into Germany for this purpose and Luther's ire was aroused by the commercial way in which these were offered to the people. He declared that such a practice was corrupt and unworthy of the support of decent men. The doctrine of indulgence was wholly unknown to the New Testament. The church of the first century knew nothing of such a practice. Persons could buy for themselves or for their friends, even though dead, a portion of the good works done by the Lord on behalf of man.

The events that brought about the dismemberment of the Catholic church and ushered in the Reformation were the actions of the clergy in making salvation a matter of merchandise. Various forms of penance was imposed upon the laity. When they became unbearable, the priests would take upon themselves the penance they had imposed upon the penitents, in payment of a sum of money. For a fast the rich were to pay twenty pence, the less wealthy ten pence, and the poor three pence. The clergy soon discovered the revenue that might be derived from these indulgences and as the need for money for the construction of St. Peter's Cathedral increased, the sale of indulgences was reduced to a system. For every sin there was a set price.

In the beginning the indulgences were for the benefit of the living, but in the thirteenth century, the living were told that by making certain sacrifices, they could shorten or end the punishment their loved ones were enduring in purgatory. The scale for the services of the priests in securing their release from punishment was in proportion to the wealth of the friends of the deceased and the nature of the crime committed. There was no sin for which the offender could not receive forgiveness by paying the set price. A price was set for incest, murder, adultery, perjury, burglary and for all other sins that violated the laws of God and man. The purchase of such indulgences assured one of the forgiveness of his sins and a home in heaven. All the people saw in them was the permission to sin.

The price to be paid varied in proportion to the offence that needed to be covered or the sin committed. This was carried to a dangerous extreme, as admitted by the Catholic church later.

In Tetzel's list of indulgences sacrilege was listed at nine ducats, and murder at seven ducats. Notices were posted stating—"The red indulgence cross, with the pope's arms outspread, has the same virtue as the cross of Christ. The pardon offered makes those who accept it cleaner than baptism, purer even than Adam in the state of innocence in Paradise."

In order to raise money Pope Leo X, early in the sixteenth century, devised the plan of selling indulgences. A regular tariff of prices was fixed for the pardon of all crimes, from murder downward. If a man wished to commit any outrage, or to indulge in any forbidden wickedness he could do so at a stipulated price, and receive from the pope a full pardon.

These permits or indulgences, as they were called, were peddled all over Europe, and an immense revenue was gathered from them. There was one man, by the name of John Tetzel, a brazen faced miscreant, who made himself very notorious as a peddler of these indulgences. He traversed Northern France and Germany, engaged in this nefarious traffic. In a cart gorgeously embellished, and accompanied by a musical band, he would approach some populous town, and tarry somewhere in the suburbs until his emissaries had entered the place and informed the inhabitants of the signal honor which awaited them from the advent of a nuncio from the pope with pardons for sin at his disposal.

All the church bells would be set ringing for joy. The whole population would be thrown into the greatest excitement to receive the brilliant pageant. At the appointed hour the cavalcade entered, bedizened with all the gorgeous finery of a modern menagerie display.

Tetzel carried, in the capacious box of his peddlers' cart, the parchment certificates of pardon for every imaginary sin. Murder, adultery, theft, sacrilege, blasphemy,—every crime had its specified price. One could purchase pardon or absolution for any crime which had already been committed, or he could purchase permission to commit the crime if it were one he wished to perpetrate. With music and banners the procession advanced to the public square.

Here Tetzel, mounted upon his box, with all the volubility of a modern mountebank palmed off his wares upon the eager crowd.

> "My brethren," said the prince of imposters, "God has sent me to you with his last and greatest gift. The church is in need of money. I am empowered by the pope, God's vicegerent, to absolve you from any and every crime you may have committed, no matter what it may be. The moment the money tinkles in the box, your soul shall be as pure as that of a babe unborn. I can also grant you indulgence; so that any sin you may commit hereafter shall be blotted out. More than this, if you have any friend now in purgatory suffering in those awful flames, I am empowered, in consideration of the money you grant the church in this its hour of need, to cause that soul to be immediately released from purgatory, and to be borne on angel wings to heaven."

"Enlightened, as the masses of people are at this present day, we can hardly imagine the effect these representations produced upon an ignorant and superstitious people who had ever been trained to the belief that the pope was equal in power to God. These peddlings of indulgences for sin were carried on all over Europe, and enormous sums of money were thus raised. The certificates, which were issued like government bonds, ran in this form: 'I, by the authority of Jesus Christ, his blessed apostles, Peter and Paul, and the most holy pope, absolve thee from all thy sins, transgressions, and excesses how enormous soever they may be. I remit to thee all punishment which thou dost deserve in purgatory on their account, and restore thee to innocence and purity, so that when thou diest, the gates of punishment shall be shut against thee, and the gates of paradise shall be thrown wide open.'"*

It was this sale of indulgences which opened the eyes of Luther and others of the reformation movement to the corruption that existed in the Roman Catholic Church.

It has been said that the indulgence certificate did not give the right to sin but only gave absolution for those sins that had already been committed, yet many recognized historians state that indulgences were granted for sins not yet committed.

"Tetzel gave letters of indulgence for sins which men intended to commit and such was the reverence in which the indulgences were held, that a papal bull was carried before him on a velvet or golden cloth and all priests, monks, the council, schoolmasters, scholars, men and women and children went in procession to meet him."†

"Pope Leo X having occasion for a great deal of money to carry on the building of the magnificent church of St. Peter's in Rome attempted to raise it by the sale of indulgences or licenses to sin, as they have been called, for these indulgences were understood not only to pardon past sins but those that might *afterward* be committed."‡

"The vendors of indulgences did all in their power to vaunt the excellency of their articles and the necessity for penitence and amendment were no longer mentioned. Indulgence was even granted for sins contemplated. Such abuses rendered anything like ecclesiastical discipline impossible."§

1517 A.D. LUTHER'S FIRST SERMON AGAINST INDULGENCES

This sermon was directed against the abuses committed by the sellers of the certificates, which brought discredit on the church of Rome and detriment to the public morals. Luther did not attempt in the beginning to discredit their power when accompanied by sincere repentance. Before his series of sermons were finished he had witnessed enough of the abuses of the sale of indulgences to

---

* *History of Christianity*—Abbott. Chapter 22, Pages 420, 421, 422.
† *Analysis of the Reformation*—Pinnock. Article 260, Page 146.
‡ *History of England*—Goodrich. Chapter 126, Pages 230, 231.
§ *Church History*—Kurtz. Section 21, Paragraph 115, Page 488.

turn him forever against them. He considered that his duty was to file a public protest against their continued sale in Germany. He wrote out "Ninety-five Propositions Concerning the Power of Indulgences" and without consulting the Bishops or Archbishop of the Wittenberg diocese, he nailed them to the door of Wittenberg church.

Luther challenged anyone to dispute the truth they affirmed. He made copies available to the public and sent copies also to the Archbishop of Mayence and to the Bishop of Brandenburg, pleading with them not to interfere in the matter. Luther's appeal to the church dignitaries profited him nothing for the archbishop was a partaker of the profits of the indulgences.

The Bishop of Brandenburg sent a private messenger to Luther saying that he should keep such teaching to himself for the sake of the peace of the church. Luther agreed to obey the instructions of the bishop, but within a short time the Theses had become known to all of Germany.

Tetzel answered the publication of Luther's Theses by a set of Counter-Theses, in which he branded Luther as a heretic. Tetzel had a great bonfire lighted in the public square of Frankfurt, where he preached a sermon against Luther and then consigned Luther's Thesis and his printed sermons to the flames. Tetzel sent printed copies of his Counter-Theses to Wittenberg for distribution. These were taken from the messenger and a crier was sent about town calling for the people to assemble at the market place at two o'clock. Here Tetzel's Counter-Theses were burned in the presence of the people.

This brought Luther many adversaries. Shortly after this incident he was compelled to write out a defence of his teaching for Sylvester Prierias, the general of the Dominican order who justified Tetzel's practices and who upheld the claims of the pope. To explain and defend his Theses, Luther wrote out his explanation of them, sending this to the pope with a personal letter expressing his personal veneration for the pontiff and declaring his willingness to abide by the pope's decision in this matter. Luther had no idea of starting a new church. He was seeking only to bring about a reform within the Roman Catholic Church because of abuses which he knew were contrary to the Scriptures. Luther did not believe the pope knew of these abuses. He believed that if the pope knew of them he would correct them. Because of the insistent clamor of Luther's enemies, Pope Leo was persuaded to convene a tribunal to try Luther's doctrines.

Within a few days after Luther sent his humble letter to the pope he was surprised to receive a summons to appear in Rome within sixty days to answer for his Theses, before a court presided over by Sylvester Prierias, his avowed enemy. Foreseeing what his fate would be should he appear before the court in Rome, the university requested that he be heard in Germany and Luther's friend, the Elector Frederick, sent the same request. The pope agreed for Luther to be heard before his legate, Cardinal Cajetan, who was then present at the Imperial Diet at Augsburg.

The pope secretly instructed Cajetan to treat Luther as a heretic, who was to be excommunicated unless he should recant along with all others who afforded him shelter or aid.

Though Luther was in poor health he proceeded to Augsburg, arriving there October 7, 1518. The Cardinal immediately sent his chaplain to Luther conveying words of friendship and kindness. Luther was admonished to throw himself upon the mercies of the cardinal, trusting the fatherly goodness of the cardinal to deal fairly with him. The cardinal was able to see the trouble that would follow if Luther was harmed and so attempted to bring about a reconciliation. Luther was received with kindness and called upon to retract his teaching on two points:

1. That the treasure of the indulgence did not consist of the merits and sufferings of Christ.
2. That faith in the partaker was needful to the efficacy of the sacraments.

Luther bowed before the legate and agreed to recant if it could be proved that he was in error from the Scriptures or by the writings of the church fathers. The cardinal demanded that he simply recant, refusing to discuss the matter.

In the discussion that followed the cardinal forgot the dignity of his office in his anger against Luther, who was more than a match for him.

When Luther confuted the cardinal by the very papal Constitutions upon which Cajetan rested his case, Luther was ordered once more to recant or to leave the assembly. Luther departed in silence, later sending a very humble letter to the cardinal begging to be convinced of his error and promising correction of his own vehemence in the hearing before the cardinal.

When no answer came within three days he wrote two letters, one to Cajetan and the other to the pope, denying the charge of heresy placed against him, appealing to the pope to have the matter properly considered.

Under the cover of darkness he now returned to Wittenberg and informed his sovereign, the elector, of his purpose to take up a residence in France. The elector persuaded Luther to wait awhile before making such a change, so Luther returned to his teaching at the University of Wittenberg.

"Luther, however, repaired to Augsburg, in the month of October 1518, and conferred at three different meetings, with Cajetan himself, concerning the points in debate. But had he even been disposed to yield to the court of Rome, this imperious legate was, of all others, the most improper to encourage him in the execution of such a purpose. The high spirits of Luther were not to be tamed by the arrogant dictates of mere authority; such however, were the only methods of persuasion employed by the haughty cardinal. He, in an overbearing tone, desired Luther to renounce his opinions, without even attempting to prove them erroneous, and insisted, with importunity, on his confessing humbly his fault, and submitting respectfully to the judgment of the Roman pontiff.

The Saxon reformer could not think of yielding to terms so unreasonable in themselves, and so despotically proposed; so that the conferences were absolutely without effect. For Luther, finding his adversary and judge inaccessible to reason and argument, left Augsburg all of a sudden, after having appealed from the present decisions of the pontiff, to those which he should pronounce, when better informed; and in this step, he seemed yet to respect the dignity and authority of the Bishop of Rome. But Leo X on the other hand, let loose the reins to ambition and despotism, and carried things to the utmost extremity; for, in the month of November in this same year, he published a special edict, commanding his spiritual subjects to acknowledge his power of delivering from all punishments due to sin and transgression of every kind. As soon as Luther received information of this inconsiderate and violent measure, he perceived, plainly, that it would be impossible for him to bring the court of Rome to any reasonable terms, he therefore repaired to Wittenberg, and, on the 28th of November, appealed from the pontiff to a general assembly."*

The pope then sent Chamberlain Miltitz to settle the controversy. Miltitz agreed that much harm had been done by indulgences; adding that though this was true, Luther should not create an uneasy condition for the pope by his methods, but respect the authority of the church. An agreement was drawn up between them embracing these points:

1. Both parties were forbidden to teach or preach on the subject or take any action on it.

2. The exact state of affairs was to be communicated to the pope, who would select a learned bishop to investigate the question.

To which Luther added, "If I am convinced of error, I will retract my teaching and not weaken the power of the church."

Dr. John Mayer of Eck, sometimes called Dr. John Eck, professor of theology in the University of Ingolstadt, was one of the outstanding scholars of the age. His ability in a discussion was recognized

---

* *Ecclesiastical History*—Mosheim. Volume 2, Chapter 2, Page 10.

in other countries where he had ably defended scholastic theses. Although he had bitterly attacked Luther's teaching upon certain points he came to Augsburg and there met Luther as a friend, proposing to hold a discussion with Carlstadt on "The Freedom of the Will." To this Luther agreed, but when Dr. Eck published the list of subjects to be discussed, it was evident that the discussion was directed against Luther rather than against Carlstadt. In justice to himself Luther was compelled to take part in the dispute.

The discussion was held at Leipzig in June of 1519. The disputation began between Dr. Eck and Carlstadt on "The Doctrine of Grace" and was continued for several days with no marked results. The discussion between Dr. Eck and Luther was based on "The Supremacy of the Pope, Purgatory, Indulgences, and Absolution." Eck attempted to sustain the supremacy of the pope by the Savior's statement as recorded in Matthew's gospel, "Thou art Peter, and upon this rock I will build my church, and the gates of hell shall not prevail against it." Luther did not deny the supremacy of the pope, but declared that it was of modern origin and unaccepted by all of Christendom. He showed by the Scriptures that Christ was the only head of the church.

Dr. Eck was the superior of Luther in theology and church history but when Luther appealed to the Scriptures he was on ground with which the famous doctor was not familiar. On the subject of indulgences Luther's opponent was compelled to surrender the points for which Luther contended. When Eck saw defeat facing him, he accused Luther as being a Hussite and a heretic. Luther replied that some of the things for which Huss contended were Christian principles and that the council had not condemned all of the teaching of Huss, but only those things in which Huss was in error. Dr. Eck replied that the council condemned all of Huss' doctrines telling Luther, "If you believe a council can err you are to me as a heathen man and a publican."

Luther concluded his speech with a defense of the writings of Huss, insisting that he was not wrong, but that the councils and the popes were wrong because they contradicted each other as well as the word of God. Each claimed the victory and the questions were eventually referred to the Universities of Wittenberg and Ingoldstadt for decision, but without result.

1520 A.D. LUTHER EXCOMMUNICATED FROM THE ROMAN CATHOLIC CHURCH

Up to this time the efforts of Luther were to correct the abuses of the papacy. He believed that when the pope was informed of the abuses he would recognize the necessity of a reform. Luther had advanced questions touching the pope's authority. Prior to this time Luther upheld and defended the pope's authority. Now with the word of God before him, he came to the conclusion that the pope was the enemy of God and of Jesus Christ, and had lifted himself up to the place of God, had corrupted the true worship of God, and had brought great harm upon all Christendom.

Miltitz put forth further efforts at reconciliation, although he had been authorized to take Luther a prisoner and bring him to Rome for trial. Miltitz believed if he attempted to do this he would forever separate Germany from the papacy.

Miltitz treated Luther with respect but heaped abuse on Tetzel for disturbing the spiritual peace of Germany by the continued sale of indulgences when he knew it was strongly opposed by Luther and other prominent church men. While the efforts toward reconciliation were going on Dr. Eck was in Rome busily engaged in procuring a bull of excommunication against Luther and his adherents, which was drawn up by the pope and the College of Cardinals on June 15, 1520. Dr. Eck was charged with the responsibility of publishing the bull of excommunication.

He selected Leipzig as the place where Luther's excommunication should first be published. Here the students tore it down and cast it in the river and insulted Eck so much that he fled from the city.

The decree of excommunication was brought to Wittenberg by the Elector of Brandenburg and the bishop, who were notified by the city official that its publication would be resisted by force.

Luther's writings were burned at Mayence, Cologne, and in other communities, and when this was known at Wittenberg a meeting of the professors, the students, and the citizens was called at the Elster Gate. There the decretals of the church, the canon law, the writings of Eck and the papal bull were all consigned to the fire and the people admonished to all oppose the pope's influence. Philip Schwartzerd, whose name was changed to Philip Melancthon by his Uncle John Reuchlin, now appeared as a colleague of Luther. He was only a lad who had taken his doctor's degree in philosophy at the age of seventeen, after which he became a professor at Tübingen. Later he became an instructor at Wittenberg, where his lecture room was always full. Here he became Luther's fellow-warrior in the contest against the papacy.

Shortly after Luther's excommunication he wrote a pamphlet addressed "To The Nobility Of The German Nation," in which he said:

"To his Imperial Majesty and The Christian Nobility of The German nation, Martin Luther wishes grace. The Romanists have raised round themselves walls to protect themselves from reform,

One is their doctrine, that there are two separate estates, the one spiritual, viz., pope, bishops, priests and monks, the other secular, viz., princes, nobles, artisans, and peasants. And they lay it down that the secular power has no power over the spiritual but that the spiritual is above the secular, whereas, in truth, all Christians are spiritual, and there is no difference between them. The secular power is of God, to punish the wicked and protect the good, and so has rule over the whole body of Christians, without exception, pope, bishops, monks, nuns and all.

For St. Paul says, 'Let every soul (and I reckon the pope one) be subject to the higher powers.' Why should three hundred thousand florins be sent every year from Germany to Rome? Why do the Germans let themselves be fleeced by cardinals who get hold of the best preferments and spend the revenues at Rome? Let us not give another farthing to the pope as subsidies against the Turks: the whole thing is a snare to drain us of more money. Let the secular authorities send no more annates to Rome. Let the power of the pope be reduced within clear limits. Let there be fewer cardinals, and let them not keep the best things to themselves. Let the national churches be more independent of Rome. Let there be fewer pilgrimages to Italy. Let there be fewer convents. Let priests marry. Let begging be stopped by making each parish take charge of its own poor. Let us inquire into the position of the Bohemians, and if Huss was in the right, let us join with him in resisting Rome."*

After a few months Luther was notified to appear before the assembled Diet of the Emperor and Estates.

Emperor Charles V, who had just come to the throne in June of 1520, had been requested by the pope's nuncio, Alexander, to order Luther's writings to be burned through all of the empire, but the Elector of Saxony, who had a great influence over Charles, requested that no action be taken against Luther until he could speak in his own defense.

Luther was anxious to testify before the Diet, though he believed they would never rest until they spilled his blood. He wrote to his friend Spalatin, "If I should be summoned, I will be carried thither sick if I cannot go sound. And then if violence be used, we must commend the matter to the Lord. Expect everything from me but flight or recantation. I will not even fly, much less recant."

The papal representatives did not desire that Luther should gain additional fame by coming before the Diet. They purposed to have him condemned unheard. Alexander spoke before the Diet for three hours, calling attention to Luther's supposed heresies and his rebellion against the papal throne. He pleaded that the sentence of condemnation be passed at once. Emperor Charles was ready to issue an order for the destruction of Luther's writings but the Estates refused to publish the order unless Luther was provided

* *The Era of The Protestant Revolution*—Seebohm. Chapter 3, Page 107. Charles Scribner's Sons.

with   fe conduct to appear before the Diet, and called upon to retract anything that was contrary to the teachings of Christianity.

If he refused to comply, then assistance would be rendered the emperor to enforce the edict. While waiting for this to be put into effect the Estates asked that the abuses that had taken place in Germany by the papal court should be immediately and fully corrected.

The Emperor accepted the proposal and called upon the nobles to prepare a statement of their grievances against the practice of the representatives of the papal church.

Luther began his journey to Worms in a conveyance provided by the town of Wittenberg. His journey to Worms resembled the triumphal march of a conquering hero. The messengers of the church of Rome everywhere posted notices calling for the burning of his books. When those who accompanied him asked if he thought it wise to proceed further, Luther replied that he would go on if they published the ban in every city, trusting in assurance of the emperor that he should have safe conduct to and from Worms. In various cities his friends called to his attention the fate of Huss at Constance, to which Luther replied, "Though they make a fire from Wittenberg to Worms and the flames blaze up to heaven, inasmuch as I have been cited I will appear in the name of the Lord."

When the pope's representatives at Worms learned that Luther was on the way there, they saw that if he were allowed to speak for himself his following would be increased.

They had hoped that he would disobey the order to appear and thus he could be condemned for his rebellion. The emperor's confessor, Glapio, addressed a letter to Luther, suggesting in a friendly way that they meet a short distance from Worms and negotiate to settle the differences between Luther and the Roman church.

This proposal was rejected by Luther in the memorable speech he addressed to his friends saying, "If there were as many devils at Worms as there are tiles upon the roofs, I would go nevertheless."

On the 16th of April, Luther entered Worms with his friends. A great number of the Saxon nobility came out to accompany him into the city. The streets were filled with people wanting to get a glimpse of him. The crowd followed him to his hotel. Here he conferred with the nobles and the clergy until late at night. Philip of Hesse came to visit him and from that time forward became one of his closest friends and advisors.

At four o'clock the next afternoon the herald of the Diet, appeared at the hotel and asked that Luther accompany him to the Diet. As he was about to go into the assembly hall George Von

Frundsberg, a soldier of repute said, "My poor monk, thou art marching to make a stand the like of which I, and many a general, in our gravest battles have never made. But if thou hast right on thy side, and art sure of thy cause, be of good courage. God will not forsake thee."

"Zwingli and Luther, having grown up apart—the one in Switzerland and the other in Saxony—were one day to meet. The same spirit and, in many respects, the same character, existed in them both. Both were filled with the love of truth and hatred of injustice; both were naturally violent, and this violence was tempered in each of them by sincere piety. . . . Both these men, ardently attached to their inmost convictions, resolved upon maintaining them, and, little accustomed to bend to the convictions of others, were to encounter each other, like two proud chargers dashing across the battle-field and suddenly meeting in the fight."

The Story of the Reformation—J. H. Merle d'Aubigné

CHAPTER 11

LUTHER AND ZWINGLI

In the assembly before which Luther appeared there were the emperor, six electors, sovereign princes of Germany, knights of the empire and representatives of the church of Rome.

Luther was asked by the emperor's representative if he admitted the books bearing his name to be his, and if so, whether he was willing to retract them. Luther admitted writing the books bearing his name, but asked for a day to consider his answer to the second question. His request for time to consider his answer was granted and he was allowed to go to his room at the inn. Luther appeared so humble before the assembly that it was supposed that he was ready to retract his writings but the next day when he appeared before the Diet all evidence of timidity was gone and he refused to retract any of his writings unless it could be shown they were contrary to the Scriptures. Luther spoke for two hours and then repeated his speech in Latin for the emperor.

He called attention to the sad plight of the church and begged the emperor to correct the evils before God's vengeance was directed against the German nation. When asked to give a direct answer as to whether he would retract Luther replied, "Unless I am convicted of error by the Holy Scriptures or by cogent and evident reasons, I neither can nor dare to retract any thing; for my conscience is held captive by God's word, and it is neither safe nor right to go against conscience. Here I take my stand. I cannot do otherwise. So help me God!"

"The chancellor of the Archbishop of Frier questioned him in the name of the emperor. Do you acknowledge these books to be yours, and will you retract what you have written? Luther answered that some of his books contained writing which had been praised by his opponents, and that he could not be expected to retract it; others were directed against manifest abuses, and that he would be false and a coward if he retracted what he and most right hearted men knew to be true, a third set contained many hasty judgments upon his opponents, and these he said, he would retract if he could be shown to be wrong. 'The emperor demanded a plain answer and not an argument,' said Eck. 'Do you retract what you have said against the church and especially what you have said against the council of Constance?'

'If you will have a plain answer,' said Luther, 'I will give you one without horns or teeth. I can retract nothing unless I be convinced either from Scripture or by clear argument. It is as clear as day that both pope and councils have often erred. My conscience must submit to the word of God, to act against conscience is unholy and dangerous; and therefore I cannot and will not retract. So help me God. Amen.''[*]

The next day the emperor brought before the Diet a proposal for the condemnation of Luther as a heretic. The nobles of Germany pleaded for time for deliberation.

The Archbishop of Treves who was in sympathy with some of Luther's declarations attempted to bring an end to the disagreement of Luther with the papacy, but Luther refused to make any concessions and so the matter ended.

"Dr. Eck was the superior to Luther in reputation, in dialectical skill, in scholastic learning. He was the pride of the universities. Luther, however, had deeper conviction, more genius, greater eloquence, and at that time he was modest. The champion of the schools, of sophistries and authorities, of dead-letter literature, of quibbles, refinements, and words, soon overwhelmed the Saxon monk with his citations, decrees of councils, opinions of eminent ecclesiastics, the literature of the church, its mighty authority. He was on the eve of triumph. Had the question been settled, as Dr. Eck supposed, by authorities, as lawyers and pedants would settle the question, Luther would have been beaten. But his genius came to his aid, and the consciousness of truth. He swept away the premise of the argument. He denied the supreme authority of popes and councils and universities. He appealed to the Scriptures as the only ultimate ground of authority. He did not deny authority, but appealed to it in its highest form. This was unexpected ground. The church was not prepared openly to deny the authority of St. Paul or St. Peter; and Luther, if he did not gain his case, was far from being beaten, and what was of vital importance to his success he had the elector and the people with him. Thus was born the second great idea of the Reformation—the supreme authority of the Scriptures, to which Protestants of every denomination have since professed to cling."[†]

Luther started for Wittenberg on the twenty-sixth of April and was taken as a prisoner to Wartburg by the order of his friend, Elector Frederick. Here at the castle of Wartburg he began the translation of the Bible. He completed the translation of the New Testament during the time he was at Wartburg castle. While there Luther learned that the churches of those who still held to the old forms of worship were being desecrated by the students of the university and a group of fanatics from Zwickau. Melancthon was

---

[*] *The Reformation*—Lindsay. Chapter 1, Page 15.
[†] *Beacon Lights of History*—Lord. Volume III, Chapter 30, Pages 234, 235.

not able to persuade them to forsake such a practice, knowing that such things would be detrimental to the Reformation.

The elector was not willing that Luther be called back to Wittenberg, fearing that his life would be taken by the papal authorities. Luther wrote to the elector that he must return to end the disorder, even at the risk of his life. He returned to Wittenberg on the 6th of March 1522 and the following Sunday began a series of sermons, which were so powerful and eloquent that his counsel prevailed and peace was restored. Luther was now able to resume the translation of the Scriptures. He was assisted in this by Philip Melancthon, who had become Luther's closest friend and counsellor. This translation was finished in 1523 and was far superior to previous translations.

1529 A.D. CONTROVERSY BETWEEN GERMAN AND SWISS REFORMERS

While Luther was bringing about a reformation of the church in Germany, Zwingli, Oecolampadius and others were attempting to bring about a reformation of the church in Switzerland. Here Thomas Wittenback, who had been one of Zwingli's instructors, openly preached that the whole system of indulgences is a delusion for Christ alone paid for the sins of mankind. Under the preaching of the Swiss reformer the churches of Zurich abolished "The Procession of Corpus Christi." Organs were removed from the churches and the loaf and cup were both administered to the laity.

The doctrinal views of the reformers of Switzerland were similar to those of Luther but on some points there was a wide difference.

Zwingli wanted to exclude from religious services anything that could not be justified by the word of God, while Luther affirmed that anything might be included unless it was expressly prohibited by the word of God.

Wittenback had boldly proclaimed that the time was ripe for a return to the word of God, for a restoration of the ancient faith and for the rejection of the doctrine of indulgences as a Roman snare and a delusion. The desire of Zwingli to know the original source of all truth, led him to study the Scriptures as the standard by which all religious activity and worship must be tested.

Once he found an old copy of the Mass book, and to his surprise he learned that in former times it was customary to give the laity both the bread and the fruit of the vine, instead of the bread alone. This caused him to question the authority of the Roman church. He asked himself the question—Can the church which claims to be unchangeable, and yet makes such alterations in its liturgy, possess the fundamental element of truth?

Zwingli definitely began to oppose papal power in 1520, when he exhorted his people to support the stand Martin Luther had taken. He advocated definite measures of reform, preaching against fastings, the worship of saints, the celibacy of the priesthood, affirming that since these were not enjoined by the Scriptures, which is the only source of authority, they could not be pleasing to God.

> "Opposition steadily arose. He was accused of heresy and at last, at his own request, a disputation was held, not in Latin but in the vulgar tongue.
>
> In this disputation, and in the presence of six hundred persons representing the council, the clergy, the burghers, and three representatives of the bishop of Constance, Zwingli defended himself from the Greek, Latin and Hebrew Scriptures. His sixty-seven theses, he claimed, contained his doctrine reduced to propositions. The replies to him were evasive. After an adjournment the people reassembled and the burgomaster rendered the decision of the council as follows—"Since no one has been able to convict Master Ulrich Zwingli of error, we, the Burgomaster and the Lesser and Greater Councils of Zurich, after mutual deliberation, have determined that Master Ulrich Zwingli shall continue to preach the genuine divine Scriptures according to the Spirit of God to the best of his ability. We also command all other priests, pastors and preachers to preach nothing else in public except what can be proved from the Holy Gospel and the canonical Scriptures."*

1529 A.D. AN EFFORT TO END THE DIVISION BETWEEN LUTHER AND ZWINGLI

Martin Bucer and Philip of Hesse attempted to heal the breach between Luther and Zwingli. They met at Marburg but were not able either in private conference or public assembly to come to an understanding. After the conference had lasted three days Philip suggested that though they were not able to reach an understanding they should both sign a statement, saying that while each retained his own opinion, they were agreed on essentials of faith and accepted each other as Christian brethren.

Those who stood with Zwingli gave consent to this and Zwingli at once offered his hand to Luther in Christian fellowship, believing their differences were not fundamental. Luther refused to accept the hand of Zwingli and by this not only frustrated the noble efforts of Philip of Hesse, but also divided the efforts of the reformers.

Luther felt that he could not fellowship with Zwingli while differences existed on points of doctrine which Luther believed to be fundamental. Luther believed that in the Lord's supper Christ was still offered as a living being, while Zwingli denied that Christ was really present in any way and that the loaf and the fruit of the vine was only a memorial of Christ's death on the cross.

---

* *A Short History of The Christian Church*—Moncrief. Pages 315, 316.

"Among the incidents that promoted animosity and discord between the friends of the Reformation, and prevented that union that was so much to be desired between persons embarked in the same good cause, the principal one was the dispute that had arisen between the divines of Saxony and Switzerland, concerning the manner of Christ's presence in the eucharist.

To terminate this controversy, Philip, Landgrave of Hesse, invited, in the year 1529, to a conference at Marburg, Luther and Zwingli, together with some of the more eminent doctors, who adhered to the respective parties of these contending chiefs. This expedient, which was designed by that truly magnanimous prince, not so much to end the keen debate, as to accommodate differences by the reconciling spirit of charity and prudence, was not attended with the salutary fruits that were expected from it.

The divines that were assembled for this pacific purpose disputed, during four days, in the presence of the landgrave. The principal champions in these debates were Luther who attacked Oecolampadius, and Melancthon, who disputed against Zwingli; in relation to which the Swiss doctors were supposed to entertain erroneous sentiments. For Zwingli was accused of heresy, not only on account of his explication of the nature and design of the Lord's supper, but also in consequence of the false notions he was supposed to have adopted, relative to the divinity of Christ, the efficacy of the divine word, original sin, and some other parts of the Christian doctrine. This illustrious reformer cleared himself, however, from the greatest part of these accusations, with the most triumphant evidence, and in such a manner as appeared entirely satisfactory, even to Luther himself. Their dissension concerning the manner of Christ's presence in the eucharist still remained; nor could either of the contending parties be persuaded to abandon, or even to modify, their opinion of that matter. The only advantage, therefore, that resulted from this conference was that the jarring doctors formed a sort of a truce, by agreeing to a mutual toleration of their respective sentiments, and leaving to the disposal of Providence, and the effects of time, which sometimes cools the rage of party, the cure of their divisions."*

In this conference at Marburg, to which Zwingli and Oecolampadius had come, at the risk of their lives, the points of Christian doctrine were discussed. The Swiss reformers set forth their beliefs on fourteen points which were accepted by Martin Luther, Melancthon, and Bucer as scriptural and evangelical, but upon the fifteenth point, which set forth the doctrine of the Lord's supper there was a wide difference of opinion.

Both groups of reformers rejected the doctrine of the sacrament of the Lord's supper taught by the Roman Catholic Church.

"Roman Catholic theologians divide this sacrament into two distinct things—the Eucharist and the Mass. The Mass is not so much a sacrament as a sacrifice. It is the prolongation through time of the sacrifice of Christ upon the cross; the bread and wine

---

* *Ecclesiastical History*—Mosheim. Volume 2, Chapter 2, Pages 20, 21.

are, it is said, the true body and blood of Christ, and when these are tasted in the act of eating and drinking done by the priest, Christ suffers in that act what he suffered on the cross. In this way Roman Catholics teach that Christians see Christ actually crucified in their midst—see his enduring the pains of the cross for them in their very presence. Thus, on this theory, there is not the distance of long centuries between the believer and the sufferings of Christ for him. The suffering of Christ and the worshipping believer are face to face in the one moment of time in the mass.

Protestants of all kinds rejected this doctrine of the Mass as idolatrous and superstitious, and taught Christians to go back in faith to the one real sacrifice of Christ on the cross on Calvary for them and for their sins.

The whole debate between Protestants is about what the Roman Catholics call the Eucharist, or sacrament of the Altar. The Roman Catholic doctrine of the Mass and their doctrine of the Eucharist have one point in common; both imply that Christ's real body and real blood are present in the bread and wine, so that these elements are no longer what they seem to be, but are the very body and blood of Christ. They teach that the priest, because he is a priest, and has been consecrated by a bishop, is able by prayer and ceremony to perform the miracle of changing bread and wine into the very body and blood of Christ, with his reasonable soul and divine nature; that he is able to work the miracle of bringing Christ down from heaven and showing him to the people to be worshipped and partaken of."*

On the subject of the power of the priests to change the bread and the fruit of the vine into the actual body and blood of the Savior, Liguori, one of the most eminent of Catholic authorities said,

"The dignity of the priest is measured again by the power he has over the real body and over the mystic body of Jesus Christ. As for the real body, it is an article of faith that, when the priest pronounces the words of consecration, the Word incarnate is obliged to obey and to come into his hands under the sacramental forms—And since he descends, he stays there at the disposition of the priest, who can transport him from one place to another, whether he shuts him up in the tabernacle, whether he exposes him on the altar, or whether he carries him out of the church. It is in his power, if he wishes to nourish himself with it or to give it to others."†

Luther and Zwingli both agreed that in whatever way Christ was present in the Lord's supper he was not brought there by a priest.

In this same year a Diet assembled at Spires issued a decree commanding the restoration of the mass and prohibiting any change in worship until the meeting of a national council.

The Roman Catholics, who were in the majority in the Diet ruled

---

* *The Reformation*—Lindsay. Part 1, Chapter 1, Pages 28, 29.
† *Works of Liguori*—Volume 12, Page 10.

that Catholics could teach their religion in Lutheran states, but prohibited the Lutherans from teaching their doctrines in Catholic communities.

Against this decree six German princes, the Elector of Saxony, George of Brandenburg, Philip of Hesse, Wolfgang of Anhalt, and Ernest and Francis of Lüneburg and fourteen imperial cities, signed a "protest," and henceforth they became known as "protestants." The name first applied to the followers of Luther, soon came to be applied to all who opposed papal power.

1530 A.D. THE AUGSBURG CONFESSION OF FAITH ADOPTED BY THE FOLLOWERS OF LUTHER

In January, Charles called upon the estates of the empire to meet at Augsburg to settle the controversy between Luther and the Roman Catholic Church, that unity might be restored.

When the elector received notice he asked Luther to prepare a summary of the Protestant articles of faith, which was later enlarged by Melancthon into the Augsburg Confession of Faith.

Luther, who had been condemned at Worms and whose life was in danger remained at the castle of Coburg, where he could be reached by Melancthon, Spalatin and Jonas, who were to represent the Protestants in the conference. Melancthon seemed to have entertained some hope that a union might be brought about between the Romanists and the Protestants, but Luther knew that could not be possible without admitting the doctrine of the infallibility of the church.

The Augsburg Confession of Faith is divided into two parts. The first part contains twenty-one articles in which the doctrines of Luther are plainly set forth. The second part is directed against the errors of the Roman Catholic Church, such as the enforced celibacy of the clergy, the sacrifice of the mass, withholding the cup from the laity, auricular confession and feast days, giving the reasons why these things could not be accepted.

Dr. Eck headed the group of Catholic clergymen who prepared a document to refute what had been set forth in the Augsburg Confession of Faith. The Diet passed a decree demanding that the followers of Luther make no further changes.

Martin Luther was the first man to teach justification by "faith only." He did a wonderful work in calling attention to the abuses of the church in Rome when they were teaching justification by works only, yet he went to the opposite extreme when he taught justification by faith only.

What caused Luther to advance this teaching? He believed the

Catholic church placed too much emphasis on justification by acts of penance and similar works.

He sought justifiation for his teaching by inserting the word "only" after the word "faith" in Romans 3:28, making it read, "Therefore, we conclude that man is justified by faith only without the works of the Law." This also contradicted the statement of James, "Ye see then how that by works a man is justified, and not by faith only."[1]

Luther was much opposed to the doctrine of the Roman church and upon the subject of infant baptism said, "It cannot be proved by the sacred scriptures that infant baptism was instituted by Christ or begun by the first Christians after the apostles." And again, "It is indeed correct to say that baptism is a washing from sins, a symbol of death and resurrection. For this reason, I would have the candidate completely immersed in the water as the Word says and the sacrament signifies."—*Luther's Works,* Volume 2, Pages 230, 231.

Martin Luther did not purpose to start another church when he first opposed the sale of indulgences. He purposed only to bring about a reform of the practices of the Roman Catholic Church, to end the abuses which had brought the church under reproach and to force Tetzel to discontinue the sale of indulgences, which he considered unscriptural. Luther was convinced that the pope did not know of the sale of indulgences and that when the facts were placed before him the traffic in indulgences would cease. Luther later learned that the pope had authorized the sale of the indulgence certificates and that the money was being used to construct St. Peter's cathedral in Rome.

Because of his opposition to the sale of indulgences, he was called upon to change his teaching and to recant. When he refused to do so he was branded as a heretic and his life was placed in jeopardy.

His continued study of the Scriptures convinced him that the teaching of the Roman Catholic Church was founded on tradition and not on the Word of God. When he called these truths to the attention of those who sat in the seats of the mighty, they laughed him to scorn and tried to take his life.

When Luther carried his case to the people calling their attention to the Scriptures, showing that the doctrines of the Roman Catholic Church were in opposition to the words of God, he received a much greater response than he had hoped for in a world where men had not had the liberty to make decisions for themselves.

---

1. James 2:24

1530 A.D. THE REFORMS OF ZWINGLI SPREAD TO OTHER SECTIONS OF SWITZERLAND

Oecolampadius became the leader of the Reformation at Basel where the Reformation was making rapid progress. Soon only five cantons remained wholly Catholic. These cantons were much opposed to Zwingli and the state of affairs in Zurich. They disliked the Reformation because of the attack which Zwingli made against the mercenary system which they supported. They accused Zwingli of slander, of treason and called upon Zurich to expel him from the city as a disturber of the peace. Eventually Zurich prohibited any supplies from passing through the city which were consigned to the five Catholic cantons. This virtually cut them off from the rest of the nation and an open rupture was about to occur when the leaders came to an agreement which did not last long. A sudden invasion of the canton of Zurich found the city wholly unprepared when the papal Swiss marched against it. Zwingli went with the men of his flock, as a chaplain, to the defense of this Protestant stronghold. He fell in the battle of Cappel on October 11, 1531. Twenty-five other leaders in the Swiss reformation also perished there.

> "Scarcely had the action begun, when, stooping to console a dying man, a stone hurled by the vigorous arm of a Waldstette struck him on the head and closed his lips. Yet Zwingli arose, when two other blows hit him on the leg and threw him down again. Twice more he stands up; but a fourth time he receives a thrust from a lance, he staggers, and sinking beneath so many wounds, falls to his knees.—Once more he uplifts that head which had been so bold, gazing with calm eye upon the trickling blood, exclaims, 'What matters this misfortune? They may indeed kill the body, but they cannot kill the soul.' These were his last words."*

The dead body of Zwingli was tried for treason and then quartered and burnt for heresy. As the flames consumed his disjointed members, the ashes of swine were mingled with his, and a mad crowd rushing in upon the remains threw them to the four winds heaven. Thus ended the life of one who was a staunch opponent of the papacy.

The war continued until a Treaty of Christianship ended the conflict. By this treaty, which was often violated, both parties agreed to tolerate each other.

The Roman Catholic Church won back many of the Reformed churches and excluded many of the members. Berne, Basel, and Zurich held fast to Protestantism. Oecolampadius did not long survive Zwingli and following his death Henry Bullinger, noted for

---

* *History of The Reformation*—D'Aubigne. Volume 4, Chapter 8, Page 450.

his learning, his zeal, and his sound judgment, became the leader
of the Reformation in Switzerland.

He was not afraid to speak his conviction and by his firmness
and his courage probably saved the Reformation in Zurich. Associated with Bullinger was Oswald Geisshusher, better known as
Myconius, who had been a life-long friend of Zwingli.

For a time he was a teacher in the schools of Lucerne, but when
the Reformation failed there he went to Basel where he became a
professor of theology in the university. Though he is noted for
his work as an educator, his greatest accomplishment was the con-
solidation of the Swiss churches, extending the Reformation along
the lines set forth by Zwingli and the publication of a biography
of the Swiss Reformer.

The death of Zwingli and Oecolampadius turned the southern
part of Germany from Zwinglianism to Luther.

1531 A.D. THE FORMATION OF THE SCHMALKALD LEAGUE

Following the formation of the Augsburg Confession of Faith
and its rejection by the Catholic representatives at Augsburg, the
papal church threatened war against the followers of Luther. The
prospect of war caused the princes of various districts and certain
cities to band themselves together in a defensive league. This
became known as the Schmalkald League. This organization was
composed of eleven cities and the territory of ten princes. It soon
developed into one of the strongest organizations of Europe, uniting
all of North Germany with the imperial cities of south Germany.

The Scandinavian countries were brought into the League when
Sweden officially rejected the papacy following the refusal of the
king to confirm the bishop-elect of the Roman Catholic Church.
The election of a Protestant archbishop took place shortly afterward. Between 1520 and 1523 the effort was made to introduce
the Reformation into Denmark. Lutheran preachers were allowed
to spread the doctrine of the Reformation through the Danish cities.
In 1525 Hans Tausen began to preach the doctrines of Luther in
Copenhagen and the Danish Diet passed a law providing "that
everyone is to enjoy freedom of conscience, the marriage of the
clergy is to be allowed and bishops are to be confirmed by the
crown and not by the pope." Thus Denmark became a stronghold
for the doctrine of Luther without the sanction of law. When Frederick I died, Christian III succeeded to the throne and a law was
passed deposing all bishops, confiscating their property, abolishing
church taxes and bringing all religious matters under the control of
the king. John Bugenhagen was brought up from Wittenberg to
prepare a church law for the kingdom. He ordained seven bishops

to take the place of those who were deposed. The church in Denmark thus became a national church under the patronage of the king, with the Augsburg Confession accepted as the standard of doctrine. The reformation of Norway followed that of Denmark, for Norway was a dependency of Denmark.

The Swedish Diet adopted a new church law for the kingdom in 1527, providing for a reformation of the church, bringing it under the control of the king, correcting financial abuses and limiting the powers of the bishops. The church in Sweden became a reformed church though it retained some customs and practices which had been abolished in other countries.

The League soon grew so strong that efforts to repress it met with failure. The following year, 1532, a religious peace was concluded which granted freedom to the Protestant states until a council should be called to settle the religious controversy.

1535 A.D. THE SCHMALKALD LEAGUE

All members of the Schmalkald League were required to accept the Augsburg Confession and the catechism as the standard of faith. In addition Luther prepared a document which was presented to the members of the Schmalkald League and accepted by them. This became known as the Schmalkald Articles and constituted the third statement of faith for the Lutheran Church. The Catholic Church became alarmed at the increase of the power of the League and in July of 1538 formed the Holy League of Nuremberg for the purpose of protecting the interest of the Roman Catholic Church. A religious war seemed inevitable but was delayed by the threat of the Turks. The Emperor of Germany needed the support of the Protestants against this enemy and so was forced to negotiate with them.

During the next few years several efforts were made to unite the Protestants and the Catholics but there were too many points of difference between them for this to be accomplished.

After a treaty was signed with the Turks the Emperor of Germany once more turned his attention to the Protestants. The king of France and the emperor agreed that all Protestants must be exterminated. They called upon the pope to call a church council at Trent as the means of re-uniting the two groups. The pope made it clear that no changes would be made in the doctrine of the Catholic Church so the Protestants refused to attend the council or to be bound by its decisions.

1545 A.D. THE COUNCIL OF TRENT CONVENED

This council was called by Pope Paul III to correct abuses which had brought in the Reformation. The Council met first at Trent, seventy-six miles northwest of Venice, though other cities became the place of their deliberations. The council remained in session for eighteen years through the reign of four popes.

All bishops and abbots of the church were called before the council to deliberate upon the means by which the Catholics and Protestants could be reunited. Many reforms were made and the doctrines of the church were clearly stated, but the changes came too late to have any influence upon the Protestants. The refusal of the Protestants to send delegates to the council gave the emperor and the pope excuse to proceed against them with armed forces, but Luther died before the actual war broke out.

Luther's last work on earth was to act as peacemaker between Count Gerhard and Count Albert. They had allowed enmity to exist between themselves over a period of years and this had created a condition of strife between their subjects. Twice in the month of October and once in December, he made a journey to Eisleben but was not able to reconcile the Counts to each other. On January 23, 1546 he set out again for Eisleben despite his infirmities. He was delayed for several days by storm and reached his destination exhausted in strength. After several days in conference with the Counts, he was able to mediate their differences, after which he returned home.

1546 A.D. DEATH OF MARTIN LUTHER

His health continued to decline and on the morning of February 18, 1546 he departed this life surrounded by his sons, his friends, the Counts, and their families. His body was brought back to Wittenberg and buried in the church where thirty years before he had nailed the thesis which shook the mighty ecclesiastical empire that had been weighed in the balances and found wanting.

Martin Luther learned that the teachings of the Roman Catholic Church were founded upon tradition and not upon the word of God. He sought to correct the abuses that had crept into the Catholic church through a departure from the divine plan but he was not able to entirely free his mind from the traditions of Rome.

The apostate church formed a catechism to set forth their doctrine. Luther, perhaps due to the great influence the Catholic church had upon his early life, said he felt compelled to draw up a catechism because of the lamentable lack of spiritual knowledge. Since Luther had given the German people the Bible in their own language, would it not have been much better to have simply directed their minds to the word of God? Certainly all that is essential to man's spiritual welfare is revealed therein.

"All scripture is given by inspiration of God, and is profitable for doctrine, for reproof, for correction, for instruction in righteousness; that the man of God may be perfect, throughly furnished unto all good works."[2]

Neither was Luther able to free his mind from the doctrine of transubstantiation, although he did teach his followers to partake of both the loaf and the cup. For centuries the Roman Catholic Church had withheld the cup from the laity.

Luther administered the Lord's supper to the laity in both kinds saying, "Therefore we beg, nay, we command in the name of our Lord Jesus Christ, that those who have received it under both kinds not to be persuaded that they have committed a sin thereby, but rather to yield up life itself."

Luther taught "with and under the bread is the body and with and under the cup is the blood." This he called the doctrine of Consubstantiation which was not different in principle to the doctrine of the Roman Catholic Church which teaches that the loaf and the fruit of the vine become the actual body and blood of Christ when blessed by the priest.

It is affirmed that the priest possesses the power to change the bread and the cup into the literal body and blood of Christ. By saying certain words he can perform the miracle of producing upon the communion altar the actual body and blood of the Savior. The members of the Roman Catholic Church believe he possesses that power. This elevates the priest in the minds of the people because they believe he has worked a miracle. As loyal Catholics, he has, they think, changed the bread and the fruit of the vine into the literal body and blood of Christ, though it is admitted that the elements are unchanged.

> "After the substance of the bread and wine had been changed into Our Lord's body and blood, there remained only the appearance of bread and wine; . . . . their color, taste, weight, shape and whatever else appears to the senses. The change of the entire substance of the bread and wine into the body and blood of Christ is called Transubstantiation.
>
> Jesus Christ is whole and entire both under the appearances of bread and wine. This change of bread and wine into the body and blood of Christ continues to be made in the church by Jesus Christ through the ministry of his priests. Only ordained priests have the power of changing bread and wine into the body and blood of Christ. When they consecrate, they act in the person of Christ, through the power received in the sacrament of Holy Orders."[*]

---

2. 2 Timothy 3 : 16, 17
* *Primer on Roman Catholicism For Protestants*—Stuber. Chapter 6, Page 67.

About A.D. 440 the Manichees, who held wine in abhorrence, attempted to introduce the practice of taking the communion under one species only, namely, the bread. Leo and Gelasius, both bishops of Rome, condemned this heresy in express terms, and ordered that the communion should be received entire, as instituted by our Lord, or not at all.

The words of Gelasius are so precise and so contradictory to the teaching of modern Rome, that we have only to quote them to convict the Roman church of imposing on believers a doctrine most emphatically condemned by a bishop of their own church. His words are: "We find that some, having received a portion of the holy body only, do abstain from the cup of holy blood, who doubtless (because they are bound by I know not what superstition), should receive the whole sacrament, or be driven from the whole, for the dividing of one and the same mystery cannot be done without sacrilege."*

Gelasius said—"Certainly the sacrament of the body and blood of our Lord, which we receive, are a divine thing; because by these we are made partakers of the divine nature. Nevertheless, the substance or nature of the bread and wine cease not to exist; and, assuredly, the image and similitude of the body and blood of Christ are celebrated in the action of the mysteries."

The decree of the Council of Trent in 1551 said—"By the consecration of the bread and wine, the whole substance of the bread is converted into the substance of the body of Christ and the whole substance of the wine is converted into the substance of his blood; which conversion is suitably called by the Catholic church, transubstantiation."

The contradiction between the decree of Pope Gelasius and the decree of the Trent Council, which now molds and directs the power and policies of the church of Rome, is so manifest, that no one can be surprised to find a desperate attempt to explain away the otherwise apparent heresy of an early bishop of Rome. Baronius and Bellarmine were foremost in their endeavors to explain the difficulty boldly confronting them. They choose the expediency of declaring that some other person of the name of Gelasius, but not Gelasius, the bishop, was the writer of the treatise in question. The Roman Catholic historian, Dupin, however, has exposed the hollowness of this "pious fraud," and proves incontestably that the work in question is the genuine production of Pope Gelasius, who was bishop of Rome A.D. 492, and by holding on to this doctrine, the church of Rome stands convicted before the intelligent world of introducing a shameful innovation into the creed of the Apostolic Church."†

* *A History of Reformatory Movements*—Rowe. Part 2, Pages 296, 297.
† *"A History of Reformatory Movements"* by Rowe. See also *"Ecclesiastical History"*—Dupin. Volume 1, Page 250.

Of the Last Supper Mark said, "And as they did eat, Jesus took bread, and blessed and brake it, and gave to them, and said, 'Take, eat: this is my body.' And he took the cup, and when he had given thanks, he gave it to them; and they all drank of it. And he said unto them 'This is my blood of the new testament.' "

No mention is here made of changing the bread and the cup into actual flesh and blood of Christ. When Paul wrote to the church at Corinth he warned them not to abuse the Lord's supper, saying, "For as often as ye eat this bread, and drink this cup, ye do show the Lord's death till he come. Wherefore, whosoever shall eat this bread, and drink this cup of the Lord, unworthily, shall be guilty of the body and blood of the Lord. But let a man examine himself, and so let him eat of that bread, and drink of that cup." (1 Corinthians 11:26-28.

What is the significance of this language? How is it to be understood? Paul did not say it was the body and blood of Christ which we eat and drink. This language is not to be understood literally. Christ also said, "I am the vine." Is this to be understood literally? Did he mean that he would leaf out in the spring and bear fruit? Certainly this is to be understood in a representative or figurative way.

Luther's ideas on baptism differed widely from those which are today held by his followers. Today it is affirmed that "the mode" is no part of the sacrament and that sprinkling is as likely as immersion. But Luther said, "Baptism is a Greek word. It can be translated 'immersion' as when we plunge something in the water that it may be completely covered."

"It is indeed correct to say that baptism is a washing from sins, a symbol of death and resurrection. For this reason I would have the candidate completely immersed in water as the word says and the sacrament signifies."*

It has been said that baptism has taken the place of circumcision and that therefore infants are to be baptized. "In the Old Testament circumcision was the sacrament of initiation. It was administered to the boy babies when they were eight days of age. If God could make a covenant with a baby in the Old Testament certainly he can and does the same thing in the new dispensation. Accordingly, we conclude, that since baptism has taken the place of circumcision, babies should be baptized." But where is the chapter and verse that teaches that baptism took the place of circumcision? Jesus said, "Go teach"; then baptize those you have taught. One can not teach babies—they are unteachable—and if infant baptism is to take the place of circumcision in the Old Testament, where is

---

* *Luther's Works*—Volume 2, Pages 230, 231.

the authority for sprinkling girl babies? Luther said, "It can not be proved by the sacred scriptures that infant basptism was instituted by Christ or begun by the first Christians after the apostles."

This brings to an end the events by which the Lutheran Church came into existence.

Its beginning dates from October 31, 1517 when Martin Luther nailed his theses to the door of Wittenberg Church in protest over the sale of indulgences. The events which followed brought about a separation from the church of Rome and brought into existence the Lutheran Church.

CHAPTER 12

GROWTH OF ENGLISH REFORMATION

Upon the death of Henry VII in 1509, Henry VIII became king, and upon his ascension he completed his marriage with Catherine of Aragon, his brother Arthur's widow. This marriage required a special bull from Pope Julius II.

There was great joy in England when Henry ascended the throne, for his father had incurred the hatred of the people by his severity and selfishness. The young king was only eighteen years old, but he gave promise of being a good sovereign, for he was well educated, pleasant in manner and skillful in all athletic exercises. The hoarded wealth of Henry VII was being squandered in expensive entertainments to the great grief of the Bishop of Winchester, when Thomas Wolsey was introduced to the king. Wolsey was the son of humble parents, a graduate of the University of Oxford and well qualified for the position of chaplain, to which he was soon appointed by Henry. He was sent as a messenger to the emperor in Flanders and when he returned in four days, Henry chided him for his delay in starting. Then he learned to his surprise, that Wolsey had gone and had returned. He was soon made Chancellor of the Kingdom, then Archbishop of York, and Henry secured from the pope his appointment as cardinal.

> "Wolsey was the son of a respectable butcher at Ipswich, in Suffolk, and received so excellent an education that he became a tutor to the family of the Marquis of Dorset, who afterwards got him appointed one of the late king's chaplains. On the accession of Henry the Eighth, he was promoted, and taken into great favor. He was now Archbishop of York; the pope had made him a cardinal besides; and whoever wanted influence in England, or favor with the king,—whether he were a foreign monarch or an English nobleman,—was obliged to make a friend of the great Cardinal Wolsey."*

In 1521 Henry entered the field as an author, against the "heresies" of Martin Luther. He wrote a book which was presented with great ceremony to Pope Leo, who rewarded him with the title "Defender of the Faith"—a title which the kings of England still retain.

---

* *History of England*—Dickens. Chapter 27, Page 221.

Henry now began to have doubts about the pope's power to allow him to marry his brother's widow and to question whether Catherine was really his wife, though he had lived with her for eighteen years. Without a doubt he was influenced, too, by the fact that their only living child was a girl (later Queen Mary), and that it was doubtful whether a woman would be permitted to occupy the English throne. Then, too, he had grown tired of Catherine and had fallen in love with a lady in waiting to the queen, Anne Boleyn. Had the Pope, Clement VII, been willing to grant Henry a divorce, all might have been well, but the pope could not grant a divorce to Henry, for his marriage to Catherine had been permitted by a special decree of Pope Julius II. If the pope refused the divorce he offended the king of England, if he granted the divorce he would offend the king of Spain and the king of Germany, Charles V, the nephew of Catherine. The pope postponed the decision for several years and Henry eventually took the matter into his own hands. He wrote a letter to the heads of the universities of England and of Europe asking the following questions.

"Is it agreeable to the law of God for a man to marry his brother's wife?"

"Can the pope dispense with the law of God?"

With the letters containing the questions he sent a gift and the heads of the institutions of learning sent back the kind of an answer that Henry wanted. Their decision was that Henry was not legally married to Catherine.

1531 A.D. HENRY ACCUSES ALL OF THE CLERGY OF ACTING AS PAPAL REPRESENTATIVES

In an assembled convocation they were forced to beg his pardon, which they obtained only in return for a large sum of money. In their petitions they addressed him as the Protector and Supreme Head of the church and clergy in England. Since Parliament had prohibited the entry of a papal edict into England, appeals to Rome were useless.

"They also offered to compound for their transgression of the 'Praemunire' (denying the sovereign's supremacy) and the over-looking of the King's supremacy, by granting to him a large sub-sidy of £ 100,044, under the name of a benevolence, in acknowl-edgement of the King's services to the church, and zeal against heresy. Henry refused all compromise unless they would acknowl-edge him to be the protector, and only supreme head of the church in England, next immediately after Christ. . . . The convocation of York, after some little demur, also assented to the entire conditions, and offered a subsidy of £ 18,840 which added to that of the

southern province, made up the enormous sum in present money
of £ 1,500,000. . . . Henry accepted the terms, and yielded to
their reservation; and thus were the clergy pardoned, and restored
to the royal favor."*

This convocation of English clergy also declared in favor of his
divorce, only twenty voting against it. The Earl of Wiltshire then
sent a letter to the pope signed by the cardinal, the Archbishop of
Canterbury, four bishops, twenty-three barons and other ecclesiastics of the papal church saying they believed Henry should have
a divorce.

Cardinal Wolsey was now sent to the pope to sue for a divorce
upon the grounds of Catherine's previous marriage to Prince
Arthur.

The pope not desiring to provoke the emperor, who was the
nephew of the queen, hesitated to give a definite reply, and after
keeping the king in suspense for a year, sent Cardinal Campeggio
to England, to decide, in company with Cardinal Wolsey, the
validity of the king's marriage to Catherine.

Cardinal Campeggio tried to persuade the king to give up the
thought of a divorce. When his efforts along this line failed he
tried to induce Catherine to retire to a nunnery. When their efforts
failed to accomplish anything, the cardinals proceeded to arrange
a trial. After hearing the evidence, they seemed to be unwilling to
come to a decision. The king's patience was now near an end and
it was evident that Wolsey's favor was declining. Soon after,
an indictment was brought against the cardinal, and all of his
property, even his clothes, was seized by order of the king and
he was banished from the court, but permitted to reside at York.

Later he was arrested for high treason. As he journeyed to the
Tower, he was seized with a high fever and could travel no farther
than Leicester Abbey, where he breathed out these words as life
departed, "Had I served my God as diligently as I have served my
king, he would not have left me in my old age."

1529 A.D. LATIMER UPHOLDS THE TRANSLATION
AND THE READING OF THE SCRIPTURES

In this year he preached at Cambridge a celebrated sermon upon
this subject.

The Friars of the church were enraged and Friar Buckingham
was selected to reply to Latimer, but his reply was wholly lacking
in sober argument, logic, and truth.

The sympathy of the people was with the reformers, who were

* *Analysis of English Church History*—Pinnock. Chapter 3, Page 169.

making the effort to restore the Bible to the people. In spite of all opposition it was being circulated and read by the people. Bishop Nikke wrote to the pope, "It is beyond my power to hinder it now, and if the spread of the Bible continues, it will undo us all." There was no longer any doubt about it, the path of the Bible was open at last and no one could close it.

This is the time in which Tyndale gave the Bible to the people of England in their own language.

> "William Tyndal . . . found the people ignorant, and the priests oftener at the ale houses than in the homes of the poor. He tells us that it was impossible to establish the lay people in any truth, unless the Scriptures were plainly laid before their eyes in their mother tongue. He also says the clergy expound the Scriptures in many senses before the unlearned lay people and amaze them when it hath but one simple literal sense, whose light the owls can not abide. . . . 'Which things only moved me to translate the New Testament.' One learned man said to him, "We were better be without God's laws than the popes." He replied, 'I defy the pope and all his laws. If God spare my life, ere many years I will cause a boy that driveth the plow to know more of the Scriptures than thou dost.' Here, then, was his motive. He would translate the Greek Testament edited by Erasmus. His life became that of a hero, an exile, a wanderer, and he closed it in the persecutor's fire at Vilvorde, Holland, praying, 'Lord, open the King of England's eyes.' But he gave the English people the New Testament in their own language. Despite the efforts of men who were burning piles of copies in London and Oxford, groups of Christian brethren were distributing it among the people:"*

1530 A.D. THE EDICT OF WORMS

This Edict placed all books and writings of teachers and preachers of the Reformation under an interdict in Netherlands. Until the end of the reign of Charles V in Netherlands, the historian Grotius says that more than one hundred thousand people were burnt, strangled, and buried alive.

In this period of time it was unlawful to give away, buy or have in one's possession any work of Luther, Calvin or Zwingli. Those guilty of violation were put to death.

1533 A.D. THOMAS CRANMER MADE ARCHBISHOP OF CANTERBURY

A court was assembled and after hearing the arguments in the case, the archbishop declared that the marriage of Henry and Catherine was not valid from the beginning and that Mary, their daughter, was not an heir to the throne. Catherine retired to Ampthill, and Henry was married to Anne Boleyn on January 25, 1533 in the present of the Duke of Norfolk, her father, mother, and brother;

---

* *The History of The Christian Church*—Blackburn. Chapter 20, Page 510

the ceremony being performed by Dr. Rowland Lee, the Bishop of Litchfield.

Cranmer now confirmed the king's marriage to Anne and she was crowned queen a few days later. When the news reached the pope that Henry had defied him by divorcing Catherine and marrying Anne Boleyn, he proceeded to annul all that Cranmer had done, threatening the king and the Archbishop with excommunication if things were not restored to their former state. The king's marriage to Catherine was declared valid and Henry was informed that he must live with her as his wife. The declaration of the pope to enforce ecclesiastical measures against him caused Henry to decide to throw off the papal yoke at once.

The king called Parliament into session and they set about to make the separation from Rome permanent by legal means.

Parliament abolished all payments to the pope, gave the two archbishops the power of granting dispensations, and all monasteries were made subject to the king's authority.

Appeals to Rome and the execution of all papal processes were denied. Henry was declared by Parliament to be the Supreme Head of the Church of England. By these acts the Church of England was brought into existence.

1534 A.D. THE ACT OF SUPREMACY

"The king our sovereign lord, his heirs and successors, kings of this realm, shall be taken, accepted, and reputed the only supreme head on earth of the Church of England . . . and shall have and enjoy, annexed and united to the imperial crown of this realm, as well the title and style thereof, as all honors, dignities, preeminences, jurisdictions, privileges, authorities, immunities, profits and commodities of said dignity of supreme head of the same church belonging and appertaining; and that our said sovereign lord, his heirs and successors . . . shall have full authority and power from time to time to visit, refer, redress, reform, order, correct, restrain and amend all such errors, heresies, abuses, offenses, contempt, enormities, whatsoever they be, which by any spiritual authority and jurisdiction ought or may lawfully be reformed . . . any usage, custom, foreign law, foreign authority, prescription, or any other thing or things to the contrary notwithstanding."

This act was also defined as granting to the king of England complete control in all matters affecting the church.

Henry's marriage to Anne was only the beginning of his troubles. After living with Anne for three years, Henry accused her of infidelity and ordered her confined to the Tower of London until her case should be tried. When Henry first met Anne he was paying court to her older sister. Though Henry paid her ardent court, she refused his attentions until he divorced Catherine.

When their first child, Elizabeth, was born, Henry became enraged when he learned that he had a daughter and not a son. When the second child was born dead, King Henry, who had prayed for a male heir, was through with Anne. He had defied Rome in contracting this marriage, now he became a law unto himself and ordered Anne brought to trial for adultery.

> "Anne was accused of adultery, and conveyed to the Tower; whither had preceded her, her brother, Lord Rochford, with Norris, Weston, and Brereton of the king's privy chamber, and Smeaton, a musician as accomplices. By the confession of Smeaton, who had been put to the torture, and therefore not a testimony to be relied on, they were all convicted of high treason and sentenced to be hanged, drawn and quartered. The unhappy queen was beheaded on the green of the Tower May 19, 1536; her marriage was declared null—and her offspring, the Princess Elizabeth, declared illegitimate.*

Divorce alone, Henry considered was not enough punishment for her unfaithfulness, so he ordered her execution. The execution spot may be seen in the courtyard of the Tower of London today. Anne went to her death gowned in gray damask, greatly composed, whispering "Lord Jesus, Lord Jesus," until the sword fell. Henry is said to have spent the time before her execution hunting in Epping Forest, but when he heard the Tower gun that announced Anne's death, he hastened to pay court to Jane Seymour and was married to her the next day.

The new queen died at the end of the year, leaving one son, who became Edward VI.

After the death of Wolsey, Sir Thomas More, the author of "More's Utopia," became Lord Chancellor. He thoroughly believed in the pope as head of the church and refused to take the oath of the king's supremacy as the rightful head of the church. He had also refused to support the king's plea for a divorce from his first wife, Catherine. For these crimes he was imprisoned in the Tower of London for twelve months. At the conclusion of his trial, when the executioner turned toward him, he bore his conviction quite serenely, giving a blessing to his son, who pressed through the crowd at Westminster Hall to receive it. He was taken back to the Tower to be executed and when he placed his head upon the block he said, "Let me put my beard out of the way; for that, at least, has never committed any treason." Then his head was struck off at a single blow. Thus died one of the outstanding men of Henry's kingdom.

One of the most active writers against the king on the side of the church, was a distant cousin of the king's, Reginald Pole, by

* *Analysis of English Church History*—Pinnock. Part 2, Chapter 4, Page 192.

name. Pole attacked the king in a most violent manner, fighting for the church night and day, with his pen.

Residing in Italy, he was beyond the king's reach, so the king politely invited him to come to England to discuss this matter. Pole knew better than to come, so the king's rage fell upon his brother, Lord Montague and several others, who were tried and executed for high treason, in corresponding with Pole. His mother, the Countess of Salisbury, was the last of Pole's relatives upon whom the king's wrath fell. When she was told to lay her head upon the block, she refused, saying, "My head never committed any treason." When she was held down upon the block by the Tower guards, she moved her head from side to side in an effort to prevent her execution.

Though the Church of England was separated from the Church of Rome, it did not become wholly Protestant. True, Cranmer set about to reform the church in England, but he was not able to introduce any Protestant doctrines. Cranmer had lived in Germany for a long time and had been deeply influenced by the teachings of Luther, yet he did not attempt to bind them upon the people of England.

Pope Paul III now made overtures to Henry for a reconciliation; but it was met by the passing of two laws by Parliament which declared—

First. That all who acknowledged the pope's authority in England would be subject to a fine.

Second—That all papal bulls, dispensations, licenses and the privileges dependent on them were null and void; wherefore those who possessed any property on that tenure were required to provide themselves with a new grant from the chancery court.

Among the few of Wolsey's servants who retained the favor of the king, was Thomas Cromwell, who rose rapidly to several offices of the state. He obtained a seat in the assembly as the king's vicar-general and Cranmer was forced to surrender his position as confidential advisor to Cromwell.

Cromwell introduced Alexander Ales into the Convocation, which had been sitting for some little time trying to reconcile many differences of opinion on points of doctrine and discipline. Ales, through the influence of Cromwell, was made a professor at Cambridge. He advocated the rejection of five out of the seven sacraments of the Catholic church, declaring that Christ instituted but two, baptism and the Lord's supper. Due to the opposition of Bishop Stokesly of London, his proposal was rejected.

There were two groups in opposition to each other, those in favor of reform under the leadership of Cranmer, the Archbishop of

Canterbury, and those opposed to religious reform under the guidance of Lee, the Archbishop of York. After much discussion, ten articles were sent to both houses of Parliament for consideration by the king. Though they were satisfactory to neither party, a compromise was worked out and they were accepted as the basis of Christian faith.

The first five were on points of doctrine and were as follows:

1. That Christian faith was comprised in the Bible, and in the three creeds, and was defined by the first four General Councils.
2. That baptism was necessary to salvation; and that children should be baptized for original sin, and procuring of the Holy Ghost.
3. That penance—repentance, confession and amendment—was a sacrament; and confession to a priest necessary.
4. That in the Eucharist, corporeal presence of Christ was to be believed.
5. That justification was remission of sins, and reconciliation with God; and a gift, through Christ's merits; yet holiness of life was necessary.

In respect to Ceremonies it was decided:

1. That images were useful helps, yet must not be worshipped.
2. That Saints were to be honored as examples of life.
3. That prayers might be addressed to Saints as intercessors, but they were not be be worshipped.
4. That the existing Ceremonies, such as vestments, holy water, candles, palms, and ashes, were highly useful as leading to devotion.
5. That prayers for souls departed were good and useful; although the existence of purgatory was uncertain.

These ten articles were signed by the chief members of Convocation, and by the king and were enforced by a royal proclamation. In order to give greater authority to the Ten Articles, Cromwell, by virtues of his high office, issued the following injunctions in the name of the king—The clergy were to preach against papal authority and vindicate the Royal Supremacy, one quarter every year, and twice in other quarters to explain the Ten Articles lately put forth by Convocation; to abrogate certain of the holy days; to discredit images, relics, and pilgrimages, and advance charity in their stead; to teach the Lord's Prayer, Creed, and Ten Commandments in the vulgar tongue, and on occasions of absence to supply their places with good Curates.

1537 A.D. JANE SEYMOUR, THE QUEEN, BECOMES THE MOTHER OF A SON

Much to the joy of the king, and the encouragement of the Reformers, a son was born to the new wife of the king, on October 12. The Reformers believed that if Princess Mary came to the throne, much of their work would be undone. Twelve days after the birth of their new heir to the throne, the queen died of a fever. The Archbishop of Canterbury, Lady Mary, and the Duke of Norfolk were the sponsors at the baptism of the royal babe.

1539 A.D. PARLIAMENT MET IN AN ATTEMPT TO END THE UNREST RESULTING FROM THE SUPPRESSION OF THE MONASTERIES

They purposed to end the diversity of opinions existing among the prelates and to form a new rule of faith that was to be enforced by law. Although those favoring the church of Rome were in the majority, yet they could come to no decision. The Duke of Norfolk, at the request of Henry, put forward The Six Articles, which became a law for the Church of England. They were said to be the production of Henry and his advisor, Gardiner. Cranmer was opposed to it, but said nothing against it before the Houses of Parliament.

The Six Articles of Religion Set Forth the Following Doctrines:
1. That in the Sacrament after consecration, the symbols are no longer bread and wine, but the real body and blood of Christ.
2. That communion in both kinds was not necessary to salvation, the flesh and blood being in each.
3. That priests by the law of God cannot marry.
4. That vows of chastity ought to be observed.
5. That private masses for souls in purgatory are necessary and ought to be maintained.
6. That auricular confession is necessary and ought to be retained.

The penalties for violating the first was to be burned as a heretic without benefit of abjuration and goods forfeited. For violating the other five the penalty was imprisonment for life; for wilful opposition to them the punishment was death.

It is evident to all students of the Scriptures that of the six articles, only one, that of chastity, was based upon the word of God. The doctrines they bound upon both the clergy and the laity show that the Church of England was still under the influence of the church of Rome.

"The Church was still a power in the land. Her prerogatives
were not assailed, and although convocation was often unduly
pressed by the king to hurry on the work of reform, neither Parliament nor the king would then have dared to alter anything without
its sanction. And the clergy through convocation, did not consent
to any changes that would impair its apostolic fellowship or Catholic
doctrine, its ministerial succession or the validity of its sacramental
ordinances."*

The immediate effect of the Act of The Six Articles, or the "whip
with six strings," as it was called, was the resignation of Latimer,
the Bishop of Worcester, and Slaxton, the Bishop of Salisbury.
Cranmer was in a precarious position, having a wife and several
children. These he hastily sent into Germany to conform to the
statute of celibacy.

Hundreds were committed to prison on account of violation of
the Six Articles, but the king was inclined to grant a general pardon
rather than to proceed against so many of his subjects.

The king this same year, by the persuasion of Cranmer, gave
his sanction for Cromwell to publish a translation of the Bible.
Letters were also granted for the free use of the Scriptures.
Cranmer wrote a preface to it and because it was published by his
endorsement, it was called Cranmer's Great Bible, although it was
only a correct edition of Matthew's Bible.

In this same year Henry began to look about for a wife. Cromwell suggested that he marry a Protestant princess, mentioning
Anne of Cleves. Hans Holbein, the famous portrait painter, was
sent to paint her picture. Cromwell and the Lutheran princes of
Germany favored the match believing that it would strengthen the
cause of the Reformation in England. The Protestantism of England did not extend beyond the rejection of papal power at this time.
When the portrait was finished, Holbein had made her so good
looking that Henry was satisfied with her beauty and the marriage
was arranged.

Henry arranged a reception for her at Greenwich, but when he
saw her he was disgusted with her appearance for she was so unlike
her picture that it was with difficulty that he was persuaded to
marry her. When Henry discovered that she was dull, lacking the
manners of a court lady, and that she could speak no language but
German, he disliked her more than before and resolved that he
would divorce her. Henry called Parliament into session, the marriage was declared void and Anne was settled in a castle and
granted an allowance of £3000 a year, as the adopted sister of
Henry, and there she passed the remainder of her life to all appear-
ances very contentedly.

---
* *Notes on English Church History*—Lane. Chapter 17, Page 294.

"The king now pushed on the dissolution of his marriage with Anne of Cleves; he desired the Parliament to consider it, and the Convocation to investigate it. In obedience to the king's known desire, the Convocation—upon the ground that the king had married her against his will, and had not inwardly consented; and that the marriage had not been consummated, nor was likely to be—authoritatively annulled the marriage, and declared both parties at liberty to marry again; this decision was sanctioned by Parliament and the queen consented to the proposal of the king, that she should be considered as his adopted sister . . . She was required also to announce to her relatives, and the foreign courts that she gave a willing acquiescence to these arrangements. Thus ended the fourth marriage of the king."*

Henry looked upon Cromwell as the one who was responsible for the objectionable match with Anne of Cleves. He, too, had incurred the hatred of the Duke of Norfolk, who was the leader of the papal party. The duke was also the uncle of Catherine Howard, in whom Henry was now interested. The king's advisor, Gardiner, and the duke persuaded Henry that by sacrificing his Vicegerent he would undo the odium of his former marriage and regain the affection of his people. A bill of attainder was prepared and Cromwell was arrested on a charge of treason and committed to the Tower of London on June 13, 1540.

Under a bill of attainder, a statute which Cromwell had been instrumental in enacting, no defense was allowed; Cromwell was accordingly condemned and executed as a traitor on Tower Hill July 28, 1540.

Within a few days Henry presented Catherine Howard, the niece of the Duke of Norfolk, to the court as queen. He was so delighted with her wit and beauty that he caused a prayer of thanksgiving to be offered for his happy marriage. It soon came out that Catherine had been guilty of indiscretions before her marriage. A bill of attainder was brought against her and her accomplices.

Catherine admitted her guilt before her marriage but denied that she had been guilty of misconduct after her marriage to the king. Judgment was given against her and those charged with her, Derham, Culpepper and Lady Rockford, her lady-in-waiting, and all were executed February 13, 1542.

Tired of marrying for beauty, Henry now looked about for someone of sense and discretion, which he found in Catherine Parr, the widow of Lord Latimer. He married her in 1543. The queen leaned toward the reformed religion and on one occasion she expressed herself rather strongly in favor of the reformed faith. When the king learned of this he actually instructed Gardiner,

* *Analysis of English Church History*—Pinnock. Part 2, Chapter 4, Pages 208, 209.

one of the bishops who favored papalism, to draw up a bill of accusations against her, which would have brought her to the block where her predecessors had died. Fortunately for her, one of her friends had picked up a paper of accusations which had been dropped in the palace and had brought it to her. When she saw what it contained she became ill with terror. When the king came to entrap her by further statements, she told him that she sometimes spoke on certain points to divert his mind and to get some information from his extraordinary wisdom. She added that she was blessed with a husband who was qualified, by his judgment and learning, not only to choose principles for his own family, but for the nation as well. The king was so flattered that he kissed her and called her his sweetheart. When the Chancellor came the next day to take her to the Tower, the king sent him on his way calling him a beast and a knave.

1545 A.D. THE COUNCIL OF TRENT

This Council convened for the purpose of correcting certain abuses within the Roman Catholic Church and endeavoring to win back those who had separated from the Catholic church.

The papal legates opened the council session in December 1545, first taking up the dogmas of the church, affirming that tradition was of equal authority with the Scriptures.

All attacks on papal power were quickly silenced. The council with short interruptions remained in session for eighteen years but failed to bring the Catholics and the Protestants together.

As Henry approached the end of his life he was troubled with a very painful disorder in his leg which prevented him from walking and added to the natural violence of his temper. Even the queen was treated with harshness while ministering to his wants. Among the last official acts of his life was the arrest of the Duke of Norfolk and son, Lord Surrey. The duke had been one of the king's favorites. He had been rewarded with honors and estates for his service to the crown. Lord Surrey was one of the most accomplished noblemen in England. He was distinguished both as a soldier and a scholar. The son was tried first and was found guilty and executed.

The Church of England now existed as a separate institution from the church of Rome.

The failure of Henry VIII to secure a papal annulment of his marriage to Catherine of Aragon brought the estrangement that severed the Church of England from the papacy. Anti-papal legislation enacted by Parliament made the separation permanent.

All payments to Rome were suspended, the monasteries closed and the church lands redistributed to the king's supporters. The formation of the Ten Articles, followed by the Six Articles revealed that England was still Catholic at heart.

> "The king was exceedingly cautious in introducing changes which affected the religious faith and practice of the people. In repudiating the authority of the pope he had on the whole the sympathy of the nation; in destroying the monastaries he was aided by the jealousy of the secular clergy and the greed of his courtiers, but he had no sympathy with Lutheranism or Zwinglianism, and he either did not wish or did not venture to tamper to any great extent with the religious life."[*]

The Liturgy or Book of Common Prayer was prepared by a group of twelve divines headed by Thomas Cranmer, the Archbishop of Canterbury. The Catholic service was retained, but simplified and translated into the language of the people. The government of the Church of England was much like that of the Roman Catholic Church except that instead of the pope being acknowledged as the head of the church the king proclaimed himself as the Supreme Head of the Church of England. By the events above recorded the Church of England was brought into existence in 1535. As the Church of England developed it was placed under an episcopacy in which the bishop ruled over several churches in a diocese with the Archbishop having jurisdiction over cities and adjacent territory. This form of ecclesiastical government was in sharp contrast with the government of the church of the first century.

The Scriptures reveal that each of the congregations of the New Testament age were under the oversight of elders, who were also called bishops or pastors. See I Timothy 3: 1-7, Acts 20: 28.

The arrangement of placing a group of churches under the jurisdiction of one man is contrary to the teaching of the New Testament. The elders had the oversight of one congregation and their rule did not extend to any other. Each congregation was independent of all others and was thus free to carry on its own work without interference from others. The New Testament does not authorize an ecclesiastical hierarchy or any organization of churches, nor the appointment of any officer above elders. God has given to no man nor to any set of men the authority to legislate for the church. He has given us His word as a guide to supply us with all things necessary for our spiritual wellbeing.

---

[*] *The History of The Book of Common Prayer*—Maude. Chapter 1, Page 2.

1547 A.D. HENRY VIII DIES AND EDWARD VI
ASCENDS THE THRONE OF ENGLAND

Edward was the son of Henry and Jane Seymour and at the time of his ascension was only ten years of age. His uncle, the Duke of Somerset, was entrusted with the affairs of the government under the title of Protector. Bishop Latimer, who had suffered much during the reign of Henry, for his zeal for the reformed faith, was appointed as the young king's chaplain.

The work of the Reformation in England was now undertaken in earnest. By the direction of the Protector, Cranmer, and Ridley a new prayer book was prepared. Few changes were made in the ritualism of the church, and, to appease those who yet held to the Papacy, many of the prayers of the Roman Catholic Church were retained.

To promote uniformity in religious practice, Archbishop Cranmer drew up forty-two articles of religious belief, which were later reduced to the Thirty-nine Articles. These set forth the doctrines of the Church of England and all subjects of the king were to be obedient to them. Those who would not accept the religion of the government were to be subjected to severe penalties.

Princess Mary was one who refused to conform to the law. The chaplains who ministered to her spiritual needs were arrested and she was threatened with punishment. She attempted to escape from England that she might place herself under the protection of her cousin, Emperor Charles. When this became known it was thought best to let her worship God according to her own desire, provided the worship was conducted in private in her own home.

Bishop Gardiner, who had been an advisor to King Henry, also refused to conform to the Thirty-nine Articles and was imprisoned for his obstinacy. Outwardly the nation was brought to conformity in religion. Some accepted the reformed religion because they believed it to be the truth, others conformed to its requirement because it was the religion of King Edward, while some favored the reforms because they had received some of the lands of the church, which they would be required to return if the papal religion was restored.

Thus the Church of England began to assume a definite Protestant character. This enabled those opposed to the papacy to secure positions of prominence in the Church.

Archbishop Cranmer appointed Latimer and Ridley, two of the outstanding Protestants of England, as Bishops of The Church of England. The Duke of Somerset, the Protector of the king, now learned that his brother, Lord Seymour, was becoming dangerous to his interests. Under the charge that he had conspired against the young King Edward, he was imprisoned in the Tower, tried and found guilty, and beheaded on Tower hill. His brother, the duke, was the first one to sign the warrant for his execution.

Now the Protector found himself accused by Dudley, the Earl of Warwick, of conspiring to seize and overthrow the government of the king. He was acquitted of the charge of treason but found guilty on other charges and executed on Tower hill.

Dudley was soon created the Duke of Northumberland, by the young king, who seemed to be completely under the control of the duke. He now set about to have one of his sons placed upon the throne as successor to Edward VI, who had been very ill, first of the measles, and then of smallpox. Edward became troubled in mind to think that at his death there would be a possibility of Princess Mary succeeding him upon the throne, by which the Catholic religion would be established again.

The Duchess of Suffolk was descended from King Henry VII, and having no sons who might succeed to the crown, she was persuaded to relinquish her claim to the crown in favor of her daughter Lady Jane Grey. The duke now arranged for his son Gilbert Dudley to marry Lady Jane Grey, after which they were named by Edward as the rightful heirs to the crowns of England. Edward delivered to the crown lawyers a document signed by himself, asserting his right to name his successor. This instrument was to be signed by all the officers of the state. Some of them hesitated to sign, but were brought to do so when the duke threatened to fight anyone who refused to agree to Lady Jane Grey's succession. Archbishop Cranmer at first refused to sign, stating that he had pledged himself to support Princess Mary's succession to the crown, but yielding to the entreaties of the young king, he signed the document with the rest of the council.

1553 A.D. THE DEATH OF EDWARD VI

Very shortly after the document which named his successor was signed, the king's health went into a rapid decline and he died on July 6, praying with his last breath that God would protect and preserve the reformed religion. The news of the death of Edward was conveyed to the Lord Mayor of London and the aldermen, and in turn made known to the people. The Princess Mary was on her way to London to see Edward when news of his death reached her. She turned aside into Norfolk. Here the Earl of Arundel told her of the selection of Lady Jane Grey as queen. A delegation of the Lords conveyed the news to Lady Jane Grey that she was to be queen. She was only sixteen when the news of her selection as the queen of England was announced to her. She was so surprised by the announcement that she fainted. When she recovered she expressed her sorrow for the king's death and said that if she was to be queen she prayed that God would direct her ways. She and her husband were brought down the Thames river to the Tower, where she was to remain until she was crowned.

The people of the city were not pleased by the selection of Lady Jane Grey and when Gabriel Pot spoke against it he was punished by having his ears cut off. Some of the nobility declared themselves in favor of Princess Mary. An army was raised to back her claims and she was proclaimed queen at Norwich. The Lord Mayor and the aldermen then decided that Mary should be the next ruler of England. Lady Jane Grey resigned the crown willingly and Mary was proclaimed queen by the Cross of St. Paul's. She passed through the streets of London to the Tower, there she released the ones who had been imprisoned because of their religious beliefs, among whom was Gardiner, later made chancellor by Mary. Mary had said that none would be persecuted or compelled to change their religion but her ideas about this were soon changed.

The Duke of Northumberland was arrested, along with five others and brought before the council. All were sentenced to death and the sentence carried out at Tower Hill.

Mary was now crowned queen and soon she was showing her desire to restore Catholicism to England. Bishop Ridley was seized and sent to the Tower of London. Archbishop Cranmer was arrested very shortly afterward. Then the aged Bishop Latimer, who was powerful among the clergy of the reformers, was ordered brought to the Tower. The prisons were soon filled with those who had favored the religious reforms of Henry VIII and Edward VI. A Parliament was called by Queen Mary and the divorce of Henry VIII and of Catherine of Aragon formerly pronounced by Cranmer, the Archbishop of Canterbury, was annulled. Parliament declared Lady Jane Grey and her husband, Lord Dudley, guilty of treason. Lady Jane Grey refused a last meeting with her husband lest she should lose her composure. She saw his lifeless body brought back from Tower Hill in a cart for burial. She was brought to the place of execution within the Tower and, as she approached the platform upon which the execution was to take place, appeared greatly composed. She acknowledged that she had erred in not firmly refusing the crown; but that respect for her father, and not her own ambition was the cause of her fault. Her execution was in February of 1554.

"One may guess the sad apprehensions the council were under for the Protestant religion, when they put the king, who was a minor, and not capable of making a will, upon this expedient, and set their hands to the validity of it. The king being dead,

Queen Jane was proclaimed with the usual solemnities, and an army raised to support her title; but the Princess Mary, then at Norfolk, being informed of her brother's death, sent a letter to the council, in which she claims the crown, and charges them, upon their allegiance, to proclaim her in the city of London and elsewhere.

The council, in return, insisted upon her laying aside her claims, and submitting as a good subject to her new sovereign. But Mary, by the encouragement of her friends in the north, resolved to maintain her right; and to make her way more easy she promised the Suffolk men to make no alteration in religion. This gained her an army with which she marched toward London; but before she came thither, both the council and the citizens of London declared for her, and on the 3rd of August she made her public entry, without the loss of a drop of blood, four weeks after the death of her brother. Upon Queen Mary's entrance into the Tower she released Bonner, Gardiner, and others, whom she called her prisoners. August 12, her majesty declared in council "that, though her conscience was settled in matters of religion, yet she was resolved not to compel others, but by the preaching of the Word."

This was different from her promise to the Suffolk men; she assured them that "religion should be left upon the same foot she found it at the death of King Edward, but now she insinuates that the old religion is to be restored, but without compulsion." Next day there was a tumult at St. Paul's, occasioned by Dr. Bourne, one of the canons of that church, preaching against the late Reformation; he spoke in commendation of Bonner, and was going on with severe reflectons upon the late King Edward, when the whole audience was in an uproar; some called to pull down the preacher, others throwing stones, and one a dagger, which stuck in the timber of the pulpit. Mr. Rogers and Bradfor, two popular preachers for the Reformation, hazarded their lives to save the doctor, and conveyed him in safety to a neighboring house; for which act of charity they were soon after imprisoned, and then burned for heresy.

To prevent the like tumults for the future, the queen published an inhibition, August 18, forbidding all preaching without special license; declaring, farther, that she would not compel her subjects to be of her religion till public order should be taken in it by common assent. Here was another intimation of an approaching storm: "the subjects were not to be compelled till public order should be taken for it." And to prevent further tumults, a proclamation was published, for masters of families to oblige their apprentices and servants to frequent their own parish churches on Sundays and holy days, and keep them at home at other times. 'The shutting up of all the Protestant pulpits at once awakened the Suffolk men, who, presuming upon their merits and the queen's promise, sent a deputation to court to represent their grievances; but the queen checked them for their insolence; and one of their number, happening to mention her promise, was put in the pillory three days together, and had his ears cut off for defamation.' "*

Queen Mary's next object was to lay hold of Princess Elizabeth. Five hundred men were sent after her at her house at Ashridge.

* *History of The Puritans*—Neal. Volume 1, Chapter 1, Page 58.

Arriving late at night, they found her ill in bed and waited until the next morning to put her in a litter to be carried to London. She sent a letter to Mary, asking the reason for such treatment, but received no answer and was sent to the Tower.

She was taken in by the Traitor's Gate, to which she objected very much, declaring that she was not a traitor. After a time she was released, and Hatfield House was assigned to her as a home, under the care of Sir Thomas Pope.

A courtship between Philip, the Prince of Spain, and Queen Mary ended in their marriage in July, 1554 before Bishop Gardiner at Winchester. Although the members of Parliament were suspected of having been influenced by Spanish money to enact laws to restore the Catholic religion, they would pass no law setting aside Princess Elizabeth or granting to Queen Mary the right to name her successor to the English throne.

A new Parliament was called and arrangements were made for the reception of Cardinal Pole, the pope's legate. Upon his arrival, he declared that all who had received church property at the hands of the former rulers would be allowed to retain it. Parliament presented a petition requesting that the Church in England be received into the fold of the papal church again.

The Cardinal made a speech in which he said that all the wrongs of the people were forgiven and would be forgotten and England became a Roman Catholic nation again. Now the persecution of the Protestants was to begin in earnest.

Queen Mary sent word to the council that none of her subjects were to be burned without some of the council being present and a good sermon being preached. The council knew what her wishes were and made preparations to carry them out.

Chancellor Gardiner opened a high court at St. Mary Overy, on the Southwork side of London Bridge for the heretic trials. In the course of the next three years more than three hundred people were burned alive, because of their religious convictions.

> "In a book corrected, if not written, by Lord Burleigh in Queen Elizabeth's time, entitled *The Executions For Treason*, it is said four hundred persons suffered publicly in Queen Mary's reign, besides those who were secretly murdered in prison; of these, twenty were bishops and dignified clergymen, sixty were women."[*]

1555 A.D. LATIMER AND RIDLEY CITED TO APPEAR AT OXFORD BEFORE THE BISHOP OF LINCOLN

When they appeared before the bishop they were entreated to return to the Catholic faith, and to acknowledge the authority of the pope as the successor of Peter. Ridley answered the arguments of the bishop and vindicated the principles of the Reformation.

---

[*] *History of The Puritans*—Neal. Volume 1, Chapter 1, Page 64.

After a lengthy debate five indictments were brought against Ridley. He was charged with denying that the body of Christ was present in the sacrament at the altar, that the sacrament remained still the bread and wine, that the mass is no sacrifice for the living and dead, that such teachings were condemned as heretical and he must appear the following day at St. Mary's church to give an answer for his beliefs.

Latimer, too, was charged with the same heresies and his answers to the Bishop of Lincoln being unsatisfactory, he, too, was ordered to appear at Mary's at the same time with Ridley. When they refused to recant and return to the Roman Catholic Church, sentence of condemnation was pronounced against them, and they were delivered into the custody of the mayor for execution.

The place of execution was near Baliol College and when everything had been made ready, they were brought here to be burned. Ridley first entered the place, and seeing the cheerful look upon Latimer's face, he embraced him saying, "Be of good cheer, brother, for God will either assuage the fury of the flame or else strengthen us to abide it."

The smith then took a chain of iron, and brought it about their middles, and as he was knocking in the staples, Ridley took the chain in his hands and said to the smith, "Good fellow, knock it in hard, for the flesh will have its course."

A Mr. Shepside, a close relative, brought a bag of gunpowder and tied it about his neck. When Ridley asked what it was, he accepted it as sent of God and requested a bag for his fellow martyr. When this was supplied, a lighted fagot was then placed at Ridley's feet and Latimer called out to him, "Be of good comfort, Master Ridley, and play the man, we shall this day light such a candle by God's grace in England, as shall never be put out." When the flames swept toward Ridley he cried out, "Into thy hands, O Lord, I commend my spirit," and Latimer cried, "O Father of heaven, receive my soul."

Thus did these two teachers of God's word die for no other crime than proclaiming what they believed to be the truth.

Five days after this scene of suffering, Gardiner went to render his account at judgment for the cruelties he had inflicted upon others.

Multitudes of people were consigned to the flames at Smithfield in an effort to destroy the seed of the Reformation and restore Catholicism to England again. Cranmer, seeking to save his life, signed a document condemning the doctrines of Luther and Zwingli. Word of this was sent throughout all England, giving joy to the adherents of the church of Rome, but bringing grief to the Reformers.

Queen Mary was determined to put Cranmer to death for the part he had taken in writing out the bill of divorce for her father, Henry VIII, when he put away Catherine, the mother of Mary. Cranmer, suspecting that though he had recanted he would be burned, prepared a true confession of his faith which he carried to St. Mary's church where he heard the Archbishop preach his funeral sermon and conclude with a promise to say many masses for the repose of his soul.

When Cranmer was permitted to speak, he read his real confession and was led away to the stake to be burned.

> "After prayers and a sermon, Dr. Cole, the preacher of the day, required him to make a public confession of his faith before the people. This Cole did, expecting that he would declare himself a Roman Catholic. I will make a profession of my faith," said Cranmer, "and with a good will too." Then he arose before them all, and took from the sleeve of his robe a written prayer, and read it aloud. That done, he knelt and said the Lord's Prayer, all the people joining; and then he arose again, and told them he believed in the Bible; and that in what he had lately written, he had written what was not the truth; and that, because his right hand had signed those papers, he would burn his right hand first when he came to the fire. As for the pope, he did refuse him and denounce him, as the enemy of heaven. Hereupon the pious Dr. Cole cried out to the guards to stop that heretic's mouth and take him away.
>
> So they took him away and chained him to the stake, where he hastily took off his own clothes to make ready for the flames. And he stood before the people with a bald head and a white and flowing beard. He was so firm now when the worst was come, that he again declared against his recantation and was so impressive and so undismayed, that a certain lord, who was one of the directors of the execution, called out to his men to make haste. When the fire was lighted, Cranmer, true to his latest word, stretched out his right hand, and crying out, "This hand hath offended!" held it among the flames until it blazed and burned away. His heart was found entire among his ashes, and he left at last a memorable name in English history. Cardinal Pole celebrated the day by saying his first mass; and the next day he was made Archbishop of Canterbury in Cranmer's place."*

Philip of Spain, now wearied of England and of the queen, departed for Flanders. The queen spent most of her time in writing him letters which he never bothered to answer. The more he neglected her the more effort she put forth to try to win him back.

---

* *History of England*—Dickens. Chapter 30, Page 254.

1558 A.D. "BLOODY" QUEEN MARY DIES

On November 17, Mary died in the forty-third year of her life and the sixth year of her reign. Cardinal Pole died the next day. When Mary's death was announced in Parliament, which was in session, the members shouted for joy and cried out, "God save Queen Elizabeth." When the news spread through the land that Mary was dead, great crowds of people went to Hatfield where Princess Elizabeth was then residing and escorted her in triumph to London. Elizabeth showed no resentment toward those who had contributed to her suffering. Those who held to the Reformed faith were anxious to know how they were to be treated. Queen Elizabeth proceeded with great caution and soon restored the religion which existed at the time of King Edward's death.

She was crowned at Westminster Abbey and returned to the Tower of London to take up her residence. When she expressed a desire to enter in through the Traitor's Gate she was told that she need not do that, but she said, "What was good enough for Elizabeth, the Princess, is good enough for Elizabeth, the Queen." Elizabeth had conformed to the rites of the Roman Catholic Church for her own safety, but now she was free to show her preference for the Protestant religion. She restored the Book of Common Prayer and made the reformed practices of the Church of England the state religion, but renounced the title "The Head of the Church." Lord Burleigh became her chief minister and one of the most important persons during the long reign of Elizabeth.

The first Parliament in Elizabeth's reign convened in 1559 and the question of religion was the first to be considered.

The course she purposed to pursue was revealed to the people. She proposed a complete separation from the Roman Catholic Church. The church in England, was to be national in character and under the direct supervision of the crown. All laws of a religious nature passed during the reign of Queen Mary were repealed and the church returned to the state it occupied under the reign of Edward VI. The Catholic religion was prohibited by law. Elizabeth knew, that to the Roman Catholic Church, she would always be regarded as an illegitimate child, for the marriage of her father, Henry VIII, to Anne Boleyn was held to be invalid. A refusal to take the queen as the "supreme governor" of the church was punishable by death. Most of the bishops appointed during the reign of Mary were relieved of their office. Pope Pius V published a bull declaring the queen illegitimate and a usurper of the throne of England. The only result this edict produced in England was to make the laws against Catholicism more strict and the enforcement of them more certain.

"Her idea was to make England independent of all earthly powers, raise the nation to a proud eminence, and bestow prosperity and happiness upon her people. This policy was her religion and the essence of her life. Government was an art; conscience often gave way to wily diplomacy, and the end was made to justify the means. One of her first acts was to inform the pope of her accession. He replied that she had no right to the throne, for England was in vassalage to him. 'Great Harry's daughter' recalled her minister instantly from the papal court, left papal insolence to discover its vanity, and soon was counted with Coligny and William the Silent, in the trio of champions who resisted the papal leagues, and with divine help, saved Protestantism in Europe.

By the will of the queen, and the votes of Parliament, the Church in England ceased to be Roman, and became Protestant. The old prelacy was continued in the new Anglicanism. Nowhere else was there a more national church. The creed and liturgy were brought into the forms which have been scarcely changed since, the sources and tests of doctrine, polity, and discipline were to be the canonical Scriptures and the first four General Councils. The queen was not the visible head of the church, but the supreme governor. She insisted upon the obedience of the bishops to her will, and uniformity of public prayers and administration of sacraments, and other rites and ceremonies.

Her political servants enforced the oath of supremacy. Her bishops and all the clergy must put in force the act of uniformity."*

Thus England again became a Protestant nation. In the reign of Henry VIII England was first a Catholic nation, later it became a Protestant nation and continued as such under the reign of Edward VI. At the ascension of Mary to the throne of England a change was again made and England was reunited with the Roman Catholic Church. When Princess Elizabeth became queen, the nation again became a Protestant nation.

These changes were accompanied with intrigue, deception, and bloodshed, but at last the Church of England stands forth as a leader in Protestantism.

---

* *History of The Christian Church*—Blackburn. Chapter 20, Pages 520, 521.

CHAPTER 13

THE WORK OF JOHN CALVIN

The Reformation in Switzerland under John Calvin had its beginning in the University of Paris. There one Jacques le Fevre lectured to a group of students upon Paul's letter to the Roman brethren. Among those who were drawn closely to their teacher was William Farel. As he learned the truth of God's word, he began to speak his convictions. The study of the Bible aroused the ire of the theological faculty who charged them with heresy and they were forced to flee for their lives. Bishop Briconnet of Meaux, who was familiar with the lack of spirituality among the clergy of Rome, invited Le Fevre, Farel, and others to assist in a reformation of his diocese. Here they carried on their work for three years, teaching the people to lead pure lives, to reject the evils of Romanism and to learn something of God's word.

The city of Meaux might have become a center of the Reformation, but for the persecution that was directed against those who saw the necessity for a reform. The Sorbonnists launched a crusade which deprived the bishop of his office, silenced the presses, filled the dungeons, and made martyrs of those who had assisted in the work.

Farel escaped to Basel where he had thousands of New Testaments printed and sent back into France. Shortly after this, John Calvin began his work as a reformer. His condemnation of folly and vice, his sobriety of mind, and his devotion to study won for him the respect and affection of his teachers at the University of Paris.

His father, becoming alarmed at the teachings of Calvin, which seemed to border on heresy, ordered him to take up the study of law. In compliance, he went to Orleans to attend the lectures of celebrated doctors of the law, becoming so proficient that he was often called upon to teach in their stead. He became acquainted with Melchior Wolmar, who taught him Greek and implanted in his mind the principles of the Reformation. He became absorbed in the study of the Bible, held many meetings in private homes, and preached to groups of inquirers in the surrounding villages.

He was greatly influenced in this work by his uncle, Peter Olivetan, who was the first Protestant to translate the Bible into the French language. Calvin again returned to Paris where his friend, Nicholas Cop, had been elected as rector of the University of Paris. Calvin helped him prepare his inaugural address, which in reality was a defense of the doctrines of the reformers. When it was learned that the address was the work of Calvin, an investigation was launched by Parliament in an effort to crush the doctrines advocated by the heretic. When an effort was made to apprehend him, he escaped from them by disguising himself as a vine dresser.

In Navarre he met the aged Le Fevre, who gave him his blessing and predicted that Calvin would yet shake France to its foundations by sending into it a theology that would bring about a Reformation within the papal church.

1535 A.D. CALVIN LEAVES FRANCE FOR SWITZERLAND

When it was no longer safe for him to remain in France, he visited Noyon for the last time, disposed of his home there, and with his brother and sister departed for the safety of Switzerland.

Arriving in Geneva, he came into contact with Farel who had been preaching the principles of the Reformation at Neuchatel, Berne and Briburg, and pleading for a restoration of the religion of Christ. Farel begged Calvin to remain in Geneva and assist in the work of the reformation there, but Calvin told of his desire to go to Germany for further study. Farel pleaded, argued, and begged Calvin to remain there to assist in the work of the Reformation in Geneva. When it seemed that his words had no effect upon Calvin, Farel told him the judgment of God would surely rest upon him if he left Geneva. Calvin afterward said that it seemed that the hand of the God of heaven rested upon him and he was afraid to leave. Calvin became a lecturer at a small salary in the cathedral where large audiences assembled every day. The council that employed him was pleased to know that he was moderate in his teaching, asking the people to believe only what was proved by the Scriptures.

Farel's Confession of Faith, which Calvin helped to prepare, was accepted by the council of Geneva. It did not include the five points which afterward were proclaimed as the foundation principles of Calvin's theology. This confession was not intended as a creed for the clergy, but as a bond by which the people would be united. Its purpose was to enlighten and strengthen, to make the church "a body of true believers." One of the articles of that confession stated "it to be expedient that all manifest idolators, blasphemers, murderers, thieves, seditious persons, strikers, and drunkards, after they had been duly admonished, if they amend not, should be separated from the communion of the faithful, till their repentance has become apparent."

Calvin attempted to bring all people to one faith and to make Switzerland a Christian nation, requiring all citizens to accept the principles of the confession. Calvin, Beza, and Farel contended that the Lord's supper should not be administered to those whose wicked lives showed that they did not belong to the Lord's body. Their request to admonish those whose conduct was wicked was refused by the council. This resulted in ridicule and abuse being heaped upon them. Groups of men who frequented taverns and ridiculed holy things paraded through the streets, taunting the reformers and bragging of their admission to the Lord's supper.

Calvin offered to leave the disposition of the matter to a general synod, but the council of the city refused and ordered that the Lord's supper should be administered to all, informing Calvin and his associates that if they refused they would be forbidden to preach. They did refuse and some of the reformers preached and the result was that Calvin, Farel, and others were ordered to leave the city, not because of an infraction of the social laws, but because they wanted to guard the Lord's supper from wicked people who gambled, became drunk, and lived immoral lives. Farel returned to Neuchatel and Calvin and several of his associates went to Strasburg, Germany. Here he became a professor of theology, lecturing daily to large groups of students on the Scriptures.

He revised the French Bible of his uncle, Peter Olivetan, and prepared a treatise on the Lord's supper which was praised by Luther. He and Melancthon labored together for the union of all Protestants. He willingly and gladly subscribed to the Augsburg Confession of Faith. He became the teacher of over a thousand French exiles, whom he organized into a church with a presbyterian form of government. Its elders and deacons met with Calvin every week for prayer, advice, and Bible study.

When it was impossible for Calvin to preach, one of the elders took his place. Calvin kept in touch with the remnant of his followers in Geneva, where persecution was more bitter. When the council of Geneva tired of the lawlessness and rioting, Perrin, one of its members, was ordered "to find means by which he could bring back Master Calvin."

1541 A.D. JOHN CALVIN RETURNS TO GENEVA

For one year the council pleaded and promised before Calvin would consent to return. He informed the council that the church must have a government such as the ancient church had as authorized by the word of God. He maintained that the Geneva church was not a union of several churches, but it was one church, composed of several congregations. No other reformer had yet suggested following the divine plan of church government, nor had any advocated the idea of one church.

The condition of the city and of the church in Geneva is revealed in the following account.

> "Bernard Ochino, an Italian reformer and refugee from persecution, wrote, in 1542: 'In Geneva where I am at present residing, excellent Christians are daily preaching the pure word of God. It is constantly read, expounded, and openly discussed, and every one may propound what the Holy Spirit suggests to him, just as it was in the early church. On Sundays the catechism is explained and the young and the ignorant taught. Cursing and swearing, . . . impure lives, so common in other places where I have lived are unknown here. Gambling is rare; benevolence so great that the poor need not beg; lawsuits have ceased; no simony, murder or party spirit; but only peace and charity. No organs here, no noise of bells, no showy songs, no burning candles (as at mass), no relics, pictures, statues, farces, nor cold ceremonies.' "*

1523 A.D. THE BEGINNING OF THE REFORMATION IN THE NETHERLANDS

The Netherlands or Low Countries were traversed by the Rhine and the Scheldt rivers and the labor of the people to keep the river beds from silting up and overflowing the adjacent land developed an industrious and reliant people.

The commerce of the nation brought a great amount of wealth to the cities of this small country. Years before the open break between Luther and the Roman Catholic church, religious liberty was granted to those who came from other countries. The clergy of the church of Rome never attained much power in the larger cities, and even in the rural districts there was an anti-clerical spirit among the people.

Charles V was the Count of Holland, the King of Spain and the Emperor of Germany when the Reformation began. The Edict of Worms, by which Luther, his writings and all who sympathized with him were put under a ban, while ineffectual in Germany, was enforced with severity in the Netherlands. Religious gatherings were prohibited and the writings of those who wrote against the Roman Catholic Church condemned.

> "Even Charles V had been nearly as severe against the new doctrines in the Netherlands as in Spain, and this had given great dissatisfaction. But between 1520 and 1530, the spread of heresy had not been very great. The first measure which had been taken against Reformation was the promulgation of the Edict of Worms,

---

* *History of The Christian Church*—Blackburn. Chapter 18, Page 450.

and the placing of all books, teaching, teachers, and confessors of the new doctrine under an interdict, and this law was carried out with sanguinary severity. In 1522 some reform movements had taken place among the Augustine Order at Brussels, and the culprits were at once seized and burnt. For years, the most cruel sentences had been pronounced upon apostates, and at the close of Charles' reign the number of those who, often on frivolous charges, had been strangled, burnt, beheaded, or buried alive, was by some, among them Hugo Grotius, set down as one hundred thousand; and by none at less than fifty thousand. The spirit of the imperial sentences, the notorious "edicts" is best seen from that of the 25th of November 1550, which Charles proclaimed in the elation of his triumph at Augsburg, and in which all the previous ones were summed up.

The next step was to repeat an edict of October 24, 1529, in which it was forbidden to print, copy, multiply, keep, conceal, buy, sell or give away any work of Martin Luther, Oecolampadius, Zwingli, Bucer, Calvin, or any other heretic. It was forbidden to destroy, or in any way injure, any image of the Virgin Mary or any canonized saint; to hold or attend any heretical conventicle; and the laity were admonished that they were neither to read the Scriptures nor to take part in any discussions or controversies respecting them, under pain of a variety of barbarous punishments. Such miscreants were to be put to death as disturbers of the public peace and order by the following methods; the men by the sword, the women to be buried alive—if they recanted; but if they are obstinate, they are to be burnt; in either case all of their property is to be confiscated.

He who omitted to accuse persons suspected of heresy, gave them shelter, food, fuel, or clothing was to be regarded as a heretic himself."*

1555 A.D. ABDICATION OF CHARLES V IN FAVOR OF PHILIP II

The efforts of Charles to overthrow the Reformation had failed, so he resolved to turn the work of restoring the authority of the papal power over to his son Philip. The efforts of Philip to crush the Reformation were likewise to meet with failure, although he did keep Europe in a state of suspense over a period of years. Philip had taken up a residence in the Netherlands when his father turned the rulership of that country over to him. He purposed to personally conduct the work of crushing religious freedom in this part of his kingdom.

He learned that the whole Bible had been translated into the language of the people and that they were familiar with its message. He also discovered that the princes of Germany and those of the Netherlands were in constant communication with each other. These facts caused Philip to carefully prepare his plans for the extirpation of the heresy.

---

* *The Period of The Reformation*—Hausser. Chapter 22, Pages 299, 300.

To execute his plans and to carry out his instructions, he chose his half-sister Margaret of Parma, who was a stranger to the people of The Netherlands and Cardinal Granvella, a close friend.

Philip, knowing that thousands of Protestants had fled from his provinces, thought the measures of punishment had not been severe enough, and so increased the powers of the Inquisition and instructed the regent to give the officials of the state every aid in punishing the heretics.

To facilitate the discovery of heretics, fourteen new bishoprics were created in the Netherlands. The people protested that their charters prohibited the increase of the clergy except by their consent but no consideration was given to their objection. When the country was divided into fifteen bishoprics under three archbishops, of whom the Archbishop of Mechlin was to be chief, added impetus was given to the Protestant cause.

When a citizen was about to be punished by the ecclesiastical courts, he was rescued by the crowd of people who had assembled at the place of punishment. Disturbances were created at the mass and in some instances the churches were attacked and the images destroyed. To end the tension, Philip removed Cardinal Granvella but left the Inquisition to carry on the work of terrorism.

The Count of Egmont was selected to carry the protest of the nobles to Philip against the proclamation of the decrees of the Council of Trent in the Netherlands. It was believed the Count of Egmont could influence Philip, because he was a Catholic. Philip received the count, listened to the message that he conveyed, and ended the interview by assuring him that the complaints of the nobles would be attended to immediately. But Philip had no intention of keeping his word. Instead he sent word that the decrees of the Council of Trent should be proclaimed in every city of the Netherlands and the bloody work of the Inquisition carried on.

The effect upon the cities of the Netherlands was tragic. The commerce of the cities ended, manufacturing was suspended, and the country ruined.

Petitions addressed to the regent failed to bring relief to the people. When a large group met at a dinner to consider the course they should take, Count Brederode told how they had been called "Beggars" and suggested they adopt the name, at the same time strapping on the leather sack of the wandering beggar.

The name and the emblem of the beggars was adopted and soon lawyers, noblemen, peasants, and burghers were seen everywhere wearing the beggar's pouch. Soon large assemblies began to be held throughout the country.

Armed sentinels guarded the crowd as they listened to the preaching of excommunicated ministers. They read portions of the Bible to the people and expounded to them the truths they had longed to hear.

These crowds grew so large that even the Spanish soldiers who had been quartered in the cities did not dare to interfere with the services.

As the hatred of the people developed against the church which had caused the death of so many of their fellow citizens, the Roman Catholic Church buildings were attacked, the images, relics and pictures destroyed and the clergy ridiculed.

Other outbreaks caused the regent to promise that the Inquisition would be abolished and the religion of the Protestants tolerated.

Philip, enraged that his regent should have in any way departed from his policy of harsh punishment for the heretics, determined to punish the country and put all of the leaders to death.

The Prince of Orange fled to Germany when he learned of the purpose of the king. The Duke of Alva, who was a staunch Catholic and hated the Protestants, was devoted to Philip. He was instructed to take bloody revenge on the leaders of the disturbances and to compel people to become Catholics to save their lives. He was to extort the wealth of the nation for the support of the Spanish troops, sending what was not thus needed to the treasury of Spain in Madrid.

His army was brought together at Genoa and from there marched overland through Savoy, Burgundy, Lorraine, and Luxemburg into The Netherlands. His first act was to imprison count Egmont and Count Horn, both of whom had supported the king against the people.

The duke now organized a Council of Disturbances, which the people soon named the "Council of Blood." This council was to deal with all past offenses. The usual accusation was "conspiracy against God and the King." Anyone who had signed a petition calling for the relaxation of the Inquisition, who had opposed the creation of the new bishoprics, who had said that the king should regard the treaties with the people, was accused as a traitor and punished by being jailed or put to death. All who had not opposed the meetings of the Beggars, who had not resisted the desecration of the churches and the destruction of the images and relics were condemned as traitors. In three months the Council of Blood put eighteen hundred citizens to death. This course was followed for years by the representatives of the church that was supposed to be the Lord's church, sanctioned by members of that organization who claimed to be Christians, authorized by the head of the ecclesiastical hierarchy whose headquarters were in Rome.

The "Beggars" were not put down by such atrocities. They marched through the country under the cover of darkness, eluding the Spanish troops, robbing monasteries, and spoiling churches.

Louis, the brother of the Prince of Orange, entered Friesland and successfully defended it against the Spanish troops for a time. The Duke of Alva now marched against the Protestant troops under Louis, but before leaving Brussels he ordered the execution of twenty noblemen, among them the Duke of Egmont and the Duke of Horn. The patriotic troops of Louis were no match for the trained soldiers of Spain, who drove them out of the Netherlands.

William of Orange recruited an army in Germany and entered the Netherlands for the purpose of engaging the Duke of Alva in battle, but the duke, learning that he was facing a superior force, kept away from an open conflict until the approach of winter compelled William of Orange to disband his army.

The Prince of Orange had up to this time been a Catholic. His patriotism rather than his religious motives had prompted him to oppose the policy of the Roman Catholic Church in the Netherlands.

Now, while he was banished from his homeland and while his country's cause seemed hopeless, he became a Protestant. He now set out to organize the sailors and the sea-traders into a marine force to prey upon Spanish shipping.

The Sea Beggars, as they came to be known, kept alive the national spirit of the people. They moved against the Spaniards on both the land and sea. They soon occupied Brill, one of the keys of the Netherlands, and from here they began a systematic attack against the cities under the control of the Duke of Alva. These attacks were successful and soon many of the towns along the coasts were in the hands of the "Sea Beggars." They invited the Prince of Orange to become the Stadtholder of the Netherlands. He was in France when the information came that Holland and Zeeland had also declared for him as Stadtholder. He entered the country disguised as a peasant, passing through the lines of the Spanish soldiers. His first act was to call a meeting at Dort where a new constitution was prepared. The provinces agreed to accept his leadership and to carry out his plans. He proclaimed religious freedom for Catholics and Protestants alike. A new army was raised and William captured a number of cities and was ready to move against Brussels. Admiral Coligny of France had promised to aid William in driving the Spanish from the Netherlands.

In the midst of his military victories the news of Coligny's death and the massacre of the French Huguenots on St. Bartholomew's Day reached William. Lacking the aid of the French, William had to disband his army and wait for a more opportune time to move against the Duke of Alva. The towns which had surrendered to William, Prince of Orange, were now seized by the Duke. His vengeance was satisfied only by burning every house and killing all of the inhabitants. All of the Dutch soldiers were murdered in cold blood. The citizens were tied together, back to back, and thrown into the lakes and rivers. It seemed to be the policy of the Catholics to kill all who were known to be Protestants.

The nation of sailors, fishermen, and shop-keepers, who had so long endured these indignities, now rose in revolt and determined to drive the Spanish soldiers from their land. The opposition became too great for the Duke of Alva and he requested that he be relieved. King Philip of Spain sent Don Louis Requescens to replace the duke, who suggested to his successor that he burn every town where he could not garrison his troops. When Don Louis promised to repeal the taxes, dissolve the Council of Blood, and grant amnesty to the people, he found that the Dutch had little confidence in Spanish promises. While negotiations were going on, Don Louis died and that brought confusion to the Spanish cause and the army began to mutiny because their pay had not been received.

The city of Antwerp suffered from the brutality and licentiousness of the soldiers, and while the mutiny was in progress, William of Orange moved into the city of Ghent and called a congress of the representatives of both the Northern and Southern provinces of the Netherlands, in an effort to unite them together.

1579 A.D. ALEXANDER OF PARMA WAS APPOINTED STADTHOLDER BY PHILIP OF SPAIN

In this same year Holland, Zeeland, Guelders, Zutphen, Utrecht, Overyssel, and Groningen sent representatives to a conference at Utrecht where they framed the Treaty of Utrecht, which outlined the constitution of the United Provinces. Two years later they threw off the Spanish yoke and a treaty of peace was arranged in 1609, which gave the Dutch their independence and by which they became a great Protestant power.

During the years of persecution the Dutch Protestants were able to organize themselves into a church and publish a confession of faith. Each group of Protestants contended for the principles of the Reformation as they had received them. Some of them had learned the principles of the Reformation from Luther, others had obtained their teaching from Zwingli, while some had gained their knowledge of the Reformation from Calvin.

The doctrine of Calvin gradually pushed the doctrine of Luther and Zwingli aside, and the Netherlands became Calvinistic in doctrine and discipline, being known as the Dutch Reformed Church.

1546 A.D. THE BEGINNING OF THE REFORMATION IN SCOTLAND

The Reformation in Scotland was closely connected with the life of John Knox, who was born in 1505 and died in 1572. John Knox was said to have attended the University of Glasgow. The date of his ordination to the priesthood is not definitely known. It is supposed to have been some time prior to 1544, for by this time we find that he had embraced the cause of the Protestants and was assisting the Scotch reformer, George Wishart.

Wishart had preached in various parts of Scotland and had influenced many against the papal church. He was arrested at the order of Cardinal Beaton, tried for heresy, and ordered to be burned. Cardinal Beaton watched his sufferings and anguish from the castle of the Archbishop of St. Andrews. Not long after the death of Wishart, the Cardinal was murdered by the friends of Wishart, who were influenced by hatred of his cruelty. This was an act of rebellion against the Roman Catholic Church in Scotland.

John Knox was not a party to this crime, but he expressed no sorrow for the act. The ones responsible for the crime took refuge in the castle of St. Andrews and Knox was invited to join them. He complied with their request after some hesitation and became pastor of the parish church in town. Here he vigorously upheld the doctrines of the Reformation which he had learned from Wishart. This castle was held for several months but was finally captured by a French fleet in July of 1547 and the leaders of the rebellion were taken to France to be punished. Among them was John Knox, who was sentence to serve as a galley slave for two years.

1549 A.D. KNOX BECOMES A CHAPLAIN TO EDWARD VI

After his release, Knox went to England where he was cordially received by Cranmer. Here he was offered the bishopric of Rochester, which he refused because he was not completely satisfied with the principles of the Reformation in England. Knox returned to Switzerland when Queen Mary came to the throne in England. Here he became a student of Calvin, remaining under his instruction for several years and assisting in the work of the Reformation there. After the death of Mary, Queen of England, he returned to Scotland and there he took a leading part in establishing the reformed religion.

"The church of Scotland acknowledges as its founder John Knox, the disciple of Calvin; and, accordingly, from its first reformation, it adopted the doctrine, rites and form of ecclesiastical government established at Geneva. These it has always adhered to with the utmost uniformity, and maintained with the greatest jealousy and zeal; so that even in the last century the designs of those who attempted to introduce certain changes into its discipline and worship were publicly opposed by the force of arms."*

While the attitude of Calvin toward sin and loose living is to be commended, there were other conditions connected with the Reformation in Switzerland that are not commendable. Calvin formed a theocracy in Geneva in which the church attempted to rule the state, during which time his rule became one of fear and hate.

An example of Calvin's intolerance is revealed in the trial and death of Michael Servetus, a Spaniard, who after spending some time in the study of law, took up the study of medicine and became one of the best physicians in France. He later lived with the Archbishop of Vienne, practicing his profession in that place. His unorthodox views upon the Trinity were responsible for his difficulties. His attitude toward those who differed with him was not conducive to friendship. He was convinced that he was the instrument of God for the restoration of truth to the world. He had entered into a discussion of his ideas with Calvin, who forwarded his letters to the Catholic Inquisition, in hopes that he might be apprehended and put to death. After being imprisoned in France, Servetus decided to seek a home in Italy. Passing through Switzerland, he reached Geneva on Sunday afternoon and decided that he would hear Calvin preach. He was recognized by Calvin and arrested before the services began. He was placed in prison until brought out for trial, without the benefit of a lawyer to plead his case. Calvin was his accuser and was responsible for his conviction. He was found guilty of heresy and was burned at the stake outside of the city on October 27, 1553.

The injustice of this act can be seen when it is recalled that Servetus was just a visitor in Geneva. None of his doctrines had been proclaimed in Geneva and therefore the government of the city had no legal right to arrest him and hold him for trial.

From Switzerland, Calvin's teaching spread into France and before his death there were thirty-six Reformed churches in France. The cause of the Protestants in France was greatly aided by Theodore Beza, who became one of the outstanding leaders of the Reformation. Because of his literary attainments, his natural ability as a teacher, and his gracious manners, he was able to reach people who were uninfluenced by either Luther or Calvin.

1559 A.D. FIVE POINTS OF CALVINISM

This year marked the beginning of the five main doctrines of religious belief developed by Calvin; the doctrine of election, of

---

* *Ecclesiastical History*—Mosheim. Volume 2, Part 2, Chapter 2, Page 105.

predestination, of a limited atonement, of total depravity and of the final perseverance of the saints. In this same year, John Knox and Whittingham finished the translation of the Geneva Bible and Knox returned to Scotland where he labored to establish the doctrines he had learned from John Calvin. After his arrival, he preached a strong sermon against idolatry at Perth and the city was soon purged of idolatry.

During this time Scotland was ruled by Mary, Queen Regent, widow of James V. Their daughter Mary Stuart had married Francis II, future King of France, and the ancient crown of Scotland was sent to France to be placed upon the head of Francis. Within a short time after the accession of Elizabeth to the English throne, Francis II of France and Mary assumed the title of King and Queen of England. They claimed the English throne through Margaret, the sister of Henry VIII, knowing the Roman Catholic Church did not recognize Elizabeth as the legitimate offspring of Henry. Mary, the Queen Regent, was worn out with the difficulties and responsibilities of trying to hold the kingdom in line for the Roman Catholic Church, and when the English fleet cut off her contact with France, she retired to the castle of Edinburgh where she died June 10, 1550.

1560 A.D. AN ACT AGAINST THE MASS

"In the Parliament held at Edinburgh, the tenth of July the year of God 1560, the said Parliament being continued to the first of August next thereafter following, with continuation of days, upon the twenty-fourth day of said month of August, the three estates being present. The which day, forasmuch as Almighty God by his most true and blessed word has declared the reverence and honor which should be given to him; and by his Son Jesus Christ has declared the true use of the sacraments, willing the same to be used according to his will and word; By the which it is perfectly known that the sacraments of baptism and of the body and blood of Jesus Christ, have been in all times bygone corrupted by the papistical Kirk, and by their usurped ministers; and presently, notwithstanding the Reformation already made according to God's word, yet none the less, there are some of the same pope's Kirk, that stubbornly persevere in their wicked idolatry, saying mass, and baptizing, conform to the pope's Kirk, profaning therethrough the sacraments foresaid, in quiet and secret places, regarding therethrough neither God nor the holy word. Therefore, it is statute and ordained in this present Parliament, that no manner of person nor persons, in any time coming, administer any of the sacraments foresaid secretly, or any other manner of way, but they that are admitted and having power to that effect, nor say mass, nor yet hear mass, nor be present thereat, under the pain of confiscation of all their goods (movable and immovable) and punishing of their bodies at the discretion of the Magistrates, within whose jurisdiction such persons happen to be apprehended, for the first fault; banish-

ing of the Realm, for the second fault; and justifying to the death
for the third fault. And ordains all Sheriffs, Stewards, Bailies, and
their deputies, Provosts, and Bailies of Burghs and other judges
whatsoever, within this Realm, to take diligent suit and inquisition
within their bounds where any such usurped ministry is used, Mass
saying or they that be present at the doing thereof, ratifying and
approving the same; and take and apprehend them, to the effect
that the pains above written may be executed upon them."

This and other acts of Parliament were designed to outlaw the
Roman Catholic Church in Scotland. At the same time another
act of Parliament was passed which ordained that the Bishop of
Rome would in time to come have no jurisdiction or authority
within the realm of Scotland. Information of these acts of Parliament was conveyed to the king and queen in France by Sir James
Sandilands for ratification, which was denied.

These acts and the policy and discipline of the Kirk revealed to
Queen Mary and her king what they might expect from their
subjects in Scotland.

The old church was thus outlawed and the foundations upon
which the new church was to build were not too secure.

There were Protestant ministers, but they were few in number,
and lacked the authority to remove the Catholic clergy from office.
On the first Sunday after Queen Mary returned from France, she
heard mass in her own chapel at Holyrood, and the clergyman who
officiated was threatened with death. John Knox took immediate
action against the attempt to restore the papal system of religion
by launching an attack upon the practice from his pulpit at St.
Giles. After his sermon Knox was summoned to an interview with
the queen and after the interview he said, "If there be not in her
a proud mind, a crafty wit, and an indurate heart against God and
his truth, my judgment faileth me."

1561 A.D. MARY, QUEEN OF SCOTS, A ROMAN CATHOLIC, ATTEMPTS TO RESTORE CATHOLICISM

She had returned from France to assume the responsibility of
ruling a Protestant nation. The General Assembly of the Protestant church recognized that an attempt would be made by such
papal representatives as remained in the land to restore the practices of the church of Rome and to control the nation. To prevent
the perpetuation of the Roman Catholic religion in Scotland, Parliament enacted laws abolishing that system of religion and accepting the Protestant Confession of Faith.

In this same year the followers of Calvin separated from the
Lutherans, forming the first division in the Protestant church.

Calvin's followers became known as the Reformed Church on the continent, but in England and Scotland they developed into the Presbyterian Church. In Holland they became known as the Dutch Reformed Church, while in France they became known as the Huguenots, a term of doubtful origin. The Huguenots became a strong political force in France and eventually included many of high rank and influence among whom were Prince Henry of Navarre, the Prince of Conde, and Admiral Coligny.

1562 A.D. ACTION OF THE GENERAL ASSEMBLY AGAINST PARISH PRIESTS

"Another meeting of the General Assembly took place in December, the same year, in which it continued steadily to advance in the course of reformation, and of what might be not inaptly termed self-construction. As many of the former parish priests continued to reside in their parishes, and, without any formal abjuration of property, pretended to act as parish ministers, the Assembly, to remedy this evil, prohibited from serving in the ministry all who had not satisfied the church of their soundness in the faith, and had not been examined and approved by the superintendent; and it was added, "This act to have strength as well against them that are called bishops, as others."*

A complete change from the teaching and practices of the Roman Catholic Church to Protestant Presbyterianism could not be effected at one step. Each change that was made was bitterly opposed by those who still hoped to bring Scotland again under the complete control of the papacy.

To combat the introduction of the mass, John Knox penned a letter calling for an assembly of the Church for the advancement of God's glory and the preservation of the Church. For sending forth this letter, he was called before the Council and a charge of treason made against him. The charge was allowed to rest following the defense of Knox, the Lords affirming that John Knox was within his right in calling an assembly of the Church.

1564 A.D. DEATH OF JOHN CALVIN AT GENEVA, SWITZERLAND —MAY 27, 1564

Calvin carried on an extensive correspondence with the religious leaders of Europe and continued to preach up until the time of his death. When he became so infirm that he could no longer sit in the assembly, the members of the group would assemble about his bed to hear his admonitions and instructions.

---

* *History of The Church of Scotland*—Hetherington. Chapter 3, Page 62.

1565 A.D. ARRIVAL OF LORD DARNLEY IN SCOTLAND

Within a brief period of time after Lord Darnley arrived, Queen Mary became his bride. This was a union in which both parties were Roman Catholics, which was a threat to the Protestants. It brought to an end the great influence that Lethington and Moray had over the queen, who now began to assert herself against both the ministers and the politicians.

The marriage, from which the queen had expected so much, soon proved to be a mistake. The reformers had objected to her marriage, but Mary had been charmed by the outward appearance of Darnley and had not bothered to consider the qualities of his mind. He proved himself to be fickle, insolent and ungrateful, and soon began to treat the queen with indifference and neglect.

She refused Darnley the crown, but took Riccio, her secretary, into her confidence, which aroused the jealousy and distrust of her husband. A plot was developed to get rid of Riccio and one evening while he was at supper with the queen and the ladies of her court, Darnley and a group of armed nobles rushed into the room and stabbed Riccio to death. Shortly after this, Lord Darnley became ill and the queen took him to her palace at Holyrood House and apparently was reconciled to him.

The location of the palace in Edinburgh, upon low ground, and the noise of the court made it necessary to move Lord Darnley to a more suitable location. The queen accompanied him and ministered to his daily wants. The marriage of one of the ladies of her court took her away from Lord Darnley, and that night the residence was blown up with a great charge of gun powder, killing Lord Darnley.

There was no doubt in the minds of the people that the death of Darnley was by design. The Earl of Bothwell, who had now become an advisor to the queen, was suspected of being involved in the murder of Darnley. He was tried for murder, but was acquitted for no one was willing to appear against him as a witness. Shortly after this, Queen Mary gave the Earl her hand in marriage. The reformers believed that the murder of Darnley had been committed with the knowledge and consent of the queen. The whole country now rose in arms against her and she was captured and taken to Locklevin Castle, where she was compelled to abdicate as queen in favor of her infant son, who was crowned James VI. The Earl of Murray, the half brother of Mary, was appointed regent of the kingdom. Mary secured her release from the castle, raised an army and met the royal forces of the infant king under Murray at Langside, where her troops were completely routed. Mary watched the battle from a neighboring hill and when she saw that her troops were defeated she fled from the field, not stopping until she came to the banks of the river which separated England from Scotland.

The Bishop of St. Andrews begged her to turn back but she was unwilling to endure the insults of her own subjects, preferring to place herself under the protection of Elizabeth, the queen of England.

These events removed some of the obstacles in the way of the growth of the Protestants in Scotland. As the strength of the Reformation grew, forms of worship, doctrines, and practices of the church of Rome were prohibited. The sign of the cross in baptizing and kneeling at the Lord's table were forbidden, and holy days abolished. The strife that later developed in Scotland caused John Knox to retire to Saint Andrews to escape death, and there in the church where he had begun his work, he preached his last sermon.

1572 A.D. THE DEATH OF JOHN KNOX

The great reformer felt that his work was at an end. He returned to Edinburgh and died on November 24. A great concourse attended his funeral and when his body was lowered into the grave it was said, "There lies he who never feared the face of man."

The doctrines advocated by John Knox were the doctrines developed by John Calvin in Switzerland. Calvin, an honest and sincere seeker for the truth came to the conclusion that God did not intend for every person to be saved, that he had predestinated or chosen the ones who would be saved and also selected the ones to be lost.

> "Predestination we call the eternal decree of God, by which he has determined in himself, what he would have to become of every individual of mankind. For they are not all created with a similar destiny; but eternal life is fore-ordained for some, and eternal damnation for others. Every man, therefore, being created for one or the other of these ends, we say, he is predestinated either to life or death."*

This teaching is further expressed in these words—"God has predestinated and ordained some men and angels to everlasting death and the number is so certain and definite that it cannot be increased or diminished."—*Westminster Confession of Faith*—Article 2, Chapter 10.

While it is true that these reformers were not able to make a complete return to the gospel of Jesus Christ and to the church established by the apostles of our Lord, yet they did much to pave the way for a return to the teaching of God's word. The doctrine of

---

* *Institutes of The Christian Religion*—John Calvin. Volume 2, Book 3, Chapter 21. Page 145.

predestination is opposed by the teaching of the Scriptures. "For the grace of God that bringeth salvation hath appeared to all men. . . ."[1] "For this is good and acceptable in the light of God our Savior; who will have all men to be saved, and to come unto the knowledge of the truth."[2]

Among the other doctrines developed by Calvin and Knox was the doctrine of the eternal security of the saints, that once a person is saved he can not so sin as to fall away to be lost. These two reformers were also advocates of the doctrine of total depravity, that every soul is born into the world in a state of sin. While these men were searching for the truth, they did not make a complete return to the teaching of God's word upon all points of doctrine. While the followers of John Calvin and John Knox today accept sprinkling, pouring and immersion as baptism, Calvin taught that baptism was a burial.

"The very word "baptize" signifies to immerse and it is certain that immersion was the practice of the early church."*

Calvin taught that the church in the New Testament age was under the jurisdiction of the elders or the presbytery and from this form of church government the church of Scotland took its name.

1. Titus 2 : 11.
2. 1 Timothy 2 : 3, 4.
* *Institutes of The Christian Religion*—Calvin. Book 4, Chapter 15.

"A dreadful and inevitable death presented itself in every shape. Some were shot on the roofs of houses, others were cast out of the windows. Some were cast into the water, and knocked on the head with blows of iron bars or clubs; some were killed in their beds, some in the garrets, others in cellars; wives in the arms of their husbands, husbands on the bosoms of their wives; sons at the feet of their fathers. They neither spared the aged, nor women great with child, nor even infants. It is related, that a man was seen to stab one of them, who played with the beard of its murderer, and that a troop of boys dragged another, in its cradle, into the river. The streets were paved with the bodies of the dead or the dying; the gateways were blocked up with them. There were heaps of them in the squares; the small streams were filled with blood, which flowed in fresh torrents into the river. Finally, to sum up in a few words what took place in those three days, six hundred houses were repeatedly pillaged, and four thousand persons massacred with all the confusion and barbarity that can be imagined."

History of France—Mezerai

CHAPTER 14

MASSACRE OF THE HUGUENOTS

1572 A.D. SAINT BARTHOLOMEW'S MASSACRE

The doctrines of the Reformation had exerted a great influence upon the people of France. Le Fevre, Farel, and Calvin had laid the foundation for a new system of religion in France. The church of Rome had fallen into disrepute because of the deficiencies of their pastors. It was said that they "took delight in worldly pleasures, and spent the greater part of the day in taverns, drinking and gambling." The publication of Calvin's "Institutes of the Christian Religion" became a text for those who were seeking spiritual enlightenment. Men of education, artisans, tradesmen, and the land owners were those who were first attracted to the teaching of the reformers.

After the accession of Charles IX, who was only eleven years old, the Huguenots gained in favor with the members of the king's court and with the people. The king's mother, with the approval of the council of State, assumed the authority, though not the title of regent. The favors shown to the Huguenots were a source of irritation to the Catholics.

Some who learned that Coligny and Conde, outstanding leaders among the Huguenots, ate meat in Lent were greatly shocked.

The Archbishop Montluc openly taught that it was not wrong to pray to God in French and that the Scriptures ought to be translated into the common tongue of the people.

The queen-mother Catherine de Medici, received the Protestant leaders with favor and appeared to be seeking after the truth. Others complained of the toleration that was shown to the Huguenot ministers who daily preached in the halls of St. Germain and Fontainebleau.

Beza, a leader among the reformers, preached in the hotel of the Prince of Conde and in the royal palace. Some of the clergy of the church of Rome adopted the doctrine and practices of the Huguenots and called for a reform in the Roman Catholic Church. It seemed that France was at the beginning of a great change and if Catherine had been sincere in her interest in the Protestant cause the future of France would have been altogether different.

The Protestants believed her to be sincere in her desire to know more of their cause and they exhorted her to but say "the word and Christ would be worshipped in truth and purity throughout the kingdom." But that word was not forthcoming.

To the south of France was the kingdom of Navarre, a land of deep valleys and towering cliffs. To the members of the French court its annexation was deemed very important. This country was ruled by Jeanne d'Albret, a Protestant. Her husband was a Catholic. They had one son, Henry, who later became Henry IV of France. The friction between the Catholics and the Protestants had now become so great that Anthony of Bourbon, the Duke of Vendome, the husband of Queen Jeanne of Navarre, had left the kingdom of Navarre to place himself at the head of the Catholic army.

That France and Navarre might be united, Catherine de Medici planned to arrange a marriage between her daughter Margaret, the sister of Charles IX, and Henry, the Prince of Navarre. This was the age in which young ladies, whether of high or low position, had but little to say in the choice of a husband.

Margaret seemed willing to comply with the desires of her mother and so the arrangements for the marriage went forward. Admiral Coligny, believing that the cause of the Protestants would be strengthened by such a union wrote to the Queen of Navarre saying, "It will be a seal of friendship with the king; and the greatest mistake you could fall into will be to show suspicion." Catherine now wrote to the Queen of Navarre inviting her to come to Blois for a visit, saying "I pray you gratify the extreme desire we have to see you among us. You will be loved and honored as you deserve to be."

The queen arrived at Blois early in March and gay parties and balls followed each other in swift succession, in honor of her royal majesty. These were not altogether pleasing to the queen, for her Calvinistic training and sober taste did not appreciate such frivolity.

The queen wrote to her son, Henry, during her stay at Blois, "Madame Margaret has paid me every honor and welcome in her power to bestow, and frankly owned to me the agreeable ideas she has formed of you. With her beauty and wit, she excites great influence over the queen-mother and the king."

"If the marriage of Henry and Margaret was part of the scheme by which the Huguenots were to be lured to their destruction, there was very little probability in March, 1572, that it would ever be accomplished. Even the mere rumor of it had aroused all the antagonism of Spain and Rome; but now that it appeared certain, those powers tried by every means to thwart it. The pope ordered his nephew, then legate at the court of Portugal, to hasten to France and stop the marriage. Alessandro actually reached Blois before the Queen of Navarre, having rudely passed her on the road. The cardinal, one of the most accomplished and eloquent men of his day, pressed the king to give Margaret to the King of Portugal, as had been once proposed, and enter into the holy alliance then forming against the Turks. The connection between these proposals is not very clear; but Alessandro probably hoped that the excitement of war, which might bring increase of territory to France, would divert Charles from subjects nearer home. 'It would be ruinous to your realm and to the Catholic church,' urged the nuncio, 'to form any alliance with the Huguenots.' "*

The difference in the religious beliefs of the contracting parties was the chief hindrance to the nuptial arrangements. Catherine de Medici pretended to hesitate to persuade her daughter to contract a marriage with a Protestant, and Jeanne of Navarre was equally doubtful of the advisability of such a union, professing to see danger on every hand. The Huguenot ministers were not enthusiastic over the proposed union, some professing to see nothing but danger to the cause of the Protestants by such an alliance. At length the negotiations were finished, the marriage contract drawn up and signed by the representatives on both sides (April 11, 1572). The only obstacle now to the wedding was the dispensation which Pope Pius V refused to grant: "I would rather lose my head than grant a marriage dispensation to a heretic." Charles wrote a letter to the pope expressing his love for the Roman Catholic Church, but also informing the pope that the lack of a dispensation would not be allowed to delay the wedding.

On the sixth of May, Queen Jeanne left Blois for Paris in preparation for the marriage that was to unite the Catholics and the Reformers. She accepted the hospitality of the Bishop of Chartres, who had been excommunicated from the See of Rome for his liberal opinions. Within a short time after her arrival she became ill and her attendants believed that she had been poisoned.

She died on June 9, and Prince Henry now became the King of Navarre. The queen's death further aroused the suspicion of the Huguenots. From every quarter Admiral Coligny was urged to be on his guard. The people of La Rochelle sent him a warning urging him not to place himself within the power of so treacherous a person as Catherine de Medici. These warnings he rejected, saying, "I confide in the sacred word of his Majesty, the king." When the Admiral entered the palace he was greeted by the king who threw his arms about him saying, "This is the happiest day of my life."

On the eighth of July, Henry, now King of Navarre, entered

---

* *The Massacre of St. Bartholomew*—White. Chapter 10, Page 346.

Paris attended by the Prince of Conde, the Cardinal of Bourbon, Admiral Coligny, and a train of nobles. The officials of the city met him and escorted him to the Louvre, the royal palace of the king. The wedding day had been set for the tenth of June but the difficulties about the papal dispensation, and the illness and death of the queen of Navarre had caused the wedding to be delayed. Final arrangements were made for it to be solemnized on the eighteenth of August. The betrothal was to be solemnized the day before at the palace of the king, to be followed by a supper and ball, after which the bride was to be conducted to the home of the Bishop of Paris where she and her ladies were to spend the night.

It was customary for the daughter of a king to be married at the Cathedral of Notre Dame. For this purpose a raised platform with a pavilion had been constructed on the great plaza in front of the Cathedral. Every roof, window, and balcony was filled with spectators awaiting the wedding procession. First came the archbishops, and then the cardinals, followed by officers of the state, then came the king and the Princess Margaret. Standing before the Bishop of Paris, Henry received the hand of his bride and the nuptial oath was administered.

After the marriage ceremony Henry escorted his bride into the Cathedral of Notre Dame to hear mass and then withdrew with Conde, the admiral, and other of the nobility, passing the time walking about the grounds beneath the shadows of its venerable towers. The marriage was followed by days of festivities which prevented the admiral from returning home. There were matters of state which Coligny desired to discuss with King Charles of France. But Charles was so much occupied with the receptions that he had no time to consider other affairs. The king requested a few days more for relaxation, promising that he would then grant Coligny a conference.

A delegation from the Huguenot churches had matters they wanted to discuss with the admiral, so he was persuaded to remain in Paris for a few days more.

After the conclusion of the promised conference, Coligny was returning to his hotel in company with two of his friends when bullets from an assassin's gun pierced his body. His friends took him to his apartment where his wounds were dressed. When word of this attempt upon the life of Coligny spread through the city, the Protestants were amazed. They now realized they had been lured into a trap. That very evening a large group of Huguenot gentlemen paraded through the streets to the Louvre shouting defiance, flourishing their swords, and discharging their pistols. When they were admitted into the king's presence, they demanded justice, threatening to take the matter into their own hands if their request was denied.

Henry of Navarre hastened to the bedside of his friend, and the king and the queen expressed their resentment toward those responsible for the crime. While Henry was visiting with Admiral Coligny, Charles and his mother, Catherine de Medici, were debating whether Henry should be included among those who were to be put to death. The decision was that he should be allowed to live because he would be powerless after all of his followers were put to death.

The Duke of Guise had been entrusted with the responsibility of directing the massacre. He had stationed his troops throughout the city instructing them to wait until they heard the bell in Saint Germain's Church begin to toll, which was to be the signal for the slaughter to begin. Charles had been persuaded that his own life would be in danger if he did not order the execution of the Huguenots, and being convinced of his own danger, gave his consent for the murder of the Protestants.

Suddenly the bell of St. Germain began to toll. The first stroke of the bell had not died away when the sound of the musketry announced that the massacre had begun. Beacon lights signaled the beginning of the slaughter in other cities. The Duke of Guise commissioned his soldiers to carry out the death of Coligny.

They forced an entrance into his apartment and as they were coming up the stairs he counseled his friends to escape over the house tops. When the soldiers burst into his room they found the admiral engaged in prayer. When he admitted his identity, a soldier thrust his sword into his body and the others fell upon him each seeking to have a part in the death of the victim. When the duke inquired whether or not they had carried out their mission, the body of the great religious leader was thrust out of the window.

The duke looked upon his features and said, "Yes, that is he," and giving the body a vicious kick, he urged his soldiers to continue the work they had begun. A group of Huguenots fled into the courtyard of the Louvre, appealing to the king for protection. He sent his own body guard into the courtyard to put them to death.

The houses which had been assigned to the Huguenots were registered and were therefore easily identified. The soldiers gained entrance to them by smashing in the doors, killing those they found without regard for the old or infirm. Restraint of every kind was forgotten, men became the victims of a vengeance which was never before equalled. Women were subjected to violence which was too horrible to mention. The streets were filled with heaps of naked bleeding bodies, others were carried to the river and thrown in so that the waters of the Seine looked as if they had turned to blood.

The houses which were built on the bridge of Notre Dame were inhabited by Protestants. Very few of them offered any resistance, though in many of them there were soldiers.

One writer of that period tells of seven or eight hundred people who had taken refuge in a prison, who were brought out in groups of ten and murdered, after which their bodies were thrown into the river. Another boasted that he had despatched eighty Huguenots with his own hands.

> "The report of guns and pistols, and of continued volleys of musketry, from all parts of the city, proved the universality of the massacre. Miserable wretches, smeared with blood, swaggered along with ribald jests and fiend-like howlings, hunting for the Protestants; corpses, torn and gory, strewed all the streets, and dissevered heads were spurned like footballs along the pavements; priests in sacerdotal robes, and with elevated crucifixes, urged their emissaries not to grow weary in the work of exterminating God's enemies; the most distinguished nobles of the court and of the camp rode through the streets with gorgeous retinue, encouraging the massacre. 'Let not one single Protestant be spared,' the king proclaimed, 'to reproach *me* hereafter for this deed.' "*

No one can describe the events of that night of murder. While the work of killing was going on, a group of soldiers entered the apartment of the King of Navarre and took him to the King of France. There Charles, inflamed with the victory over the Huguenots, demanded that Henry renounce the religion of the Protestants or prepare to die. Henry, to save his life, yielded to their demands and was compelled to send an order to his own kingdom, forbidding the exercise of any religion except that of the Roman Catholic Church.

The massacre continued until October third, during which time more than one hundred thousand people were put to death, and assumed such proportions that the Duke of Guise refused to bear the responsibility for it alone.

Charles, in company with his mother, brothers, and a group of nobles, moved in a stately procession through the streets of Paris, where he was welcomed with shouts of joy by the people. Some of those who had taken part in the massacre proudly exhibited their bloody weapons and boasted to the king of the number of Huguenots they had killed.

The king proceeded to the Cathedral of Notre Dame to give thanks to God that without shedding the blood of one believer, the kingdom had been delivered from the control of heretics.

From the Cathedral he went to the Palace of Justice, where

---

* *History of Christianity*—Abbott. Chapter 23, Pages 460, 461.

Parliament was assembled and there he assumed all responsibility for the massacre saying that it was not prompted by any religious motive, that it was ordered to prevent Admiral Coligny and his followers from carrying out a plan to murder the king, his mother, his brothers and the King of Navarre.

His royal speech was amplified and published as a manifesto. It accused the Huguenots of murdering the Catholics and of plotting against the king. When the news of this revolting crime of slaughter reached Rome, the pope ordered a religious ceremony to be held in gratitude for the death of the heretics.

The papal courts of Spain and the Netherlands sent a message of thanks to Charles and Catherine for having effectually abolished heresy from France.

But the Protestant nations of Europe were filled with indignation. The stories of murder and pillaging that the refugees from France repeated in Germany, Switzerland, England and Scotland, filled the hearts of all who heard them with horror.

"If I were to say that I had devoted myself to the study of the Christian religion because nothing else can so effectually rescue the lives and minds of men from those two detestable curses, slavery and superstition, I should seem to have acted rather from a regard to my highest earthly comforts, than from a religious motive.

But since it is only to the individual faith of each that the Deity has opened the way of eternal salvation, and as he requires that he who would be saved should have a personal belief of his own, I resolved not to repose on the faith or judgment of others in matters relating to God; but, on the one hand, having taken the grounds of my faith from divine revelation alone and on the other having neglected nothing which depended on my own industry, I thought fit to scrutinize and ascertain for myself the several points of my religious belief, by the most careful perusal and meditation of the Holy Scriptures themselves."

Treatise of Christian Doctrine—John Milton

CHAPTER 15

THE PROTESTANT NONCONFORMISTS

1558 A.D. THE RISE OF THE PROTESTANT NONCONFORMISTS. THE ACCESSION OF QUEEN ELIZABETH

Queen Elizabeth had come to the throne of England when she was only twenty-five years old. Every circumstance seemed to be against her. Her nation was at war with France. Taxes imposed upon the people were grievous. The money of the kingdom had been debased by a mixture of inferior metals and the rivalry and jealousy of the courtiers was a source of continual discord. She immediately set about to remedy these conditions.

Her selection of Lord Burleigh as her treasurer and of Walsingham as her secretary showed that she recognized men of ability and integrity.

Shortly after Elizabeth ascended the throne, a contention developed among the clergy respecting ecclesiastical vestments and certain rites and ceremonies which had been developed by the reformers who fled to Germany and the Netherlands, during the reign of Mary. The dissension became so great that Queen Elizabeth called upon her advisors to enforce the Act of Uniformity, which provided "that all ornaments for churches and the ministers thereof, shall remain as they were in the second year of Edward VI."

The greatest objection to the garments was the square cap and the surplice. The ecclesiastical Commission issued Canons or Articles for enforcing uniformity of doctrine and discipline. The majority of the clergy conformed to the general practice but those clergymen who would not conform received the name Nonconformists.

Among those who refused to comply with the orders of the Commission, were Dean Sampson and Humphrey, President of Magdalene College. George Withers, a preacher of Bury, preached against the vestments but ceased to speak against them when rebuked by Archbishop Parker. The Nonconformists said they were advocating a purified religion. In derision they came to be called Puritans because they said they advocated purity of doctrine and discipline, free from all human inventions. They affirmed that the Church of England had retained many things that were once a part of the church of Rome even though they professed to have reformed.

"In reviewing the Liturgy of Edward VI no alterations were made in favor of those who now began to be called Puritans, from their attempting a purer form of worship and discipline than had yet been established."*

They objected to kneeling at the Lord's Table, to the cross in baptismal service, to the custom of bowing at the name of Jesus, to the Episcopacy in the government of the church, to many forms of prayer, and to the use of organs in the worship of the church. Here we notice an effort to leave some of the practices of the Church of Rome which had been carried over into the Church of England.

The continued objection of the Puritans caused an injunction to be issued by royal proclamation requiring uniformity of practice in religion. This injunction was called the Advertisements. Because of their opposition to them, thirty-seven of the London clergy were deprived of their offices in the Church of England. They began to worship in private meetings.

1566 A.D. DEATH OF POPE PIUS IV

Pope Pius V became head of the Church of Rome and finding religious matters in England beyond hope of reclaiming, he issued a "bull" of excommunication against Queen Elizabeth who was declared a usurper of the English throne and a vassal of iniquity. This "bull" was nailed to the gate of the Bishop of London by a man named Felton, who was hanged for the act. Up to this time the Catholics in England had been in communion with the Church of England but now they separated from the Church of England.

1568 A.D. THE BISHOPS' BIBLE

Bishop Parker engaged the bishops of the Church of England to each take a part of the Bible for revision. When they had finished their revision they were put together and printed as the Bishops' Bible. The Puritans now separated from the Church of England, maintaining that the Scriptures ought to be followed in all matters concerning the government of the church, and·that every congregation ought to have the power to decide its own doctrine, government, and discipline. From this they came to be called Congregationalists. The Puritans sent petitions to the House of Commons

* *History of The Puritans*—Neal. Volume 1, Chapter 3, Page 76.

listing their grievances. The harsh language of their "Admonition" caused the leaders to be sent to prison.

Queen Elizabeth, believing these things questioned her supremacy, issued a proclamation for enforcing the "Act of Uniformity." This caused a number of the Puritan clergymen to be deprived of their privilege of preaching the gospel. Under the guidance of Cartwright the Puritans formed themselves into societies under the name "Prophesyings of the Clergy" which were sanctioned by some of the Bishops, although Archbishop Parker tried to suppress them. Later Queen Elizabeth called upon all bishops and archbishops to put a stop to these meetings which were originated by the Puritans and eventually spread over all of England.

The effort of the Puritans was to push the Reformation still farther, to abolish the Episcopacy, the use of vestments, and ceremonies. They also began the publication of pamphlets of a satirical nature, which caused Parliament to pass a law stating that whoever printed or circulated anything designed to defame the Queen's Majesty should be put to death and his property given to the Crown.

These edicts caused many to withdraw from the Church of England and to accuse it of being an ecclesiastical-political organization that was contrary to the law and mind of Christ. The purpose of their separation they claimed was to regain the simplicity of the church as it was in the beginning. They denied the right of any civil power to prescribe by law the things that they should believe and the worship to which they should conform. All citizens within the limits of the borders of England, it was claimed, were held to be under the government of the Church of England and therefore under the authority of the bishops of the church. From these bishops were selected those who were to constitute the "High Commission for Causes Ecclesiastical."

These commissioners were to have jurisdiction over all spiritual or church matters, to correct all heresies, errors, and abuses within the realms of England and Ireland. All law enforcement officers were to be at their service in apprehending anyone who might have been guilty of neglecting the worship or speaking against the established worship of the church. Sometimes those who served as ministers to the people were prosecuted in the ecclesiastical courts, suspended from their labors and sentenced to prison for long periods of time because they refused to conform to the established customs of the Church of England. The persecutions imposed upon the Puritan clergy only made the people more obstinate in their opposition to the formality of the Church of England. The growing dislike of the people for the system of religion that was being bound upon them led them to consider the idea of a church that was separate from the state church, formed of believers governed by Christ's teaching and independent of any potentate.

The first to attempt to form such a body were John Copping, Elias Thacker, and Robert Browne, who were clergymen in the Church of England. John Copping was confined to jail at Bury for refusing to conform to the established customs of the English Church and there he remained for seven years.

Robert Browne, a young man of great zeal, was active in condemning the practices of the established church for which he had often been called to account and for which also he had been imprisoned. When he was released at the request of Lord Burleigh, the counsellor of the queen, he fled to Middelburg, Netherlands, and gathered together a church of English exiles who had fled from their mother country to escape religious persecution. Here he printed two books against the Church of England. The first of these was titled—"A Book Which Showeth The Life and Manners of All True Christians." The second was titled "Of Reformation Without Tarrying For Any." Nothing is known of its contents other than the fact that it was a call for believers to withdraw from the queen's ecclesiastical establishment and gather themselves into separate churches.

At this time Copping had been in prison for five years for his disobedience to the laws of the land. Elias Thacker was a fellow prisoner with Copping and assisted him in putting the books of Browne into circulation. For this they were tried on a charge of sedition and burned at the stake as heretics, their crime being that they held to the doctrine of Congregationalism.

After Copping and Thacker had been put to death for maintaining that Christians ought to separate from the Church of England and form churches of the New Testament pattern, Greenwood was put in prison because of his Puritan views and his friend, Henry Barrow, went to visit him. The jailor refused to let him depart when the visit ended, but hurried to inform Archbishop Whitgift of Lambeth of the capture of Barrow.

Barrow, who had studied law, contended that to keep him under arrest without a warrant was contrary to English law. When he was called upon to swear to the answers to the questions of the High Commission, he refused, saying that he would join no creatures to the name of God in an oath, so they proceeded to question him on such opinions as he held.

His answers to their questions reveal that here was a man who was searching for the truth and who had found at least a part of it. His direct and fearless answers to the several "articles of inquiry" show clearly enough that the controversy was between him and the church of Queen Elizabeth, and what the crimes were of which Barrow and the so-called Barrowists were guilty.

1. "In my opinion, the Lord's Prayer is rather a summary than an enjoined form, and, not finding it used by the apostles, I think it may not be constantly used."

2. "In the word of God I find no authority given to any man to impose liturgies or forms of prayer upon the church; and it is therefore high presumption to impose them."

3. "In my opinion, the common Prayer,"—the form of worship actually imposed in England—"is idolatrous, superstitious, and popish."

4. "The sacraments of the Church of England, as they are publicly administrated, are not true sacraments."

5. "As the decrees and canons of the church are so numerous, I can not judge of all; but many of them, and the ecclesiastical courts and governors, are unlawful and antichristian."

6. "Such as have been baptized in the Church of England are not baptized according to the institution of Christ; yet they may not need to be baptized again."

7. "The Church of England, as it is now formed, is not the true church of Christ, yet there are many excellent Christians in it."

8. "The queen is supreme governor of the whole land, and over the church, bodies and goods; but may not make any other laws for the church of Christ than He hath left in his word."

9. "I can not see it lawful for any one to alter the least part of the judicial law of Moses without doing injury to the moral law, and opposing the will of God."

10. "The question being, whether a private person may reform the church if the prince neglect it; No private persons may reform the state; but they ought to abstain from all unlawful things commanded by the prince."

11. "The government of the church of Christ belongeth not to the ungodly, but every particular church ought to have an eldership."*

It was apparent to the inquisitors that such opinions would be dangerous to the realm if the man who held them was permitted to be free, so he was again confined to prison. Twice Barrow and Greenwood were granted a stay of execution, but when there was no indication that they would submit to the will of the High Commission they were brought to Tyburn and hanged.

---

* *Genesis of New England Churches*—Bacon. Chapter 6, Pages 97, 98.

1586 A.D. THE DISCOVERY OF THE PLOT AGAINST QUEEN ELIZABETH

A plot to assassinate Queen Elizabeth and place Mary, Queen of Scots, upon the throne of England was brought to light by Lord Burleigh. Mary had been kept a prisoner for sixteen years following her entrance into England after she abdicated the throne of Scotland. Fourteen of those who were involved in the plot to place Mary upon the English throne were condemned and executed before Mary knew that the plot was discovered. The Earl of Shrewsbury was relieved of the guardianship of Mary and she was taken to Fotheringay Castle. Officials from the High Court soon made their appearance at the Castle to try her for her part in the conspiracy against Elizabeth. She was found guilty of treason and sentenced to death October 25. Parliament met and approved the sentence and requested the queen to have it executed. Queen Elizabeth asked Parliament to consider whether it was possible to save Mary's life without endangering her own. Parliament replied in the negative. Lord Burleigh drew up the death warrant on February 1, 1587 and it was taken to Queen Elizabeth for her signature, by Secretary Davison. A few days later the Earls of Kent and Shrewsbury, with the Sheriff of Northamptonshire came with the warrant to Fotheringay Castle to tell the Queen of Scots to prepare for death the next morning.

Mary received the message with composure and occupied herself during the remainder of the day in writing letters and dividing her few possessions among her servants. She retired to rest at her usual time, but after having slept a few hours she arose and spent the remainder of the night in prayer. When the Sheriff came for her he found her ready to accompany him to the place of execution. Two of her women and four of her men were allowed in the hall to witness her execution. While the sentence of death was being read she sat upon a low stool and when it was finished, she again denied her guilt, announced that she died in the Catholic faith, allowed one of her women to fasten a cloth over her eyes, placed her neck upon the block where it was severed from her body.

King James of Scotland, the son of Mary, wrote a letter to Elizabeth expressing great resentment over the murder of his mother and threatened to declare war on England. King Philip of Spain also threatened to declare war on England, re-establish the Catholic religion, and to punish the Protestants.

Elizabeth, hearing of the great preparations that were being made for this purpose, sent Sir Admiral Drake to Cadiz, where he set fire to a hundred ships that were filled with stores and equipment for the invasion.

The invasion was thus postponed for a year and a half. When the Armada sailed for England it consisted of one hundred thirty ships compared to the eighty ships of Admiral Drake. The fire ships which he sent against the Spanish, destroyed their sails, rendering them helpless. A storm arose which drove many of them upon the rocky shores where they were wrecked. The remainder of the fleet sailed around Scotland and Ireland and eventually made their way back to Spain.

1593 A.D. THE CONTINUED GROWTH OF THE PURITANS

The Puritans continued to make attacks upon the Church of England. Several books were secretly printed which brought the enactment of severe laws which affected both the Catholics and the Puritans. The Puritans were asking for a reformation of the Church of England by the government. Queen Elizabeth and Parliament were requested to change the prevailing form of public worship, to exclude all things that pertained to idolatry, and to end all ritualistic ceremonies. These changes were requested in an effort to get back to the purity and simplicity of the primitive church. The Puritans, having free access to the Scriptures, were convinced that such officials as archdeacons and archbishops were not known in the days of the apostles; that the bishops referred to by Paul were not officials over a group of congregations but officers of local congregations only. The Puritans humbly requested that these things which were at variance with God's word be changed by the authority of the queen and the National Government.

They had no intention of separating from the Church of England, for that would bring discord and strife. When the Puritan ministers conducted the worship without wearing the surplice, a loose fitting broad sleeved white vestment, when they administered their rite of baptism without making the sign of the cross, or served the Lord's supper to the congregation without having them to kneel, they did not consider that they were in rebellion against the established religion, but only endeavoring to return to the simplicity of the church as it was in the beginning. For their failure to conform to the accepted practice of the Church of England they were sometimes removed from their position and deprived of their living. This led them to meet with those of like faith in the privacy of their homes. Even then they did not plan to organize another church in opposition to the Church of England. The efforts of the church officials in positions of authority to compel them to conform to the established custom caused Thomas Cartwright, a leader of the Puritans, a scholar and a preacher, to investigate the episcopal form of church government and to raise the question whether the Church of England was truly a church of Christ in any particular.

The continued study of the New Testament convinced them that neither the Church of England nor any other national church sustained any resemblance to the church of the apostolic age.

Questions now arose which had never before been investigated. The Puritans raised the question of the difference between the Church of England and the church of the time of the apostles. From the study of God's word they were convinced that the congregations of the New Testament age were not bound together in a synod or a conference. Whenever people responded to the gospel they came together to edify and admonish each other upon the first day of the week and to remember the Lord Jesus in the breaking of bread. They spoke of each other as brethren or saints, and their help to each other in times of distress was an indication of their deep and abiding love for one another. The marked contrast between the Church of England and the church of which they read in the New Testament brought them to the conclusion that they were not the same institution.

Instead of an ecclesiastical hierarchy they found the teaching of the New Testament indicated a simple government for the church under elders appointed by those who had revisited each city where they had made converts and ordained elders.

> "When a missionary, the modern evangelist, in some unevangelized country, gathers his converts into churches, leads them in the choice of officers necessary to the completeness of their organization, trains them to habits of self-support and self-government, and at last leaves them to the protection of God's providence and the guiding influence of God's word and Spirit, the difference between him and those whom he ordains in every city is surely intelligible. Such was the difference between those primitive evangelists, the apostles, with their fellow-laborers, and the presbyter-bishops in every city. Such was the simplicity of organization in the primitive churches. There was no complex constitution, no studied distribution of powers, no sharp distinction of ranks. Each congregation like a patriarchal tribe, like a Hebrew village, like a synagogue—had its elders. Some were to preside in the assembly, leading and feeding the flock; others to serve in the communion of the saints, almoners for the church to the needy, comforters to the afflicted. Bishops or deacons, they were the servants of the community, not lords over it. In a brotherhood where all were "kings and priests to God," no elder was king over his brethren or stood as a priest between them and the Father of their Lord Jesus Christ."*

* *Genesis of New England Churches*—Bacon. Chapter 1, Pages, 32, 33.

1593 A.D. SEVERAL GROUPS SEPARATE FROM THE CHURCH OF ENGLAND

Several groups who refused to accept all the teaching of the Church of England separated from it and fled to Holland. Among them was John Smith who had been a preacher of the Church of England. In Holland he became acquainted with the Mennonites who had rejected infant baptism. Their strong opposition to it caused him to begin a careful study of the subject. By his study he was convinced that infant baptism was unscriptural.

Brewster, a prominent Puritan, turned his home into a place of worship, where his friends assembled every Lord's Day. The efforts of these people were directed toward purifying the Church of England. When eventually they gave up their efforts to do so and separated from they Church of England they were called Separatists.

> "Whereas the Puritans were for keeping close to the Scriptures in the main principles of church government, and for admitting no church officers or ordinances but such as are appointed therein.
>
> Our Reformers maintained that things indifferent in their own nature, which are neither commanded nor forbidden in the Holy Scriptures, such as rites, ceremonies and habits, might be settled, determined and made necessary by the command of the civil magistrate; and that in such cases it was the indispensable duty of all subjects to observe them. But the Puritans insisted that those things which Christ had left indifferent ought not to be made necessary by any human laws, but that we ought to stand fast in the liberty wherewith Christ has made us free; and farther, that such rites and ceremonies as had been abused to idolatry, and manifestly tended to lead men back to popery and superstition, were no longer indifferent, but to be rejected as unlawful."*

Here is an effort to get back to God's word as the source of authority for the worship of the church. Barrow rejected all liturgies and condemned all forms of prayer such as were found in the Book of Common Prayer. All of these men might have come much nearer to the truth if death had not cut short their work, for they pleaded for their followers to accept all enlightenment that came to them from the Scriptures.

Another reformer of the same period of time was John Penry. He became a student at the University of Cambridge where his religious interest was quickened by the Puritan influences of that institution. He was not so much concerned with ritualism and vestments as with the desire to preach the gospel of salvation to the people of Wales. Penry published a small treatise on the necessity of preaching the gospel to the poor people in Wales, presenting

---

* *History of The Puritans*—Neal. Volume 1, Chapter 3, Page 79.

also to Parliament an humble petition on behalf of his fellow-countrymen. No objections were made to the petition, but the book which he had published was an offence to Archbishop Whitgift, who issued orders for the suppression of the book and the arrest of the author.

He was thrown into prison and for a month no charge was placed against him, then he was brought before the Archbishop to be interrogated and scolded like a schoolboy. Though he was charged with "heresy," he was later released.

He continued to write against the hierarchy of the Church of England, not because of its methods of government or its forms of worship, but because it hindered the preaching of the Gospel to the people. He accused the ecclesiastics of bringing about a "famine of the word of the Lord."

This was very distasteful to the High Commission who now set about to find the secret press which was printing his tracts. During his absence from home, his study was entered and searched by an officer of that court who carried away several books and papers, affirming that they contained treasonable matter. He requested the arrest of Penry as a traitor to the nation.

A few days after the seizure of his books an edict was issued against seditious books. The representatives of the High Commission immediately instituted a search for such books and for their authors and publishers. An order for his arrest caused Penry to flee with his wife and child into Scotland, where he was received with kindness. He was allowed to proclaim the doctrines of the Puritans and to continue the publication of his books.

Queen Elizabeth begged James of Scotland not to harbor traitors and those guilty of sedition but to return them to England or banish them from his land. King James issued an order that "John Penry, Englishman, should depart from the kingdom within ten days, and not return under pain of death." The friendly clergy of Scotland prevented the order from being executed.

After several years in Scotland he returned to England seeking to obtain an-interview with the queen. He knew of a group of persecuted disciples in London who were endeavoring to form themselves into a church after the pattern of the primitive disciples. Sometimes he spoke in their assembly. Often their meetings were held in his home. In all ways possible he endeavored to promote their spiritual welfare. The authorities of the High Commission were now searching for him and the place of concealment became known to them and he was arrested on March 22, 1593.

After spending several weeks in jail, he addressed his farewell letter to his wife, saying,

"To my beloved wife, Hellenor Penry, partaker with me in this life of the sufferings of the gospel of the kingdom and patience of Jesus Christ, and resting with me in undoubted hope of that glory which shall be revealed. I see my blood laid for, my beloved, and so my days and testimony drawing to an end, for ought I know. I beseech you, stand fast in the truth which you and I profess. Let nothing draw you to be subject unto Antichrist. Consecrate yourself wholly unto the Lord. Fear not the want of outward things. He careth for you. My love be with thee now and ever, in Christ Jesus."

Penry was brought to trial two months after his arrest, and of course he was convicted. A few days later, Archbishop Whitgift and other members of the queen's High Commission signed their names to his death warrant and he was taken from his prison at Southwark to the place of execution where he was hanged for sedition.

Four years after the execution of the three Separatist martyrs, William Brewster came to Nottinghamshire, with his father.

Brewster had been educated at Cambridge University and was acquainted at the court of the queen and informed on the affairs of the state. He had been employed by William Davison, a Puritan, who was a trusted servant of the queen. He had been ambassador to the Netherlands and was later a secretary of state. The relationship of Davison and Brewster was more like that of a father with a son than that of a master and his servant.

After several years of faithful service to the queen, Davison was disgraced by the queen, deprived of his possessions and sent to prison in the Tower of London, under the pretense that he had acted contrary to her will in the matter of the execution of Mary, Queen of Scots. Two years later Brewster was acting for his father in the office he held in the service of the queen. Later Brewster became the postmaster at Scrooby, on the road between London and York, and in his home those who were opposed to the anti-Christian bondage of the Church of England, met as the Lord's free people for worship. As his guests, the little group came together on Lord's day. They came one or two at a time to avert suspicion. Among those who assembled at the home of Brewster was John Smith, who had received his training at Cambridge, and who, as a clergyman of the Church of England, held a benefice at Gainsborough, some miles from Scrooby. He conformed to the established customs and ceremonies of the Church of England, but when he investigated the question of conformity he cast his lot with the Puritans. When the place and purpose of their meeting became known, they were arrested and placed in prison. Hearing of the religious freedom that was granted in the Netherlands, those who

had escaped imprisonment resolved to seek refuge there until conditions changed in England. Brewster and his friends had hired
a ship to take them to Holland. When the shipmaster had them
and all of their goods on board he betrayed them into the hands of
the state authorities. They were arrested and placed in prison
for a month, after which Brewster and six others were bound over
for trial. A second attempt to leave England also failed, but later,
one by one they made their way to Amsterdam and there met together to rejoice in their new freedom. In Amsterdam they found
their old friend John Smith and many who had been members of
the church at Gainsborough. They soon discovered that Smith had
adopted some ideas from the Dutch Anabaptists which were contrary to their belief.

> "John Smith was almost the last man whom a judicious adviser
> would have selected to neutralize the elements of discord in such a
> church. Evidently, there was some sort of magnetism in his
> enthusiastic nature. He was not only a good preacher, but had
> also other able gifts. In his moral character he seems to have
> been unblamable. The fearlessness with which he sought for truth
> and the fidelity with which he obeyed his convictions could not
> but command respect. But with all his "able gifts" and estimable
> qualities, he had not the gift of good common sense; his mind's
> eye was microscopic, incapable of seeing things in their perspective
> and proportions. Such a man could not but bring with him, into
> such a community as that of the English exiles at Amsterdam,
> new questions to be debated and new contentions . . . Nor can we
> certainly conclude against him when we are told that he became
> scrupulous about baptism, and denied that it could be properly
> administered to the children of Christian parents."*

After living in Amsterdam for some time, a part of the Puritans
removed to Leyden where a few of them became merchants, others
silk workers and wool carders. Here they received kind and hospi-
table treatment and their numbers were increased by the many who
came from England to escape the religious persecution that had
been directed against them. Outstanding among those in the church
at Leyden were Brewster and Robinson who became elders in the
church there.

On the first day of the week one of the elders would lead the
assembly in prayer and the giving of thanks, as indicated by Paul
in writing to Titus, "that, first of all, supplication, prayers, inter-
cessions, and giving of thanks be made for all men." Following
their prayers, their voices were blended together in one of the Old
Testament psalms arranged in verses. A portion of the worship
period was given to the exercise of the Word, in which two or three

---

* *Genesis of New England Churches*—Bacon. Chapter II, Pages 222, 223.

chapters of the Scriptures were read with an explanation of their meaning.

One of the elders expounded and explained these passages of scripture with admonitions and exhortations, another psalm followed, after which came the Lord's supper and the baptism of believers of the Word. Nor did the worship end with the contribution in which each gave according to his ability for the relief of the poor and the support of the church. These things indicate the desire of these people to return to the pattern of the church as it was in the New Testament age. However imperfect their understanding of some of the teaching of God's word may have been, here, at least, was an effort in the right direction. Robinson said that it was not possible that Christians, who had so lately come out of darkness, would enjoy full knowledge at once, and that they therefore, must be ready to accept all enlightenment that came to them from any source, so long as it was in harmony with the word of truth. As the number of Puritans increased who were leaving England for the religious liberty offered to them in Holland, Parliament passed a law confiscating the property of all who acted without authority in this matter.

1598 A.D. THE EDICT OF NANTES

The massacre of St. Bartholomew's Day had deprived the Huguenots of their greatest leaders, leaving them scattered but not destroyed. They still held control over many of the cities in the southern part of France.

Catherine de Medici, the mother of King Henry III, now lost control over him and he granted to the Huguenots a broad toleration in 1576. The Huguenots acknowledged the leadership of Prince Henry of Navarre, who at the time of the massacre had been compelled to renounce Protestantism and embrace Catholicism. The Catholics had formed a league called the Holy League, which was headed by Henry, the Duke of Guise.

The purpose of the Holy League was to restore the Catholic church to power, to support the pope, and to make an effort to destroy Protestantism. This League had the support of the pope and of Philip II of Spain. Henry III, the dissolute king of France, was now placed in a subordinate position to Henry, Duke of Guise, whom the Holy League wanted to make king.

The king, learning that his crown was in danger, invited the duke to come into his cabinet and when he had complied the king had him stabbed to death.

The Cardinal of Lorraine, a brother of the duke, was put to death in prison and that brought the house of the Guises to an end.

In 1589 a Dominican monk assassinated Henry III, the king of France, and that brought to an end the house of Valois and placed Henry of Navarre next in line of succession.

Henry was under the ban of the pope for the aid he had given the Hugenots, so in order to win the pope's approval and unite all parties he once more became a Romanist. When he entered Paris as king in 1594, the power of the Holy League was broken and he became the King of France.

In January of the next year he declared war on Spain, for Spain still occupied large sections of France which had been taken by the Duke of Savoy. The Peace of Vervins restored these lands, so the Roman Catholic Church had to retract all decrees that had been issued against Henry and announce that he had returned to the church.

Henry promised toleration for both religions and this promise was fulfilled in the Edict of Nantes. By this edict the Huguenots secured the religious liberty for which they had long contended. All nobles were allowed to teach Calvinism and were allowed to admit persons to their services, unless they lived in places under Catholic jurisdiction. In all towns and villages where Calvinistic services had at one time been held, they were to be restored. The privileges of the Protestants were to be the same as those of the Catholics. These provisions were to be recognized as a perpetual right.

This edict did not satisfy either party. The Catholics objected to its toleration and the Huguenots to its limitation, yet it remained the religious law for almost one hundred years though it was often violated by both parties.

"In 1598 the famous Edict of Nantes was signed, which went further in the path of religious toleration than any other edict of the sixteenth century. Its great fault was that the circumstances of France made it impossible to guarantee religious liberty without granting to the Protestants political privileges, which made them a separate state within the state, and thus in time prevented the fusion of the two parties into one government.

This edict granted complete liberty of conscience; henceforth no one was to be persecuted for his religious opinions, all nobles possessing what was called superior jurisdiction were allowed to teach Calvinism, and anyone might share their teaching. Nobles not possessing this jurisdiction had the same privilege, and might admit any number of others to their services, unless they lived in places where Roman Catholics possessed the superior jurisdiction. Public worship, after the fashion "so-called reformed," was allowed to be continued or restored in all towns where it had been held up to August 1597.

Where Protestants were scattered over a country district, a place was appointed in a suburb or village where services might be held. Public worship was forbidden to Protestants in Paris, or within five miles of it, and in the following Roman Catholic towns;

Rheims, Toulouse, Dejon, and Lyons. Elsewhere the Protestants could possess churches, church bells, schools, etc. The chief limitations of religious liberty were, that the Romanist religion was declared the established religion, Protestants had to pay tithes to the established clergy, to refrain from work on festival days, and to conform to the marriage laws of the Romanist church."*

This edict was revoked by Louis XIV under the pretense that the greater part of the "pretended Reformed have embraced Catholicism." All Huguenot pastors were ordered to leave France within fifteen days or they would become galley slaves. The Huguenot people were denied the right to leave the country and soldiers were placed along the roads and the frontiers to prevent them from so doing.

In spite of these methods, eight hundred thousand of them fled from France in the next few years and found a welcome in other lands.

* *The Reformation*—Lindsay. Chapter 3, Page 50.

"It was on the one hand the feeling that the Geneva Bible was a better translation than any of the Great Bibles, and on the other hand the dislike of many, including King James, for the tendentious glosses, that led to the resolve, at the Hampton Court Conference, to prepare yet another version. Three committees were appointed, for Oxford, Cambridge and Westminster, and the work divided among them. Instructions were issued of which only one or two need be cited: the Bishops' Bible (1572) was to be followed as closely as possible. The older ecclesiastical words to be kept instead of Tyndale's innovations; there were to be no marginal glosses except to explain some Hebrew or Greek word."

The English Bible—Sir Herbert Grierson

CHAPTER 16

A NEW TRANSLATION OF THE BIBLE

1603 A.D. THE DEATH OF QUEEN ELIZABETH

On the tenth of March, Queen Elizabeth became ill. Her condition became worse and when she was asked who should succeed her, she named her cousin, James, of Scotland. Early on the morning of March 24 she breathed her last breath. She had ruled England for forty-five years. Her reign had been a glorious one; a reign in which the Protestant religion had prospered. Though the queen had a haughty temper and a stubborn will, she was loved by the people who long afterward referred to her as "Good Queen Bess."

The accession of James VI of Scotland to the throne of England was accomplished very quietly. He became James I of England. His character was difficult to describe. He was naturally shrewd, but very conceited. His person was awkward and his manners uncouth and without dignity. These defects made him the object of contempt to those who had been accustomed to the stately majesty of the court of Elizabeth.

> "James was fond of study; he read much, but it was chiefly on religious subjects, upon which he was a warm controversialist. Argument was his delight and his glory; he loved to exhibit his wisdom and learning in long harangues. But though he could talk, he could not act; he wanted both decision and exertion; and the Parliament, soon finding out his weakness, listened to his speeches, but paid no attention to them; and contrived by degrees to strengthen its own power at the expense of the crown's; so that while he was perpetually talking of his royal prerogative, he gradually lost much of it."*

In an effort to persuade King James to make some concessions to them, the Puritans sent a petition to him requesting an audience and an opportunity to present their grievances. The king called together an assembly of the Puritan divines at Hampton Court in January of 1604, at which he presided.

The objections presented were chiefly against the government of the church.

When the hearing was finished James calmly told the Puritans, "I will have one doctrine, one discipline, and one religion in Eng-

---
* *History of England*—Goodrich. Chapter 150, Page 287.

land and I alone will decide what that shall be, and you will conform to it or I will hang you every one." He refused to permit them to leave England but secretly Brewster and others made their plans to go to Holland. These plans became known and they were arrested and thrown in jail. After many weeks of suffering they were released.

1605 A.D. THE GUNPOWDER PLOT

Before the death of Queen Elizabeth the popes had declared it was useless to try to bring England back into the realm of the Roman Catholic Church. When it became apparent that James was to be the next king of England, Pope Clement VIII wrote to James to assure him of the support of the papacy in the event of his accession.

James did not at first enforce the fines that Elizabeth had imposed upon those who refused to obey the act of conformity. The members of the Roman Catholic Church who yet remained in England took this as an indication of his good will toward them and they gave out word that he had become a member of the Roman Catholic Church.

This brought so many Jesuits into the country that James was compelled to order all priests of the Roman Catholic Church to leave England. This so angered some of the Catholics that they agreed to attempt the destruction of the king, of the House of Lords, and the House of Commons, at one stroke. This was to be accomplished by blowing up the Parliament House when it next convened to hear the message of the king. Among those who planned the destruction of the government of the nation were Robert Catesby, Guy Fawkes, Robert Kay, Thomas Percy, and John Wright.

After having rented a house near the Parliament, they found that the basement of the Parliament building was rented to a fuel dealer. They came into possession of it by some means and stored thirty-six barrels of gun powder there with other combustible materials. As the time drew near for the opening of Parliament, others were taken into the plot, among whom were Sir Edward Boyham, Sir Everard Digby, Ambrose Rookwood, and Francis Tresham. Most of these men were wealthy and were to assist; some with money, others with horses upon which they were to ride through the country and arouse the Catholics after Parliament was blown up. As the time for Parliament to convene drew near, the conspirators began to think of their friends who would be in the building on that day. Some of those involved expressed a wish to warn their friends to keep away from Parliament on the fifth of November, the opening day. They were not much comforted by Catesby's declaration, that in such a case he would blow up his own son. Tresham's brother-in-law was certain to be in the House, and when Tresham found he could devise no other means of saving his life he wrote a letter to Lord Monteagle warning him to keep away from Parliament at its opening "for God and man had concurred to punish the wickedness of the times," adding, "that Parliament should receive a terrible blow but should not see who hurt them." The conspiracy was thus discovered and those who were involved were all hanged, drawn and quartered; some at St. Paul's Church yard, others at Ludgate Hall and the remainder before the Parliament House. A Jesuit priest named Garnet, was tried with two of his servants and another priest who was taken with him. All were found guilty and executed. The laws that were then imposed upon the members of the Church of Rome were more severe than before.

1607 A.D. THE FIRST ORGANIZED BAPTIST CHURCH

Smith came into contact with those who had separated from the Church of England, whose baptism had been administered by the apostate church. Thirty-six of Smith's followers stood with him in rejecting the baptism which had been administered to them in infancy; Smith baptized himself and then those who stood with him. These people were first called Anabaptists because they baptized again all of those who had been baptized as infants. When it became known that Smith had baptized himself, he was called a Se-baptist, later this group were called Baptists. The baptism they practiced in the beginning was by sprinkling. It was not until later that they began the practice of immersion.

This marks the beginning of Baptist Churches. It is true that some of that faith have tried to establish a visible line of churches reaching back to the days of the apostles, but this assertion does not agree with the facts of history and is rejected by Baptist historians of note.

> "The very attempt to trace an unbroken line of persons duly baptized upon their personal trust in Christ, or of ministers ordained by lineal descent from the apostles, or of churches organized upon these principles, and adhering to the New Testament in all things, is in itself an attempt to erect a bulwark of error."*

Henry C. Vedder, who was professor of Church History at the Southern Baptist University of Louisville, Kentucky, said, "Smith is generally called a Se-baptist, which means that he baptized himself. Such acknowledgement exists in his own handwriting"——

> "True the attempt has been made at one time or another to identify the Baptists with nearly every sect that separated from

---

* *History of The Baptists*—Armitage. Introductory Chapter, Page 2.

the Roman church. It is impossible to show that any one group of persons or sect for a period of more than a thousand years held the teaching that the Baptists now believe."

In the "New Directory For The Baptist Church," on page 34 we find these words:

"Strange to say, some Baptists have been courageous enough and indiscreet enough to assert that an unbroken succession of visible organized congregations of believers similar to their own, and therefore substantially like the primitive churches can be proven to have existed from the apostles until now.

Such claims may well be left to papal audacity. For those who learn from that storehouse of truth, the New Testament, what are the spirit, ordinances and doctrine of the church of Christ, and practice the same, it matters not whether the chain may have been broken or may not have been broken a thousand times."

1611 A.D. KING JAMES TRANSLATION OF THE SCRIPTURES COMPLETED

The translation of the Scriptures known as the King James translation was made at the request of the Puritans at the Hampton Court Conference. Wyclif's translation made from the Latin about 1430 was used until it was supplanted by Tyndal's translation which was finished at Antwerp, Holland in 1526. This translation of the Scriptures was smuggled into England by the sailors who traveled between the ports of the two countries. Copies of it were hidden in bundles of cloth and in barrels of flour that were shipped into England. In this way it became widely circulated, giving to the English people a knowledge of God's word in a language they could read and understand. This increased their desire to know more about the will of the Lord and paved the way for the Reformation. During the Reformation, various translations of the Holy Scriptures made their appearance in England.

"In the year 1535 the whole Bible was printed for the first time in folio, adorned with wooden cuts and Scripture references; it was done by several hands and was dedicated to King Henry VIII by Miles Coverdale. On the last page it is said to be printed in the year of our Lord 1535, and finished the fourth day of October.

This Bible was printed in quarto in 1550, and again, with a new title, 1553. Two years after the Bible was reprinted in English, with this title, 'The Holy Byble, which is all the Holy Scripture, in which are contayned the Olde and Newe Testament, truelye and purelye translated into English by Thomas Matthew (a fictitious name), 1537.' It has a calendar with an almanac, and an exhortation to the study of the Scripture, signed J. R. John Rogers, a table of contents and marriages, marginal notes, a prologue; and in the Apocalypse some wooden cuts. At the beginning of the prophets are printed on the top of the page, R. G. Richard Grafton, and at the bottom of the page, E. W. Edward Whitechurch, who were the printers. This translation, to the end of the book of Chronicles, and the book of Jonah, with all the New Testament, was Tyndal's; the rest was Miles Coverdale's and John Roger's.

In the year 1539 the above mentioned translation, having been revised and corrected by Archbishop Cranmer, was reprinted by Grafton and Whitechurch, "cum privileges ad imprimendum solum." It has this title, 'The Bible in Englyshe, that is to say, The Content of the Holy Scriptures, both of the Olde and Newe Testament, truely translated after the veritie of the Hebrue and Greke Texts, by the diligent study of divers excellent learned men, expert in the foresayde Tongues.' In this edition Tyndal's prologue and marginal notes are omitted. It was reprinted the following year in a large folio, proper for churches, begun at Paris and finished at London. In the year 1541 it was printed again by Grafton, with a preface by Cranmer, having been revised by Tonstal and Heath, bishops of Durham and Rochester. But after this time, the popish party prevailing at court, there were no more editions of the Bible in this reign.

Soon after King Edward's accession (1548-49), the Bible of 1541 had been reprinted with Cranmer's prologue; and the liturgy of the Church of England; being first composed and established, the translation of the Psalter, commonly called the old translation, in use at this day, was taken from this edition. Next year, Coverdale's Testament of 1535 was reprinted, with Erasmus's paraphrase, but there was no new translation.

In the reign of Queen Mary (1555) the exiles at Geneva undertook a new translation, commonly called the Geneva Bible; the names of the translators were Coverdale, Goodman, Gelby, Whittingham, Sampson, Cole, Knox, Badleigh and Pullain, who published the New Testament first in small twelves, 1557, by Conrad Bodius. This is the first that was printed with numerical verses.

The whole Bible was published afterward with marginal notes, 1559, dedicated to Queen Elizabeth.

The translators say they had been employed in this work night and day with fear and trembling; and they protest, from their consciences, that in every point and word, they had faithfully considered the text to the best of their knowledge. But the marginal notes having given offense, it was not suffered to be published in England till the death of Archbishop Parker, when it was printed by Christopher Barker, in quarto, and met with such acceptance that it passed through twenty or thirty editions in this reign.

Cranmer's edition of the Bible had been reprinted in the years 1562 and 1566, for the use of the churches. But complaint being made of the incorrectness of it, Archbishop Parker projected a new translation, and assigned the several books of the Old and New Testaments to about fourteen dignitaries of the church, most of whom being bishops, it was then called the Bishops' Bible, and was printed in an elegant and pompous folio, in the year 1568, with maps and cuts. In the year 1572 it was reprinted with some alterations and additions, and several times afterward without any ammendments.

In the year 1582 the Roman Catholic exiles translated the New Testament for the use of their people and published it in quarto, with this title 'The New Testament of Jesus Christ, translated faithfully into English out of the authentic Latin, according to the best corrected copies of the same, diligently compared with the Greek and other editions in divers languages; with arguments of Books and Chapters, Annotations, and other necessary helps for the better understanding of the Text, and especially for the Discovery of the Corruptions of divers late Translations, and for clearing the Controversies in Religion of these Days. In the English College of Rheims, Printed by John Fogny.'

The Old Testament of this translation was first published at Doway (Douai) in two quarto volumes, the first in the year 1609, the other 1610, by Lawrence Kellam, at the sign of the Holy Lamb, with a preface and tables; the authors are said to be Cardinal Allen, sometime principal of St. Mary Hall, Oxford; Richard Bristow, fellow of Exeter College; and George Martyn, of St. John's College. The annotations were made by Thomas Worthington, B.A., of Oxford; all of them exiles for their religion, and settled in popish seminaries beyond the sea.

The mistakes of this translation, and the false glosses put upon the text, were exposed by the learned Dr. Fulke and Mr. Cartwright. At the request of the Puritans in the Hampton Court Conference, King James appointed a new translation to be executed by the most learned men of both universities, under the following regulations,

1. That they keep as close as possible to the Bishops' Bible.
2. That the names of the holy writers be retained according to vulgar (common) use.
3. That the old ecclesiastical words be kept; such as church not to be translated congregation.
4. That when a word has divers significations, that be kept which has been most commonly used.
5. That the division of chapters be not altered.
6. No marginal notes but for the explication of a Hebrew or Greek word.
7. Marginal references may be set down.

The other regulations relate to the translators comparing notes and agreeing among themselves; they were to consult the modern translations of the French, Dutch and German, but to vary as little as possible from the Bishops' Bible.

The king's commission bears date 1604, but the work was not begun till 1606, and finished 1611. Fifty-four of the chief divines of both universities were originally nominated; some of whom dying soon after, the work was undertaken by forty-seven, who were divided into six companies; the first translated from Genesis to the First Book of Chronicles; the second to the prophecy of Isaiah; the third translated the four greater prophets, with Lamentations and twelve smaller prophets; the fourth had the Apocrypha, the fifth had the four Gospels, the Acts, and the Revelation; and the sixth, the canonical epistles. The whole being finished and revised by learned men from both universities, the publishing it was committed to the care of Bishop Bilson and Dr. Miles Smith, which last wrote the preface that is now prefixed. It was printed in the year 1611, with a dedication to King James and is the same that is read in all the churches."*

---

* *History of The Puritans*—Neal. Volume 1, Part 2, Chapter 2, Pages 255-256.

The Douai Version does not differ widely from non-Catholic versions. It contains the Apocrypha, which are omitted in Protestant Bibles and which were not included in Catholic Bibles until placed there by the order of the Council of Trent in the sixteenth century. The Douai Version is translated from the Latin Vulgate, which was in turn translated from the Greek and Hebrew. Being a translation of a translation it lacks the accuracy of non-Catholic Bibles.

The Catholic Digest of October 1946 contained an article entitled, "Best Seller of the Ages" by Michael J. Early C.S.C., which contains the following statement. "Up to now Catholics have been using the Douay version, an English translation made hurriedly at Rheims and Douai, France. . . . This version, although accurate and approved by the church, is inferior in style and diction to the Protestant King James Version."

As new discoveries of ancient manuscripts became available, the King James translation was revised from time to time. It is said that seven-tenths of the King James translation follows the reading of Tyndal's translation. The King James translation is not without its faults. During the three hundred years since it was translated the English language has undergone many changes and many words which were in common use in the seventeenth century are now obsolete.

One of the requests of King James relative to the translation of the version which bears his name was that the arrangement of the chapters be not changed. When the Bible was first written it was not divided into chapters and verses. It was not until 1248 that the Bible was divided into chapters by Hugo Cardinal DeSanto Caro. Rabbi Mordecai Nathan divided the Old Testament into verses in 1445. Robert Stephen divided the New Testament into verses in 1555.

The Roman Catholic Church has never seriously encouraged the study of the Bible. Indeed at various times they have counselled against the reading of the Scriptures in the common tongue. On June 29, 1816, Pope Pius issued a decree against Bible societies in which he refers to the councils as authority for refusing the Bible to people in their own language. Concerning the circulation of the Bible by Bible Societies, the pope said—

"It is a crafty device by which the very foundations of religion are undermined, a pestilence which must be remedied and abolished, a defilement of the faith—eminently dangerous to souls, a nefarious scheme, snares prepared for men's everlasting ruin, a new species of tares which an adversary had abundantly sown"—to which he added that "the Bible printed by heretics, (Protestants) is to be numbered among the prohibited books."

The Pilgrim Fathers—where are they?
  The waves that brought them o'er
Still roll in the bay, and throw their spray
  As they break along the shore:
Still roll in the bay, as they rolled that day,
  When the Mayflower moored below,
When the sea around was black with storms,
  And white the shore with snow.

The Pilgrim spirit has not fled:
  It walks in noon's broad light;
And it watches the bed of the glorious dead,
  With the holy stars, by night.
It watches the bed of the brave who have bled,
  And shall guard the ice-bound shore,
Till the waves of the bay, where the Mayflower lay,
  Shall foam and freeze no more.

                    —Pierpont.

CHAPTER 17

PILGRIMS SEEK RELIGIOUS FREEDOM

1620 A.D. BREWSTER AND HIS FOLLOWERS ESTABLISH A SETTLEMENT IN THE NEW WORLD

The people who fled to Holland to escape the wrath of King James for their refusal to abide by the Act of Conformity were called Puritans because of their plea that they wanted only to purify the worship of the Church of England. Because of the desire of the people that each congregation be allowed to decide for itself just what its worship should be they were also called Congregationalists. When they obtained a charter from King James allowing them to come to America they received the name Pilgrims because they were making a pilgrimage to the New World. In this year, Brewster obtained from the king a charter granting them the right to settle in Virginia. The group assembled for the last time on English soil at Plymouth, July 21, 1620. John Robinson preached to the little group on the wharf. Every face was stained with tears as the pilgrims boarded the Mayflower and the Speedwell, which later proved unseaworthy.

The Mayflower took all passengers on board and they set sail. After many weeks, land was sighted. They skirted the coast for some distance and on November 21, they anchored near Provincetown, and later anchored at Plymouth. Before leaving the ship, they assembled in the cabin and drew up a document which was signed by all. This became known as the Mayflower Compact and assured them a government of the people, by the people and for the people.

The visitor to Plymouth, Massachusetts, is shown the place where they stepped ashore and fell upon their knees and thanked God for a safe trip to the new world and for the religious freedom they were to have.

In the Plymouth Museum one may see Brewster's Bible and many of his other books. This is the first Congregational church in America, though others existed prior to this date in England and Holland.

"The Puritans affirmed that the office of arch-deacons, deans, bishops, and archbishops had no foundation in the Scriptures or primitive antiquity and only infringed upon the privileges of the presbyters. They disapproved of the sundry church festivals or holy days as having no foundation in the Scriptures. (We have no

days in either the Old Testament or New Testament appointed to
the commemoration of saints, and to observe the fast of Lent is
superstitious.) Nor did they approve of musical instruments, as
trumpets, organs, and etc., which were not in use in the church
for about 1200 years after Christ."*

"The Ministers of the town of Northampton with their bishop,
the Mayor of the town and the justice of the county, agreed upon
the following regulation for worship—That singing and playing
organs in the choir shall be put down and common prayer read in
the body of the church, with a psalm before and after the
sermon."†

The Plymouth Colony was often referred to by the Governor,
William Bradford, as "pilgrims and strangers." The term "Pilgrims" eventually was applied to them. They were in some respects
like the Puritans but were not identical with them. They grew out
of Puritanism and were known in England as Separatists because
they separated from the Church of England. When they first left
England they emigrated to Leyden, Holland, and later to America
at which time they became known as Pilgrims.

The Puritans were a group within the Church of England who
insisted on purifying the ritual and doctrine of the Church of
England, making it conform to the word of God. They did not
desire, as the Separatists, to leave the Church of England. When
they emigrated to America they settled at Boston, Charleston and
other points along the coast.

1628 A.D. THE KING JAMES VERSION REVISED

To assist the translators in this revision, the Patriarch of Constantinople, Cyril, presented the King of England, Charles I, a copy
of the Septuagint translation of the Scriptures. This later became
known as the Alexandrian Manuscript. Where Cyril obtained it is
not known. It contains seven hundred seventy three leaves of
vellum and is now bound in four volumes and is kept in the British
Museum.

1633 A.D. AN EFFORT TO UNITE THE PROTESTANTS TO THE GREEK CATHOLIC CHURCH

The Protestant world had always maintained an interest in the
Greek church because of their opposition to the papacy. Cyril
Lucar, a Greek Christian, made the effort to unite the Calvinists
to the Greek Church. During his travels in Europe he adopted the
Protestant faith. When he returned to Constantinople he prepared
a Confession of Faith, which contained many Protestant dogmas.

---

* *History of The Puritans*—Neal. Volume 1, Chapter 5, Pages 106-107.
† *History of The Puritans*—Neal. Volume 1, Chapter 5, Page 117.

The Jesuits were active in their opposition against him and his printing press was destroyed and he was deposed from the office of Patriarch of Constantinople to which he had been elevated. He was charged with high treason a few years later and executed by the Sultan of Turkey. No permanent results followed his efforts to unite those who differed religiously. The patriarch had a worthy purpose in mind but the procedure was wrong. The efforts of men to unite on creeds or confessions of faith has always met with failure. The divisions that exist among religious people have been produced by failing to follow the divine plan. The only method of restoring unity is to return to the teaching of the New Testament Scriptures.

When the Savior prayed for those who would believe on him through the teaching of the apostles, he prayed that they might be united in a common faith, so that the world might believe that he was the Son of God.

All confessions of faith, creeds, church manuals, and books of discipline are produced by some ecclesiastial organization for the purpose of bringing the minds of men into submission to the tenets of that institution.

Neither the Savior nor the apostles gave authority to any man or any group of men to produce such documents. If such had been considered essential for the guidance of the church and its members, certainly provision would have been made for them.

The church stood united when there was nothing to which men must subscribe but the word of God, but after the formation of the Nicean creed, division and strife developed within the church. In the apostolic age of the church there was nothing given for the guidance of the divine body but the apostles' doctrine. Human creeds are prohibited by the word of God. When Paul said, "All Scripture is given by inspiration of God and is profitable for doctrine, for reproof, for correction, for instruction in righteousness," all other source of guidance were excluded.

1639 A.D. ROGER WILLIAMS ESTABLISHES THE FIRST BAPTIST CHURCH IN AMERICA

Roger Williams came to America in 1631 and was invited to become a teacher in the church at Boston under the pastor, John Wilson. He openly declared that he would not unite with the church there because they had not separated themselves from the Church of England, which he held to be antichristian. He insisted that the New England Christians should have broken off fellowship with the Church of England while they were yet in England. He denied the right of the King of England to grant the patent on which the government of the colony was based.

Some of his followers at Salem were persuaded to cut the cross out of the royal ensign, since it was said to have been granted to the king by the pope of the Roman church. Many of the colonists believed that such things would incur the wrath of the government in England.

Williams became the pastor of the Salem church upon the death of Skelton. Numbers of those who had been identified with the Plymouth colony came to Salem to receive the "more light" which was said to come from his ministry. The people of Plymouth protected him as much as possible from the persecution which was directed against him from other towns and churches. He insisted that the colonies had no right to the lands they occupied, even though they had been granted to them by Christian kings.

Williams was called upon to appear before the colonists' court on three different occasions to answer for his public utterances in which he attacked the patent which granted their land, and his opposition to the Freemen's oath, which required that each man was to take an oath pledging obedience to the laws, to promote the peace and welfare of the community, and to reveal any plots against the colony. When he appeared before the court the last time, a sentence of banishment was pronounced upon him and he was compelled to leave Salem.

> "Whereas Mr. Roger Williams, one of the Elders of the Church of Salem hath broached and divulged divers new and dangerous opinions, against the authority of magistrates, has also writ letters of defamation, both of the magistrates and churches here, and that before any conviction, and yet maintaineth the same without retraction, it is therefore ordered, that said Mr. Williams shall depart out of this jurisdiction within six weeks now next ensuing, which if he neglect to perform, it shall be lawful for the governor and two of the magistrates to send him to some place out of this jurisdiction, not to return any more without license of the court."*

The small city of Salem was overwhelmed with grief at the banishment of their friend and pastor. Many of them later joined him in his exile and shared with him the sufferings he endured as an outcast. Roger Williams was driven into the wilderness in the depth of winter, without a weapon of any kind to protect him from the wild beasts that roamed that vicinity.

The friendship he had formed with the Indians through his kindness to them now bore fruit. They sheltered him from the storms of an extremely cold winter and provided him with food. He bought

---

* *History of The Baptists*—Armitage. Section American Baptists, Chapter 2, Page 630.

land from the Indians on the Narragansett Bay and founded the town of Providence, the freest city on earth. Here he founded a new society upon the principle of entire religious liberty. On the site now occupied by the city of Providence, he organized the first church of the Baptist faith in America in 1639. This marks the beginning of the Baptist Church in America.

1648 A.D. THE ORIGIN OF THE SOCIETY OF FRIENDS, SOMETIMES CALLED QUAKERS

The founder of the Society of Friends was George Fox, the son of a weaver. He was first instructed in religion by his father, who was a Presbyterian, but in later life he became closely associated with the Anabaptists. When a difficulty developed in his life concerning personal conduct, he sought the advice and help of a clergyman. The advice he received did not satisfy his mind so he turned away from the established church and its ministers. He later believed he had received a direct revelation from the Lord, an inner light which guided him in his actions, in his speech, and in enabling him to properly interpret the Scriptures. Fox became a wandering preacher, visiting all parts of England and Scotland. He and his converts rejected all churches and sacraments. They bound themselves to lives of purity and simplicity. They refused to bear arms, to take oaths, or to pay taxes for the support of the state church.

The refusal of the Friends to obey laws which they believed to be evil brought them into conflict with the government of England and thousands of them were imprisoned and persecuted. When Fox was brought before a judge at Derby he threatened the judge with the prophetic statement, "Thou shalt quake at the judgment," to which the judge replied, "No, thou shalt be the quaker." This name was applied to the followers of Fox in derision, but later was accepted by them as a name of honor. Fox spread his views both by writing and by preaching. Because Fox interrupted religious services, he was imprisoned under the Blasphemy Act. He was considered an opponent of law and order because he denounced all religious groups. The Quakers multiplied rapidly in England and within a few years Fox had twenty-five preachers assisting in the spread of his doctrines. The most prominent convert to the teaching of Fox was William Penn, the son of an English admiral. Penn had been sent by his father to Oxford where he attended the worship of Christ's church. The ritualism of the church was so repulsive to Penn that he refused to attend services, for which he was first fined, and then banished from the school.

When he announced to his family that he had accepted the doctrines of the Quakers, he was whipped and beaten by his father and ordered to leave home. His mother interceded for him and he was sent to France and Italy. When he returned, he again turned his attention to preaching the truths of the Quakers which caused him to be imprisoned in the Tower of London for eight months. Here he wrote "No Cross, No Crown," an outstanding work on Christian living. For addressing unlawful assemblies, he was again imprisoned in the Tower of London. After his release from his second imprisonment in the Tower of London, he obtained from Charles II a land grant of forty-five thousand acres of land, part of what is now Pennsylvania and Maryland, in payment of a loan made by his father to the king. Over this territory he was to rule as he wished. Thousands of English people who were seeking religious freedom became colonists in this new territory.

All religious faiths were welcome in this new colony and many who were persecuted elsewhere in America now sought refuge among the Quakers. The colonists who had settled around Massachusetts Bay were the first to refuse religious liberty to those who were of a different faith. Though they desired religious liberty for themselves they did not grant it to others. The first Quakers who landed in Massachusetts were two women, Ann Austin and Mary Fisher, who came from the Barbados. When it was known they were Quakers, Governor Richard Bellingham ordered their trunks searched and their books burned. They were then brought ashore and placed in prison, though there was no law against them in Massachusetts at this time. They were stripped of their clothing and forced to submit to an examination to determine if they were witches. After being confined for more than a month in jail, they were placed on board the ship and sent back home. Later, after a ship arrived from England with eight Quakers aboard, a law was passed providing harsh treatment for any Quakers who would seek to enter the colony.

No declaration of faith in the form of a creed has ever been published by the Quakers, though they have issued from time to time statements as to their belief. These have been issued to acquaint non-members with their teachings. These declarations have not been used as a creed for church government nor for the purpose of erecting a standard to which their members must conform. The prominent points of their doctrine must be learned from different statements made through a period of years. They believe in the personal guidance of an "inner light."

They rejected all outward ordinances, such as baptism and the Lord's supper, contending that there was no command for their continuance. They believed they received a spiritual baptism and had no need for an outward sign or ceremony. They met in complete silence in divine worship until one was led to speak by the Holy Spirit.

They held that anyone who pretended to speak under the direction of the Spirit and whose words were contrary to the Scriptures was under the delusion of the devil. They believed that marriage was God's ordinance and that nothing more was required of the contracting parties than a public statement before an assembled group of Friends that they intended to abide with each other as husband and wife. The Friends had a reputation of being a peace loving, honest and honorable group of people. Through their suffering they obtained toleration for themselves and for other independent religious groups both in England and in America.

1648 A.D. THE PEACE OF WESTPHALIA

The Peace of Westphalia was signed by the representatives of the sovereigns of the states involved in the Thirty Years War which was the last conflict of any note between the Protestants and the Catholics. This was started as a conflict between the Protestants and Catholic princes of Germany, but gradually inolved all the nations of Europe in a contest for power and territory. The extent of the destruction of life can not be determined. Multiplied thousands died of starvation while hundreds of thousands of women and children died in the destruction of the towns and cities. Bohemia had a population of two million at the beginning of the war, of whom the greater part were Protestants. At the end of the war there were left eight hundred thousand Catholics and no Protestants.

When the war began, the population of Germany was thirty millions; when the war ended, the population had been reduced to twelve millions. Everywhere were the ruined homes of the peasants and the palaces of the nobility. The fine arts had virtually perished. Education had been neglected. Moral laws were forgotten and vice prevailed everywhere.

The Peace of Westphalia is an important date in history. It marks the end of the Reformation period and the beginning of political revolutions. From this time men will be concerned more with civil government than with church government.

> "The causes of this war were mainly: 1. The smoldering religious hatred of half a century, kindled afresh by the Bohemian troubles; 2. The church lands which the Protestants had seized and the Catholic princes sought to reclaim; 3. The emperor Ferdinand's determination, backed by Spain, to subjugate Germany to his faith and house.
>
> *Opening of the War.* The Bohemians, enraged by Ferdinand's

intolerance, revolted, threw two of the royal councilors out of a
window of the palace at Prague, and chose as king the elector-
palatine Frederick, son-in-law of James I. of England. War en-
sued, . . . the old Hussite struggle over again. But Frederick's
army was defeated near Prague in its first battle, and the "Winter
King," as he was called, for he reigned only one winter, instead
of gaining a kingdom, in the end lost his Palatinate, and died in
poverty and exile. Meanwhile Ferdinand was chosen emperor.

As the seat of the war passed from Bohemia into the Palatinate,
the other German states, in spite of their singular indifference and
jealousy, became involved in the struggle. Finally Christian IV.,
of Denmark, who, as Duke of Holstein, was a prince of the empire,
espoused Frederick's cause. In this crisis, Count Wallenstein
voluntered to raise an army for the emperor, and support it from
the hostile territory. The magic of his name and the hope of
plunder drew adventurers from all sides. With 100,000 men he
invaded Denmark. Christian was forced to flee to his islands, and
finally to sue for peace (1629).

Ferdinand's triumph now appeared complete. Germany lay
helpless at his feet. The dream of Charles V., an Austrian monarch,
absolute, like a French or a Spanish king . . . seemed about to be
realized. Ferdinand ventured to force the Protestants to restore
the church lands. But Wallenstein's mercenaries had become as
obnoxious to the Catholics as to the Protestants, and Ferdinand
was induced to dismiss him just at the moment when, as the
event proved, he most needed his services: for at this juncture . . .

Gustavus Adolphus, King of Sweden, landed with a small army
on the Baltic coast. A pious, prudent, honest, resolute, generous
man; maintaining strict discipline among his soldiers, who were
devoted to their leader; holding prayers in camp twice a day;
sharing every hardship with the meanest private, and every danger
with the bravest; treating the enemy with humanity, respecting the
rights of the inhabitants of the country, and paying for the food
he took; improving the art of war by breaking the heavy masses
of the army into small battalions, by throwing off their armor,
by reducing the weight of their weapons, and by mingling the
cavalry, pikemen, artillery, and musketeers so as to support one
another in battle, such was the man who now appeared as the
Protestant champion. In Vienna they laughed at the "Snow King,"
as they called him, and said he would melt under a southern sun.
But by the next summer he had taken eighty towns and fortresses.
France, then ruled by Richelieu, made a treaty promising him money
to pay his army; and, though England did not join him, thousands
of English and Scotch rallied around the banner of the Lion of
the North.

Tilly, the best imperial general after Wallenstein, now laid
siege to Magdeburg (1631). Gustavus hastened to its relief. But,
while he was negotiating leave to cross the Protestant states of
Saxony and Brandenburg, Magdeburg was taken by storm. For
three days Tilly's bandit soldiers robbed and murdered throughout
the doomed city. From that time this hero of thirty-six battles
never won another field. On the plain of Leipsic, Gustavus captured Tilly's guns, turned them upon him, and drove his army
into headlong flight. The victor, falling on his knees amid the

dead and dying, gave thanks to God for his success. The next year, at the crossing of the Lech, Tilly was mortally wounded.

Count Wallenstein was now recalled, the humbled emperor giving him absolute power over his army. He soon gathered a force of men, who knew no trade but arms, and no principle but plunder. After months of maneuvering, during which these skill-full generals sought to take each other at a disadvantage, Gustavus, learning that Wallenstein had sent his best cavalry-officer, Pappenheim, with ten thousand men, into Westphalia, attacked the imperial forces at Lützen, near Leipsic (1632). After prayer, his army sang Luther's hymn, "God is a strong tower," when he himself led the advance. Three times that day the hard-fought field was lost and won. At last Gustavus, while rallying his troops, was shot. The riderless horse, galloping wildly down the line, spread the news. But the Swedes, undismayed, fought under Bernard of Weimar more desperately than ever. Pappenheim, who had been hastily recalled, came up only in time to meet their fierce charge, and to die at the head of his dragoons. Night put an end to the carnage. Wallenstein crept off in the dark, leaving his colors and cannon behind. Gustavus had fallen, like Epaminondas, in the hour of victory.

After the Death of Gustavus, the war had little interest. As the Swedish crown fell to Christina, a little girl of six years, the direction of military affairs was given to the chancellor Oxenstiern, an able statesman; under him were Bernard, Duke of Weimar, the Generals Horn and Baner, and later the brilliant Torstenson. Ferdinand, suspecting Wallenstein's fidelity, caused his assassination. At Nordlingen (1634) the Swedes met their first great defeat, and the next year most of the Protestant states of Germany made terms with the emperor. Still for thirteen years longer the war dragged on.

The character of the contest had now entirely changed. It was no longer a struggle for the supremacy of Catholic or Protestant. The progress of the war had destroyed the feelings with which it had commenced. France had openly taken the field against Spain and Austria. Ferdinand died, and his son, Ferdinand III, came to the throne; Richelieu and Louis XIII. died, but Louis XIV. and his minister, Mazarin, continued the former policy. Both French and Swedes strove to get lands in Germany, and Ferdinand struggled to save as much as possible from their grasping hands. The contending armies, composed of the offscourings of all Europe, surged to and fro, leaving behind them a broad track of ruin. The great French generals, Condé and Turenne, masters of a new art of war, by the victories of Rocroi, Freiburg, Nordlingen, and Lens, assured the power of France. Maximilian of Bavaria made an heroic stand for the emperor; but at last, Bavaria being overrun, Bohemia invaded, a part of Prague taken, and Vienna itself threatened, Ferdinand was forced to sign the Peace of Westphalia (1648). This treaty, the basis of our modern map of Europe, brought to an end the religious wars of the Continent. It recognized the independence of Holland and Switzerland; granted religious freedom to the Protestant states of Germany; and gave Alsace to France, and a part of Pomerania to Sweden."*

* *Brief History of Ancient, Medieval, and Modern Peoples*—Steele. "The Seventeenth Century." Page 480-485.

1726 A.D. THE INDEPENDENT CHURCHES OF
ENGLAND AND SCOTLAND

In the previous century independent churches began to make their appearance in both England and Scotland. These churches differed widely in doctrine and practice with the established churches of England and Scotland. Among the religious leaders of this period was John Glass who separated from the Church of Scotland and established independent churches in many cities of Scotland.

These churches were wholly unlike the churches of Scotland. They were established upon the following principles:

1. That national establishments of religion were unlawful and inconsistent with the true nature of the church of Christ.

2. That the church being spiritual, ought to consist only of true spiritual men.

3. That a congregation of Jesus Christ, with its leaders, is in its discipline subject to no jurisdiction under heaven, save that of Christ and his apostles.

4. That each church should have a plurality of elders or bishops, chosen by the church according to instruction given to Timothy and Titus, without regard to previous education for the office, continuous engagement in secular employment being no disqualification.

5. That the church observe the Lord's Supper on the first day of every week; and that love feasts be held, after the example of the primitive Christians.

6. That mutual exhortations be practiced on the Lord's day; any member able to edify being at liberty to address the church.

7. That a weekly collection be made in connection with the Lord's Supper in aid of the poor, and for necessary expenses.

The principles for which Glass contended shows an effort to restore the New Testament church and to be guided alone by God's word.

Glass was followed by Robert Sandeman, who began to plead with people to return to God's word for spiritual guidance. Here is another definite step toward the restoration of God's word as a guide for religious conduct. Sandeman rejected the theory of a direct operation of the Holy Spirit upon the heart of the sinner for the purpose of producing faith.

He believed that the one thing necessary to justify one in the sight of God was the acceptance of the redemption provided for all men in the death of Christ, that when these facts, as set forth by the apostles, were accepted as being true, the individual who thus accepted them was justified. While he did not stress the importance of obedience to the commands of the Lord, yet he did see the necessity of a faith based upon the word of the Lord. His teaching in general was much like that of John Glass who taught that the Lord's Supper must be observed weekly, that all Christians should contribute weekly to aid the poor, that the church should edify itself, and that each congregation should have a plurality of elders.

> "In this special field, Glass and Sandeman, from our distant point of view, appear to have been adventurous pioneers, leading bravely out into what doubtless seemed to them to be the most promising paths of inquiry which the researches of the fathers of Protestantism had left open to their descendants. They were keen thinkers if not profound, and their speculations, though often unfruitful, as judged by the standard of our times, must be admitted to have been ingenious, and sometimes absolutely convincing. They did more than attract the attention of the best thinkers, they made a marked impression upon the thought of their age."*

Some of the things that Sandeman advocated were not readily accepted by the people. His influence was felt over much of Ireland, in England and in America. Because of the nature of his teaching, which emphasized purity of life and strict conformity to the word of God, he was severely persecuted. He later came to America where much that he taught was readily accepted. He died at Danbury, Connecticut, and his monument there bears this inscription,

"Here lies until the resurrection the body of Robert Sandeman, a native of Perth, N. Britain, who in the face of continued opposition from all sorts of men, long and boldly contended for the ancient faith, that the bare work of Jesus Christ, without a deed or thought on the part of man is sufficient to present the chief of sinners spotless before God. To declare this blessed truth as testified in the Holy Scriptures he left his country, he left his friends, and after much patient suffering finished his labors at Danbury April 2, 1771. Age 53 years."

While the labors of Sandeman did not result in the restoration of the church of the first century, yet his labors were directed toward that end.

The work of Glass and Sandeman was followed by that of the Haldanes. These brothers were members of the Church of Scotland. Though they were laymen they became itinerant preachers and traveled extensively through Scotland, calling upon the people for a closer walk with God and a better understanding of His word.

Recognizing the needs of the poor and the unlearned, these men devoted their time and means to giving such people the opportunity

---
* *Origin of Disciples of Christ*—Longan. Chapter 2, Page 20.

of hearing God's word proclaimed as they believed it. Those who desired a better knowledge of the Scriptures were brought together in groups for study. The opposition of the clergy of the Church of Scotland and of the synods was revealed in the decrees that were issued—

> "That as lay preaching has no warrant in the word of God, and as the synod has always considered it their duty to testify against promiscuous communion, no person under the inspection of the synod can, consistently with these principles, attend upon or give countenance to public preaching by any who are not of our community; and if any do so they ought to be dealt with by the judicatories of the church, to bring them to a sense of their offensive conduct."

This decree against the proclamation of God's word is comparable to the decree issued by the council in Jerusalem against preaching in the name of Jesus. (See Acts 4: 16-18.) The Haldanes desired only to revive the work of the Lord. With this in mind they began a search of God's word for a remedy for the religious indifference of the times. This investigation of God's word revealed the difference between the church of the apostolic age and the practice of the Church of Scotland. They began to advocate a complete return to the commandments of the Lord, and the necessity of faith in Christ as the Son of God as a means of salvation.

Practices that were characteristic of the Church of Scotland were discontinued in the churches established by the Haldanes. They endeavored to bring all acts of worship and all doctrine into harmony with the word of God. The Church of Scotland observed the Lord's Supper two times a year, but the Haldanes taught that it should be observed every Lord's day. They taught that immersion was the only scriptural baptism. These brothers established a church in Edinburgh in which James Haldane served as pastor for above fifty years without salary. By the end of 1807 there were eighty-five independent churches in Scotland.

1762 A.D. OTHER EFFORTS TOWARD THE RESTORATION OF NEW TESTAMENT CHURCH

In Scotland another group in search of the truth made its appearance under the leadership of Archibald McLean, who had been associated with one of the independent churches of Edinburgh. Friction over the conduct of some of the members caused McLean, Carmichael, and several others to separate themselves from the independent group. They then directed attention to the subject of baptism as taught in the New Testament. They became convinced that baptism was a burial of the entire body in water. Those who had separated from the independent church were immersed, forming a church under the leadership of McLean, which later became known as a Scotch Baptist church from their practice of immersion. Other congregations of like faith were formed in other cities and they received the same name.

They had no direct connection with the English Baptists who had their beginning with John Smith in 1607.

The Scotch Baptists taught that the Lord's Supper should be observed upon the first day of every week and that it required the presence of an ordained elder to administer the loaf and the fruit of the vine. Others among them called attention to the fact that the church existed where there was no eldership and thus in every place where people had named the name of the Lord this ordinance should be observed with regularity. Other congregations of like faith were established in England, Wales, and Ireland. Prominent among those who were seeking for the truth in Ireland were John Walker, George Carr, and Dr. Darby. These men established congregations in various parts of the country which differed with each other only on a few points of doctrine. They professed to be searching for the truth that existed among the disciples of Jesus Christ in the days of the apostles.

They taught that any deviation from the teaching of the New Testament, which they believed God had given for guidance to all nations, for all time and in all places, would bring punishment upon the guilty for such transgressions.

They believed there was no basis upon which they could have full fellowship with the established systems of religion by which they were surrounded.

They affirmed that any group obedient to the commands of the gospel of Christ, who were guided alone by His word and who assembled upon the first day of the week, constituted the Lord's church in that community. These groups were in harmony with God's word on many points, but on others they failed to conform to the divine requirements. We have before noticed that it required a great number of years for the true church to get away from the truth, therefore, we may expect also that many years will be required for seekers after the truth to make a complete return to the divine plan.

Certainly the thing necessary for such a return would be the rejection of all such ideas, doctrines, and practices as have been obtained from creeds, church manuals, prayer books, and confessions of faith, (for these are human documents based on portions of verses taken from the context, verses taken out of their connection, verses that are irrelevant to the subject under consideration, verses that are misapplied, verses that are perverted to suit the preconceived ideas of the clergy by whom the creeds were formulated) and return to the apostles' doctrine as taught in the New Testament.

This would produce here upon the earth the gospel of Christ; those who obeyed these commands would be Christians just as they were in the beginning, and when they came together in the capacity of worshippers they would constitute the church of the Lord in that community. Will it be possible to find people who are willing to do this? We shall see.

1729 A.D. JOHN WESLEY AND THE METHODISTS

John Wesley, the son of Samuel and Susannah Wesley, was born at Epworth on June 17, 1703. The father had been for many years the rector of the Epworth parish of the Church of England. Wesley's education in his early youth was received from his mother, but at the age of eleven he entered a private school in London where he remained for six years. Because he was a charity student, he was subject to the taunts and ridicule of those who were better situated than he.

When he was seventeen years old he entered Christ College at Oxford, England. Here he acquired a knowledge of Hebrew, logic, and the classical literature of that age. The reading of "The Christian's Pattern" by Thomas à Kempis, and "The Christian Perfection" by William Law, made a deep impression upon his mind and centered his mind upon religion.

At the age of twenty-one he was ordained deacon and was elected Fellow of Lincoln College. Here he applied himself to the study of Greek, Latin, philosophy, and history. Here, too, a little band was formed whose members expressed a desire to learn and to do the Lord's will. Their number increased rapidly and shortly attracted the attention of the student body who began to call them "The Holy Club," "Bible Moths," and "Sacramentarians."

They came together for mutual benefit alone, reading the Bible, praying, singing psalms, visiting the sick, and those who were in prison.

> "The 'Holy Club' was formed at Oxford in 1729 for the sanctification of its members. The Wesleys there sought purification by prayer, watchings, fastings, alms, and Christian labors among the poor. George Whitefield joined them for the same purpose: he was the first to become 'renewed in the spirit of his mind;' but not till he had passed through a fiery ordeal, till he had spent whole days and weeks prostrate on the ground in prayer, . . . He was hooted and pelted with missiles in the streets by his fellow-students, but was preparing meanwhile to go forth a sublime herald of a new 'movement;' a preacher of Methodism in both hemispheres."*

* *History of The Methodist Episcopal Church*—Stevens. Chapter 1, Page 25.

Their strict methodical manner, their punctuality and their close attention to religious duties caused them to be styled Methodists. They were accused of being hypocrites, of using religion only as a shield to cover their own wickedness, of pretending to be more pious than their neighbors to cover up their own lack of righteous living.

1735 A.D. WESLEY LEAVES ENGLAND FOR AMERICA

While Wesley was still at Oxford his father died. Soon after he was offered the Church at Epworth, but chose instead to come to America where an opportunity to preach the gospel to the Indians had been offered by Governor Oglethorpe, a close friend of the Wesley family. Under the protection of a royal charter, an English settlement had been planted on a tract of land between Carolina and Florida.

This territory had been named Georgia in honor of George II of England. It was to become a place of refuge to all foreign Protestants who were seeking to escape from the domination of the papacy.

On his voyage to America, Wesley came into contact with some Moravians and was impressed with their peace of mind during a severe storm when it seemed that the ship was in danger of destruction. After his arrival in Savannah, he again conferred with them upon religious subjects, and was impressed with their trust in God, the simplicity of their religion, and their desire to live a righteous life.

"There was a tract of land in North America, lying between South Carolina and Florida, over which the English held a nominal jurisdiction. It was a wild, unexplored wilderness, inhabited only by Indian tribes. Under the sanction of a royal charter, in 1732, a settlement was made in this territory, and, as a compliment to king George II., it was named Georgia.

The object of such a settlement was twofold: first, to supply an outlet for the redundant population of the English metropolis; and secondly, to furnish a safe asylum for foreign Protestants who were the subjects of popish intolerance. No Roman Catholic could find a home there. James Edward Oglethorpe, an earnest friend of humanity, was appointed the first governor of the territory; and he, with twenty others, were named as trustees, to hold the territory twenty years in trust for the poor.

The first company of emigrants, one hundred and twenty-four in number, had already landed at Savannah, and were breathing its balmy air; and the enthusiastic governor was on his return, to inspire in the mind of the English people increased confidence in the new enterprise.

Having long been a personal friend of the Wesley family, Oglethorpe knew well the sterling worth of the two brothers—John and Charles—who were still at Oxford. An application was made to some of the Oxford Methodists to settle in the new colony as clergymen. Such sacrifices as they were ready to endure, and such a spirit as seemed to inflame them, were regarded as excellent qualities for the hardships of such a country as Georgia. Mr. Wesley was earnestly pressed by no less a person than the famous Dr. Burton, to undertake a mission to the Indians of Georgia, Dr. Burton telling him that "plausible and popular doctors of divinity were not the men wanted in Georgia," but men "inured to contempt of the ornaments and conveniences of life, to bodily austerities, and to serious thoughts." He finally consented, his brother Charles, Benj. Ingham, and Charles Delamotte joining him. . . .

He submitted his plans to his widowed mother, asking her advice. She replied, 'Had I twenty sons, I should rejoice if they were all so employed.' His sister Emily said, 'Go, my brother'; and his brother Samuel joined with his mother and sister in bidding him God-speed.

All things being in readiness, on the 14th of October, 1735, the company embarked on board the Simmonds, off Gravesend, and after a few days detention set sail for the new world.

The Georgia to which Wesley came was very different from the Georgia of to-day. It had only a few English settlements, the most of the territory being the home of savage Indians. These tribes being at war with each other, all access to them was cut off. Not being able to extend their mission among them, Wesley and his co-laborers turned their attention to the whites, hoping that God would before long, open their way to preach the gospel to the Indians. In the prosecution of their mission they practiced the most rigid austerities. They slept on the ground instead of on beds; lived on bread and water, dispensing with all the luxuries and with most of the necessaries of life. They were in season and out of season, everywhere urging the people to a holy life. Wesley set apart three hours of each day for visiting the people at their homes, choosing the midday hours when the people were kept in doors by the scorching heat.

Charles Wesley and Mr. Ingham were at Frederica, where the people were frank to declare that they liked nothing they did. Even Oglethorpe himself had become the enemy of his secretary, and falsely accused him of inciting a mutiny.

Their plain, earnest, practical public preaching and private rebukes aroused the spirit of persecution, which broke upon them with no mixture of mercy. Scandal, with scorpion tongue, backbiting with its canine proclivities, and gossip, which always does immense business on borrowed capital—these ran like fires over sun-scorched prairies, until these devoted servants of God were well-nigh consumed.

At Frederica, Charles narrowly escaped assassination. So general and bitter was the hate, that he says: 'Some turned out of the way to avoid me.' 'The servant that used to wash my linen sent it back unwashed.' 'I sometime pitied and sometimes diverted myself with the odd expressions of their contempt; but found the benefit of having undergone a much lower degree of obloquy at Oxford.'

While very sick, he was unable to procure a few boards to lie on the ground in the corner of Mr. Reed's hut. He thanked God that it had not as yet become a 'capital offense to give him a morsel of bread.' Though very sick, he was able to go out at night to bury a scout-boatman, but 'envied him his quiet grave.' He procured the old bedstead on which the boatman had died, upon which to rest his own sinking and almost dying frame; but the bedstead was soon taken from him by order of Oglethorpe himself. But through the mercy of God and the coming of his brother and Mr. Delamotte, he recovered.

After about six months (February 5 to July 25) spent in labors more abundant, and almost in stripes above measure, Providence opened his way to return to England." . . .*

In England he again came into contact with the Moravians, conferring frequently with Peter Bohler, who organized a society known as the "Fetter-lane Society" of which Wesley was a charter member. Bohler's teaching had a great influence upon the life of Wesley. On one occasion, while Bohler was reading Luther's comments upon the Roman letter, emphasizing the doctrine of justification by faith, Wesley said that he felt his heart "strangely warmed and filled." This he took to be an indication of conversion. Later, however, Wesley found certain practices and doctrines of the Fetter-lane Society not to his liking and withdrew, taking with him a group of Moravians. These he formed into a Methodist society.

His supreme desire was to abolish the coldness that existed in that body and to plant there instead a true piety and a warm spirituality.

"The labors of John Wesley were prosecuted in the teeth of opposition such as seldom falls to the lot of man to endure. And what made it more dastardly and cruel was the fact that it was instigated and principally conducted by the officials of that church of which he was a worthy member and ordained minister to the day of his death. It is a sad fact, but nevertheless true, that most of the opposition encountered by reformers and revivalists has come from the churchmen of the times. It has been the church opposing those who were honestly seeking her own reformation. When the church substitutes forms for godliness, and devotes herself to ecclesiasticism instead of to soul saving, and place-seeking takes the place of piety, she is ready to resist all efforts for her restoration to spirituality as irregular and offensive. No sooner had Wesley exposed the sins of the church, especially those of the pulpit, than the pulpit thundered as though the end of the world had come. Then the idle rabble rushed to the front, and mob violence and mob law was the order of the hour.

The flaming denunciations of the pulpits of the establishment against Mr. Wesley and his people have never been surpassed in the history of the English nation. . . . The Wesleys were represented as 'bold movers of sedition, and ring leaders of the rabble, to the disgrace of their order.' They were denounced by the learned divines as 'restless deceivers of the people,' 'babblers,' 'insolent pretenders,' 'men of spiritual light and cunning craftiness.' They were guilty of 'indecent, false, and unchristian reflections on the clergy.' "*

---

* *John Wesley and His Doctrine*—McDonald. Chapter 2, Pages 12-19.

Wesley's purpose was to end the cold formality of the Church of England and to this end he banded together those who had come under the influence of his teaching. He considered them to be members of the Church of England, concerned only with her welfare and subject to those in authority. He never thought of preaching his gospel outside of the walls of the Church of England until he was prevented from doing so in all of her pulpits. He was firmly convinced that he should not allow the ecclesiastics to stand between him and his obligation to God.

Churches were closed against them, but those without a knowledge of God were not in the churches and to reach these people with the word of God they entered the hospitals, the prisons, and even the mines in their efforts to give the people some knowledge of the truth. When they were prohibited from carrying the word of God to the hospitals, and the prisons, they turned to the fields and the streets of the cities, using the steps to a home, a table or a horse block for their pulpit. People who before knew little about God's Word now rejoiced that they were privileged to hear some portion of it proclaimed to them.

Wesley believed the membership of the Methodist societies should be restricted to those who had experienced a regeneration. In such meetings as Wesley held, the people were taught that they were still a part of the Church of England.

In 1744 a conference was held in London, England, which outlined the doctrine and the discipline of the societies which Wesley formed. In America, the first Methodist service was conducted by Philip Embury, who had emigrated to America in 1760. He was encouraged to conduct services in his own home by his cousin, Mrs. Barbara Heck. Only five people came to hear him preach but these were quickly organized into a class. Embury continued to preach in his home and was soon joined by a Captain Webb, a retired soldier of the king. Webb entered heartily into the work and soon the construction of a "preaching house" was begun. Those who were dissenters were prohibited from building regular churches, so the building had to be constructed with a fire place like a residence to keep within the limits of the law.

As the number of Methodist societies increased, a request was sent to Wesley for preachers to assist in the work. He sent Richard Boardman and Joseph Pilmoor to assist in the work. They were followed by Francis Asbury and Richard Wright, but when the Revolutionary War developed between the colonies and the mother country, all of the preachers returned to England except Asbury. The Methodist societies were still a part of the Church of England, but when the war ended the colonies having severed their connection with England, considered their separation from the Church of England a necessity.

Asbury announced the separation of the Methodist societies from the Church of England and became the superintendent and later was elected as a bishop of the infant church by Conference.

Wesley regarded the ordination of a minister by a bishop as a scriptural practice and so endeavored to have the bishops of the Church of England to ordain the missionaries which he was ready to send forth. This the bishops of the Church of England refused to do. Being a presbyter in the Church of England, and knowing that the office of presbyter and bishop were one in the New Testament age, he ordained Thomas Coke as bishop for the new church. Thus the episcopal form of church government was fastened upon the church which was formed of the Methodist societies.

"Unfortunately, the annals of the Church, like those of civil and political transactions, remind us too plainly that the actors have been human beings. If anything could deter a believer in revelation from composing a History of the Christian Church, it would be his unwillingness to disclose to the world the succession of miseries which, in one sense, may be traced to religion as their cause. He would wish to throw a veil over those dismal periods when ignorance and superstition combined to make men slaves to error, or when all the worst passions of the heart appeared to be let loose in polemical warfare. But we have no reason to think, that the Almighty Disposer of events, who allowed these impurities to defile his Church, intended the record of them to be lost. That he had wise reasons for allowing them to take place, cannot be doubted; but even our limited faculties can see, that a faithful description of such misfortunes may serve as a merciful warning to those who are to come after."

History of the Christian Church—Edward Burton

CHAPTER 18

DIVISION OF THE CHURCH OF ENGLAND

1776 A.D. THE BEGINNING OF THE EPISCOPAL CHURCH IN AMERICA

The enforcement of the "Act of Uniformity" caused many of the people of England to seek religious liberty in the new world. The "Act of Uniformity" was designed to compel all congregations to use the book of Common Prayer in their public worship. Many of the members of the Church of England, including a part of the clergy, objected to the liturgy as containing part of the practice of the church of Rome. They contended that the Reformation in England was not complete when authorities of the church and state were still influenced by papal ritualism.

They regarded the Reformation in Switzerland under Calvin and Farel as a complete separation from Rome.

The method by which the book of Common Prayer was bound upon the Church of England was held to be contrary to Christian principles. Those who were opposed to its use were sometimes sent to the stocks, but more often sent to jail, and those who stubbornly refused to accept it were burned at the stake. The "Act of Uniformity" thus destroyed liberty of worship.

After the separation of the Church of England from the church of Rome a variety of forms of worship prevailed. In some places there was little difference between the worship in the Church of England and the mass of the papal church. The clergymen who conducted the services were unmarried and wore vestments, while in other communities the ministers were married and officiated in the worship without wearing clerical garments.

These conditions ultimately became unbearable to the authorities of the church. They attempted to make all classes conform by resorting to violence. This seemed to the church officials the proper course to pursue. It did not occur to them that such severity would eventually separate many honest and sincere people from the church. The Separatists, the Puritans, the Quakers, and the Methodists had each in turn been lost to the Church of England by harsh treatment. The first effort toward colonization in America was made in 1585 by Sir Walter Raleigh, who brought together a group of a hundred people and sailed for America. They gave the name Virginia to the country where they settled in honor of Elizabeth, the virgin queen of England.

The colony was not successful, being brought to want and despair by frequent quarrels with the Indians and disagreements among themselves. A part of this colony returned to England and the remainder disappeared altogether.

Later, Captain John Smith received a land grant from the king giving the colony he led, the right to settle any place from the Bay of Fundy to South Carolina. They sailed from England with the prayers of the archbishop still sounding in their ears and with the good will of the people following them. A mistake in their reckoning caused them to sail into Chesapeake Bay in April of 1607, and when they landed they named the settlement Jamestown, in honor of King James of England.

Being under the law of England as well as the Church of England, their first act when they landed was to have their clergyman read a prayer of thanksgiving for a safe voyage.

Their first meeting place was a pen of poles set in the ground with a ship sail for a roof, and a bar of wood fastened between two trees served as their first pulpit. Here in this crude structure the Lord's Supper was observed according to the liturgy of the Church of England on June 21, 1607.

Virginia was a royal colony with its parish church, its minister, its Prayer Book, customs, and ritualism planted in a new country. Cold, hunger, and sickness reduced them to a state of despair and they planned to return to England on the relief ship when it came.

The arrival of the ship brought supplies and new people which so encouraged them that they set about to construct a better structure for worship. Money had been collected in England to supply them with Bibles, Prayer Books, and a silver service to be used in the Lord's Supper.

Other ministers who were well learned came to assist their chaplain. The colony at Jamestown prospered until the great massacre of May 22, 1622, in which the ministers, their converts and the colonists were all put to death. Other colonists later arrived from England and viewing the ruins at Jamestown decided to establish a new colony at Williamsburg, which later became the capital of Virginia. The clergymen of the Church of England became the owners of great plantations. Their zeal to spread the religion of the Church of England slowly died. The church relaxed its law against dissenters and allowed them to construct their buildings undisturbed. The Pilgrims who came to the New World in 1620 had rebelled against the Act of Supremacy, which named the reigning monarch as the head of the Church of England. To them there could be no head but Christ. To force one to swear allegiance to an earthly ruler as the supreme head of the church was very repulsive to them. They held it to be a doctrine of Satan and rather than submit to it, they were willing to go to jail and to suffer any form of persecution. Under their leader, John Robinson, they first emigrated to Holland, but later set sail for America, establishing a colony at Plymouth.

The sponsor of this enterprise was Bishop Arthur Lake of Bath and Wells. Their pastor was John White, who had the assistance of Francis Skelton and Francis Higginson. These colonists took themselves from under the control of the Crown. While they sought religious liberty for themselves, they denied it to others. One John Morton had settled in Massachusetts bringing with him his household servants, stock, and furniture. He lived as a country squire, reading prayers before his household and acting as their leader in devotions on Sunday morning. Before his home stood a flagpole from which the English pennant unfurled itself in the breeze. In the beginning, no one interfered with his practice but later these things became a source of annoyance to his neighbors, and he was notified that his religious service must end. He was also ordered to cut his flagpole down. When he objected he was fined, and when he refused to pay his fine, he was jailed. His servants and tenants were compelled to become Puritans and he himself was sent back to England.

"While the Salem people were diligently purging their colony of the Church leaven, a Church of England clergyman was quietly living and prospering, far away from neighbors, where Boston now stands,

The Rev. William Blaxton was a quiet, peaceable man, who, wearied with the din of religious controversy at home, had come to America to be at rest. He had taken up a farm, built a comfortable house, planted orchands, and made for himself and family a pleasant home, before the Salem people came.

It was not to exercise his ministry he had come, but to escape the strife of tongues. One day in 1630, Winthrop, with a little band of land-hunters, laid down their packs and built their fire at Charlestown. Blaxton's servants reported their presence, and the kindly man brought the cold and hungry hunters to his house. They admired his place 'as a paradise,' being chiefly delighted with his apples, whose fragrance reminded them of home. From his house they went morning by morning to their clearings, building their cabins in Charlestown, to which they soon removed. New settlers flocked in, and the town of Boston grew apace.

Soon Blaxton was surrounded. His peaceful solitude was gone. A town was built and a community organized around him. He was graciously permitted to become a 'freeman'; but his Episcopal neighbors Maverick and Walford were denied the same privilege. No attempt was made by Blaxton to hold services of the church.

But gradually and surely he was made to feel that 'New England was no place for such as he.' When the town passed an order that only those of the 'Established Order' should be counted as freemen, thus taking away his citizenship, he sadly accepted its paltry offer of one hundred fifty dollars for his property and moved away. 'I left England,' he says 'because I misliked my lords the bishops: I leave here because I like still less my lords the brethren.' "*

Among the Puritans were two brothers by the name of Brown who refused to join in the action by which they had separated themselves from the Church of England. These men brought their families together and read to them their daily prayers. This was at first permitted by their neighbors but when others joined with them in these services, the Browns were called before the ministers. They were informed that the Prayer Book was the cause of their leaving England and they did not propose that it should be introduced in America.

The town council held that the speech of the Browns tended to mutiny and they were ordered sent back to England.

The zeal of the Puritans in opposing the Prayer Book closed it to all in Massachusetts. By vexation, legal process, and by still harsher methods they drove all clergymen of the Church of England from the New England colonies.

The Baptists had been banished to Rhode Island, the Quakers had been whipped and driven into the uninhabited sections of the country and the churchmen had been exiled by the Puritans. When the news of these things reached England, the charter of the Puritans was withdrawn, and their territory again became part of the kingdom, and the religion of the Church of England the established religion.

In May 1686, the British ship Rose sailed into Boston harbor bringing the first governor. Boston had three meeting houses but none of them opened their doors to the new clergyman, Mr. Ratcliffe. He had to be content with reading the service and preaching in the Town House. During the week he asked the town council for the use of one of the meeting houses for services. The request was refused and he was invited to continue to use the Town Hall. The congregation, composed of those who had held the doctrines of the Church of England from their childhood, continued to grow until the Town House would not accommodate the people. The vestrymen tried to borrow one of the meeting houses when it was not in use by its own people. This was refused with the statement that they could not consent that it be used for Common Prayer worship.

When Andros, the new governor arrived, in obedience to royal

---

* *The History of the American Episcopal Church*—McConnell. Chapter 3, Pages 39, 40.

instructions, he took no part in the religious controversy. He attended the meeting in the Town House and sat upon the uncomfortable seats while the Puritans sat in ease in their comfortable pews in their meeting houses.

The governor now ordered that the Old South Meetinghouse should be used by the Church of England for their morning service and used by the Puritans in the afternoon. Later this was changed to permit the two groups to use it on alternate Sunday mornings. This did not prove satisfactory, for the Church of England extended their services until mid-afternoon before releasing the building to the Puritans. The next Sunday, the Puritans continued their preaching until little time was left for the evening prayers. When the Church of England decided to construct a building for their own use, no one was found who was willing to sell land for this purpose. The governor again came to the relief of the English Church. The council was persuaded by threats to set aside enough land for the purpose. On this land, the King's Chapel was constructed, and there it stands today. With a meeting-house of their own the church grew rapidly.

Other church buildings were constructed throughout the colonies. The services of the Church of England were ritualistic, lacking in warmth and spiritual life. The clerk announced the songs with the words, "Let us sing to the praise and glory of God." The congregation remained seated while singing, and when the custom of standing was introduced, it was held to be a ritualistic innovation. More and more there was a tendency to drop the practices of the Church of England and to substitute in their stead, simple forms of worship. Very few of the clergy now wore vestments.

The interests of the colonies and those of the mother country were widely separated and it was only natural that their spiritual interests should be also. When the subject of taxation came up, the phrase, "Taxation without representation is unjust," became the slogan of the colonists. John Adams said, "If Parliament can tax us, they can establish the Church of England with all of its creeds, articles, tenets and titles, and prohibit all other churches."

The sending of a ship load of tea for the American colonists and the denial of the right of peaceable assembly brought about the "Boston Tea Party." The grievances of the colonists brought about an open break between the mother country and themselves. The clergy were largely in sympathy with the king. The authority which taught them to fear God also taught them to honor the king. Above all they desired to be delivered from taking sides in the strife now developing. When a congress convened, they appointed July 20, 1775 for a day of fasting and prayer, and called upon all Christians to assemble at their accustomed places of worship. The clergy were thus forced into a corner. To disregard the proclamation would openly place them in support of the mother country. To publicly pray for the king and the royal arms would be too much to risk. To pray against the king and the country they would not do. All but four of the clergymen in the country opened their doors for services. Never were fasting and prayer more needed. The sentiments of the clergy were revealed in their sermons. The burden of their discourses was compromise. If that could not be done, then, it was intimated rather than said, submission would be the duty.

Public indignation was aroused, the laymen declaring that the clergy did not voice the real feelings of the colonists. Newspapers reviled the clergy as Tories, traitors, and British emissaries. "No more passive obedience" was chalked on the church doors. The clergy stood condemned in the eyes of those who were to carry through the war for independence and to build the republic.

> "The Connecticut clergy assembled at New Haven and determined to suspend all services and wait for better times. Those in New York retired to the seclusion of private life, exiled themselves to Nova Scotia, or moved within the British lines. Dr. Seabury became a chaplain to a regiment of British infantry.
>
> The church in Virginia was formally disestablished by the colonial government, but neither seclusion, insignificance, nor high character was able to save the clergy from the fury of the populace. Their churches were wrecked, defiled, and burned. Their property was confiscated. Their cattle were killed. They were hooted, pelted, arrested, imprisoned, ducked in the pond, shot at, starved, and banished. The baneful old alliance of Church and State here produced its inevitable results. The Church, which in itself was not disliked by Americans was wrecked because its fortunes were bound to a state which they hated."*

A large part of the people were indifferent, dreading the possibility of war and hoping the differences could be adjusted peaceably. The patriots were eager to have the issues settled, peaceably, if possible, but by war if necessary.

Eventually, two groups, the Tories and the patriots were about evenly divided until the conflict weakened the ranks of the Tories. Several of the colonies, in which the Tories and the patriots were about equal were first opposed to war, but later they developed an extreme hatred for each other and endeavored to outdo the other in acts of violence. At the beginning of the Revolutionary war, thousands of Tories enlisted in the King's army, and thousands of others, finding their lives in danger returned to England or emigrated to Canada. Eleven hundred left Boston in a single day and

---

* *The History of The American Episcopal Church*—McConnell. Chapter 19, Pages 209, 210.

thousands left New York when it was evacuated. Those who expressed sympathy for the mother country were severely treated. They were defrauded of their debts, tarred and feathered and driven from their homes.

Sixty of the clergymen who stayed at their homes were mistreated, robbed of their possessions and then banished from the country.

1783 A.D. A TREATY OF PEACE SIGNED BY THE COLONIES AND ENGLAND

The signing of the treaty of peace brought an end to the Church of England in America. No longer could the church be called the Church of England for the colonies were no longer a part of England.

The Church in England was a part of the English state, as such it could have no existence where the state did not exist. The bonds by which the church in America had been bound to England were now severed and the partisans composing the church were scattered. Many of the members of the church who had cast their lot with the nation were now under a political and social ban. The feeling against them was so hostile that they left everything behind and fled for their lives. Some sought the protection of the Spanish flag in Florida while others returned to England.

This mass emigration further weakened the church, leaving it without resources and in some instances, without members.

The hostility against the church itself quickly disappeared, when the independence of the colonies was assured by the treaty of peace signed in Paris September 3, 1783. Now those who had been identified with the church set about to rebuild its structure and restore its doctrine. The question of the ownership of property held by the Church of England arose. It was affirmed that this property was simply held in trust by the state and now that a new state had been formed the old state had no claims upon it. The members of the church felt that the church property belonged to each individual congregation. While the war was still in progress, Dr. William Smith, president of Washington College, called a meeting of clergymen and laymen to consider the right of ownership of all church property. He suggested that the name, The Church of England, be dropped and the name, The Protestant Episcopal Church, be adopted.

It was accepted as the title which best expressed the fact that they were Protestants and that they believed in an episcopal form of church government, a government of the church by the bishops.

Thus the name Protestant Episcopal Church became the official name of what had been the Church of England in America.

A meeting was called at Annapolis which was attended by many of the leading clergymen who had cast their lot with the colonies and the name Protestant Episcopal Church was adopted, and all lands and property belonging to the Church of England were now declared to be the property of the Protestant Episcopal Church.

Other colonies accepted the decision of the council and the Protestant Episcopal Church became a reality.

Samuel Seabury was selected as their candidate for bishop and was sent to England to be consecrated. Here he met with difficulty for the English bishops hesitated to consecrate one a bishop who would not take the oath of allegiance to the king. After much delay Seabury proceeded to Scotland where the Bishops of the Scotch Episcopal church consecrated him as bishop. He returned to America and became rector of a parish at New London, calling a convocation of Connecticut clergymen. Together, he showed them his certificate of consecration, and they pledged their obedience to him as a bishop and from that time forward the Protestant Episcopal Church functioned under the supervision of her bishops. At a later date (February 4. 1786) Dr. White and Bishop Provost were consecrated bishops at Lambeth Chapel in London and upon their return to America they were accepted and acknowledged by Bishop Seabury, and all later assisted in the consecration of Bishop Bass, thus uniting the Scottish and English lines of episcopacy in America.

From this time forward the efforts of all Episcopal bodies in America were blended together.

CHAPTER 19

DEVELOPMENT OF DENOMINATIONS

Thomas Coke came to America shortly after his appointment and appeared before the conference which was in session at Baltimore. He was recognized as bishop by the preachers who were there assembled. Asbury was accepted as his fellow bishop and several of the preachers present were ordained as elders and deacons.

Wesley had supplied Bishop Coke with a ritual for conducting the church services and also with the Articles of Religion which were in part taken from the Book of Common Prayer of the Church of England. Bishop Coke presented the conference with a letter written by Wesley giving his reasons for the ordination of the bishop and advising the conference as to their future course of action. The letter follows:

"To Dr. Coke, Mr. Asbury and our brethren in North America: By a very numerous train of providences many of the provinces of North America are totally disjoined from their mother country, and erected into independent states. The English government has no authority over them either civil or ecclesiastical, any more than over the States of Holland. A civil authority is exercised over them, partly by Congress, partly by the state assemblies. But no one either exercises or claims any ecclesiastical authority at all. In this peculiar situation some thousands of the inhabitants of these states desire my advice, and in compliance with their desire I have drawn up a little sketch.

Lord King's Account of the Primitive church convinced me many year ago, that bishops and presbyters are the same order, and consequently have the same right to ordain. For many years I have been importuned from time to time to exercise this right by ordaining part of our traveling preachers. But I have still refused, not only for peace sake, but because I was determined, as little as possible, to violate the established order of the national church, to which I belonged. But the case is widely different between England and North America. Here there are bishops who have a legal jurisdiction. In America there are none, and but few parish ministers; so that for some hundred miles together there is none to baptize or to administer the Lord's Supper. Here, therefore, my scruples are at an end; and I conceive myself at full liberty, as I violate no order and invade no man's right, by appointing and sending laborers into the harvest. I have accordingly appointed Dr. Coke and Mr. Francis Asbury to be joint superintendents over brethren in North America. As also Richard Whatcoat and Thomas Vasry to act as elders among them, by baptizing and ministering the Lord's

Supper. If any one will point out a more rational and Scriptural
way of feeding and guiding those poor sheep in the wilderness I will
gladly embrace it. At present I cannot see any better method than
that I have taken. It has indeed been proposed to desire the English
bishops to ordain part of our preachers for America. But to this I
object.

1. I desired the Bishop of London to ordain one only, but could
not prevail;

2. If they consented, we know the slowness of their proceedings;
but the matter admits of no delay;

3. If they would ordain them now they would likewise expect
to govern them. And how grievously would this entangle us!

4. As our American brethren are now totally disentangled, both
from the state and from the English hierarchy, we dare not
entangle them again, either with one or the other. They are
now at full liberty simply to follow the Scriptures and the
primitive church. And we judge it best that they should stand
fast in that liberty wherewith God has so strangely made them
free."*

This document was accepted by the conference and it was agreed
that they should form themselves into a Methodist Episcopal church,
following the liturgy as prepared by John Wesley.

Wesley, though having a thorough knowledge of the teaching of
the New Testament, did not attempt to restore the practice of the
church established by Christ through the apostles. Like other reformers who had preceded him, Wesley sought only to reform the
Church of England, to do away with the cold formality of that
ecclesiastical organization, and to instill into its worship fervent
zeal and true spirituality.

His teaching upon baptism for the remission of sins, for the
necessity of observing the Lord's Supper every Lord's day, and his
opposition to mechanical music in the worship reveal that he was
not lacking in knowledge of the New Testament. In the preface of
his Notes on the New Testament he said, "Would to God that all
the party names and unscriptural phrases and forms, which have
divided the Christian world, were forgot; and that we might all
sit down together as humble, loving disciples at the feet of our
common Master, to hear His word, to imbibe His spirit, and to
transcribe His life into our own."

Though John Wesley thus spoke upon the need for unity upon
the part of those who professed to be the people of God, yet he was
so biased by his own ecclesiastical background that he made no
effort to sever his connection with the church with which he stood
identified, and to restore the church of Christ as it was in the
apostolic age.

* *History of The Methodist Episcopal Church*—Stevens. Chapter 13, Pages 185, 186.

John Wesley's writings often call attention to apostolic procedure and to the great fundamental truths proclaimed by them, yet he labored to establish a denomination and to formulate a creed by which his followers were to be governed. The idea of a Conference to govern the church and to legislate for it was wholly foreign to God's word, yet he delivered the powers and properties of Methodism to a Conference composed of about one hundred ministers of the Methodist societies, and discontent immediately developed among those whose names had not been included in that body.

William Thompson and others separated and formed The New Connection. Another group became known as the Primitive Methodists and they introduced Camp Meetings and Retreats.

Other divisions among the followers of Wesley produced nine subdivisions of the Methodist body in England and fourteen different kinds of Methodists here in America.

None of these groups came into being by following the teachings of the apostles, nor can they be traced beyond the eighteenth century. The legislative authority vested in the bishops when they assemble in Conference, which allows them to enact and to abrogate laws by which the Methodist Church is governed, is without authority in God's word and is entirely different from the government of the church of the first century.

Reformation, such as John Wesley attempted, has always met with failure. Martin Luther tried to reform the Roman Catholic Church by calling attention to the sinfulness of the doctrines of indulgences. He failed in his efforts to bring about a reformation within the church and only succeeded in bringing into existence a new religious institution of which he became the head. John Calvin and John Knox tried to bring about a reformation within the same church by calling attention to the many departures from God's Word but the efforts only produced the Presbyterian Church.

The Church of England, which combines doctrines and practices from both Catholics and Protestants, was brought into existence by King Henry VIII following his separation from the church of Rome over the matter of divorcing his wife, Catherine of Aragon.

Wesley attempted a reform of the Church of England without an open separation from the parent church. From the societies he sponsored came the Methodist Episcopal church.

It was not Wesley's purpose to establish a religious body to compete with the Church of England nor to sever his association with that body. Only a short time before his death he made a statement to that effect. He said, "I declare once more that I live and die a member of the Church of England and that none who regard my advice will ever separate from it." He was of the opinion that very few of his followers would leave the Church of England to form a separate organization, predicting that if any were so unwise as to do so, they would dwindle away.

1791 A.D. THE DEATH OF JOHN WESLEY

During the lifetime of Wesley he is said to have traveled two hundred thousand miles on horseback, preaching from two to five sermons each day, publishing more than fifty volumes upon religious subjects, a complete dictionary of the English language, four volumes of Ecclesiastical History, a History of England, a History of Rome and six volumes of church music. Of his last birthday, Wesley wrote, "For above eighty six years I found none of the infirmities of old age, my eye did not wax dim, neither was my natural strength abated. But last August I found almost a sudden change; my eyes were so dim that no glasses would help me; my strength likewise forsook me, and probably will not return in this world."

His last public work was to preside at the Conference held at Bristol, England, on July 26, 1790, later visiting Cornwall, London, and the Isle of Wight. His last sermon was preached at Leatherhead, February 3, 1791, and on March 2 he breathed his last, surrounded by a few friends and his devoted wife.

When Bishop Coke learned of the death of Wesley, he left America in May, 1791 and remained in England for a year and a half, returning in October 1792, prior to the opening of the General Conference in Baltimore.

THE DEVELOPMENT OF DENOMINATIONS

The gradual development of apostasy overshadowed the church established by Christ through the apostles, resulting in the formation of the apostate church. From the apostate church came the Greek Catholic Church in the Eastern part of the Roman Empire and the Roman Catholic Church in the Western part. Later the work of the reformers brought into existence the Lutheran Church, The Church of England, The Reformed Church, The Episcopal Church and the Methodist Church. Did any of these religious bodies exist in the days of the apostles? Students of church history readily agree that these churches were unknown in the days of the apostles. No student of the Bible will claim that any of them were in existence in the beginning of the gospel age. How many churches existed in the days of the apostles? There was only one. What kind was it? It was the kind that Christ wanted it to be. How was it designated? It was called "the church," "the churches of Christ" or "the church of God." In it there was no developed clergy composed of Bishops, Archbishops, Patriarchs, Metropolitans, Cardinals and Popes.

> "It may be settled that there is no mention of the clergy, in the modern sense of the term, in the New Testament. In the church in the beginning there was no place for ambitious men for the highest position one could occupy was that of Bishop or Elder in a local church. Only when men became dissatisfied with this order of things did they set about to make a change. This change began in Paul's day and the development of the 'mystery of Iniquity' brought into the world the Roman Catholic Church.
>
> Little by little it grew, waxing strong in about the sixth century when the Bishop of Rome was acclaimed 'Head of the Church.' The societies which were instituted in the borders of the Roman Empire were united only by ties of faith and charity. Elders and bishops were the two appellations which in their first origin appear to have distinguished the same order of persons. The name presbyter was expressive of their age, or gravity and wisdom. The title bishop denoted their inspection of the Christians who were admitted to their care."*

Such is the picture of the church as presented by authors who wrote of the church as it was in the apostolic age. Before the crucifixion of Christ, He spoke of the establishment of the church, promising that it would be built. He also promised to send the apostles the Holy Spirit to guide them into all truth.

"Howbeit, when he, the Spirit of truth, is come, he will guide you into all truth; for he shall not speak of himself; but whatsoever he shall hear, that shall he speak; and he will show you things to come."[1]

On the day of Pentecost these promises were fulfilled in the coming of the Holy Spirit and the establishment of the church. The apostles understood that they were vested with authority, for when the question was asked by those who had assisted in the death of Christ, "What shall we do?" the apostle replied, "Repent and be baptized every one of you in the name of Jesus Christ for the remission of your sins, and ye shall receive the gift of the Holy Ghost."[2]

Those who asked the question recognized the authority of the apostles for they obeyed their instructions and we later read that "they continued steadfastly in the apostles' doctrine and fellowship and in the breaking of bread, and in prayers."

In the beginning, the apostles imparted their teaching by word of mouth under the guidance of the Holy Spirit. Before their deaths, that same Holy Spirit guided them in writing the New

---

* *Decline and Fall of The Roman Empire*—Gibbon. Chapter 15.
1. John 16: 13
2. Acts 2: 38

Testament Scriptures, that future generations of Christians might have the written word to guide them. After the death of the apostles, the church continued to accept the New Testament as the only source of authority for the church and for every act of work and worship.

Through the years immediately following the apostolic age, the church grew and prospered. From a small beginning at Pentecost it increased until its influence was felt throughout the Roman Empire. This period of growth and prosperity began to decline after the death of the apostles when men began to reject the apostles' doctrine as the source of authority, substituting their opinions for the inspired word of God. The erroneous doctrines that were developed by false teachers did not divide the church, but caused the early church historians to reaffirm their faith in the teaching of the apostles as revealed in the New Testament, as constituting the only source of authority for the church.

As the apostasy developed, the authority of the apostles was rejected and placed in the hands of uninspired men. Up to the year 325 A.D. people were received into the church upon confession of their faith in Christ as the Son of God and their obedience to the command of baptism. But the bishops of the fourth century insisted that the confession did not indicate the relationship that existed between God and Christ and it should be more comprehensive. They prevailed upon Constantine to call a church council at Nicea which was attended by three hundred eighteen bishops, who formed the Nicean Creed which was accepted as the basis of religious faith.

This was the beginning of the complete rejection of the New Testament as a source of guidance for those who professed to be servants of God. In the Scriptures, God gave to no man nor to any group of uninspired men the authority to legislate for the church in matters of faith or doctrine. The Nicean creed marks the beginning of the apostasy. It represented the effort of uninspired men to improve upon the inspired word of God. In the passing years, human laws took the place of divine laws in the plan of salvation and the government of the church, because the membership of the church neglected the study of the word of God.

Gradually an ecclesiastical hierarchy was developed which prohibited the reading of God's word. Man-made laws for the government of the church reached their supremacy when Pope Leo proclaimed a general indulgence, the income of which was to be used for the building of St. Peter's Cathedral in Rome.*

* See *D'Aubigné's History*—Vol. 1, Page 227.

Luther vowed that if God would give him strength, he would deliver the church from the group of those who were endeavoring to make of it a commercial organization. Luther believed that the whole difficulty lay in the failure of those in power to let the people read the Bible. He believed that if people knew what the Bible taught, they would not condone the evils that were being practiced in the church. He made the effort to give the people the Bible in a language they could read and understand.

But after Luther separated from the Roman Catholic Church, he and his co-laborer, Philip Melancthon, wrote out the Augsburg Confession of Faith. All who entered the Lutheran church accepted this creed. If Luther could not accept the decrees of the papacy, why should he have supposed that future generations would accept what he had written in the Augsburg Confession?

Indeed Luther found that many objected to his confession of faith in his own generation.

Zwingli objected to many of Luther's doctrines and prepared his own confession for the consideration of the Diet of Augsburg. This confession known as the Helvetic Confession, was not even considered by the diet. After the break between Henry VIII and the Roman Catholic Church, it was not long until Thomas Cranmer prepared The Book of Common Prayer, which became the creed to which all members of the Church of England were asked to subscribe.

After the death of Henry VIII, his daughter, Mary, who was an ardent Catholic, had a brief reign, and following her death, England once more became Protestant under the reign of Elizabeth. So firmly did Protestantism become entrenched in England, that when Charles I tried to drive it from England, Parliament refused to co-operate with him but called the Westminster Assembly into session to prepare a statement of principles by which the church could be ruled. This statement, which became known as the Westminster Confession of Faith, was readily accepted by the Presbyterians and became the standard of that church. While the people of the Baptist faith recognize the right of local church independence, they first adopted the Philadelphia Confession of Faith as an expression of their religious belief. Church manuals followed which set forth their religious convictions and which are today accepted by most of their religious groups. When John Wesley attempted to end the formality of the Church of England, he only succeeded in forming the Methodist societies out of which developed the Methodist Church. The creeds did not serve to keep those who produced them united. Mead's "Handbook of Denominations" lists twenty-one Lutheran groups, twenty-one Baptist groups, ten Presbyterian groups, and nineteen branches of the Methodist Church. From the standpoint of unity, human creeds and human denominations have been "weighed in the balances" and found wanting.

All denominations claim to be a part of the church established by Christ or to be that church itself. The study of God's word shows that the ONE church established by our Savior was not divided into various groups teaching different doctrines. Neither can a religious body whose teaching contradicts the doctrine of the apostles be the church of the Lord.

The Roman Catholic Church claims to have been established by Christ through the apostles. This religious organization affirms that Christ established the church in a visible form, as a hierarchy made up of superiors who ruled the church from the beginning. It is said that Christ founded the church upon Peter, appointing him as the supreme head.

It is assumed that Christ invested Peter with this authority and built the church upon him, when he said, "And I say also unto thee, That thou art Peter, and upon this rock I will build my church; and I will give unto thee the keys of the kingdom of heaven; and whatsoever thou shalt bind on earth shall be bound in heaven; and whatsoever thou shalt loose on earth shall be loosed in heaven."[3]

Now let us study these verses of scripture with care. Consulting a lexicon to determine the meaning of the words "Petros" and "petra," we find the word "Petros" is masculine gender and means a stone, and this word was applied to Peter. The word "petra" is feminine gender and means a great ledge of rock. This word is applied to the truth that Christ was the Son of God, and upon this fact the church was to be built. Thus Christ did not found the church upon Peter, but upon the truth that Peter had just confessed, that Jesus was the Christ, the Son of God.

If the words "Peter" and "rock" are read in the Greek, these verses would then read "Thou art 'Petros', and upon this 'Petra', I will build my church, and the gates of hell shall not prevail against it."

Paul said, "Other foundation can no man lay than that is laid, which is Jesus Christ."[4]

Peter did not indicate in his epistles that he was the foundation of the church. "To whom coming, as unto a living stone, disallowed indeed of men, but chosen of God and precious."[5]

The supposed supremacy of Peter was not recognized by the church. When the apostle Paul and Barnabas came to Jerusalem to place the matter of circumcision before the other apostles, it was

3. Matt. 16 : 16-19.
4. 1 Cor. 3 : 11.
5. 1 Pet. 2 : 4.

the apostle James who rendered the final decision. "Wherefore my sentence is that we trouble not them, which from among the Gentiles are turned to God."[6] James was the leader of that assembly. Paul and Barnabas came to Jerusalem to confer with those who seemed to be the pillars of the church, James, Cephas and John; of them Paul said, "Whatsoever they were, it maketh no matter to me; God accepteth no man's person: for they who seemed to be somewhat in conference added nothing to me."

Paul did not acknowledge Peter as the supreme authority in the church. When Peter came to Antioch he freely associated with the Gentile converts there, but when brethren came from Jerusalem he separated himself from them and Paul withstood him to his face. "But when Peter was come to Antioch, I withstood him to the face, because he was to be blamed."[7]

Had the apostle Peter been the supreme authority, Paul would not have rebuked him. Thus Peter was not infallible as claimed for those who occupy the papal throne.

A booklet published with this title, "The Catholic Religion Proved by the Protestant Bible" contains this statement, "The Bible teaches that Christ founded but one church and that this is the church which has Peter for its head. Hence the only church having Peter and his lawful successors for its head can logically claim to be the Church of Christ."

The Bible does teach that Christ founded but one church, but it does not teach that Peter was the head of the church. "And hath put all things under his feet and gave him (Christ, not Peter) to be the head over all things to the church."[8] "And he (Christ) is the head of the body, the church."[9]

It is clearly a misrepresentation to say that Peter was the head of the church. The Bible does not so teach! Peter made no claim to being head of the church. True, he preached the first gospel sermon on Pentecost, but he was never named as head of the church. Peter could not be the head of the church since it had only one head and that was Christ.

There is nothing in the New Testament that states that Peter was ever in Rome. There is no recognized non-Catholic history that so teaches. There was a church in the city of Rome and when Paul penned a letter to it he saluted person after person by name, but made no mention of Peter, a strange way to treat Peter if he was a bishop in the city of Rome.

True, some historians have sought to place Peter in Rome as a

6. Acts 15 : 19.
7. Gal. 2 : 11.
8. Eph. 1 : 22.
9. Col. 1 : 18.

bishop, asserting that he presided there for twenty-five years. According to Paul's letter to the Galatians about twenty years after the death of Christ, Peter was still at Jerusalem and from there he went to Antioch where he remained for a period of time. From the death of Christ to the end of Nero's reign, under whose reign they assert Peter was slain, there were only thirty-seven years. From this must be taken the twenty years that Peter was in Jerusalem. This would leave only seventeen years which must be divided between his time in Antioch and Jerusalem so Peter could not possibly have been in Rome for twenty-five years.

When Paul was a prisoner in Rome he addressed several letters to the church in other localities, making mention of those who were with him, but saying nothing of Peter.

To the young man Timothy, Paul said, "At my first answer no man stood with me, but all men forsook me: I pray God that it may not be laid to their charge."

Where was the apostle Peter when Paul made his defense? If it is contended that he was there in Rome, how great is the disgrace that is placed upon him by Paul's letter.

The claim of the Roman Catholic Church that it is the first church can not be proven to be true.

It is true that it is older than any of the so-called Protestant denominations, but the histories that confirm this fact also show that the Catholic church was started by men only a few centuries earlier than the denominations. The first church was not called the Catholic church, nor did the church in the city of Rome occupy a position of prominence over any of the other congregations. The apostles foretold the development of the papacy, and the effort of the city of Rome for the supremacy, but the efforts of Rome to assume authority over other congregations was bitterly contested for five hundred years by the congregations of Alexandria, Antioch, Jerusalem and Constantinople.

The councils of the church held up to the year 869, convened in the East and were conducted in the Greek language. In these seven councils there were one thousand four hundred eighty-six Greek bishops and twenty-six Roman bishops. These councils were called by the emperors of the Eastern Roman Empire. The church historians for centuries were Greek historians, Eusebius, Socrates, Scholasticus and Theodoret.

The words that are used in describing the government and structure of the Roman Catholic Church, hierarchy, diocese, patriarch, ecclesiastic, synod and catholic, are borrowed from the Greeks. These words are all used in the Roman Catholic Church but were borrowed from the Greek Catholic Church. The papacy did not start with the apostle Peter. It developed in a later period from the ambition of certain bishops who desired to be honored above their fellow elders.

We have learned in other chapters that in the New Testament church there was no higher official than the elders who were sometimes called bishops because it was their duty to oversee the flock.

The bishops or elders were charged with the work of tending, feeding and overseeing the flock of God over which they were appointed. In the apostolic age no elder assumed authority over other congregations. In later years, after the study of God's word was neglected, some bishops began to desire a place of honor and distinction above their fellow elders. In attending to matters of business or discipline, one elder would be called upon to preside over the assembly. He was referred to as the bishop, while the others were called the elders. Here a distinction was made which was without warrant from God's word.

It has before been shown that the bishops in the centers of religious influence began to assume authority over other congregations in a given district. A contest for supreme authority began to develop between the bishops in the city of Rome and those in the city of Constantinople, with the bishop of Rome gaining the supremacy when Boniface was appointed universal bishop by Emperor Justinian in 533. Fifty-five years from this time the bishop of Constantinople, John, the Faster, assumed the title of Universal Bishop, and Gregory the Great, the bishop of Rome, was the first to condemn him for taking such honor unto himself. The office of Pope and apostolic succession do not have any real support from either the Bible or history.

The claim has been made by the Roman Catholic Church that they have an unbroken line of popes from Peter down to Pope Pius XII. The Catholic church has made her own line of popes from the bishops of the church in Rome, but for five hundred years after the church was established those bishops were not popes. And even the line of popes the Roman Catholic Church has prepared has been broken several times. Here is a word-for-word dispatch from Vatican City, dated January 18, 1947,

"Vatican City—As the result of years of investigation into the nineteen hundred year line of succession of the popes of the Roman Catholic Church, the Vatican's new directory has dropped six popes from its old list. It placed two others in doubt as possible anti-popes and lists as a true pope one who had not been included until now."

Information was changed on a number of popes and Pope Dono II who was listed as pope in 173 never really existed at all.

The papacy itself is foretold by the apostle Paul. "Let no man deceive you by any means; for that day shall not come, except there come a falling away first, and that man of sin be revealed, the son of perdition; who opposeth and exalteth himself above all that is called God, or that is worshipped; so that he as God, sitteth in the temple of God, showing himself that he is God."[10]

The pope has borne at various times such titles as "Lord of the Church," "Pontifex Maximus," "Vice Regent of God," and is also described as "God on Earth."

The popes have placed their hands upon every ordinance of the church and changed its meaning as well as the method of performance. They have instituted new ordinances and filled the church with innovations. They have pretended to pardon the sins of the people. They have taken the Bible from the hands of men and have substituted instead human traditions. Catholicism demands that every individual accept as truth whatever the priest teaches, denying that laymen are qualified to teach God's word. It takes the interpretation of the Roman Catholic Church to make the Scriptures valid. Bally, a Jesuit priest said, "Without the authority of the church I would no more believe St. Matthew than Titus Livius." Cardinal Hosius said that apart from the authority of the church, the Scriptures would have no more authority than the fables of Aesop. Thus the words of men are set above the words of God.

On June 29, 1816, Pope Pius issued a decree against Bible societies in which he referred to the councils as authority for refusing the Bible to people in their own language. Concerning the circulation of Bibles by Bible Societies, the pope said, "It is a crafty device by which the very foundations of religion are undermined, a pestilence which must be remedied and abolished, a defilement of the faith, eminently dangerous to souls, a nefarious scheme, snares prepared for men's everlasting ruin, a new species of tares which an adversary has abundantly sown."

It is an admitted fact that the Roman Catholic Church is the oldest of all denominations. It is true that the Roman Catholic Church and her sister, the Greek Catholic Church, are older than the Lutheran Church, the Church of England, the Reformed Church, the Presbyterian Church, the Episcopal Church, the Congregational Church, the Baptist Church or the Methodist Church. But long before any of the above denominations existed, the church established by Christ was in the world. If we trace history back through the ages we come to the place where no denominations exist, where no Roman Catholic Church exists, where there is no

---

10. 2 Thess. 2: 3, 4.

Greek Catholic Church, where the apostate church disappears and only the church of Christ is revealed as a divine institution through which God designed to save the world. No, the Roman Catholic Church is not the first church, it is only a human institution built upon tradition and not on the word of God.

The assertion that the Roman Catholic Church has never changed from the doctrine and practice of the apostles is a fallacy known to all students of Church History. History confirms the fact that it is possible to find the time when the church of Rome changed from immersion to sprinkling for baptism. In ancient Roman Catholic Churches built up to the twelfth and thirteenth centuries the baptistry was a large pool for immersion. Such buildings remain standing to this present day.

Students of the Bible know that the Roman Catholic Church left the apostolic teaching and practice of administering both the loaf and the fruit of the vine to all members of the body. When they abolished giving the fruit of the vine to the members of that body they formed a new tradition.

The requirement of the Roman Catholic Church for its clergy to practice celibacy is contrary to the teaching of Christ and the apostles. Peter himself was a married man. Paul taught that a bishop must be married. The Roman Catholic Church admits that "Priestly celibacy as a law is of later ecclesiastical institution." Any "ecclesiastical institution" like compelling priests not to marry is a human tradition. "Now the Spirit speaketh expressly, that in the latter times some shall depart from the faith, giving heed to seducing spirits and doctrines of devils; Speaking lies in hypocrisy; having their conscience seared with a hot iron; Forbidding to marry, and commanding to abstain from meats, which God hath created to be received with thanksgiving of them which believe and know the truth."[11] Here Paul shows that "forbidding to marry and commanding to abstain from meats" is a departure from the faith. To say that the Roman Catholic church does not change its doctrine is contrary to facts. There have been many changes in Roman Catholic tradition and practice, as well as theology. Where were the masses in the days of the apostles? All students of Church History know that the mass and its tradition did not develop until a long time after the apostles.

The doctrine of the confessional does not come from the New Testament. It is the invention of men, a perversion of the teaching of Christ and the apostles. The Catholic Church once sold indulgences. This practice became universal, resulting in many abuses.

---

11. 1 Tim. 4 : 1-3.

It was supported only by the tradition of the church and not by the teaching of the Scriptures.

Once the Roman Catholic Church burned people at the stake for reading the Bible; now the church, under the pressure of public opinion and the example of the Protestants, permits the reading of the Bible by the laity. Truly Roman Catholic tradition has been an unstable thing. Wherever Catholic tradition and superstition reigns there is spiritual and intellectual darkness. In Latin America the Roman Catholic Church has had the opportunity of showing what Catholic teaching could do. With little competition from the Protestants and all aid possible rendered by the state what has been the result? The people are backward, civilization is retarded and illiteracy prevails. In contrast, wherever the Bible is accepted as authoritative, where it is loved and taught, enlightenment, morality and righteousness have prevailed.

When the true church in some communities departed from the teaching of the Scriptures and errors crept into the church and creeds began to be formed they were absolutely free from Roman Catholic influence or doctrine. In the Nicean Creed, the first creed that was ever written, there is not one phrase that is Roman Catholic. If the Roman Catholic Church had been in existence from the beginning certainly the creed would have had something in it about the pope, about purgatory, about the mass, about penance or some of the other doctrines of the Roman Catholic Church.

When the creed was reaffirmed by the Council of Chalcedon in 451 there is no trace of Roman Catholic doctrine in the findings of that Council. Can you picture a council under the influence of the Catholic church writing a creed and then reaffirming it, and yet making no mention of the papacy, of the worship of saints, the sacrifice of the mass, auricular confession, holy water, lent, the worship of Mary or the sign of the cross? Not one of these practices is named in the worship of the church of the first century. This is sufficient to show that the church of which we read in the New Testament is not the Roman Catholic Church.

Sometimes reference is made to the fact that the Bible of the Roman Catholic Church contains more books than the King James translation of the Bible. These books are called "The Apocrypha." They are so called because they were hidden and of uncertain origin. They were not accepted by the Jewish people as inspired books, but only as a history of the nation. "The Apocrypha" contains fourteen books, namely, I Esdras, II Esdras, Tobit, Judith, the rest of Esther, Wisdom, Ecclesiasticus, Baruch, The Song of the Three Children, The Story of Susannah, Bel and the Dragon, The Prayer of Manasses, I Maccabees and II Maccabees.

It is true that by some of the fathers of the Christian Church a few of these books have been quoted as canonical, but they were not looked on in this light; nor were their titles included in any list of canonical writings during the first four centuries after the birth of our Lord. It was not, indeed, until the Council of Trent, in 1545, that they were definitely declared to be an integral portion of the Holy Scripture as acknowledged by the Roman church.

The doctrine of the Roman Catholic Church is not the doctrine of the New Testament. There is no mention of the doctrines which are characteristic of the church of Rome. The doctrine of celibacy did not have its beginning until the council of Elvira prohibited the marriage of the elders of the church in 303. In the qualifications of an elder as given in the New Testament, the elders were to be married men. "For this cause left I thee in Crete, that thou shouldest set in order the things that are wanting, and ordain elders in every city as I had appointed thee: If any be blameless, the husband of one wife, having faithful children, not accused of riot or unruly, . . ."[12]

Paul affirmed that to forbid to marry was a departure from the faith and a doctrine of devils. Marriage was ordained of God in the beginning of time because he saw it was not good for man to be alone. It was not required of Christians who did not desire to enter into the marriage relationship. Any person (or institution) who requires one to abstain from marriage violates the teaching of an inspired writer of the scriptures. "Marriage is honorable in *all*, and the bed undefiled; but whoremongers and adulterers God will judge."[13]

Millions of Roman Catholics every day speak or pray to Mary in the "Hail Mary," addressing her as the Mother of God. It is not difficult to understand how Roman Catholics might honor and respect the memory of the mother of Jesus, but other religious groups are at a loss to know why anyone should pray to Mary, why one should venerate her, believe in her immaculate conception, and in her alleged bodily assumption into heaven. Nothing in the Scriptures teaches that she was resurrected the third day and ascended into heaven. Jesus loved and respected his mother, but he did not ascribe to her a place above the angels of heaven. When Jesus was told that his mother and brethren stood without seeking to see him, he said, "Who is my mother? and who are my brethren? For whosoever shall do the will of my Father which is in heaven, he is my brother and sister and mother." Those who exalt Mary are doing what the scripture does not authorize. The theory that Mary

12. Titus 1 : 5-6.
13. Heb. 13 : 4.

is the ruler of heaven, that she commands, and that God obeys her will, that through her we obtain salvation, that she is more merciful than Christ and God, is an ecclesiastical fiction which has grown with the centuries. No one needs the intercession of Mary to reach God, for we are told, "And if any man sin, we have an advocate with the Father, Jesus Christ, the righteous; And he is the propitiation for our sins; and not for ours only, but also for the sins of the whole world."[14]

The head of the Roman Catholic Church is the pope, who has the titles of Bishop of Rome, Vicar of Jesus Christ, Prince of the Apostles and Successor of St. Peter. The Scriptures teach that the apostles were witnesses, for one of the requirements for one to take the place of Judas was that he must be a witness of the resurrection of Jesus. Witnesses do not have successors. The government of Christ's church was under the oversight of a plurality of elders. The idea of one man having supreme control over all churches is foreign to God's word.

Neither is the mass of the church of Rome founded upon the teaching of God's word. The mass is defined in the following words:

"The Mass is the Sacrifice of the New Law in which Christ, through the ministry of the priest, offers himself to God in an unbloody manner under the appearance of bread and wine."

In the consecration of the wafer the bread and the wine are changed into the body and blood of Christ who then is actually present on the altar. Is this actually true? "Jesus took bread and blessed it, and brake it, and gave it to the disciples, and said, Take, eat; this is my body. And he took the cup, and gave thanks, and gave it to them, saying, 'Drink ye all of it, for this is my blood of the New Testament, which is shed for many for the remisssion of sins."[15]

Are the loaf and the fruit of the vine the actual body and blood of Christ after being consecrated by the priest? When Jesus instituted this memorial supper his blood had not yet been shed. The disciples knew the loaf and the cup were not his literal body and blood. Jesus said "I am the door" but no one believes he actually became a literal door.

None of the doctrines mentioned here are taught in the New Testament which is the only source of authority Christ has left us. Christ commanded his apostles to teach whatever he had taught them. He sent the Holy Spirit to bring to their memory all things that he had said unto them. "But the Comforter, which is the Holy Ghost, whom the Father will send in my name, he shall teach you

14. 1 John 2 : 1-2.
15. Matt. 26 : 26-28.

all things. and bring all things to your remembrance, whatsoever I have said unto you."[16]

Since they were under the guidance of the Holy Spirit, their teaching was the same as that of Christ. The divine will of Christ which they committed to writing was perfect so far as the spiritual needs of man are concerned. "All Scripture is given by inspiration of God, and is profitable for doctrine, for reproof, for correction, for instruction in righteousness; that the man of God may be perfect, throughly furnished unto all good works."[17]

Whatever is not taught in the Scriptures can not be the will of Christ. This fact excludes making the sign of the cross, the doctrine of celibacy, the adoration of Mary, the doctrine of indulgences, the sacrifice of the mass, the doctrine of purgatory and the practice of auricular confession, as well as many other doctrines of the Roman Catholic Chuch.

Not one of these practices is found in the worship of the church of the first century. This shows that the church of the New Testament and the Roman Catholic Church are not one and the same thing.

---

16. John 14 : 26.
17. 2 Tim. 3 : 16-17.

"Dearly beloved brethren, why should we deem it a thing incredible that the Church of Christ, in this highly favored country, should resume that original unity, peace and purity which belong to its constitution and constitute its glory? Or is there anything that can be justly deemed necessary for this desirable purpose but to conform to the model and adopt the practice of the primitive Church, expressly exhibited in the New Testament? Whatever alterations this might produce in any or in all of the churches, should, we think, neither be deemed inadmissible nor ineligible. Surely such alteration would be every way for the better and not for the worse, unless we should suppose the divinely-inspired rule to be faulty or defective. Were we, then, in our church constitution and management, to exhibit a complete conformity to the apostolic Church, would we not be in that respect as perfect as Christ intended us to be? And should not this suffice us?"

Declaration and Address—Thomas Campbell

CHAPTER 20

EFFORTS TOWARD RESTORATION

As the Reformation developed, groups of religious people separated themselves from the Church of Rome. These religious groups developed into churches, but lacking a knowledge of God's word, they substituted their creeds for what the Lord had said.

They went outside of the New Testament for their religious practices. When they withdrew from Rome, they brought many things with them for which there was no authority in God's word. The practices they had learned from Rome had a secure hold upon their religious convictions. The leaders of the Reformation claimed to follow the Bible, but there was no Bible authority for the traditions they brought with them.

This caused them to pervert the Scriptures to try to make them teach what they had adopted from Rome. From this came legislative bodies to govern the church, church officials that were unknown to the word of God, doctrines that bound upon the denominations such practices as infant baptism, ritualistic services, instrumental music, and many other things that are characteristic of the Protestant churches of today.

Attention has been called to the union of church and state under Constantine about 325 A.D. As the papacy began to develop, men were forced to accept the findings of the Roman Catholic Church under penalty of confiscation of property, and death.

This is the reason that for so long a time there were no rival churches established in opposition to the Catholic church. When the great schism came that separated the Catholic Church into the Greek Catholic Church and the Roman Catholic Church in 1054, neither the part of the church in the East nor the part in the West was able to prevent the separation.

The same was true of the Lutherans, The Church of England, and the followers of Calvin; but when we come to the smaller groups such as the Donatists, the Waldenses and the Albigenses, the strength of the Roman Catholic Church prevented them from existing as rival churches for any length of time.

The approach to the close of the eighteenth century reveals that strife, enmity, and jealousy reigned among the churches that were then prominent. As the result of this condition, religious indifference began to sweep over the world.

Sinful men, whose hearts might have been touched and won by the gospel of Christ, were embittered and turned away from Christianity by the envy and strife that everywhere prevailed among those who professed to be the followers of Christ.

The failure of the churches of Christendom to measure up to the church of the days of the apostles caused sincere men to begin a search for the truth. They recognized that the efforts of men to force creeds and confessions of faith upon people had brought only strife and discord.

The Roman Catholic Church was in the clutches of an ecclesiastical hierarchy and the Protestants were divided into rival sects until they were powerless to do what God intended for the church to do.

1792 A.D. THE BEGINNING OF THE GENERAL CONFERENCE AT BALTIMORE

On November 1, the General Conference of the Methodist Church convened at Baltimore. Bishop Coke, who had been in England for a year and a half, was present. Francis Asbury, the superintendent of the Conference, had claimed the right to appoint preachers to their several circuits. It was believed that Asbury was planning to obtain control of the Methodist church in America which caused many of the preachers to turn away from him. Asbury had appointed preachers whom he disliked to some of the circuits which were difficult fields in which to labor. In 1790 James O'Kelly wrote to Asbury requesting a change in this practice, threatening to withdraw from the Conference unless preachers should have the right to appeal their appointment if they considered it unsatisfactory.

He insisted that the practice of the bishops of the Methodist churches making the appointments gave them a power that was not vested in them by the New Testament. The opening day of the Conference was spent in considering the rules of order. On the second day, James O'Kelly introduced a motion that any preacher should have the right to appeal to the Conference if he did not like his appointment. This motion was directed against the power of the Episcopacy. It called in question the administration of Asbury. In anger, he left the Conference leaving Bishop Thomas Coke in charge.

The debate on this matter occupied the attention of the Conference for several days. After a debate of several days, a vote was taken and O'Kelly's motion lost by a large majority. O'Kelly and those who stood with him now served notice that they were with-drawing from the conference.

A few days later they met at Reese Chapel in Charlotte Co., Va., and sent a request to the Conference for amendments to their first motion. This was rejected. A meeting was held at Piney Grove, in Chesterfield Co. Va., on August 2, 1793. A request was sent to Asbury to meet with them and to examine the government of the Methodist church by the Scriptures.

This Asbury refused to do. This brought about the complete break which came on December 25, 1793 at a meeting at Manakin-town, Virginia. At their next meeting, O'Kelly and those who stood with him, decided to lay aside all creeds and to take the Bible as their only guide. In this meeting Rice Haggard and others affirmed that the Holy Scriptures were sufficient as a rule of faith and prac-tice, and that "Christian" was the only authorized name for God's people.

The five points of their teaching were:

1. Christ is the only head of the church.
2. The name Christian to be used to the exclusion of all other names.
3. The Scriptures of the Old and the New Testaments to be our only creed, ard our only rule of faith and practice.
4. Christian character shall be the only test of church fellowship and membership.
5. The right of private judgment and the liberty of conscience, the privilege of all.

These men did not learn all of the truth but they were headed in the right direction. Step by step the people who professed to be the servants of God, departed from the truth. Step by step men began to seek for the right way that they might return to the Lord. In writing of the foregoing events an able historian said,

> "But the chief subject of its deliberations was the proposition of O'Kelly to so abridge the Episcopal prerogative that 'after the bishop appoints the preachers at conference, to their several circuits, if any one thinks himself injured by the appointment he shall have liberty to appeal to the Conference and state his objections; and if the Conference approve his objections, the bishop shall ap-point him to another circuit.' The motion was obviously a reflection on his administration, but he bore it with admirable magnanimity.
>
> Having secured the organization of the body, with Coke for moderator, he (Asbury) retired anxious and sick, but his 'soul breathing unto God, and exceedingly happy in his love.' The dis-cussion, as we have seen, occupied nearly a week; it was the first of those great parliamentary debates which have given pre-eminence to the deliberative talent of the body. It was lead chiefly by O'Kelly,

Ivey, Hull, Garrettson, and Swift, for the affirmative and by Willis, Lee, Morrell, Everett, and Reed for the negative, all chieftains of the itinerancy and eloquent preachers. Coke, however anxious for the issue of the controversy, sat in the chair rapt in admiration of the talent it elicited. 'On Monday,' says Lee, 'We began the debate afresh, and continued it through the day; and at night we went to Otterbein's church, and again continued it till near bedtime, when the vote was taken, and the motion was lost by a large majority.'

The next morning after the decision of the question the Conference was startled by a letter from O'Kelly and a few other preachers, declaring that they could no longer retain their seats in the body, because the appeal was not allowed. A committee of preachers was immediately appointed to wait upon them and persuade them to resume their seats. Garrettson, who had taken sides with them in the controversy, was on this committee.

'Many tears,' he says, 'were shed, but we were not able to reconcile him to the decision of the Conference. His wound was deep and apparently incurable.'

After the withdrawal of O'Kelly, peace and the old brotherly spirit again pervaded the Conference. On Thursday, the fifteenth, and last day, the business being ended, Coke preached before the Conference. O'Kelly returned to Virginia prepared to upturn the foundations he had helped to lay. Asbury hastened thither also and held a conference in Manchester. Already O'Kelly had begun his pernicious work; some of the most devoted people and preachers had been disaffected; and, in this day, we are startled to read that William M'Kendrer, afterward one of the saintliest bishops of the Church and Rice Haggard, sent to Asbury, their resignations in writing. It was a period of general excitement in Virginia by the political contests of the Republicans and Federalists, the former being the dominant party. O'Kelly adroitly availed himself of these party agitations, and formed his associates into a church with the title 'Republican Methodists.' Their organization gave them a temporary power, and disastrous results followed."*

1801 A.D. OTHER EFFORTS TOWARD A RESTORATION

Dr. Abner Jones of Hartland, Vermont left the Baptist Church and established churches at Lyndon, Vermont and Pierpont, New Hampshire. The members of this group called themselves Christians and adopted the New Testament as their only rule of faith and practice.

Similar to this movement was that of Elias Smith of New Hampshire. With less than twenty members a church was established whose only designation was "The church of Christ." They agreed that Christ was its only head and Christian the only name by which it could be identified. Later the efforts of Jones and Smith were blended together at Portsmouth, New Hampshire. Like cther reformers these men did not make a complete return to New Testament Christianity but they were headed in the right direction.

---

* *History of The Methodist Episcopal Church*—Stevens. Chapter 19, Pages 270, 271.

CHAPTER 21

BARTON W. STONE AND RESTORATION

Is is not common knowledge that Barton W. Stone holds a position of prominence in the work of the Restoration. This man had been preaching the doctrine of the Restoration for several years prior to his exclusion from the fellowship of the Presbyterian church. The churches of Christendom had at this time lost their power because they had lost the use of God's word and had substituted instead human creeds for their guidance. They had lost also their ability to direct the hearts of men to the salvation God had provided through his Son.

> "The spiritual deadness which followed the Revolutionary war caused widespread dismay. Year after year the General Assemblies, in their reports on the state of religion throughout the Church, expressed to the people the deepest concern as to the state of society. It looked to good people as if the very foundation of morality and social order were going to destruction. It is possible that this sense of their great need led God's people to renewed and earnest prayer. By 1797 the symptoms of better times began to appear; and the closing years of the century were at once seasons of great religious awakening and great moral desolation. Infidelity and atheism were bold, confident, and defiant. Christians grew weak in their own eyes and sought their strength from God. The earliest symptoms of this great awakening were manifest in Kentucky. The ministers of that region were zealous and faithful itinerants. The people were bold on either hand—in sin and in religion."*

Barton W. Stone was born at Port Tobacco on the Potomac on December 24, 1772. His family was affiliated with the Church of England, which was the state church of Maryland from 1692 to 1776.

After the father's death, at about the time of the Revolutionary war, the family moved to Pittsylvania County, Virginia. When about twenty years old, Barton Stone began to attend David Caldwell's school near Greensboro, North Carolina. David Caldwell was a graduate of Princeton University and had been ordained a minister of the Presbyterian Church.

Caldwell and his wife were outstanding church leaders. Stone confided to his teacher that he would like to preach but that he had received no call. Dr. Caldwell informed him that he should not

---

* *Presbyterians*—Hays. Chapter 7, Page 145.

expect a miracle, and that if he had a desire to save sinners and to glorify God he should hesitate no longer.

After teaching for a year, he returned to North Carolina and sought license to preach from the Orange Presbytery.

In the fall of 1798 Barton Stone received a call from the congregations of Concord and Cane Ridge through the Transylvania Presbytery. Knowing that the Presbytery would require him to adopt the Westminster Confession as the doctrine taught in the Scriptures, he planned to tell them of his difficulty and ask for more time to study the Confession of Faith. In conversation with James Blythe and Robert Marshall he stated his difficulties. They asked him how far he could receive the Confession and he replied that he would accept it just as far as he saw it was consistent with the Word of God. This was acceptable with them and no objections were offered to his reply before the Presbytery, so he was ordained.

The Cane Ridge meeting house was built in 1791, one year before Kentucky was admitted to the Union as a state. The meeting house was built by a group of pioneers from North Carolina under the leadership of Robert Finley. This old meeting house, constructed of blue ash logs, is fifty feet long and thirty feet wide. The building entrance was at the West, with the pulpit at the center of the North side of the building, being about two or three feet by six or seven feet in length. Here on the grounds of this old meeting house, Barton Stone and his companions are buried, as well as many of the members of the church at Cane Ridge.

On July 2, 1801 Barton Stone was married to Elizabeth Campbell, the daughter of Col. William and Tabitha Campbell. Leaving the home of the bride's mother at Muhlenberg, they hurried to Cane Ridge where the meeting was to begin on Thursday or Friday before the third Lord's day in August.

1801 A.D. THE CANE RIDGE MEETING

When the appointed time came for the meeting the whole countryside became alive with wagons, carriages, and those on foot. It was estimated that between twenty and thirty thousand people came together to hear the gospel. Four or five preachers would be speaking at the same time in different parts of the encampment. Both Methodist and Baptist preachers aided in the work, preaching salvation by obedience to Christ. Other Presbyterian preachers who assisted Stone and who came to a knowledge of the truth were Richard McNemar, Robert Marshall, David Purviance and John Thompson. Barton Stone attempted to prove to Robert Marshall that infant baptism was taught in the scriptures and soon came to the conclusion that it was unauthorized by the Bible.

In the Cane Ridge meeting no attention was given to the doctrines which separated the various denominations at that time. Because these men taught a doctrine different from the Confession of Faith, others who were identified with the Presbyterian faith attempted to end their work.

The Presbytery of Springfield brought charges against Barton Stone and others. After appearing before the Presbytery he was then called upon to appear before the Synod at Lexington, Kentucky. During the course of their deliberations, the Synod indicated that the others who had rejected the Confession of Faith would also be called to account.

When it became evident that the decision would be against McNemar, Stone and his companions left the assembly and drew up a protest against the treatment of McNemar, announcing also their withdrawal from the jurisdiction of the Synod, but not from the Presbyterian church. When a committee sent by the Synod was unable to reclaim them, the Synod proceeded to suspend all and to declare their doctrine of the Westminster Confession of Faith. Barton Stone contended that the Presbytery and Synod did him an injustice in saying he was suspended because he had departed from the the Westminster Confession of Faith. He supplied this evidence that he did not accept the Confession of Faith in full at his ordination.

> "It is well known by some of the members of that Presbytery, that I did make exception to the Confession of Faith, and declared to them that I would not receive it farther than I saw it agreeable to the word of God. This the following certificate will show; We, the subscribers, do certify that we were present at the ordination of Barton W. Stone, at Cane Ridge, by the West Lexington Presbytery. That when the question was put to him by the Presbytery,
>
> 'Do you receive and adopt the confession of Faith,' etc., the said Stone answered aloud,
>
> 'I do, as far as I see it consistent with the Word of God.' Witness our hands, this 20th of Dec. 1818.
>
> Moses Hall
> John Snoddy
> David Knox"*

Barton Stone had taken issue with the church with which he stood identified, agreeing to accept the Westminster Confession of Faith only as far as he believed it to be in harmony with the word of God. He believed the Bible to be the only source from which man could learn of his obligation to God. Prior to this time the Bible had been considered only as a book to be used to confirm the Westminster Confession of Faith.

---

* *Works of Elder B. W. Stone*—Mathes. Chapter 5, Pages 83, 84.

Shortly after the Cane Ridge meeting Barton Stone and those who were associated with him in that meeting rejected all creeds, all church manuals, and all confessions, taking their stand upon the word of God alone.

After their separation from the Synod, these servants of the Lord formed the Springfield Presbytery, addressing a letter to each of the churches they had served, giving a full account of their separation.

Under the name of the Springfield Presbytery they continued to labor, preaching the gospel of Christ and establishing congregations.

In less than one year all came to the conclusion that the Presbytery was a human institution which would only perpetuate division. It was decided that it should be rejected along with the human creeds they had before surrendered. They rejected also the name Presbyterian and took the name Christian, the name given to the disciples of the Lord at Antioch.

This decision caused them to prepare the Last Will and Testament of the Springfield Presbytery.

"The Presbytery of Springfield, sitting at Cane Ridge, in the county of Bourbon, being through a gracious Providence, in more than ordinary bodily health, growing in strength and size daily, and in perfect soundness and composure of mind, but knowing that it is appointed for all delegated bodies once to die; and considering that the life of every such body is very uncertain, do make, and ordain this our last Will and Testament, in manner and form following, viz:

Imprimis. We will, that this body die, be dissolved, and sink into union with the Body of Christ at large; for there is but one body, and one Spirit, even as we are called in one hope of our calling. Item—We will, that our name of distinction, with its Reverend title, be forgotten, that there be but one Lord over God's heritage and his name one.

Item—We will, that our power of making laws for the government of the church, and executing them by delegated authority, forever cease; that the people may have free course to the Bible, and adopt the law of the Spirit of life in Christ Jesus.

Item—We will, that candidates for the gospel ministry henceforth study the Holy Scriptures with fervent prayer, and obtain license from God to preach the simple Gospel, with the Holy Ghost sent down from Heaven, without any mixture of philosophy, vain deceit, traditions of men, or rudiments of the world. And let none henceforth take this honor to himself, but he that is called of God, as was Aaron;

Item—We will, that the church of Christ resume her native right of internal government—try her candidates for the ministry, as to their soundness in the faith, acquaintance with experimental religion, gravity and aptness to teach; and admit no other proof of their authority but Christ speaking in them. We will that the church of Christ look up to the Lord of the harvest to send forth laborers into his harvest; and that she resume her primitive right of trying those who say they are apostles and are not.

Item—We will, that each particular church as a body, actuated by the same spirit, choose her own preacher and support him by a free will offering, without a writen call or subscription, admit members, remove offences; and never henceforth delegate her right of government to any man or set of men whatever.

Item—We will, that the people henceforth take the Bible as the only sure guide to heaven; and as many as are offended with other books, which stand in competition with it, may cast them into the fire if they choose; for it is better to enter into life having one book, than having many to be cast into hell.

Item—We will, that preachers and people cultivate a spirit of mutual forbearance, pray more, and dispute less; and while they behold the signs of the times, look up, and confidently expect that redemption draweth nigh.

Item—We will, that our weak brethren who may have been wishing to make the Presbytery of Springfield their king, and wot not what is now become of it, betake themselves to the Rock of Ages and follow Jesus for the future.

Item—We will, that the Synod of Kentucky examine every member, who may be suspected of having departed from the Confession of Faith, and suspend every suspected heretic immediately; in order that the oppressed may go free, and taste the sweets of gospel liberty.

Item—We will, that Ja———, the author of two letters lately published in Lexington, be encouraged in his zeal to destroy partyism. We will, moreover, that our past conduct be examined into by all who may have correct information; but let foreigners beware of speaking evil of things which they know not.

Item—Finally we will, that all our sister bodies read their Bibles carefully, that they may see their fate there determined, and prepare for death before it is too late.

Springfield Presbytery) L.S.
June 28, 1804)
Witnesses
Robert Marshall
John Dunlavy
Richard M'Nemar
B. W. Stone
John Thompson
David Purviance

The Witnesses' Address

"We, the above named witnesses of the Last Will and Testament of the Springfield Presbytery, knowing that there will be many conjectures respecting the causes which have occasioned the dissolution of that body, think it proper to testify, that from its first existence it was knit together in love, lived in peace and concord, and died a voluntary and happy death.'

'Their reasons for dissolving that body were the following; With deep concern they viewed the divisions, and party spirit among professed Christians, principally owing to the adoption of human creeds and forms of government.

While they were united under the name of a Presbytery, they endeavored to cultivate a spirit of love and unity with all Christians but found it extremely difficult to suppress the idea that they themselves were a party separate from others. This difficulty increased in proportion to their success in the ministry. Jealousies were excited in the minds of other denominations; and a temptation was laid before those who were connected with the various parties, to view them in the same light. At their last meeting they undertook to prepare for the press a piece entitled 'Observations on Church Government,' in which the world will see the beautiful simplicity of Christian church government, stript of human inventions and lordly traditions.

As they proceeded in the investigation of that subject, they soon found that there was neither precept nor example in the New Testament for such confederacies as modern Church Sessions, Presbyteries, Synod, General Assemblies, etc. Hence they concluded, that while they continued in the connection in which they then stood, they were off the foundation of the Apostles and Prophets, of which Christ himself is the chief cornerstone. However just, therefore, their views of Church government might have been, they would have gone out under the name and sanction of a self-constituted body.

Therefore, from a principle of love to Christians of every name, the precious cause of Jesus, and dying sinners who are kept from the Lord by the existence of sects and parties in the Church, they have cheerfully consented to retire from the din and fury of conflicting parties, sink out of the view of fleshly minds and die the death. They believe their death will be great gain to the world. But though dead, as above, and stript of their mortal frame, which only served to keep them too near the confines of Egyptian bondage, they yet live and speak in the land of gospel liberty; they blow the trumpet in jubilee, and willingly devote themselves to the help of the Lord against the mighty. They will aid the brethren, by their counsel, when required; assist in ordaining Elders or Pastors, seek the divine blessing, unite with all Christians, commune together, and strengthen each other's hands in the work of the Lord.

'We design, by the grace of God, to continue in exercise of those functions, which belong to us as ministers of the gospel, confidently trusting in the Lord, that he will be with us. We candidly acknowledge, that in some things we may err, through human infirmity; but he will correct our wanderings, and preserve His church. Let all Christians join with us, in crying to God day and night, to remove the obstacles which stand in the way of His work, and give Him no rest till He make Jerusalem a praise in the earth. We heartily unite with our Christian brethren of every name, in thanksgiving to God for the display of His goodness in the glorious work He is carrying on in our western country, which we hope will terminate in the universal spread of the gospel, and the unity of the church.' "*

Only by believing that God was leading them can you account for the fact that these men living in widely separated communities,

---

* *Works of Elder B. W. Stone*—Mathes. Chapter 2, Pages 21-26.

unknown to each other, were devoting their efforts to one subject, the restoration of the church as it was in the apostolic age. Years elapsed before James O'Kelly, Abner Jones, Elias Smith and Barton Stone learned of each other's work in their respective fields, but when they learned of the work of restoration that was being carried on by others, they saw that they were all striving for the same thing. They were not working for the reformation of any religious group, but for the restoration of the ONE CHURCH of the New Testament. So we have religious leaders who once called themselves Methodists, Baptists and Presbyterians, all working for unity, all wanting to wear no other name but Christian, all working for the restoration of the word of God as the only safe guide in religious matters.

They were searching for unity. Not a unity achieved by one group giving up their creed and adopting the creed of another group, but the unity brought about by all of them giving up their respective creeds, confessions of faith, church manuals, and taking their stand upon the divinely inspired word of the Lord. Here was a guide all could accept. They did not ask their religious neighbors to reject their own creed and accept one formed by them, but only to do as they had done, to surrender their belief in and their obedience to all human doctrines and accept in their stead the doctrines proclaimed by Christ and his apostles. Their efforts toward the restoration of the church as it was in the beginning met with strong opposition.

About this same time, too, Barton Stone became dissatisfied with his infant sprinkling. At a meeting of the brethren, the subject of baptism was brought up and discussed freely. It was agreed that baptism was a matter to be decided by each one personally. Those who desired to be immersed should do so *at once,* but *no* reproach was to be directed toward those who were not immersed.

Then the question arose as to who was qualified to baptize them. They decided that since the New Testament authorized them to preach the gospel it also authorized them to administer baptism.

The preachers first baptized each other and afterwards immersed those who requested it. Barton Stone did not arrive at a full understanding of God's word at one step. Even after the Cane Ridge meeting, after deciding that the Bible should be the source of authority for all religious conduct, he still followed the custom of that age in inviting mourners to assemble before the pulpit for prayers. He stated that though prayers were offered daily for the same people they failed to find the comfort for which they sought. While he questioned himself for the cause of this, the words of Peter at Pentecost came to his mind, "Repent and be baptized every

one of you in the name of Jesus Christ for the remission of your
sins, and ye shall receive the gift of the Holy Ghost." He quoted
the words of the apostle Peter to them and urged them to comply.
Here was the beginning of his teaching on the remission of sins,
though he did not grasp the full force of this truth until he heard
it proclaimed at a later date by Alexander Campbell.

1812 A.D. STONE BAPTIZES WILLIAM CALDWELL,
A PRESBYTERIAN PREACHER

The Separate Baptists were holding their annual association in
Meigs County, Ohio, and they requested the aid of Barton Stone in
their deliberations.

When the subject of church government came up for discussion,
he was asked to express his views. He spoke openly upon the
subject, calling attention to the fact that creeds were insufficient
as guides in church government and religious matters, holding forth
the Bible as the only divine guide.

The association agree to discard their human guide and to take
the Bible alone as their rule of faith and conduct, to discard the
name Baptist and accept the name Christian, to disband their association, and to blend their efforts with those of Stone and his co-
laborers in the great work of Christian union. This resulted in multitudes being added to the Lord. The entrance of Alexander Campbell into Kentucky caused no small stir among the people. Some
accepted him as a messenger of God while others accused him of
deceiving the people.

Barton Stone stated that he heard him often in public and in
private and could see no difference between the teaching of Alexander Campbell and that which he and his brethren had taught for
many years, except on baptism for the remission of sins. This, too,
Barton Stone had once taught, but had not emphasized it as Alexander Campbell did. It became evident that they were both teaching
the same truth and it was not long until their efforts were blended
together.

1834 A.D. BARTON STONE MOVED TO ILLINOIS

In this state he continued to labor to build up the cause of Christ.
A few years later he was stricken with paralysis which greatly
impaired his labors.

Believing that the time was not far distant when he should leave
the things of this life behind he began his last trip through Indiana,
Ohio and Kentucky. He arrived at Noblesville, Indiana, on the
tenth of June and visited with several preachers of that state.

Passing through Ohio, Barton Stone came to Cane Ridge, the second Lord's Day in August, where forty-two years before he had pleaded for a restoration of the church for which Christ died.

Here he spoke from Acts 20: 17-21 and as he left the meeting house he turned and looked at the old building, at the graves and the surrounding groves, and then said, "I shall see this place no more."

In October of the following year, he, in company with his wife and youngest son, made a visit to a number of congregations in Missouri, among them, an annual meeting near Columbia, in Boone County. His discourse, filled with admonitions and warnings, was directed to both saints and sinners. After spending a few days with his son, he left for his home at Jacksonville, Illinois, but got no farther than the home of his son-in-law, S. A. Bowen, at Hannibal, Missouri, where he passed away on November 9, 1844.

His mortal remains were laid to rest upon the grounds of the Cane Ridge meeting house and the stone marking his final resting place states that it was erected to his memory by "his friends of the Church of Christ."

"What dreary effects of those accursed divisions are to be seen, even in this highly favored country, where the sword of the civil magistrate has not yet learned to serve at the altar! Have we not seen congregations broken to pieces, neighborhoods of professing Christians first thrown into confusion by party contentions, and, in the end, entirely deprived of gospel ordinances; while, in the meanwhile, large settlements and tracts of country remain to this day destitute of a gospel ministry, many of them in little better than a state of heathenism, the churches being so weakened by divisions that they can not send them ministers, or the people so divided among themselves that they will not receive them? Several, at the same time, who live at the door of a preached gospel, dare not in conscience go to hear it, and, of course, enjoy little more advantage in that respect than living in the midst of heathen."

Declaration and Address—Thomas Campbell

CHAPTER 22

CAUSES OF RELIGIOUS DIVISION

Jesus said, "Upon this rock I will build my church and the gates of hell shall not prevail against it." The word "churches" was used only when the writer spoke of the congregations in a given district, as the "churches of Galatia" or "The seven churches which are in Asia."

The churches of the New Testament age had accepted the same gospel, were obedient to the same commands, had the same kind of government, and followed the same worship.

While the churches of Christendom admit the authority of the Scriptures, it is certain that all of the doctrines of the religious world do not come from the Bible. Among the causes of division may be listed the following:

1. A lack of knowledge of God's word. Though people profess to have a love for God and his word, they do not study it as they should to learn God's will. God revealed his will to the Jewish people in the Old Testament Scriptures and when his people neglected the study of his word they were led into evil. The New Testament reveals the will of God for all mankind and we are commanded to let it be our guide. "If any man speak let him speak as the oracles of God, if any man minister, let him do it as of the ability which God giveth, that God in all things may be glorified through Jesus Christ, to whom be praise and dominion for ever and ever. Amen."[1]

Since the Scriptures furnish us unto all good works and are profitable for doctrine, certainly every person who desires to do the will of God should have an understanding of his word.

2. Division among those who want to be the children of God is caused by following human creeds. Many of the practices of the religious world are taught in some creed but are not taught in the word of God. Creeds, confessions of faith, church manuals and prayer books are the product of some human council. They possess no divine authority because neither God, Christ, nor the apostles ordered them to be made. The very fact that the Savior gave no authority for their existence is proof that they infringe upon the Bible. It is sometimes affirmed that they are more easily understood than the Bible. If this is true then man is wiser than God

---

1. 1 Pet. 4 : 11.

and better able to express himself than the heavenly Father. Such is the conclusion we are forced to accept if creeds are to be preferred above the Scriptures.

It is often asserted that the acceptance of creeds will bring unity among religious groups. When the church was first established it was united, but after the Nicean creed was formed, division resulted from the interpretations which were placed upon it. Creeds have always produced division. This is shown by the fact that there are ten different kinds of Presbyterians, yet all of them subscribe to the same creed. There are nineteen different branches of the Methodist church which subscribe to the principles of the Methodist creed. There are twenty-one Lutheran groups. In the beginning, the Lutherans were united in one body, but after the Augsburg Confession of Faith was produced division entered their ranks.

3. Division is produced by wearing names that are not found in the New Testament. Christ prayed that those who believed on him through the teaching of the apostles might all be one. As long as human names, such as Presbyterians, Methodists, Lutherans, are worn by religious people division will exist among those who want to serve God. The name by which the followers of Christ were called in the New Testament is a scriptural name and the only one that honors Christ.

4. Division is produced by the form of church government that is advocated. There are several forms of church government in existence today, only one of which is revealed in the word of God.

A. The papal form of church government is characteristic of the Roman Catholic Church. The pope is regarded as the viceregent of Christ and the supreme bishop of the Church. He is regarded as infallible in his decisions and when elected by the college of cardinals and invested with authority he is accountable to no man or group of men. It required centuries to develop this form of church government and the doctrine of the infallibility of the pope.

B. The Episcopacy is the form of church government accepted by the Church of England and the Episcopal Church in America. They profess to have an unbroken line of bishops from the days of the apostles and through this line of bishops they claim to trace the church back to the apostles. But these theories do not coincide with the teaching of the Scriptures and the facts of history.

In the New Testament the elders and the bishops were the same officials, the term "elder" denoting that they were men of age and experience, while the word "bishop" indicated their work as overseers of the flock. "For this cause left I thee in Crete, that thou shouldest set in order the things that are wanting and ordain elders in every city, as I had appointed thee: If any be blameless, the husband of one wife, having faithful children not accused of riot or unruly. For a bishop must be blameless as the steward of God; not self willed, not soon angry, not given to wine, no striker, not given to filthy lucre."[2] This shows that the elders and the bishops were the same officials, so the theory of a government by bishops over a group of churches is not in harmony with the New Testament.

> "At first these terms, "Presbuteroi," "Episcopoi," as well as the offices which they represented, were identical and an entire equality of rank and authority appears to have existed among all members of the council in each church. That the titles were interchangeable in the days of the apostles, the Sacred Records clearly show (Acts 20: 17, 28, and Titus 1: 5, 7, 9.); the same parties being spoken of as Elders and Bishops or Overseers."*
>
> "The Apostles wished in accordance with the spirit of Christianity not to govern alone; but preferred that the body of believers should govern themselves under their guidance. Thus they divided the government of the Church with tried men, who formed a presiding council of Elders, similar to that which was known in the Jewish synagogues under the title of 'Presbuteroi.' But with the Hellenic Gentiles, another name was joined, more allied to the designation of civil and social relations among the Greek,—"Episcopoi," which designed Overseers over the whole Church, and its collective concerns."†

This is sufficient to show that the Episcopacy was not the government of the churches in the days of the apostles.

C. The Congregational form of church policy makes the congregation absolute in authority within its own borders. While it was true that the congregation selected those who were to be ordained as elders, if approved, the authority of the congregation did not extend beyond this work.

D. The Presbyters or Elders were the highest officials in the local congregations in the New Testament church. When men were qualified they were selected by the congregation and appointed by the evangelist.

Not until apostasy developed within the church was this procedure changed. When Paul and Barnabas returned to visit the churches they had planted they ordained elders in every church and prayed and fasted and commended them to God. Here is an example of a scriptural form of church government and the only form that is in harmony with the word of God.

5. Division is caused by those who claim to be God's people when one verse of Scripture is used as a basis for some doctrine, without considering what God has said elsewhere upon the same subject.

The will of God can not be learned by such a method. The only

---

2. Titus. 1: 5-7.
* *The Early Christian Church*—Kimber. Church Organization. Pages 102, 103.
† *History of the Church*—Neander. Volume 1, Pages 85, 143.

means by which we can learn the will of the Lord is to read all that God has revealed upon any subject. This method of Bible study is responsible for the doctrine of salvation by faith only, the doctrine that God has elected some to be saved and others to be lost, the doctrine of sinless perfection, which teaches that we become so perfect we will never sin.

This method of reasoning, concluding that God has expressed his will upon the subject by one verse of Scripture, to the exclusion of all that he has revealed in other verses, has brought into existence the doctrine that every person who comes into the world is born in sin, and the doctrine that the Holy Spirit must operate upon the heart of man separate and apart from the word of God before one can be saved.

Let us remember that *all Scripture* is profitable for doctrine, and not just one verse separated from all other.

6. Division is caused among religious people because of rejecting what the Bible says upon the subject of baptism. Some religious groups sprinkle water upon the candidate, others give the candidate the choice of having water poured upon him, or of being immersed. Some groups practice triune immersion and some do not practice either sprinkling, pouring or immersion. Multitudes of sincere people have been led to believe if they do not have their babes sprinkled they will be lost should they die. One who studies the New Testament will find therein no command or example, by Christ or the Apostles for infant baptism. Those who contend for it, contend for something which is not taught in the Bible. Immersion only is baptism.

> "The sacrament of baptism was administered in this century without the public assemblies in places appointed and prepared for that purpose; was performed by the immersion of the whole body in the baptismal font . . ."*

This agrees with what we read in God's word. "Buried with him in baptism, wherein also ye are risen with him through the faith of the operation of God, who hath raised him from the dead."[3] Let us follow the teaching of God's word and we will always be right.

7. Division is caused over what constitutes acceptable worship in the sight of God. Worship is adoration rendered unto God. It is not just the outward performance of some certain act.

True worship is something that takes place in the heart. The outward act only reveals what is in the heart. For that which we do as worship to be acceptable in God's sight, it must be prompted by the right motive and rendered in harmony with God's will.

---

* *Ecclesiastical History*—Mosheim. Century II, Part II, Chapter 4, Section 8, Page 28.
  3. Col. 2:12.

To practice anything as worship that is not authorized by God's word. renders that worship vain.

Jesus said to the woman at the well, "God is a spirit and they that worship him must worship him in spirit and in truth." We read that the church in Jerusalem continued steadfastly in the apostles' doctrine and fellowship, and in breaking of bread and in prayers. They came together upon the first day of the week for the breaking of bread.

This establishes the time when the Lord's Supper was observed in the apostolic age. There is no evidence that it was ever observed on Thursday, on Friday, or Saturday. The Lord's Supper is the great memorial of the church, by which we remember Christ. Some religious groups observe this memorial once a month, others once every three months, asserting that the Bible does not say to observe it on the first day of every week, but the fact that every week has a first day shows how often it must be observed.

Others affirm that, when thanks are given for the loaf and the fruit of the vine, they become the actual body and blood of Christ, the same body which was nailed to the cross. This conclusion is drawn from the words of Christ, "This is my body; this is my blood." But Christ also said, "I am the vine," yet we do not think of him as a literal vine.

Prayer was also a part of the worship. If our prayers are to be answered, they must be in harmony with the teaching of God's word. There were no stereotyped forms to be followed in the church of the Lord, for their prayers came from the heart. The disciples of the Lord taught and admonished one another in psalms, hymns, and spiritual songs. There is no indication in the New Testament that instrumental music was used in connection with the worship of the church.

The lack of unity upon the part of those who profess to be the people of God is more productive of infidelity than any other cause. There is need to get back to the word of God, to the purity and simplicity of the church of the Lord. All religious people profess to believe in the same God, to accept the same Bible, and to acknowledge the same Christ. Would it not be a wonderful thing, if all who want to serve the Lord, would renounce the things that now divide religious people, and the strife that now separates one group from another, and all belong to the one body?

The Lord never expected his church to be divided and subdivided into groups, parties and factions for which there is no authority in his word. Christ prayed for the unity of God's people, saying, "Neither pray I for these alone, but for them also which shall believe on me through their word, that they may all be one."

The Cane Ridge Meeting-House

The Brush Run Meeting-House

Chapter 23

A PLEA FOR CHRISTIAN UNITY

The moral condition of the people of this nation was very low at the beginning of the Restoration movement. Infidelity influenced a great many people. Many had lost confidence, not in God, nor in the Bible, but in the many churches that dominated the religious scene. The majority of the people who were religiously inclined held to Calvinism. They believed that God had selected a definite number of people to be saved, and that this number could not be increased, neither could it be diminished. People had little reason for living a righteous life, for if they were to be saved, they were saved already, and if they were to be lost, righteous living would not save them.

Religious leaders taught that no one could understand the Bible but themselves. It was a common teaching that man was born totally depraved, and could do nothing to save himself, but must wait until God purposed to save him. Conversion was considered a miracle. Sinners were taught to seek God in prayer, to renounce sin, and just believe that Jesus was the Son of God, and that God would then be reconciled to them and save them.

Honest seekers could not understand why a friend would profess to be saved while they must yet continue in prayer. When they failed to experience any change, they concluded they were among the lost, sometimes turning to atheism.

There was in Ireland at this time, a young man who was teaching school at Sheepbridge, who had been born February 1, 1763. A friend who had been impressed with the ability of Thomas Campbell, the young teacher, offered to defray his expenses at the University of Glasgow. After three years of study there, he turned his attention to the study of theology at the Anti-Burgher School, where Archibald Brown was a teacher. When this period of theological training ended, Thomas Campbell appeared before the Presbytery for his examination and became a probationer, being allowed to preach under the supervision of the Synod.

1787 A.D. MARRIAGE OF THOMAS CAMPBELL

Thomas Campbell again turned to teaching school, to supplement his meager income as a preacher. He had married Jane Corneigle, whose ancestors were French Huguenots.

1798 A.D. THOMAS CAMPBELL PRESENTED A PLEA FOR UNITY

Thomas Campbell gave his attention to the unity of two Burgher groups of the Presbyterian church. The Seceder group of Ireland was ready for the restoration of unity, and selected Thomas Campbell to present their case before the Synod at Glasgow. He directed his efforts to uniting these two bodies which had the same teaching and practice. It was said that "in the Synod he out-argued his associates, but they out-voted him." The plea for unity was rejected by the Synod at that time, but was adopted several years later.

The Seceder Presbyterians were divided into several branches, all subscribing to the same creed, and each claiming to be the true church. The branch to which Thomas Campbell belonged was especially strict. One man was excluded from fellowship because he listened to the preaching of James Haldane.

The arduous work of teaching school and looking after the small congregation to which he had been assigned, impaired the health of Thomas Campbell, and his physician prescribed a rest and a sea voyage. When the son of the family informed his father of his intentions to go to America when he became of age, the father seriously considered the son's suggestion that the father go first and get located, and the rest of the family would follow.

Some of the friends and parishioners of Thomas Campbell had left Ireland for America, taking up residence near Washington, Pennsylvania. Here, too the father purposed to locate if he found conditions suitable. He set sail for America in 1807, carrying with him his certificate of church membership which stated his ministerial standing, his Bible, and possibly a few books.

When he arrived at Philadelphia he learned that the Synod of the Presbyterian church was in session and so presented himself and his church letter.

> "We, the remaining members of the Presbytery at Market Hall, March 24, 1807, do hereby certify that the bearer, Thomas Campbell, has been for about nine years, minister of the gospel in the seceding congregation of Ahorey, and co-presbyter with us, during which time he has maintained an irreproachable moral character; and, in the discharge of the duties of his sacred functions has conducted himself as a faithful minister of Christ; and is now released from his pastoral charge over said congregation at his own request, upon good and sufficient reasons for his resignations of said charge, particularly his intention of going to America. Given under our hands at our presbyterial meeting, the day and year above written. The above, by order of the Presbytery, is subscribed by David Arrott, Moderator."*

---

* *Memoirs of Elder Thomas Campbell*—Campbell. Chapter 1, Page 20.

Mr. Campbell established a residence in Washington, Pennsylvania, and was assigned to the Chartiers Presbytery.

The Presbytery sent Thomas Campbell to minister to some of the scattered brethren who lived along the banks of the Allegheny River. His preaching drew together families who were identified with other groups of the Presbyterian church. He looked upon them as sheep without a shepherd.

In his sermon prior to the memorial supper of the Lord, he mentioned the strife and division existing among those who professed to be the people of God. When thanks had been given for the Lord's Supper, he invited all who were so disposed to join in the observance of this institution. A young minister who was present carried this information to the Presbytery where charges were preferred against him for failing to follow the practices of the church. Others found fault with his preaching in which he called attention to the fact that the Scriptures were sufficient as a guide without resorting to human documents. Other complaints filed against Thomas Campbell by his fellow ministers seemed to indicate that they looked on him as an intruder in their territory.

The investigation of the Presbytery of Chartiers found Thomas Campbell guilty as charged, which caused him to appeal to the Synod of Philadelphia. Here he was cleared of part of the charges, but was rebuked and admonished by that body. He protested against the unjust treatment which he had received at the hands of his own brethren who seemed determined to inflict upon him as much persecution as possible. When he returned to the jurisdiction of the Presbytery at Chartiers he found that no assignments had been made for him to work there as a minister.

Thomas Campbell therefore separated himself from the Synod of the Seceder Presbyterian Church, sending them notice of his separation, saying in part—

"It is with sincere reluctance, and at the same time, with all due respect and esteem for the brethren of this reverend Synod who have presided in the trial of my case, that I find myself in duty bound to refuse submission to their decision as unjust and partial; and finally to decline their authority, while they continue thus to overlook the grievous and flagrant maladministration of the Presbytery of Chartiers.

And I hereby do decline all ministerial connection with, or subjection to, the Associate Synod of North America, on account of the aforesaid corruptions and grievances; and do henceforth hold myself altogether unaffected by their decisions. And that I may be properly understood, I will distinctly state that while especial reference is had to the corruptions of the

Presbytery of Chartiers, which constitute only a part of this
Synod, the corruptions of that Presbytery now become also the
corruptions of the whole Synod; because when laid open to this
Synod, and unprotested against, the Synod pass them over
without due inquiry and without animadversion."

—Thomas Campbell.

Those who stood with Thomas Campbell in his opposition to the
treatment he had received from the Chartiers Presbytery organized
the Christian Association of Washington, Pennsylvania, and erected
on the Sinclair farm, three miles west of Mount Pleasant, a log
building for religious services. At a meeting of the Association,
twenty-one persons were appointed for recommending the best
means of promoting the purpose of this Association. Mr. Campbell
was selected to write out their report. This report called "The
Declaration and Address" was read to the Association on September
7th, and approved by the committee.

This document contained thirty thousand words and is of course
much too long to be given in its entirety in this work.

Briefly stated, "The Declaration and Address" embraced the following points:

1. The church of Christ on earth is essentially, intentionally,
   and constitutionally one, consisting of all those in every place
   that profess Christ and obedience to him in all things, according to the Scriptures, and that manifest the same by their
   tempers and their conduct.
2. There should be no schisms or uncharitable divisions among
   congregations of believers. The churches should walk by the
   same rule and speak the same thing.
3. Nothing should be inculcated as articles of faith nor required
   as terms of communion but what is expressly taught in the
   word of God, either in expressed terms or approved precedent.
4. The Old and New Testaments make a perfect revelation of
   the divine will; the New Testament is a perfect constitution
   for the worship, discipline, and government of the New
   Testament church.
5. Human authority has no power to impose new commands
   and ordinances not enjoined by the Lord. Nothing ought to
   be received into the faith or worship of the church, or be
   made a term of communion among Christians, that is not as
   old as the New Testament.
6. Faith must stand in the power of God, not the wisdom of men.
7. Doctrinal exhibitions of divine truth ought not be made
   terms of communion.

8. Admission into the church is permissible to those who realize their lost condition, recognize the way of salvation through Jesus Christ, confess him, and render obedience to him.

9. All that are enabled to make profession, and to manifest it in their conduct, should consider others in the church as the saints of God, and should live together as the children of the heavenly Father.

10. Divisions among Christians is a horrid evil. It is anti-Christian and anti-scriptural. It destroys the love that should obtain among brethren.

11. A partial neglect of the revealed will of God, and an assumed authority for making human opinions terms of communion, have been causes of divisions.

12. Those are to be received as members of the church who have a due measure of scriptural knowledge and profess their faith in Christ and obedience to him in all things. Ordinances are to be carefully observed after the example of the primitive church exhibited in the New Testament.

13. Human expediences are never to be permitted to produce contentions nor divisions in the church."

While these events were transpiring, the wife and children of Thomas Campbell were yet in Ireland. He had expected that his family would arrive in America some time in July, or August, of 1808, so he requested a two months' appointment in Philadelphia.

The departure of the family had, however, been delayed by illness. After they recovered, Alexander went to Londonderry and booked passage on the Hibernia for the family to come to America. The captain of this ship proved to be very stubborn, and the crew young and inexperienced. After several unsuccessful starts they finally set sail and on October 7, during a sudden squall, the ship ran aground on a rock. The family suffered the loss of part of their goods and fearing to sail again at that season of the year, they decided to spend the winter in Glasgow.

Here, Alexander enrolled in the University as a student of French, New Testament Greek, Latin, Logic, and Philosophy, having as instructors two professors who had taught his father more than twenty years before.

He also availed himself of hearing some of the great religious leaders of that day. He seemed to be more influenced by the teaching of the Haldanes than by any others. The Haldanes were two brothers, independent preachers, who were seeking for a remedy for the low spiritual condition of that age.

One of the subjects that claimed the attention of the young

student was the history of the church. He was surprised at the numerous groups into which the church had divided. His attention was first claimed by the Roman Catholic Church with its superstitions and ritualism. But when he looked at the Protestant side of the picture it was far from attractive. Instead of being able to present a united front against the corruption of Rome, he found that strife and discord controlled their activities. Even the Presbyterians to which he belonged were divided into Seceders, Burghers, Anti-Burghers, Old Lights and New Lights, all adding their part to filling the world with religious confusion.

> "At last his doubts led him to question his right to continue in the fellowship of the Seceder Church. The crucial hour came at the semi-annual communion service, near the close of his sojourn in Glasgow. It was the custom to supply all who, according to the rules of the church, were entitled to a place at the Lord's Supper with a metallic token, thus shutting out those who seemed unworthy of this solemn privilege. Though filled with conscientious misgivings about sanctioning a religious system which he no longer approved, he finally decided to apply for a token. As he had no letter of recommendation from his home church in Ireland, it was necessary for him to pass an examination on the previous Saturday before the elders. This he did to the satisfaction of all.
>
> But when the hour for the celebration of the Lord's Supper arrived, his scruples overcame him, and instead of taking his place among the communicants, he cast his token into the plate that was passed around, and declined to partake with the rest.
>
> The ring of that token, as it fell from his hands, was like the ring of Martin Luther's hammer on the door of Wittenberg Cathedral, announced his renunciation of the old church ties, and marks the moment at which he forever ceased to recognize the claims or authority of a human creed to bind upon men the conditions of their acceptance with God."*

1809 A.D. ALEXANDER CAMPBELL COMES TO AMERICA

On August 7, 1809, the family again embarked for America and after many difficulties landed in New York, September 29, and after spending a few days there reached Philadelphia, on October 7. Here they loaded their household possessions into a Conestoga wagon and started on the long journey of three hundred fifty miles to Washington, Pennsylvania.

When the father learned the family had left Ireland, and perhaps were already in America, he immediately set out for Philadelphia. Somewhere on the National Pike, about three days journey from Washington, Thomas Campbell and his family met and had a pleasant reunion after a separation of two years.

---

* *Life of Alexander Campbell*—Grafton. Chapter 2, Pages 40, 41.

During this separation both the father and the son had changed their attitude toward the Seceder Presbyterian church.

Thomas Campbell rehearsed to his son all the events that transpired between himself and the Chartiers Presbytery. When the father told the son of his complete separation from the Seceder church, the son confessed that he, too, now had different religious convictions. The father then submitted to his son the first copy of the statement which he had prepared at the request of the Christian Association. What the father had written in "The Declaration and Address" were also the convictions of the son. He expressed himself as being willing to devote his time and talents to the proclamation of the principles therein set forth. Thomas Campbell had not acted upon impulse. He was well qualified by his university training for the course he expected to pursue. He purposed to unite a separated and divided church. He stressed the necessity of unity. He taught that all should walk by the same rule, mind the same thing, be joined in the same mind and be guided by the same judgment.

Weekly the Christian Association came together to worship God, and those who attended, heard Thomas Campbell speak of the evils of division and the necessity of devising a way to end them. He advocated the acceptance of the Scriptures as all sufficient for their guidance. Here was the creed he affirmed that guided the New Testament Church, "for they continued steadfastly in the apostles' doctrine." Here was a creed that need never be revised. These people, in their endeavor to restore the church as it was in the days of the apostles, purposed to call Bible things by Bible names. They believed nothing should be included in the worship, nor held as a matter of faith, unless it was clearly taught in the word of God.

Their purpose to speak only where the scriptures spoke, brought about a separation of some because they would have to surrender some of their human doctrines, notably among them, the doctrine of infant baptism, the title of Reverend, and a government vested in an ecclesiastical body separate from the church.

The Restoration had its beginning at the right time. The reformation of Luther, Knox, Zwingli, and others, prepared the way for a complete return to the word of God and to the church of the New Testament.

The men of the Restoration movement accepted all that the Reformers taught that was in harmony with the Bible, but they did not produce any creeds, confessions of faith, or church manuals, but accepted the word of God alone. Their efforts were directed not to reforming any church, but to the fulfillment of the prayer of the Savior, "That they may all be one."

Thomas Campbell wanted to see the church exactly as it was in the beginning. He wanted to see it on the same foundation upon which it stood in the days of the apostles, proclaiming the gospel as God's power unto salvation.

This was something more than Luther, Calvin or Zwingli proposed. They purposed the reformation of the Catholic church, but the thing for which Thomas Campbell contended was not a reformation in which some unscriptural doctrines were to be rejected and some abuses corrected. It was to be a complete restoration of Christianity as it was in the beginning.

1810 A.D. THOMAS CAMPBELL URGED TO BECOME AFFILIATED WITH THE SYNOD OF PITTSBURGH

Many of his friends, including several Presbyterian ministers, suggested that he request an ecclesiastical union with the Synod of Pittsburgh. In the interest of unity he made his request for union with this Synod, speaking at length and answering such questions as were propounded. The Synod voted not to receive him. It condemned his plan as one which would promote division and provide for corruption in discipline. They added that "other important reasons" existed for not receiving him. When he requested an explanation of the phrase, they pointed out that he declared the baptism of infants unscriptural, and that he encouraged his son to preach when he had not been licensed to do so. He thus discovered that his own original church would not receive him. As the time for the spring meeting drew near, a step was taken that up to this point had been undesirable. The society of believers did not consider that it was a church, but only advocates of church reformation and church unity. Their rejection by the Synod now convinced them that they must declare themselves a church. This was done at their May meeting.

1811 A.D. THE CHURCH OF CHRIST ESTABLISHED AT BRUSH RUN

Thomas Campbell was selected to serve as elder, four were appointed deacons, and Alexander Campbell was licensed to preach. Those who were banded together were searching for the primitive church as it existed in the days of the apostles. They accepted the authority of the scriptures as the only foundation for faith. Their objective was the unity of all who professed to be the people of God.

In their assembly on the first day of the week they attended to the Lord's Supper. Some who assembled with them did not partake because they believed they had not been scripturally baptized.

"An episode occurred at this first meeting which soon led to important changes in the practice of this infant church. It was resolved that the Lord's Supper should be celebrated weekly, in conformity with the example of the primitive church; but at the first communion service it was observed that several who were regarded as members did not partake of the emblems. On inquiry, it was discovered that they did not consider themselves as scriptural subjects, as they had not been baptized. Upon further inquiry, it was learned that they would be satisfied with nothing but immersion as scriptural baptism. Though Thomas Campbell had himself been sprinkled in infancy, and did not yet question the validity of his baptism, he did not scruple to accede to the demands of these members, since they had never been baptized. So they were taken to a pool in Buffalo Creek, and with due ceremony immersed. It is curious to observe the manner of this first immersion in the new church, which would now scarcely be regarded as befitting the solemnity of the occasion. He requested the candidates to wade out into the pool, to the depth of their shoulders, while he climbed out on an overhanging root, and bent their heads beneath the water, repeating as he did so the baptismal formula."*

Up to this time neither Thomas Campbell, nor his son Alexander, had given much consideration to the subject of baptism. The birth of a daughter in the home of Alexander Campbell now brought the question before them for immediate consideration. Though he had before held that it would be unscriptural to make the matter a test of fellowship, he now began a search of the Scriptures for an answer that would satisfy his conscience. At the conclusion of his study he was satisfied that the baptism of infants and the practice of sprinkling was unscriptural, and that he therefore had never been baptized. His wife agreed with him in this, and they purposed to obey the command of Christ as soon as possible. He asked a Baptist minister, Matthias Luce, to assist him in obeying the command. He made it clear to the administrator that he wanted to be baptized only on confession of his faith in Christ as the Son of God. The minister at first hesitated about the matter, stating that it was contrary to Baptist usage, but later agreed to administer the ordinance to those who desired it.

He informed his father of his purpose and though he offered no objection, he had little to say to his son upon the subject. On the day when the son and his wife were to be baptized, Thomas Campbell, his wife, and oldest daughter, appeared ready to comply with the divine command. Thomas Campbell preached a sermon on that day, June 12, 1812, to those who had assembled at the home of David Bryant, giving the reasons for believing that immersion was New Testament baptism. Alexander Campbell spoke after his

---

* *The Life of Alexander Campbell*—Grafton. Chapter 5, Pages 82, 83.

father, declaring that penitent believers alone were scriptural subjects for baptism. James Hansen and his wife were persuaded by his teaching, which was confirmed by the word of God, that they, too, should be baptized.

The next day thirteen others were baptized by Thomas Campbell, and immersion became the accepted practice of the congregation.

Soon after this event the Brush Run church was invited to become a part of the Redstone Baptist Association. The matter was placed before the Brush Run church and it was decided that, if they were granted the privilege of being independent of all human creeds, and were allowed to preach whatever they learned from the Scriptures, they would become a part of the Redstone Association.

For some time the relationship of the Campbells and the Association was all that could be desired, but eventually the popularity of Alexander Campbell among the churches of the Association caused some of the ministers to show their resentment against his method of presenting Bible truths.

The delivery of the "Sermon on the Law" by Alexander Campbell before the Association aroused so much criticism, that charges of heresy were brought against him. He was acquitted of the charge but the persecution and misrepresentation continued.

Each year the charge was repeated, and this convinced Alexander Campbell that he could expect nothing else from his brethren in the ministry.

Following the establishment of a new congregation at Wellsburg, Virginia, the Mahoning Baptist Association extended an invitation for all of the churches which had been established to become identified with them. This invitation was accepted. The clerk of the meeting entered this statement in the minutes of the meeting: "At the request of the church of Christ at Wellsburg, it was received into this Association."

At this time this congregation had grown to forty members.

1820 A.D. CAMPBELL-WALKER DEBATE

This debate was held at Mt. Pleasant, Ohio, beginning on June 19, between Mr. Campbell and John Walker of the Presbyterian church. The subject discussed was "Baptism." During the debate Mr. Campbell said, "Baptism is connected with the promise of the remission of sins and the gift of the Holy Spirit." Later this truth was emphasized as a necessary part of the restoration of the gospel.

The Presbyterians agreed that Walker lost the debate. His reputation as a debater was also lost. At the conclusion of the debate,

Mr. Campbell issued a challenge to meet any Presbyterian in debate upon the same subject.

This debate convinced the public that the doctrine of immersion had an able defender in the person of Alexander Campbell. With the publication of the debate, his fame spread, and brought requests for Campbell to visit various communities.

In the spring of 1823, a circular was issued announcing the publication of a religious magazine which was to be devoted to the promulgation of truth and the condemnation of error in doctrine or practice. It was to promote no cause except that of Christianity.

In presenting the picture of the primitive church under the title, "The Christian Religion," the editor of the new publication said,

> "The societies called churches, constituted and set in order by those ministers of the New Testament, were of such as received and acknowledged Jesus, as Lord Messiah, the Savior of the world, and had put themselves under his guidance. The ONLY BOND OF UNION among them was faith in him and submission to his will. No subscription to abstract propositions framed by synods; no decrees of councils sanctioned by kings; no rules of practice commanded by ecclesiastical courts were imposed on them as terms of admission into, or of continuance in this holy brotherhood. In the 'apostles' doctrine' and in the 'apostles' commandments' they steadfastly continued. Their fraternity was a fraternity of love, peace, gratitude, cheerfulnes, joy, charity, and universal benevolence.
>
> Their religion did not manifest itself in public fasts or carnivals. They had no festivals—no great and solemn meetings. Their meeting on the first day of the week was at all times alike solemn, joyful, and interesting. Their religion was not of that elastic and porous kind, which at one time is compressed into some cold formalities, and at another expanded by prodigious zeal and warmth. No, their piety did not at one time rise to paroxysms, and their zeal to effervescence, and by and by, languish into frigid ceremony and lifeless forms.
>
> It was the pure, clear, and swelling current of love to God, of love to man, expressed in all of the variety of doing good. The order of their assemblies was uniformly the same. It did not vary with moons or seasons. It did not change as dress nor fluctuate as the manners of the times. Their devotion did not diversify itself into the endless forms of modern times.
>
> They had no monthly concerts for prayer; no solemn convocations, no great fasts, nor preparation, nor thanksgiving days.
>
> Their churches were not fractured into missionary societies, Bible societies, educational societies; nor did they dream of organizing such in the world. The head of a believing household was not in those days a president or manager of a board of foreign missions; his wife, the president of some female education society; his eldest son, the recording secretary of some domestic Bible society; his eldest daughter, the corresponding secretary of a mite society; his servant maid, the vice president of a rag society; and his little daughter the tutoress of a Sunday school. They knew nothing of the hobbies of modern times.

In their church capacity alone they moved. They neither transformed themselves into any other kind of association, nor did they fracture and sever themselves into divers societies.

They viewed the church of Jesus Christ as the scheme of heaven to ameliorate the world; as members of it, they considered themselves bound to do all they could for the glory of God and the good of men.

They dared not transfer to a missionary society, or Bible society, or education society, a cent or a prayer, lest in so doing they should rob the church of its glory, and exalt the inventions of men above the wisdom of God. The church they considered the 'pillar and ground of the truth'; they viewed it as the temple of the Holy Spirit; as the house of the living.God. They considered if they did all they could in this capacity, they had nothing left for any other object of a religious nature."*

1823 A.D. CAMPBELL-McCALLA DEBATE

This debate was held at Washington, Kentucky, beginning on October 15, and concluding on the 22nd.

"Mr. McCalla, a Presbyterian preacher of Kentucky, in the spring of 1823, intimated his willingness to engage Mr. Campbell in a discussion of the question of baptism, that he might retrieve the injury which had been done his cause by Mr. Walker's admitted failure. Mr. Campbell, having ascertained his standing, agreed to meet him, and arrangements were made for the discussion to take place in October, in the town of Washington, Ky. The low stage of the Ohio River necessitated Mr. Campbell's making the entire journey on horseback. Here, as in his former discussion, the entire bearing of the baptismal question was carefully canvassed. It is not necessary, at this point, to go into the details of the arguments pro and con. Each controverted point was hotly contested in the presence of a vast assemblage, which had been drawn together by Mr. Campbell's reputation and their interest in the question at issue. During this discussion, which lasted seven days, in addition to his defense of the scriptural mode and subject of baptism, Mr. Campbell gradually, for the first time, unfolded it's design and true place in the economy of the Gospel, though it was several years before any use was made of it in urging obedience to Christ"†

In this same year, Alexander Campbell began the publication of the Christian Baptist, at Bethany, Virginia. "The Christian Baptist" was published for several years and then gave place to "The Millennial Harbinger," a monthly paper which was much larger than the first periodical. The articles appearing in the Harbinger created much discussion among all religious groups. Some of his friends thought he was too severe in his condemnation of the clergy whom he designated as hirelings and scrap doctors.

They were condemned for their clerical dress, for their pretended piety and for their use of the titles of Doctor, Bishop or Reverend.

---

* *The Christian Baptist.* Volume 1, Number 1, Pages 6, 7.
† *Life of Alexander Campbell*—Grafton. Chapter 7, Pages 110, 111.

Alexander Campbell was strongly opposed to the use of creeds and confessions of faith. He held them to be responsible for much of the strife, sectarianism and division existing in the world. He affirmed that "had the founder of the Christian faith been defective in wisdom . . . then his religion might be improved, or reformed, or better adapted to existing circumstances. But as all Christians admit that he foresaw and anticipated all the events and revolutions in human history, and that the present state of things was as present to his mind as the circumstances that encompassed him in Judea, or in the judgment hall of Caiaphas; that he has wisdom and understanding perfectly adequate to institute, arrange, and adapt a system of things, suitable to all exigencies and emergencies of men and things, and that his philanthropy was not only unparalleled in the annals of the world, but absolutely perfect and necessarily leading to and resulting in, that institution which was most beneficial to man in the present and future world."

The creeds and the councils which produced them, Mr. Campbell charged, were responsible for the lack of understanding of God's word. He further stated that "in the ancient order of things there were no creeds or compilations of doctrine in abstract terms, nor in other terms, other than the terms adopted by the Holy Spirit in the New Testament."

"Therefore, all such are to be discarded, from the fact that none of those now in use, nor ever at any time in use, existed in the apostolic age. But as many considerations are urged why they should be used, we shall briefly advert to these and attempt to show that they are perfectly irrational, and consequently foolish and vain. It is argued that confessions of faith are, or may be, much plainer and of much more easy apprehension and comprehension than the oracles of God. Men, then, are either wiser or more benevolent than God. If the truths in the Bible can be expressed more plainly by modern divines than they are by the Holy Spirit, then it follows that God either would not or could not express them in words so plainly as men."

Of course such teaching met with strong opposition from those who believed them necessary for the unity of the church.

The Philadelphia "Confession of Faith" was accepted by most of the Baptist churches through which Alexander Campbell was seeking to bring about a restoration of the New Testament church.

1824. A.D. THE FIRST MEETING BETWEEN BARTON STONE AND ALEXANDER CAMPBELL

Each of these reformers had long heard of the work which the other was doing. In their meeting together they learned that their aims were one, though they differed on some points as to methods. Barton Stone, in speaking of their meeting said, "We plainly saw we were on the same foundation, in the same Spirit, and preached the same gospel." Of Alexander Campbell, Barton Stone said, "I will not say there are no faults in brother Campbell, but that there are fewer, perhaps in him, than any man I know on earth; and over these few my love would throw a veil and hide them from view forever. I am constrained, and willingly constrained, to acknowledge him the greatest promoter of this reformation of any man living. The Lord reward him!"

In speaking of the work of Alexander Campbell, Stone said, "He boldly determined to take the Bible alone for his standard of faith and practice, to the exclusion of all other books as authority. He argued that the Bible presented sufficient evidence of its truth to sinners, to enable them to believe it, and sufficient motives to induce them to obey it—that until they believed and obeyed the gospel, in vain they expected salvation, pardon, and the Holy Spirit—that now is the accepted time, and now is the day of salvation. These truths we had proclaimed and reiterated through the length and breadth of the land, from the press and from the pulpit many years before A. Campbell and his associates came upon the stage as aids of a good cause. Their aid gave a new impetus to the reformation which was in progress among the Baptists in Kentucky; and the doctrine spread and greatly increased in the West."

1827 A.D. REDSTONE BAPTIST ASSOCIATION REJECTS SISTER CONGREGATIONS WHO REFUSE TO ACCEPT THE PHILADELPHIA CONFESSION OF FAITH.

Alexander Campbell attended this meeting as a messenger of the Mahoning Baptist Association. At this meeting thirteen congregations were excluded from the sessions because they refused to accept the Confession as a statement of their faith.

Alexander Campbell condemned this course of action, pointing out that the Philadelphia Confession of Faith was nothing more than a human document.

> "At the annual meeting of the association in 1827, the crisis came. Mr. Campbell had been appointed corresponding messenger from Mahoning to the Redstone association that year. As his letter of greeting made no reference to the Philadelphia Confession, the accepted standard of the Baptist Church, it was determined by his enemies that he should not be received. Upon a canvass it was found that they could rally to their support but ten of the twenty-three churches of the asociation; but with these ten they ventured the hazardous experiment of excluding the other thirteen, and organized themselves upon the basis of their cherished creed. The thir-

teen churches denied admission, then formed a new association, declaring as the second article of their constitution, "We receive the Scriptures as the only rule of faith and practice to all the churches of Christ." Thus began the conflict which within the next three years resulted in the complete separation of Baptists and those who accepted the principles of the reformation."*

This incident laid the foundation for his complete separation from the Baptist church, which came later.

As the truths of the New Testament were unfolded to the people and the church of the Lord thus revealed, multitudes gave up their denominational names and creeds and took the name Christian. The plea to speak only where the Bible speaks, attracted the attention of some of the outstanding preachers of that age, and soon they were blending their efforts with those of the Campbells for a restoration of the ancient order. Outstanding leaders who assisted in the work of restoration were P. S. Fall, John T. Johnson, John Smith, Walter Scott, Barton Stone and William Hayden. Wherever Mr. Campbell and his fellow-laborers went, people accepted the good news.

They gave up their denominational names, their creeds, and customs for the simple religion of Christ. Numerous Baptist congregations rejected the Philadelphia Confession of Faith and accepted the New Testament as their only rule of faith. The Methodist Church at Deerfield gave up the name Methodist Church and took the name, the church of Christ.

Thomas Campbell and Alexander Campbell were much opposed to religious division. In the beginning of their association with the Baptist Church it was agreed that the Campbells should be allowed to teach whatever they learned from the word of God.

Because of their strong opposition to religious division, they did not purpose to establish another church, but to make an effort to return to the church revealed in the New Testament.

The circulation of the Christian Baptist brought others into contact with Alexander Campbell. In his tours among the Baptist Churches of Kentucky and Tennessee he was everywhere cordially received by large audiences who listened attentively to his plea for a return to the word of God. Those among the Baptist clergy who saw their prestige and their pastorates in danger, began to denounce the work of the Campbells and their fellow workers.

Alexander Campbell had trusted that the Baptist Church would make a complete return to apostolic Christianity. When his enemies began to attack him, he said, "If there be a division, gentlemen, you will make it, not I. The more you oppose us, the faster we will

* *Life of Alexander Campbell*—Grafton. Chapter 8, Pages 122, 123.

grow. I am for peace, for harmony, for co-operation with all good men." As the issue became clear, some churches divided, some were excluded from Baptist Associations, but in other places whole associations ceased to call themselves Baptists and announced that they were Christians.

The Mahoning Baptist Association embracing fifteen congregations renounced the name Baptist, burned their confession of faith as unscriptural, and took the name the church of Christ, bringing the total number of congregations that were laboring for New Testament Christianity to twenty-one.

1828 A.D. ALEXANDER CAMPBELL ACCEPTS THE CHALLENGE OF ROBERT OWEN, SCOTCH INFIDEL

Mr. Robert Owen, a man of wealth and learning, was the acknowledged leader of infidelity in England as well as in America. He had purchased a large tract of land and founded a town called New Harmony, in Indiana. In this town all forms of religion were excluded. No church buildings could be erected and the gospel could not be preached. To spread his doctrine throughout the United States he travelled extensively, conducting a campaign against the Christian religion and the Bible, challenging the clergy to defend the Book they professed to believe.

Mr. Owen issued the following challenge to the clergy of New Orleans, where he was lecturing.

"To the Clergy of New Orleans:

Gentlemen: I have now finished a course of lectures in this city, the principles of which are in direct opposition to those which you have been taught it is your duty to preach. It is of immense importance to the world that truth upon these momentous subjects should be now established upon a certain and sure foundation. You and I, and all of our fellow-men are deeply interested that there should be no further delay. With this in view, without one hostile or unpleasant feeling on my part, I propose a friendly public discussion, the most open, that the city of New Orleans will afford; or, if you prefer it, a more private meeting; when half a dozen friends of each party shall be present, in addition to half a dozen gentlemen whom you may associate with you in the discussion. The time and place of the meeting to be of your own appointment. I propose to prove, as I have already attempted to do in my lectures, that all of the religions of the world have been founded on the ignorance of mankind; that they are directly opposed to the never changing laws of our nature; that they have been and are the real source of vice, disunion and misery of every description; that they are now the only real bar to the formation of a society of virtue, of intelligence, of charity in its most extended sense, and of sincerity and kindness among the whole human family; and that they can be no longer maintained except through the ignorance of the mass of the people, and the tyranny of the few over that mass. With feelings of perfect good will to you, which extend also in perfect sincerity to all mankind, I subscribe myself your friend in a just cause.

—Robert Owen

New Orleans

Jan. 28, 1828

P.S. If this proposal should be declined, I shall conclude, as I have long most conscientiously been compelled to do, that the principles which I advocate are unanswerable truths.—R. O."

This challenge was unnoticed by the clergy of New Orleans and Mr. Owen asserted that no one would debate the issue with him.

When the news of the defiant challenge reached Mr. Campbell in far away Virginia, he promptly accepted the challenge. The arrangements for the debate provided that it should be held in Cincinnati, Ohio, in April of 1829.

The debate attracted large crowds at each session, many being turned away because of lack of room in the building where the discussion was held. Those whose belief coincided with that of Mr. Owen believed the Bible would be overthrown, but as the discussion continued it became apparent that the cause of Christianity had a very able defender. On the concluding day of the debate Mr. Owen stated that he had exhausted his resources, that he had no new evidence to present. He agreed to let Mr. Campbell continue to speak until he had presented all of his material.

Mr. Campbell spoke for twelve hours upon the evidence of Christianity as a divinely revealed religion. The debate was published and remains at the present one of the greatest works ever published in defense of Christianity.

1828 A.D. THE FIRST MEETING BETWEEN THE FELLOW-WORKERS OF BARTON STONE AND ALEXANDER CAMPBELL IN THE INTEREST OF UNITY

Several years prior to this time, Barton Stone and Alexander Campbell had become acquainted with one another. In their conversations together, they discovered that they were both teaching the same thing. The meeting, held at Lisbon, Ohio, in October, 1828, prepared the way for uniting the forces of these two great men of the restoration movement.

The doors of the Baptist Churches now began to be closed to Alexander Campbell, and this brought about a complete separation between the Baptist Churches who refused him admittance to their buildings, and those who accepted his plea for a return to New Testament Christianity.

This separation resulted from differences on points of doctrine.

The Baptists of this period believed that both the Old and the New Testaments were of equal authority. Alexander Campbell believed that the law of Moses was addressed to the Jewish people alone, and that it was blotted out or brought to an end at the death of Christ. He contended that all people upon the earth were now subject to the law of Christ.

The Baptist churches that opposed Campbell, differed with him on the subject of baptism. They considered baptism as an ordinance to be obeyed because one's sins had been forgiven. Alexander Campbell pointed out that baptism was a command to be obeyed because it promised the remission of sins. The Baptists accepted the Philadelphia Confession of Faith as a statement of their belief and practice.

The men of the Restoration taught that creeds were only human documents and as such they produced division among those who claimed to be the people of God. The plea of Alexander Campbell was for a return to the New Testament as a guide that was sufficient to direct us into all truth.

These points had often been discussed in the meetings of the Associations without any decision being reached. As the opposition grew and other differences developed, the line of separation was drawn and the Campbells and their fellow-laborers were forced from the ranks of the Baptist Church.

1836 A.D. CAMPBELL ADDRESSES TEACHERS' COLLEGE

In October of this year Mr. Campbell was invited to deliver an address before the students of the College of Teachers of Cincinnati. At that time an attempt was being made to exclude the reading of the Bible from the public schools.

Mr. Campbell chose for his subject "Moral Culture," in which he lauded the march of modern civilization, attributing it to the spirit of inquiry that had been awakened by the Protestant Reformation.

Bishop Purcell, of the Roman Catholic Church, attacked the speech of Mr. Campbell, asserting that the "Protestant Reformation had been the cause of all of the contention and infidelity in the world."

Alexander Campbell did not allow this statement to go unnoticed. He sent word to the bishop that he was prepared to defend what he had said in public debate. The bishop ignored Mr. Campbell's reply, so he delivered another address in which he publicly signified his willingness to defend six propositions which covered the subject of their differences on the Reformation.

A petition was presented to Alexander Campbell urging him to publicly expose the arrogant claims of the Roman Catholic Church. The pressure became so great against the bishop, that he consented to meet Mr. Campbell in debate.

The debate was to be held in Cincinnati, beginning on January 13, 1837, and the propositions for discussion, all of which he affirmed, were as follows:

"1. The Roman Catholic institution, sometimes called the Holy Apostolic Church, is not now, nor was she ever catholic, apostolic, or holy, but is a sect in the fair import of that word, older than any other sect now existing; not the Mother and Mistress of all churches, but an apostasy from the only true, apostolic, and Catholic church of Christ.

2. Her notion of Apostolic succession is without any foundation in the Bible, in reason or in fact; an imposition of the most injurious consequence, built upon unscriptural and anti-scriptural traditions, resting wholly upon the opinions of interested and fallible men.

3. She is not uniform in her faith or united in her members, but mutable and fallible as any other sect of philosophy or religion, Jewish, Turkish, or Christian, a confederation of sects under a politico-ecclesiastic head.

4. She is the Babylon of John, the man of Sin of Paul, and the Empire of the youngest Horn of Daniel's sea-monster.

5. Her notions of purgatory, indulgences, auricular confession, remission of sins, transubstantiation, supererogation, etc., essential elements of her system, are immoral in their tendency, and injurious to the well being of society, religious and political.

6. Notwithstanding her pretensions to have given us the Bible and faith in it, we are perfectly independent of her for our knowledge of that book and its evidences of a divine original.

7. The Roman Catholic religion, if infallible and unsusceptible of reformation, as alleged, is essentially anti-American, being opposed to the genius of all free institutions, and positively subversive of them, opposing the general reading of the Scriptures and the diffusion of useful knowledge among the whole community, so essential to liberty and permanence of good government."*

The knowledge Alexander Campbell had of the history of the church, his acquaintance with the priest-craft of his native country, and his hatred for shams in religion, fitted him to become the defender of Protestantism. In this discussion, Mr. Campbell sustained the propositions he had signed to the satisfaction of his friends, and the Protestants of Cincinnati. This debate was published and was widely circulated.

---

* *Campbell-Purcell Debate.* Page 7.

1843 A.D. CAMPBELL-RICE DEBATE

In November of this year Mr. Campbell debated with N. L. Rice of Paris, Kentucky. The arrangements for this debate had their beginning in September of 1842, but were not concluded till August of 1843. This debate which lasted sixteen days involved six propositions, covering the differences between the Presbyterians and the Christians. The debate was held at Lexington, Kentucky, and was attended by two thousand people, or more, at each session.

The propositions for debate were as follows:

1. The immersion in water of a proper subject, into the name of the Father, the Son and the Holy Spirit, is the one, only apostolic or Christian baptism.

Mr. A. Campbell—affirms
Mr. N. L. Rice—denies

2. The infant of a believing parent is a scriptural subject of baptism.

Mr. Rice—affirms
Mr. Campbell—denies

3. Christian baptism is for the remission of past sins.

Mr. Campbell—affirms
Mr. Rice—denies

4. Baptism is to be administered only by a bishop or ordained presbyter.

Mr. Rice—affirms
Mr. Campbell—denies

5. In conversion and sanctification, the Spirit of God operates on persons only through the word of truth.

Mr. Campbell—affirms
Mr. Rice—denies

6. Human creeds, as bonds of union and communion, are necessarily heretical and schismatical.

Mr. Campbell—affirms
Mr. Rice—denies

The debate was published by the Presbyterians as a defense of their doctrines but when it was learned that many, after having read the debate, embraced the teaching of the Scriptures as presented by Mr. Campbell, the Presbyterians ceased to publish it. It is still accepted by the churches of Christ in support of what they believe to be the truth.

Alexander Campbell departed this life March 4, 1866, at his home at Bethany, West Virginia, and was laid to rest in the family cemetery at that place.

CHAPTER 24

SCOTT AND THE RESTORATION

Walter Scott was born at Moffatt, Scotland, October 31, 1796. His father and mother, who were cultured people, died while he was yet very young. He finished his education at Edinburgh University, and came to New York in 1818, taking a position as a Latin teacher in a private school at Jamaica, Long Island. A year later he went to Pittsburgh where he became a teacher in the school of George Forrester. Forrester, also a native of Scotland, had been greatly influenced by the teaching of the Haldane brothers. He had become the preacher for a small group of Independents. Scott had been reared in the Presbyterian church and the religious atmosphere among the Independents was altogether different.

The Haldanes had preached the restoration of the New Testament, the weekly observance of the Lord's Supper, baptism by immersion, a plurality of elders and the edification of the church by the members. All of these points were part of the doctrine and practice of the Independent church in Pittsburgh. Scott attended the services of this group and became convinced that they were following the New Testament pattern and was baptized and shortly thereafter began to preach occasionally in the Independent church. In the winter of 1821-22 he became acquainted with Alexander Campbell and both were surprised that their views on so many subjects coincided. Both believed that baptism was for the remission of sins. Scott returned to New York and visited with the Independent churches in and around New York and then returned to Western Pennsylvania, later blending his efforts with those of the Campbells. From his study of the Scriptures he recognized that the church of the New Testament was being restored, that the worship of the congregations established by the Campbells was like the worship of the church in New Testament times, but that something was yet lacking because they did not seem to be able to reproduce the church in new communities, as the church did in the apostolic age. Scott devoted himself to the study of God's word over a long period of time searching for a reason for the lack of growth. He reasoned that if Christ established his kingdom for the redemption of mankind, he would also reveal the means by which one entered that kingdom.

Up to this time those desiring to become the children of God had been taught that under the conviction of sin they must pray for God to give them faith through the Holy Spirit. This period of praying and mourning might be extended for months or years. In this state of conviction the seeker would wait for a miraculous experience, a sign of God's grace being directed toward him. He could then relate to the church his experience, and to make it sound equal to, or better than that of his neighbors, he would add just a few more details, embellishing it with an exaggerated account of the events that transpired in connection with his prayer for salvation. After relating his experience a vote would be taken to decide whether he should be received into the church. If his Christian experience was accepted, he was declared saved and received into the church upon his baptism.

The investigation of Walter Scott convinced him that those who became members of the church did so by obeying the commands of Christ. Jesus had said: "Therefore whosoever heareth these sayings of mine and doeth them, I will liken him unto a wise man, which built his house upon a rock."[1] The importance of hearing Christ speak was emphasized, Scott believed, by the words of God when he said, "This is my beloved Son; hear him."[2] To hear the word would produce faith, for Paul said, "So then faith cometh by hearing and hearing by the word of God."[3] John, in his gospel record, proclaimed the same truth, saying, "Many other signs truly did Jesus in the presence of his disciples, which are not written in this book; but these are written that ye might believe that Jesus is the Christ, the Son of God; and that believing ye might have life through his name."[4]

Christ had made that belief, or faith in him as God's Son, a condition of salvation. "I said therefore unto you, that ye shall die in your sins: for if ye believe not that I am he, ye shall die in your sins."[5] This was not some newly formed practice, for these things were taught by the apostles, for when the jailer at Philippi asked what he must do to be saved, he was told, "Believe on the Lord Jesus Christ and thou shalt be saved, and thy house."[6] Paul, knowing that no one could believe in something which they had never heard, spoke unto him the word of the Lord, and to all that were in his house.

Scott was sure that he was right in the conclusions he had formed. Here were terms of salvation clearly set forth in the word

---

1. Matt. 7 : 24.
2. Mk. 9 : 7.
3. Rom. 10 : 17.
4. Matt. 20 : 30, 31.
5. John 8 : 24.
6. Acts 16 : 30.

of God. Because repentance occupied a place of importance in the Scriptures, Walter Scott gave this subject serious consideration also. His continued study of the Scriptures revealed the meaning of the word as used by Christ. "A certain man had two sons, and he came to the first and said, Son, go work today in my vineyard: He answered and said, 'I will not' but afterward, he repented and went."[7] Here was a change of mind; the son, believing he was wrong, repented and went. Repentance is therefore a turning from sin. No one could be saved without repentance, hence, he said, "I tell you, Nay, but, except ye repent, ye shall all likewise perish."[8]

The Savior ascribed to the act of repentance a place in the gospel order, for on the occasion of his last conversation with his disciples, he said, "Thus it is written, and thus it behooved Christ to suffer and to rise from the dead the third day: and that repentance and remission of sins should be preached in his name among all nations beginning at Jerusalem."[9]

The apostles taught the same thing in the first gospel sermon at Jerusalem on the day of Pentecost. Hear the apostle Peter as he sets forth the terms of pardon, "Now when they heard this, they were pricked in their heart, and said unto Peter and to the rest of the apostles, Men and brethren, what shall we do? Then Peter said unto them, Repent, and be baptized every one of you in the name of Jesus Christ for the remission of sins and ye shall receive the gift of the Holy Ghost."[10] Here again Scott discovered that the terms of forgiveness of sins named by the Savior, were also taught as conditions of salvation by the apostles. Jesus taught, "Whosoever therefore shall confess me before men, him will I confess before my Father which is in heaven."[11] When the eunuch asked Philip, "What doth hinder me to be baptized?" Philip said, "If thou believest with all thine heart thou mayest." And he answered and said, "I believe that Jesus Christ is the Son of God."[12]

Paul confirmed this when he said, "If thou shalt confess with thy mouth the Lord Jesus, and shalt believe in thine heart that God hath raised him from the dead thou shalt be saved."[13]

Walter Scott knew that baptism was for the remission of sins. The importance of this command was not ridiculed by the lost in apostolic days. Luke testified, "And many of the Corinthians hearing, believed, and were baptized."[14] Why? Because Jesus had made

---

7. Matt. 21 : 28, 29.
8. Luke 13 : 3.
9. Luke 24 : 46, 47.
10. Acts 2 : 37, 38.
11. Matt. 10 : 32.
12. Acts 8 : 36, 37.
13. Rom. 10 : 9.
14. Acts 18 : 8.

obedience to this command a condition of salvation. "He that believeth and is baptized shall be saved."[15]

Never since the great apostasy had the terms of salvation been so clearly pointed out in plain, simple, and scriptural language.

1827 A.D. WALTER SCOTT SELECTED TO TRAVEL AMONG THE CHURCHES AND PROCLAIM THE GOSPEL

"The Mahoning Baptist Association did one good work at their last regular meeting. They agreed to support one active, spiritually minded, and able brother as a messenger of the churches, who is to labor every day, for one entire year, all things concurring, in the word and doctrine, among the churches in the association. He is to proclaim the word to those without, and to teach those within to walk in the Lord. Brother Walter Scott, who is now in the field, accepted of the appointment; and few men on this continent understand the ancient order of things better than he. His whole soul is in the work, and there is great room for many such at home. It is to be hoped that all Christians will turn their attention more to good works and to the conversion of those around them, and to the union of all disciples on primitive grounds, in order that the whole world may be brought under the dominion of the Root and Offspring of David."[*]

Walter Scott had been selected by the Mahoning Association to travel among the churches and conduct gospel meetings. His preaching was altogether new to that age. Up to the time that Scott began his labors there seemed to be no clearly defined teaching among the men of the restoration as to what steps a sinner must take to become a child of God. Those who became identified with the church announced their intentions and were baptized. Walter Scott purposed to put into practice those things he had learned from the study of God's word.

1827 A.D. WALTER SCOTT PROCLAIMS THE NEW TESTAMENT TERMS OF SALVATION

In October of this year, Scott was conducting an evangelistic meeting at New Lisbon, Ohio, and on the eighteenth day of that month as he concluded his sermon, he set forth what he understood to be the divine plan of redemption, calling upon the unsaved to believe that Christ was the Son of God, to repent, to acknowledge Christ, and to be baptized for the remission of their sins. The first man to accept the invitation to obey the gospel was William Amend, whom he baptized without calling upon him to relate a Christian experience, or without having the congregation to vote him into

---

15. Mk. 16 : 16.
* *The Christian Baptist.* Volume 5, No. 1, Page 382.

the church. For the first time since the church was led away from the truth and swept into the great apostasy, the ordinance of baptism was obeyed in perfect accord with apostolic teaching.

The preaching of Walter Scott was the beginning of a period of great growth for the church of Christ. He had been a diligent student of the Scriptures for several years and their truths were deeply imprinted upon his mind. He purposed to preach just what Peter preached on Pentecost. Arriving in a town or village he would use the school children to announce the beginning of the meeting. He would tell the children to tell their fathers and mothers to come to the services and hear a man preach the gospel on five fingers. Pointing to his fingers he would say, "Here are five things to remember—Hearing, Faith, Repentance, Confession, Baptism. Now close your hand, put it in your pocket and when you get home show your parents what you have learned. Tell them to come hear a man preach on these things."

The meeting place would be filled and Walter Scott would give them the ancient gospel of Christ, showing that it consisted of facts to believe, commands to obey, promises to enjoy, and threats to avoid.

The meeting of the Mahoning Association brought hundreds into the churches. News of the great numbers brought into the church reached the Campbells at Bethany and they wondered if he was overstepping the bounds of the gospel.

Thomas Campbell decided to go to Ohio and see just what was taking place. After hearing Walter Scott preach and seeing the numbers that were converted, Thomas Campbell wrote to his son saying,

> "We have spoken and published many things correctly concerning the ancient gospel, its simplicity and perfect adaptation to the present state of mankind, for the benign and gracious purposes of its immediate relief and perfect salvation, but I must confess that in respect of the direct exhibition and application of it for that purpose, I am, at present, for the first time, upon the ground where the thing has appeared to be practically exhibited to the proper purpose. 'Compel them to come' saith the Lord, 'that my house may be filled.' Mr. Scott has made a bold push to accomplish this object, by simply and boldly stating the ancient gospel and insisting upon it; and then by putting the question generally and particularly to males and females, old and young; 'Will you come to Christ and be baptized for the remission of your sins and the gift of the Holy Spirit? Don't you believe this blessed gospel? Then come away'; etc, etc. This elicits a personal conversation; some confess faith in the testimony, beg time to think; others consent, give their hands to be baptized as soon as convenient; others debate the matter friendly; some go straight to the water, be it day or night, and upon the whole none appear offended."

William Hayden traveled with Scott as a singer, and Scott was so much impressed with his fellow-worker, that he said, "Brethren, give me my Bible, my head, and Bro. William Hayden, and we will go out and convert the world."

Soon all the preachers saw the simplicity of this gospel message and began the proclamation of the same story. The success of Scott's evangelistic efforts brought an invitation for him to visit the Baptist Church at Sharon, Pa. The labors of Scott at this place resulted in a great many confessing their faith in Christ and being baptized. After Walter Scott left, part of the church rejected the new converts, saying that they had not conformed to Baptist customs and, therefore, could not be received as members. Those who were excluded formed a new congregation on New Testament principles. In the presentation of the gospel Walter Scott stressed the fact that faith changes the heart or mind, repentance changes the life, confession changes the attitude, and baptism changes the state of the obedient.

The rapid growth of the restoration is revealed in a report published in the Christian Baptist. The preaching of Vardeman, Smith, Scott, Rigdon, Morrison, and Lane, had brought two thousand forty-nine converts into the church in a period of about six months.

Scott was a contributor to the Christian Baptist under the name, "Philip."

Scott edited "The Evangelist" which was published at Cincinnati, from 1832 to 1844. He was also the author of several books, the best known of which are "The Gospel Restored" and "The Messiahship." Through the years of his labors he had several young men with him, teaching them the word of God, assisting them in the preparation of sermons, preparing them for a place of usefulness in the kingdom of God. The last few years of his life were spent at Mayslick, Kentucky, where he died on April 23, 1861. He was buried there, and these words are carved on the stone that marks his grave, "The words which Thou gavest me I have given unto them"—John 17: 8.

CHAPTER 25

THE WORK OF JOHN SMITH

John Smith, the son of George Smith and Rebecca Brown Smith, was born in Sullivan County, Tennessee, in October, 1784. The parents lived at that time on a small farm, and there it was that John Smith's childhood was spent. His early education was received from teachers who travelled from place to place conducting schools for the children of the pioneers in the unsettled sections of the state. From these teachers he learned to read from the New Testament, and as he improved his reading, his father gave him the duty of reading from the Bible at family devotions. Thus the Bible became his reading book, making a lasting impression upon his mind.

The people of the community in which the Smiths lived were of the Baptist faith, a part of the Holston Association. At the services of the church the preachers called upon the hearers to pray to God for the forgiveness of their sins, holding before them the horrors of a never-ending hell. John Smith questioned whether he was one of God's elect, and anxiously day after day, and night after night, he prayed for some indication that he was one of the elect of God. When John was about eleven or twelve years old the father sold his farm in Tennessee, and taking with him John and an older brother, he set out for Kentucky in search of a place where all of the family could settle around him. At the time of the removal of the family to Kentucky a great religious awakening was spreading through the land, bringing thousands of people together to hear the word of God. John's study of God's word convinced him that he was a sinner and he constantly sought peace with God. Day after day he entered a dense thicket to pour out his soul to God in earnest prayer. When he related his difficulties and desires to his brother William, he was told that he was converted. Later, doubt filled his mind, and again he returned to his place of prayer to call upon God to save him.

Because of his doubts he was persuaded to go before the church and relate his difficulties to them. This he agreed to do, so on the 26th of December, 1804, he related his experience to the assembled church in that community. The moderator placed his case before the church and asked that "all who believed that his experience was a work of grace should raise their right hand." All persons present raised their hands and John Smith was declared saved. The next day he was immersed in the waters of Clear Creek and received into the fellowship of the church.

After the father's death, John Smith assumed the responsibility of leading the family in prayer and directing their spiritual life. At the meeting of his fellow members of the Baptist church he was often asked to give a few words of exhortation, but always refused because of his lack of ability. On one occasion after the songs had ended and the prayer had been offered he arose to speak, but when he looked into the faces of those assembled he became so confused that the words he had intended to speak fled from his mind and he left the cabin in embarrassment. In the darkness he tripped over some object and fell to the ground, immediately the words he purposed to speak filled his mind, and he returned to the cabin and gave an exhortation to those assembled.

In 1806 he was married to Anna Townsden and they took up residence on the two hundred acre farm he had purchased in Horse Hollow. His devotion to God and his ability to exhort and lead in prayer caused his neighbors to regard him as their leader. A church building was erected in the community and Isaac Denton came from Stockton's Valley to set the members apart as a church and place them under the pastoral care of Richard Barrier. Soon afterward, John Smith was urged to submit to being ordained as a preacher of the gospel. At his ordination he was asked if he accepted the Philadelphia Confession of Faith to which he replied that he did and that he accepted all the articles that it taught. The Presbytery having prayed, placed their hands upon his head and declared that he was empowered to preach the gospel, administer the Lord's Supper, and attend to the ordinance of baptism.

John Smith now gave all of his spare time to the study of the Scriptures and to the Confession of Faith. He lost no opportunity to improve his talents, and when the Cumberland River Association convened in the summer of 1810, he attended the meetings and renewed acquaintance with Jeremiah Vardeman, who urged him to come visit some of the congregations of Northern Kentucky. He later accepted the invitation and was well treated by the churches he visited, but a realization of his lack of learning and culture prevented him from accepting a call to labor among them. When he returned home he learned that some of the public lands of Alabama were to be opened for settlement. He therefore sold his farm and moved to Huntsville, Alabama, where he secured several hundred acres of land. He rented an unoccupied cabin until he could build one on his own land. He had been invited by friends of his parents to visit them and to preach to them the second Lord's

Day, in January, 1815. Leaving his wife and children he hastened to deliver a message to the people who had known his parents in Kentucky. That same night the home was destroyed by fire during the absence of the wife, who had gone to a nearby home to comfort a dying woman. Everything the family possessed was destroyed by the fire, which also took the lives of the two older children. When John Smith arrived at the ruins, he tried to comfort his bereaved companion by assuring her that she had gone where duty called her. Another home was provided, but very shortly after this the wife became ill and died. Within a few weeks John Smith became ill and for many months lay at the point of death. When he recovered from his long illness his hogs and cattle had wandered away and were lost. Seeking the solace and comfort of his pious brother, William, he returned to Kentucky. Jeremiah Vardeman wrote to him inviting him to come to Crab Orchard where the Association was soon to convene.

He accepted the invitation to return to Crab Orchard, arriving there after the sessions were in progress. He spoke before those who were assembled outside of the meeting house and so great was the interest that was aroused by his preaching that the business of the Association was suspended that all might hear. After the Association adjourned he returned to Stockton's Valley to the home of his brother, Jonathan, who had offered to care for his children until he could provide for them a home. He brought his children from Alabama, left them in the care of his brother, and again purchased a small farm on the Little South Fork. He visited again the congregations near Lexington, contacting his old friends Jacob Creath and Jeremiah Vardeman, who urged him to locate in that section of Kentucky. But John Smith's heart was filled with a desire to labor among the poor people of the hills of Kentucky, so he returned to the Little South Fork, and then on the twenty-fifth of December, was united in marriage to Nancy Hurt. After residing on the farm for several months they removed to Montgomery County, in October of 1817. He studied carefully the Philadelphia Confession of Faith, comparing it with the Scriptures, searching for proof for the doctrine of predestination and the personal election of individuals, which he had questioned in his own mind since the death of his children. He ultimately gave up the doctrine of infants being born totally depraved. While preaching at Spencer's Creek on one occasion, he called upon sinners to repent and believe the gospel, but, he reflected, if they were the elect and did not believe, they would not be saved, and if they were not the elect and did believe, it would do them no good, so they could not be saved in either case. He looked over his audience and said "Brethren, I am in the dark, and how to lead you to the light, I know not." He dismissed the congregation, returned to his home, related the confusion of his mind to his wife and they both fell upon their knees in prayer.

He asked God to give him light, giving a promise to the Father of all light that he would take the Bible as his only guide, that he would follow wherever it might lead. This was the beginning of the religious reformation to which John Smith contributed so much in Kentucky. Very soon after the foregoing events he learned that a preacher from Virginia, one Alexander Campbell, was to preach at Flemingsburg. He rode the twenty miles to hear him preach and complained that Campbell had preached only thirty minutes, when, in truth the sermon had taken two and a half hours.

1825 A.D. JOHN SMITH PURPOSES TO PREACH NOTHING NOT AUTHORIZED BY THE BIBLE

From this time he began to declare that the Bible was God's only revelation to mankind, and that the New Testament, when believed and obeyed, was sufficient to save the soul of any individual. The truths that he preached to the people were indeed new to them. Gradually the word went forth that John Smith was departing from the faith. Then charges were brought against him by the Association.

First—That he read from a new translation published by Alexander Campbell, rather than from the King James translation.

Second—That he failed to follow the Baptist practice in baptism, saying instead, "By the authority of Jesus Christ I immerse you into the name of the Father, and of the Son, and of the Holy Spirit."

Third—That instead of breaking the loaf into small particles, he left it in large pieces, teaching that each person should break it for themselves.

To these charges he replied briefly at the time of their presentation, but when they came up for general discussion he was denied the right of defending himself because he had already spoken twice upon the subject. It was agreed that action against Smith should be deferred for one year.

Returning to his home, he began to preach in the homes of his neighbors, and when a young man expressed his desire to be baptized upon the confession of his faith in Christ as the Son of God, Smith baptized him upon this simple confession and he was accepted into the fellowship of the church. He admonished those who attended his preaching to discard their creeds and to take the word

of God alone as their only guide in matters of faith and conduct.
He endeavored to impress upon their minds the necessity of reading
the Bible for themselves rather than accepting the teaching of the
clergy. Wherever opportunity presented itself he preached the
truth that Christ died for all and that those who believed on him
and were obedient to his words had the promise of the remission
of their sins.

1826 A.D. SMITH INVITED TO FRANKFORT TO PREACH

When Philip S. Fall, a friend of John Smith's, attempted to
secure a place for the services, he found that all the church buildings had been closed against him. He appealed to the judge of the
court which was then in session. The judge then offered to adjourn
court to provide a place for John Smith to preach. When inquiry
was made as to which John Smith was to preach, people were
informed that it was "Raccoon" John Smith, from Montgomery.
This name was afterward used to identify him wherever he went.

1829 A.D. SMITH SEPARATES FROM THE GRASSY LICK
BAPTIST CHURCH

During the early part of this year, John Smith was absent from
the Grassy Lick Church, laboring in distant parts of the state.
In prior years it had been the practice of the congregation to have
the fifteen articles of the Covenant, their creed, read at every
monthly meeting. That procedure had not been followed for some
time, but at the regular meeting in May a member of the church
asked that it be read. After the reading he publicly stated that he
could no longer accept it as a Christian. John Smith arose after
the discussion of the Covenant ended and taking up several of the
articles of the Covenant showed wherein they were at variance with
the Scriptures. The church was called upon to express themselves
as to whether the Covenant should be retained or dropped. When
two-thirds of the congregation expressed their opposition to it, the
clerk was instructed to write the Association and place the matter
before them for acceptance or rejection. When the Association
convened, it was learned that those in favor of the Covenant had
also sent a letter and a representative to that assembly declaring
that only those whose names were affixed to the New Covenant
constituted the church at Grassy Lick.

John Smith asked the church to give him a letter of fellowship
that he might identify himself with some congregation that was
not opposed to his views. Others also asked for their letters and
ultimately one hundred twenty were dismissed from the congrega-

tion by letter. That week they met at the Grassy Lick meeting-house, and declared themselves to constitute a church of Jesus Christ, with no creed but the Bible, pleading for a return to New Testament Christianity. A church building was constructed two miles east of Grassy Lick, and six miles north of Mount Sterling. Here they continued to grow in numbers and spiritual strength. Wherever John Smith went he was asked why he had left the Baptist faith to which he gave the following answer—

"1. I did not believe the doctrines of the Philadelphia Confession of Faith to be in accordance with the Word of God; and of course, I could not conscientiously teach them.

2. I could not find such a thing as the Baptist church named in the Bible.

3. I found that the kind of experience they required was unknown to any of the saints of the New Testament. I recalled my own experience, and compared it with the conversions in the Bible; and I was astonished to find that sinners, when convinced of sin and desiring salvation, instead of agonizing for months, as I had done, did not wait a single day to find it; except, perhaps, Saul of Tarsus, who waited and prayed three days before he was told what to do. In bringing everything to test, however, I found these points in my experience:

I. I believed sincerely in the Lord Jesus; this I knew the word of God required, and I felt conscious of its qualification.

II. I was conscious that I had repented of all my sins; this also, I knew the word of God demanded.

III. I knew that I had been immersed; and this, I saw, the Lord required of every believing penitent. I saw clearly that instead of being required to tell all the workings of my mind, they should have required these three things and nothing more, in order to my admission into the Church. True, when I was immersed, I submitted to it simply as a command of God, without knowing the blessings connected with it.

4. I found, also, this glaring inconsistency among the Baptists; while they taught that a man must be a Christian in the Bible sense of that term, before they could admit him to baptism, yet, until he was baptized, they allowed him no more privileges among them than a pagan or publican.

5. I was well persuaded that God never authorized any man or set of men to make articles of Faith or Rules of Practice for the subjects of his kingdom.

6. I was convinced, moreover, that it was not the custom of the ancient and apostolic churches to eat the Lord's Supper, monthly, or quarterly, but that the disciples met together for that purpose every first day of the week.

Now, convinced as I was that the Baptists taught many erroneous, and some dangerous doctrines, that they had given their church a name unauthorized, that they assumed the authority to make laws and rules for the government of Christ's church, and that they neglected to celebrate the Lord's death more than two, or four, or twelve times a year; seeing all these things, I could not conscientiously remain a Baptist, especially when they were not willing for me to preach and practice among them what I believed to be the truth."—*

1829 A.D. IN JULY OF THIS YEAR THE NORTH DISTRICT ASSOCIATION MET AT SPENCER'S CREEK

Only eighteen congregations were represented. The congregations that had opposed John Smith, which included Lulbegrud and Grassy Lick, did not send representatives. Cane Spring, which had before been represented by David Chenault, sent four delegates. This congregation had accepted all that John Smith taught in opposition to the Philadelphia Confession of Faith. The congregation at Somerset sent representatives but refused to be called a Baptist church. Many prominent brethren who were interested in primitive Christianity were present at this meeting, among whom were Jacob Coons and Absalom Rice, who were among the first to be baptized for the remission of their sins. Jacob Creath, Sr., David S. Burnet, and Thomas Campbell, sometimes called the fathers of the American Reformation were also in attendance. These religious leaders had not yet made a complete return to New Testament Christianity but they were on their way. They had rejected the Philadelphia Confession of Faith as their rule of faith and practice, had surrendered their Covenant, and had adopted the New Testament as their only source of guidance. They had declared that Conferences and Associations are unscriptural, that the Lord's Supper must be observed each Lord's Day, and that baptism was for the remission of sins. The proclamation of these truths brought them into conflict with many of the congregations. The doors of the Baptist meeting houses now began to be closed against them.

* *Life of Elder John Smith*—Williams. Chapter 26, Pages 237, 238.

1830 A.D.

A three-day meeting was held in May at Mayslick, Kentucky, which was attended by John Smith, Jacob Creath, Sr., William Morton, Josiah Collins, Jacob Creath, Jr., Thomas Campbell, and Alexander Campbell. A report of the meeting appearing in the Millennial Harbinger said:

> "We had the pleasure of meeting with many public, bold, and powerful advocates of the Reformation, and of uniting with them in prayers, praise, reading, exhortation, and in breaking the symbolic loaf. It was a very happy meeting, and, I trust, a very profitable one. All was harmony, Christian affection and intense zeal for the purity, peace, and union of the disciples on earth. I could have wished that all opponents of the Ancient Order of things had witnessed this meeting, and heard and seen all that passed. . . . The brethren, both public and private (and there was a large assemblage of them present), parted as they met, in the strong bonds of Christian affection, with increased zeal and renewed energy in the great and good cause of emancipating the brotherhood from the deadly influences of human systems, and from the galling yoke of human authority in the kingdom of Immanuel."

1831 A.D. NORTH DISTRICT ASSOCIATION DISSOLVED

The last meeting of the North District held July 23 was attended by representatives of fourteen congregations. All observed the Lord's Supper together and peace and harmony prevailed. It was agreed that there was no command or example for an Association, neither was there an express command against it. It was suggested that, even if Associations were not essential for the well being of the church, it would be all right for them to convene in an advisory capacity. But, it was pointed out, that while they were supposed to come together only to advise with each sister congregation they soon developed into legislative bodies.

Each year as the assembly drew to a close a friendly competition developed among the congregations for the privilege of having the Association assemble at their meeting house or grove the following year. But this year no congregation extended an invitation or offered to provide a meeting place. The question was asked, "Is there any authority in the word of God for this Association to meet at all?" It was agreed that there was no precept or example for such a practice. Their decision was presented in the following words, "No church requesting the next Association to be appointed at any of their meeting houses, and this body not having authority to force it upon any; and every church which appeared here by her letter and messengers unanimously agreeing that the word of God is the only rule of faith and practice for Christians, on motion and second, that the Constitution of the North District Association of Baptists be dissolved, after consultation among the brethren, when the question was put, was carried in the affirmative; and the said Association was thereby dissolved."

This concerted action in dissolving this unscriptural body as stated in the foregoing paragraph was comparable to the action taken by the Springfield Presbytery, when that body wrote out its last will and testament in 1804. This took place five years before Thomas Campbell wrote out his "Declaration and Address" by which he and those who stood with him separated themselves from the Presbyterian Church.

After Barton Stone separated from the Presbyterian church he traveled extensively and established congregations throughout Kentucky, Tennessee and Ohio. Wherever he had the opportunity of preaching he called upon the members of denominational churches to lay aside their human creeds and names and accept the Bible as the only safe guide and to work for the unity of all who professed to be the people of God. A spirit of brotherly love existed between those who had obeyed the gospel under the preaching of Barton Stone and his fellow-laborers, and those whose obedience had been brought about by the preaching of John Smith, Jacob Creath, Absalom Rice, and Alexander Campbell.

As they frequently met and discussed their problems, it became evident that both were pleading for a return to New Testament Christianity, both were preaching the same gospel, and standing on the same foundation. Even those who were not identified with either group often asked "Why are the Disciples and the Christians not united?" The more they came into contact with each other, the more they realized that such was not only possible, but desirable.

John T. Johnson, a fellow-laborer of John Smith, and Barton Stone lived near each other at Georgetown, Kentucky. The close of this year found Barton Stone laboring with John T. Johnson, at Great Crossings, to build up the congregation of disciples at that place. After the meeting ended Barton Stone invited Johnson to become co-editor of the Christian Messenger which he was publishing at Georgetown. A meeting of a number of brethren from the Disciples and Christians was held at Georgetown and the subject of the union of the two groups was discussed. John Smith devoted his efforts to visiting the congregations of both Christians and Disciples. A meeting was held at Georgetown, which embraced the twenty-fifth of December, and a similar meeting was to be held at Lexington, Kentucky, over the New Year's day. At an early hour on that day, a large assembly began to gather at the meeting house of the Christians on Hill Street in that city. It included Jacob

Creath, Barton Stone, John T. Johnson, Samuel Rogers, John Smith, and others. Barton Stone and John Smith were selected by their respective groups to present the basis upon which they could unite in the work of the Lord. John Smith was informed that he had been selected to speak first. He arose before the assembly, and realizing the responsibility that had been placed upon him he carefully weighed his words. He said in part:

"God has but one people on the earth. He has given to them but one Book, and therein exhorts and commands them to be one family. A union, such as we plead for—a union of God's people on that one Book—must then, be practicable.

Every Christian desires to stand complete in the whole will of God. The prayer of the Savior, and the whole tenor of his teaching, clearly show that it is God's will that his children should be united. To the Christian then such a union must be desirable.

But an amalgamation of sects is not such a union as Christ prayed for and God enjoins. To agree to be one upon any system of human invention would be contrary to his will and could never be a blessing to the church or the world; therefore the only union practicable or desirable must be based on the word of God, as the only rule of faith and practice. For several years past I have tried to speak on such subjects only in the language of inspiration; for it can offend no one to say about those things just what the Lord himself has said. In this scriptural style of speech all Christians should be agreed. It cannot be wrong, it can not do harm. If I come to the pasage, "My Father is greater than I," I will quote it, but will not stop to speculate upon the inferiority of the Son. If I read, "Being in the form of God, he thought it not robbery to be equal with God," I will not stop to speculate upon the consubstantial nature of the Father and the Son. I will not linger to build a theory upon such texts, and thus encourage a speculative and wrangling spirit among my brethren. I will present these subjects only in the words which the Lord has given to me. I know he will not be displeased if we say just what he has said. Whatever opinions about these and similar subjects I may have reached, in the course of my investigations, if I never distract the church of God with them, or seek to impose them on my brethren, they will never do the world any harm.

I have the more cheerfully resolved on this course, because the Gospel is a system of facts, commands, and promises, and no deduction or inference from them, however logical or true, forms any part of the Gospel of Jesus Christ. No heaven is promised to those who hold them, and no hell is threatened to those who deny them. They do not constitute, singly or together, any item of the ancient and apostolic Gospel.

For several years past, I have stood pledged to meet the religious world, or any part of it, on the ancient Gospel and order of things, as presented in the words of the Book. This is the foundation on which Christians once stood, and on it they can, and ought to stand again. From this I can not depart to meet any man, or set of men, in the wide world. While for the sake of peace and Christian union, I have long since waived the public maintenance of any speculation I may hold, yet not one gospel fact, commandment, or promise, will I surrender to the world. Let us, then, my brethren, be no longer Campbellites or Stoneites, New Lights or Old Lights, or any other kind of lights, but let us all come to the Bible, and to the Bible alone, as the only book in the world that can give us all the Light we need.'

He sat down and Stone arose, his heart glowing with love, and every pulse bounding with hope.

'I will not attempt,' said he, 'to introduce any new topic, but will say a few things on the same subjects already presented by my beloved brother. I have not one objection to the ground laid down by him as the true scriptural basis of union among the people of God; and I am willing to give him, now and here, my hand.'

He turned as he spoke, and offered to Smith a hand trembling with rapture and brotherly love, and it was grasped by a hand full of the honest pledges of fellowship, and union was virtually accomplished!

It was now proposed that all who felt willing to unite on these principles, should express that willingness by giving one another the hand of fellowship; and elders and teachers hastened forward, and joined their hands and hearts in joyful accord. A song arose, and brethren and sisters, with many tearful greetings, ratified and confirmed the union. On Lord's day, they broke the loaf together, and in that sweet and solemn communion, again pledged to each other their brotherly love." . . .*

This was not the surrender of one group to the doctrine or practice of another. It was a true scriptural union of the people of God upon the word of God as their only guide in religious matters.

When they were asked to which group new converts would be added, Smith answered that they would not be added to any party, but only to the church of Christ. To apprise the brethren of the unity that now prevailed among the congregations at Georgetown, it was suggested that John Smith and John Rogers should visit all the churches of Kentucky. Some brethren had heard only that John Smith had accepted the teaching of Barton Stone and had become uneasy, fearing that the cause of Christ had been injured by the course he had taken. After having placed before the brethren the principles upon which they came together, to take the Bible as their only guide in matters of faith and to hold opinions as such and to keep them private, the opposition to the union of the Disciples and the Christians disappeared. John Smith continued to travel among the congregations of Kentucky, extending his labors also into Indiana, Alabama, Tennessee and Missouri. His labors in Missouri carried him as far west as Chillicothe, where his preaching brought a goodly number into the church by obedience

* *Life of Elder John Smith*—Williams. Chapter 39, Pages 371-373.

to the gospel of Christ. In spite of the infirmities of old age he continued to preach the gospel as opportunity afforded. He became ill on the ninth of February and passed away on February 28, 1868.

His final resting place in the cemetery at Lexington, Kentucky, is marked by a stone bearing this inscription, "In memory of John Smith, an elder of the church of Christ."

CHAPTER 26

BENJAMIN FRANKLIN, GOSPEL PREACHER

Benjamin Franklin, the son of Joseph and Isabella Franklin, was born on the first day of February, in the year 1812, in Belmont County, Ohio. In 1833, Joseph Franklin and his family moved to Henry County, Indiana, and settled near where Middletown now stands. When Benjamin became twenty-one, he married Mary Personett and soon began to labor as a carpenter. The community in which they resided was divided into different religious groups. Among those in the neighborhood were the Baptists, the Episcopalians, the Presbyterians, and the Congregationalists.

Most of these religious groups were guided by their Confessions of Faith, Articles of Religion or Disciplines. Just at this time the preaching of the men of the Restoration reached Indiana. Samuel Rogers moved into Henry County, Indiana, and began to preach in a schoolhouse.

Joseph Franklin and a neighbor decided to hear what the newcomer had to say. The preacher created a state of excitement in the neighborhood by affirming that "baptism is essential to salvation." To Joseph Franklin, who was a member of the Methodist Episcopal Church, such preaching was a heresy. Benjamin Franklin had accompanied his father and the neighbor to the religious services but had paid but little attention to the doctrine which had been proclaimed. Though he was at this time irreligious, he had heard the Bible read regularly in the home of his father, and had gained some knowledge of its teaching. As the controversy continued between his father and the neighbor, Benjamin asked whether baptism was commanded by Christ. Being assured by the men that it was commanded by Christ, he said, "Well, isn't it necessary to obey the commands of Christ?" The men were so surprised by his logic that they did not attempt an answer. His interest in the preaching of Samuel Rogers continued to grow, and early in December, of 1834, he and his brother, Daniel, were baptized. Within a short period, thirty or forty persons obeyed the gospel, among whom were Joseph Franklin and his wife.

From the time that Benjamin Franklin confessed Christ he began to admonish people to obey the gospel of Christ. He made the word of God his constant companion and was soon able to quote long passages of Scripture.

Benjamin Franklin was a believer in the gospel of Christ and was always ready to tell it to any who might believe and obey.

In 1842, Benjamin Franklin moved to a village about ten miles southeast of New Castle, Indiana. During his residence here he held a public debate with the Universalist preacher, George W. McCune. In this period of time the plan of preaching once a month had its beginning. Benjamin Franklin never voiced any objection to that plan but he did deplore the result.

"Very gradually, but steadily, the churches learned to rely on these monthly visits for their spiritual edification. Very gradually and very steadily, they learned to feel more interest in these monthly meetings than in the acts of devotion and worship which might be observed on any Lord's day. Very gradually, the preachers left off their efforts to develop the talent in the churches to which they ministered, and finally adopted the habit of merely delivering their three sermons and then going home. Occasionally they roused themselves in a spasmodic effort 'to set in order things that were wanting' and preached a sermon or two on the ancient order of worship, 'the apostles' doctrine, and fellowship, the breaking of bread, and prayers.' The brethren would indulge in a little pleasantry about how their preacher had 'hauled them over the coals,' and then, people and preachers would lapse into the old routine again. Today, hundreds of churches never meet unless they have a preacher present to discourse to them. A plan which suffers churches to fall into such helplessness is in some way deficient. Some are inclined to urge more frequent visits, or a stationed preacher, as the remedy. But how will it help the matter to have a preacher present every Lord's day who never calls for a prayer, a thanksgiving, or an exhortation from any member of the congregation?"*

1845 A.D. BENJAMIN FRANKLIN BEGAN THE PUBLICATION OF "THE REFORMER" AT CENTERVILLE, INDIANA.

The subjects discussed in this paper were quite numerous for a small periodical. Among them were Secret Societies, Amusements, Temperance, Evidences of Christianity, Support of Preachers, Church Government and Its Relation to Human Government.

The editor of "The Reformer" showed no desire for speculative theology. All questions were decided by this rule, "Is it taught in the Bible?"

---

* *The Life of Elder Benjamin Franklin*—Franklin and Headington. Chapter 5, Page 73.

1847 A.D. FRANKLIN-MANFORD DEBATE

Benjamin Franklin held a debate in Milton, Indiana, with Erasmus Manford, a Universalist minister who was the editor of "The Western Universalist." The subjects for debate were as follows:

1. Do the Scriptures teach that the coming of Christ to judge the world is future?

> Mr. Franklin, affirms
> Mr. Manford, denies

2. Do the Scriptures teach the final holiness and happiness of all mankind?

> Mr. Manford, affirms
> Mr. Franklin, denies

3. Do the Scriptures teach that those who die in disobedience to the Gospel will suffer endless punishment?

> Mr. Franklin, affirms
> Mr. Manford, denies

The debate lasted four days. Each of the disputants wrote out his speeches and introduced no arguments not used in the oral discussion. Benjamin Franklin travelled extensively during the following years, preaching the gospel of Christ wherever opportunity afforded. During these years he also engaged in a number of religious discussions.

1849 A.D. ORGANIZATION OF MISSIONARY SOCIETY

The American Christian Missionary Society was organized in this year at Cincinnati, Ohio. A group comprising many of the prominent preachers had assembled at this city to attend to the business of the Bible and Tract Societies which had been formed at a previous time. By the unanimous approval of all assembled the organization of the society was effected.

Benjamin Franklin was present and gave his approval to the formation of this society. The judgment of the brotherhood at large, following the Last Will and Testament of the Springfield Presbytery, and the dissolution of the Mahoning Association, was that the church should stay clear of every form of ecclesiastical organization. When the news of the formation of this society became known it produced a lengthy discussion. Though Benjamin Franklin at first approved of its organization and served the society in an official way, in later years he reconsidered the questions involved and became an opponent of the society and like organizations.

1856 A.D. BENJAMIN FRANKLIN BEGAN THE PUBLICATION OF
THE AMERICAN CHRISTIAN REVIEW

For a period of years he remained its editor and endeavored to make it a review of Christianity in America. He was able to see the coming conflict between those who contended that the times called for a more cultivated ministry, and those who believed that a knowledge of God's word was of far more importance than literary excellence. Some of the older evangelists were being moved aside to make way for a generation of younger evangelists who had more culture.

The minds of many were turned from the older evangelists who had indicated their ability by their years of success, to younger evangelists who had the desire to become pastors over a congregation. This resulted in a decline in the spread of the gospel.

"The situation and the remedy for it were appreciated by Benjamin Franklin and he was not slow in sounding the trumpet in tones of warning, nor did he fail to act in accordance with his own views in the case. He was by no means indifferent to the 'oversight of the churches' by men who were 'apt to teach' but he regarded the plea for the 'pastorate' as an unscriptural thing. In the Review for February, 1856, we find an editorial on 'Evangelizing,' from which we make the following extract: 'If we are not sadly mistaken, here is where the attention of the brotherhood needs directing now. It is no matter how many schemes the brethren engage in nor how good their object, if they neglect evangelizing, the cause will fail. In every city, town, village and neighborhood where evangelical labors are not enjoyed, the cause is languishing and suffering. The attention of the Evangelists has been divided and distracted by unavailing and useless schemes to the neglect of the great evangelical work. Schemes of organization have been commented upon until the brethren have become sickened, and they turn from the subject at the first sight of the caption of an article treating upon it, feeling conscious that it will not afford relief. Long articles upon officers and their qualifications, and fine descriptions of the details of the pastorate appear in prints; but the churches fall soundly asleep under their fine themes. If we intend to save the cause, we, as evangelists of Christ, have something more to do than to seek good places, ease and earthly comfort. The Lord did not intend Evangelists to open an office, and sit down in it and wait for sinners to come to them to be converted. But he intended the living preachers to go to sinners and with the living voice preach to them the word of the living God. The command is to go, go and keep going, while God shall give us life; go, believing in God with a strong faith, trusting in the Lord for a support now, and eternal glory in the world to come. A little preaching on Lord's day will not do the work. The word should be preached every day and every night as far as possible. We cannot confine our labors to cities, towns and villages, expecting preaching to be brought to us, as work to a tailor, hatter or shoemaker; but we must go out into the country, among the people, and be one of them, as messengers sent from God to take them to Heaven. We are not to confine ourselves to the fine meeting houses; but, when we can do no better, go to the court house, the town or city hall, the old seminary, the schoolhouse, or the private dwelling, and preach to the people."*

In the college founded by Alexander Campbell, Benjamin Franklin was much interested. He contributed to its support and aided it by his influence but when he became aware of the changes that were being made in the college he withdrew his support from that institution.

Such colleges as had been established were founded for the purpose of perpetuating the principles of the Restoration. In the beginning, all of the faculty members were members of the one body, but this was gradually changed. Some teachers were later employed who were believed to be doubters of the truths recorded in the Bible.

Benjamin Franklin became a sharp critic of the colleges established for the purpose of teaching the Bible and freely expressed his disappointment in the Bible colleges, and concluded that all schools ought to be as secular as any business enterprise and that all religious instruction should be supplied "entirely through the church and Sunday school, or by the enterprise of individuals."

1876 A.D. FRANKLIN OPPOSES CHURCH COLLEGES

The liberal views of the professors of various colleges established by brethren of the church of Christ, such as Bethany College and Abingdon College, caused Benjamin Franklin to express himself in an editorial in The American Christian Review in the following words:

"We do not disguise the fact that we are not working for Bethany College, we are taking no interest in it. We worked for it all the time till Bro. Campbell died, subscribed and paid $100 to its support since his death. Things have been occurring all along since to cut our affections off from it till we have no sympathy with it. We do not believe it is doing the cause any good. We are now measuring every word we write, and understand the meaning of every word. We can give reasons for what we are saying to any extent the reader may desire. We shall put down a very few things briefly here:

1. We have become perfectly satisfied that education, in the popular sense, is purely secular, and is not a church matter. The church ought to be connected with no educational enterprise. We are in favor of no church college. This is a matter that may be discussed at length, but we enter into no discussion of it now. Still this would not utterly cut off our sympathy with Bethany College, other matters being equal.

---

* *Life of Elder Benjamin Franklin*—Franklin and Headington. Chapter 14, Pages 274-276.

> 2. One of the main pleas Alexander Campbell made for a college under the control of Christians was, in view of the moral training, that no man was educated in the true sense who was not cultivated in heart. This we hold to be as true as any principle yet uttered. To this end there should be sound professors to train students, and there should be a sound church in the vicinity of the college, maintaining the highest order of morality, order and discipline."*

Benjamin Franklin was a tireless worker in spreading the gospel of Christ. He debated with S. M. Merrill of the Methodist Church in Portsmouth, Ohio, on the subject of baptism and remained for one day after the debate which, including three persons who obeyed the gospel before the debate began, resulted in twenty-eight additions to the church.

After that debate he visited his home for a few days and then journeyed to Decatur, Illinois, where he preached for two weeks and baptized twenty-eight persons. Before returning to his home he went to Chillicothe, Missouri, where he debated with W. M. Rush, a presiding Elder of the Methodist Church, on baptism. At the conclusion of the debate Benjamin Franklin preached for a week and this resulted in twenty-five persons being added to the church. Three meetings in Kentucky resulted in sixty-eight additions to the church. His extensive labors weakened him physically and his health began to decline late in 1876. For a period of two years he lingered between life and death. It became apparent that his work on earth was near an end.

His health improved during 1878, and he had hopes for a complete recovery but on October 22, he suffered a relapse and died that afternoon. His body was buried at Anderson, Indiana.

Benjamin Franklin was blessed with a strong physical body. The great amount of physical and mental labor that he performed over a period of fifty years is evidence of his great strength.

The great number of people who came to hear him is an indication of his wonderful power over an audience. Because of the simplicity of his style of preaching the masses were continually calling for his services. They considered him as their man, their special representative.

His method of teaching was to present the doctrine of the denominational world and then to return to the Bible and show the contrast between truth and error. He did not resort to emotionalism to win converts but presented to his hearers the gospel of Christ. Those who obeyed the gospel under his preaching were soundly converted.

* *Life of Elder Benjamin Franklin*—Franklin and Headington. Chapter 18, Pages 397, 398.

His illustrations, as revealed by his sermons, were drawn from real life, his own experiences and observations. The effect of his preaching was indeed wonderful. All classes of men, the rich and the poor, the educated and the unlearned, the exalted and the lowly were all alike interested in the great subjects he discussed. He is believed to have travelled more in his effort to spread the gospel of Christ than any other evangelist of the Restoration period. The fruits of his labors may be summed up as follows:

1. An example of faithfulness to the teaching of the scriptures revealed in his daily walk before men.
2. Two volumes of sermons published to point out to sinners and saints their obligation to God.
3. Multitudes of Christians grounded and settled in the faith of Jesus Christ.
4. For thirty-seven years he filled the editorial chair with grace and dignity.
5. More than ten thousand sinners converted to the Lord by his preaching.

The secret of his power to lead men to obey the truth was founded on his great knowledge of the Bible, his knowledge of human nature, his close adherence to the Scriptures and his refusal to depart from them, the simplicity of his speech, his boldness in exposing error and his great love for the gospel, the church, and his brethren in Christ.

His influence for good will be felt by generations yet unborn.

APOSTOLIC AGE 33	APOSTATE AGE 100 (325)	DARK AGES 533	REFORMATION 1517	RESTORATION 1793 1956
Christ the Head	Universal Bishop	Papacy takes form	Church not under Prelates —Wycliff	All Human Heads Rejected
Scriptures the Guide	Creeds to Regulate	Councils Legislate	Bible restored to the People—Tyndal	Scriptures the only Guide
Elders to rule	Priests to Officiate	Hierarchy Develops	Papacy Rejected—Henry VIII	Elders the only Pastors
Salvation by Obedience	Salvation by Works	Salvation by Money	Salvation by faith only— Luther	Salvation by faith and obedience
Simple worship	Ritualistic worship	Mass-Penance	Worship guided by Bible —Zwingli	Nothing unauthorized in worship
Prayer	Pray to Statues	Auricular Confession	Christ our only Mediator —Knox	No human intercessor needed
Self-edifying	Clergy to teach	No Prelate No worship	Worship without a clergy —Wesley	The Body self-edifying
Lord's Supper	Lord's Supper changed	Transubstantiation	Weekly Lord's Supper— Calvin	Lord's Supper for the Lord's People
Contribution Gave as prospered	Tithing	Taxed by the Clergy	Give as prospered— Brewster	No Pledges no Assessments
Vocal Music	Harps in Worship	Instrumental Music	Vocal Music only— Gregory	Mechanical Music Unauthorized—
Baptism Immersion	Clinic Baptism	Sprinkling	Immersion only is Baptism —Luther	Baptism a burial in water
Christian	Arians Montanists	Followers of men	Christian the spiritual name	One name for the Lord's people O'Kelly-Jones Stone-Scott Smith-Campbell

CHAPTER 27

SUMMARY OF THE RESTORATION

Prior to the religious reformation, which had its beginning in 1793, many people did not believe in God or the Bible. Those who were accepted as teachers of the word of God knew nothing about rightly dividing the divine revelation. No distinction was drawn between the Patriarchal, the Jewish, and the Christian ages of religion. It was believed that what one read from the Old Testament was just as binding on man as any thing recorded in the New Testament. The position of the clergy was exalted. They were believed to be the only class of people who understood the will of God. To contradict or oppose their interpretation of the Scriptures marked one as a heretic.

In this period of time most religious people were subject to creeds and confessions of faith. All who entered the churches must accept them as portraying the will of God. Some held to the Westminster Confession of Faith, others to the Philadelphia Confession, the Book of Common Prayer, or Wesley's Discipline. It did not occur to them that the creeds blinded men to their duty towards God. The creeds taught that only the elect would be saved, and if one was not of the elect he was doomed to be lost. Those who professed to be Christians were at variance one with another. Such were the conditions in America when Thomas Campbell began to plead for people to come back to the Bible. He pleaded for the unity of all who professed to be the people of God on the one foundation of God's word.

James O'Kelly, Dr. Abner Jones, Rice Haggard, and Barton Stone, were well along in the work of the restoration when Thomas Campbell came to this country. All that the leaders of the Protestant Reformation had taught that was right was readily accepted by the men of the Restoration movement. The work Luther, Knox, Zwingli, and Calvin attempted was a reformation of the Roman Catholic Church, but these men were not working for the reformation of any religious group. Their purpose was to bring about a restoration of the teaching of the ONE CHURCH of the New Testament.

Those who had once called themselves Methodists, Baptists, or Presbyterians, surrendered those names that they might wear a

Bible name. All became interested in the spread of the Gospel and the extension of the Kingdom of Christ. The unity they brought about was not the result of one group surrendering their creed and adopting the Prayer Book, The Confession of Faith, or the Church Manual, of another group. This unity was the result of all of them surrendering their respective creeds and taking their stand upon the New Testament. In their efforts to restore the church for which Christ shed his blood, they did not ask their religious neighbors to surrender their creed and accept one formed by them. They asked only that they reject all human documents and accept the doctrine proclaimed by the inspired apostles of Jesus Christ. The scriptures would supply all things needed for their spiritual guidance. "All scripture is given by inspiration of God, and is profitable for doctrine, for reproof, for correction, for instruction in righteousness: that the man of God may be perfect, throughly furnished unto all good works."[1] "Therefore, brethren, stand fast, and hold the traditions which ye have been taught, whether by word, or our epistle."[2]

These men who pleaded for a return to God's word, purposed to worship God after the pattern revealed in the New Testament. That worship they learned was not marred by human inventions. The singing of the church was a part of its teaching and admonishing, for Paul said, "Teaching and admonishing one another in psalms, hymns and spiritual songs, singing and making melody in your hearts to the Lord." They learned this was addressed to the church. They believed, therefore, that the use of instrumental music could not be introduced into the worship without transgressing the divine will. This was new teaching to the religious world but it was not new to the word of God. They learned from a close study of God's word that when the church gathered for worship the teaching and admonishing was the work of the members of the church. When Paul wrote to the church at Rome, he said, "Ye are filled with all knowledge and able to edify one another." The members were taught to have part in the service because it contributed to their own spiritual growth and welfare. The reformers were convinced, by the reading of God's word, that every member had his work to do. When Paul wrote to the church at Ephesus he said, "But speaking the truth in love, may grow up into him in all things, which is the head, even Christ, from whom the whole body fitly joined together and compacted by that which every joint supplieth, according to the effectual working in the measure of every part, maketh increase of the body unto the edifying of itself

1. 2 Tim. 3:16, 17.
2. 2 Thess. 2:15.

in love."[3] Thus, in the church established by Christ through the apostles, there was no need for a clergyman to do the teaching and the preaching. They were not dependent upon a minister, for as ability permitted and opportunity afforded, the members served as ministers, supplying the teaching, the exhortations and the admonitions. The congregation in each community, with its elders and deacons, guided by the apostles' doctrine attended to its own affairs. There were no official boards, no synods or any other form of ecclesiastical government, created by uninspired men to make rules or laws by which the church was to be controlled.

The simplicity of the government and worship of the New Testament church was not originated by Thomas Campbell, Barton Stone, Walter Scott, Alexander Campbell, Rice Haggard, or John Smith. They were revealed in God's word and were the teaching and practice of the church throughout the apostolic age.

The effort of these men was not to reform some existing religious body, neither were they trying to produce a new church, but only to restore the teaching and practice of the church for which our Saviour died. They did not purpose to produce another confession of faith, they did not want another creed, they were not advocating the introduction of a new discipline. They simply wanted people to accept the one given by the Holy Spirit through the apostles. They believed a complete restoration of the teaching of God's word was necessary. This would take them back beyond all creeds, beyond the decrees of all church councils, assemblies and synods, to the church as it was in the beginning. This would effect a restoration of the teaching from which the religious world had departed during the Dark Ages. These men were not seeking for reformation but for restoration. What is the difference?

Perhaps an illustration will assist us. A man buys an old residence. He builds on an ell, provides for an extra room by changing the pitch of the roof, adds on a front porch, and changes the interior. When he has finished he has changed the house, it has been reformed. It does not now have the same appearance. It does not have the same lines.

Many years later another man becomes the owner. In an old chest in the attic of the home he finds the architect's drawings, the original plans and specifications by which the house was built. As he looks at the original plans and the drawing of the house he is impressed with the beauty of the house as it was when first constructed. He calls in a contractor, shows him the plans, and tells him, "I want the house put back as it was in the beginning. I want it to bear the same lines it had when first built."

---

3. Eph. 4 : 15, 16.

Is that possible? Certainly! He has the plans, the pattern by which the house was constructed. The contractor has his men remove the front porch. They give the roof the same pitch it once had, the ell is removed and the interior is replaced as it was originally. New material has been added, to be sure, but it has been of the same kind, cut according to the specifications, and of the same dimensions. The appearance of the house is just the same now as it was when first built. It has been restored to its original lines. Here is restoration.

Such is the thing these men purposed to do for the church. They had the original plans of the church of the New Testament. The forms of worship, the rituals, the officers, and the names that had been added through the ages, they purposed to cast aside.

They wanted the Lord's house just as it was when first built. It is freely admitted by all students of God's word that the passing of the years has brought many changes in the doctrine and practice of those who claim to have fellowship with Christ. Things unknown in the days of the apostles have been added by the religious world, while doctrines, practices, and commands, that were a part of the Lord's church were dropped by those who claimed to be servants of the church. These changes came about as the result of the teaching of men that if the church was to meet the needs of all ages, it had to be kept modern, lest it become obsolete and fail to serve the purpose for which God gave it.

Had the church been of human origin this might have been true, for men cannot produce a perfect institution. It is admitted that all organizations created by men need to be changed in plan or design as new conditions arise, but the church is different. It is not a human production. It is a blood-bought, divinely established institution, created just as God wanted it to be through all generations. God knew what men would need through all time and he designed the church to fill that need. When men tamper with the word of God, they virtually say that they are wiser than the Lord.

The changes made by men in the pattern of the church resulted in a misunderstanding of the purpose of the church. It was not designed by the Lord of heaven as an institution for promoting good health, it was not created for the purpose of carrying on an educational program or interesting people in social activities. It was designed solely for the salvation of man and for the betterment of his spiritual welfare. God gave to no one the right to change its original pattern or abrogate any of its divine requirements. To end the changes, and to restore the church as it was in the beginning, a complete return to the teaching of the New Testament was necessary.

If the men of the Restoration period had formed a church as Martin Luther did in 1517, as Henry VIII did in 1535, as John Knox did in 1572, as John Smith did in 1607, or as John Wesley did in 1728, it would have been just like any other human institution. But they realized that salvation was not in men, but in Christ; so they said, "Let us give up Luther's name, let us discard any name suggestive of a nation or form of government, let us reject any name that honors John Knox, let us not accept any name that calls attention to some specific command, let us not march under John Wesley's standard, but let us find out what Christ's followers were called at Jerusalem, at Ephesus, and at Antioch." They searched the Scriptures and studied as they read. In the book of Acts of Apostles they found that Christ's followers were called "Christians." That name was given by inspiration. It was called a "worthy name." It was the name they purposed to wear. They said, "That is a Bible name, that is the name we will wear."

They planned that nothing should be accepted which was not taught in the Scriptures. Remember, they were not trying to form a new organization, neither were they attempting the reformation of some existing church. They were pledged to return to the teaching and practice of the church as it was when established in Jerusalem on Pentecost. They asked, "What should the church be called?" They reasoned that it could not be called Luther's church, because they did not purpose to follow Luther or be guided by the Augsburg Confession of Faith; it could not be called Calvin's church for his creed was no better than any other human document. They could not call it Smyth's church, or Wesley's church, for they did not purpose to be led by their teachings, but by the teaching of Christ. Attention has been called to the truth that obedience to the will of Christ made Christians, and when those Christians in any community were banded together they constituted the church. But whose church? Just any one's church? Indeed not! Christ said he would build his church. Paul said the church had been built, and when he penned his letter to the church in Rome, he said the churches of Christ sent their salutations to the saints in that city. Here was a name that suggested the ownership of the body. It was placed in the divine record by inspiration.

The restoration of Christ's church, with the Bible as their guide, was the thing for which they hoped. What a glorious thought! Could this be brought about? Only by rejecting the creeds of men. Some affirmed that it would be an impossibility to be guided by the Bible alone, contending that its meaning could only be understood by men who were trained for that purpose.

For hundreds of years the gospel plan of salvation had been rejected. Walter Scott was the first of the Restoration group to teach that if God gave the word as a guide, then the plan by which one became a Christian was contained therein. Diligent study of God's word revealed that the gospel of Christ required faith in Jesus Christ, repentance of sins, confessing Christ before men, and being buried with Christ in baptism. All who entered the church obeyed these commands. Nowhere did the leaders of the Restoration period find that infant baptism, and sprinkling or pouring were a part of the practice of the New Testament church. This divine institution had its beginning in Jerusalem on the day of Pentecost, which the apostle Peter called the beginning. This is the ONE BODY of which Paul spoke when he said, "There is one body and one Spirit, even as ye are called in one hope of your calling." He identified that one body as the church saying, "And he is the head of the body, the church." In the church of the Lord there were only two classes of officials, elders and deacons. The elders were sometimes called bishops, because they were to oversee the local congregation. They were the pastors of the flock because they supplied the spiritual food. The evangelists were not officials in the local congregations, but were proclaimers of the word to the unsaved, not to the church. There was no example of a New Testament congregation calling an evangelist in from the work of preaching the gospel to the world, to become the "minister" of a congregation with elders, to do their work of feeding the flock.

The church at Jerusalem was guided by the apostles' doctrine. Whatever the apostles taught by command or example, the leaders of the Restoration believed they could safely teach. What the apostles' doctrine, as revealed in the epistles, did not teach, they rejected as unauthorized by the Lord. They believed that in every way the church should measure up to the divine pattern in its worship and work. That church met on the first day of the week in some private home or some upper room. As they came together, there was no sound of flute or stringed instruments, for these things did not come into the worship until hundreds of years later. That Christian assembly sang praises to God, making melody in their hearts to the Lord. Their prayers were part of their worship, coming from the heart and not from the pages of some church manual or prayer book. The elders, or bishops as they were called, qualified according to God's word, supplied their spiritual food. As occasion demanded and ability enabled, others had a part in edifying the body.

When Paul wrote to the church in the city of Rome he admonished them to follow after the things which make for peace and the things wherewith they could edify one another. In that worship they observed the Lord's Supper upon the first day of every week. Just as often as the first day of the week occurred, these men knew that God meant for the Lord's Supper to be observed. "Upon the first day of the week, when the disciples came together to break bread, Paul preached unto them ready to depart on the morrow and continued his speech until midnight."[4]

Here was teaching that had been overlooked by the religious world.

It was a new idea that the church of the apostolic age commemorated the death of Christ every Lord's day, but it was not new to the word of God. There is no apostolic example that it was ever observed on Thursday, on Friday, or on Saturday. There are some religious people who observe this memorial once a month, once every three months, or once a year, asserting that the scriptures do not say every first day of the week. God told the children of Israel, "Remember the Sabbath day to keep it holy." The children of Israel did not believe that this command meant to keep one Sabbath every month or one every three months. They knew that just as often as the Sabbath occurred they were to keep it holy.

When the question of the support of the gospel and the care of the poor came before the reformers, they were sure some provision was made for the support of the gospel, for Paul taught that those who preached the gospel should live of the gospel. When the church at Jerusalem was in distress, Paul reminded the Roman brethren that the Macedonian church and the disciples at Achaia, had made a certain contribution to the saints there. Here was an example of how the church took care of these conditions in the New Testament age. They had no other means to raise money to carry on the work of the church. There were no suppers, fairs, or festivals, to raise finances to carry on the work of the Lord. They contributed of their means as they had been prospered. No one had a right to tell another how much to give. These acts of worship, rendered to God in spirit and in truth, constituted the simple, yet impressive worship of the early church. As these truths were presented to the religious world, the leaders of the Restoration period were charged with teaching a new religion. But these acts of worship were pleasing to the Lord, for we read that the hand of the Lord was with them. They were the Lord's plan of worship for the church then, and should be for all time. Such was the teaching of Barton Stone, Alexander Campbell, Jacob Creath, Absalom Rice, John T. Johnson, John Smith, and others as they pleaded for a return to the will of the Lord. What were these men trying to do?

---

4. Acts 20 : 7.

Their endeavor was to get people to return to the word of God. As they consulted God's word for guidance and put into practice what they learned, did this make them a new church? Indeed not! It is the same old religion, the same doctrine of the same church which men had forgotten so long ago.

Wherever the apostles and evangelists of our Lord went preaching the word, they established churches. These churches were all alike. They had obeyed the same gospel, they believed the same doctrine, they worshipped the same way. When Philip preached in Samaria, he did not establish a Philipite church. It was the church of the Lord. When Paul preached in Thessalonica, he did not established a Paulite church. It was a church of the Lord. When Peter preached the gospel at Caesarea, and those who believed were baptized, it was not a Cephasite church, but a church of the Lord. Wherever the gospel is preached in any age of the world's history, and people obey it and assemble themselves on the first day of the week to obey Christ, to partake of the Lord's supper, to give as they have been prospered, to praise the Lord in psalms, hymns and spiritual songs, there you have, not a Philip-ite church, a Paul-ite church or a Cephas-ite church, but a church of Christ.

Because of his natural ability, Alexander Campbell became one of the acknowledged leaders of the Restoration. He preached the gospel with such power that thousands accepted the truth. The religious organizations then prominent, to conceal their embarrassment in losing thousands who turned from denominationalism to the purity of the church of Christ, began to call the church the "Campbellite church" and the truths he preached "Campbellism." This was only an effort to turn attention from the truth, seeking by derision to bring the preacher into disrepute. But those who sought to ridicule Barton Stone, John Smith, Walter Scott, Alexander Campbell, Rice Haggard, Jacob Creath, and others, were unable to show that what they taught was not what the apostles taught, that the name Christian was not the name the disciples of Christ wore, that the requirements for salvation were not the requirements of the New Testament, and that the worship for which they contended was not the worship of the church of the Lord.

Sometimes the question is asked, "How could the church that these men preached about and established in Pennsylvania, Virginia, Indiana, Kentucky, Illinois, Ohio, Tennessee and Alabama, be the church established by the apostles of Jesus Christ?" Perhaps an illustration will enable the reader to see how this was possible. After the war between the states ended, a group of unscrupulous citizens from the northern states flocked to the South to exploit the new citizens of the colored race, who had received the right to vote. These men who invaded the South became known as "carpetbaggers," because they were said to carry all their possessions in their carpet bags. A state of unrest developed throughout the South because of the tactics of these politicians. An organization to combat their influence came into existence at Pulaski, Tennessee, in 1865. It was called the Ku Klux Klan. This organization increased in members and power until it spread over all the southern states and into some of the northern states also. It became an empire within an empire, with laws that were more powerful than those of the commonwealth, which it dominated. Its affairs were administered by a grand wizard, his ten geni and the cyclops of the local organization, and his subordinates. They had their code of laws, their rules, and the form of procedure outlined in the Klan Manual. Because of the corruption within the Klan, an act was passed by the Congress of the United States in 1871, which brought an end to the Klan. All members and officers of this organization were called upon to surrender their arms and disguises, and to cease meeting, bringing an end to their organization.

But the Klan manuals were not destroyed. From generation to generation they were handed down. In 1916, a copy of this manual came into the possession of William Simmonds. He studied its laws and its organization. He read about the duties of its members and officers, then he set about to bring this organization back into the world. How could he do it? He had the Manual, the book of rules, with all of the information about the officers, and the form to be followed in the meetings. He called a few of his neighbors and close friends together, outlined to them the purpose of the society and they agreed to be guided by what was set forth in the Manual.

Was this a new organization? No, it wore the same name, had the same officials, carried on the same kind of meetings, and had the same ceremonies and rites that were used by the Klan in generations past. How was this possible? Because they were guided by the same Manual, the same book that was used by that organization when it first came into being.

Now here is the application. The church of our Lord was planted upon the earth in 33 A. D. It was controlled by its head, Jesus Christ. He legislated, or enacted laws, through his twelve apostles. Congregations were established throughout the world. Over these local congregations elders and deacons were appointed. They were guided in their meetings by the apostles' doctrine. This doctrine was set forth in the New Testament Scriptures. Eventually corruption found its way into this institution; its light and influence were blotted from the face of the earth. But the guide book of the church, the New Testament, was handed down from generation to generation. The study of this book brought about a desire to restore the Lord's church to the world. Could this be done? Yes, as long as they had the guide book, the New Testament, the same church could be produced. Barton Stone, Alexander Campbell, Walter Scott, Jacob Creath, John Smith, and others, only called people back to the old book which had been forgotten so many years before. They began to practice only what was authorized in the word of God. They met for worship on the first day of the week, they praised God in song and prayer, studied His word, exhorted each other to live righteous lives, partook of the Lord's supper, and gave of their means to care for the poor and support the preaching of the gospel. Was this a new church? Indeed it was not! It had the same gospel, the same officials, observed the same worship, kept the same ordinances that were kept by the church of the Lord in generations past. To restore the church to the world in its purity and simplicity it was necessary to go back beyond the councils, back beyond the Westminster Confession of Faith, back beyond the Augsburg Confession of Faith, back beyond the Nicean Creed, and come to the apostles' doctrine as set forth in the New Testament. Here all that the Lord requires man to do to be saved is revealed, here all that we must do in worship of the heavenly Father is clearly set forth, and here the life that we must live is portrayed.

As the plea of the men of the Restoration period spread among the people of the nation which had so recently secured religious liberty and freedom of speech, it was readily accepted.

Its rapid spread, no doubt, grew out of the fact that during the Dark Ages, when the persecutions of Rome became unbearable, fathers and grandfathers conducted worship in the home in secret. They held to such truths as had been handed down from generation to generation. They met under the cover of darkness in some convenient place, and there offered unto God a simple worship based upon such copies of the Scriptures as they had been able to preserve from the Inquisitors of papal Rome. One generation taught the coming generation that once a church existed whose doctrine was the doctrine of Christ and the apostles, whose sole guide was the word of God and not the words of men, whose worship was without ritualism and pomp, whose pastors did not fleece the flock, but looked after its spiritual needs, whose requirements for entrance were belief in God's son and obedience to his commands. The members of each family constituted the church in each home. As the children and grandchildren grew to maturity they assumed their place in the work of the church. Here was the church in the wilderness. As the church of Rome developed, the true church of Christ was obscured. Because of the severity of the persecutions which were directed against her, she was compelled to go under cover. God sent the church into the wilderness for her own protection, where she remained for twelve hundred sixty years. Evidence of the existence of the church in the wilderness has come down to our time. A Catholic authority requesting information on how best to proceed against those who would not acknowledge the rulership of Rome said,

> "Their heresy is this—They say the church is only among themselves, because they alone follow the ways of Christ and imitate the apostles, not seeking secular gain. The apostolic dignity, they say, is corrupted by engaging itself in secular affairs, while it sits in the chair of Peter. They do not hold the baptism of infants, they place no confidence in the intercession of the saints and all things in the church which have not been established by Christ they call superstition. These who have returned to our church tell us they had great numbers scattered almost everywhere. And as for those who were burnt they, in the defense they made for themselves, told us that this heresy had been concealed from the time of the martyrs and that it had existed in Greece and other countries."*

This information coming from an enemy of the true church is very valuable. Not only does it show the existence of Christians, but it proves that great numbers of them existed in many countries. Concerning the existence of primitive Christians in England, Newburg, the historian said,

> "Being interrogated about their religion they said they were Christians and believed in the doctrine of the apostles."†

Another authority states that the houses where the early Christians assembled were the homes of those of like faith and they were identified by a secret mark. These congregations had bishops or elders. The members were above reproach in their morals, dress and conduct.

When the Haldanes, Glass, Sandeman, and others, began to plead for a return to the word of God as the only source of guidance, the twelve hundred sixty years of the wilderness bondage of the church drew to a close.

The departure from God's word had not been made at one step. Little by little men changed the doctrine of Christ, altered the plan of salvation, and corrupted the worship of Christ's church.

The return to the Bible will not be made by one step, but little by little as the doctrine of Christ is learned, it will be accepted, as the plan of salvation is unfolded it will be obeyed, and as the purity of the worship is revealed, it will be adopted.

---

* *Ancient Churches of Piedmont*—Page 140.
† *Live Religious Issues*—Kendrick—Page 852.

"Had the morning of the day of Pentecost found the disciples assembled in strife or split into factions, can we imagine that the Divine Spirit would have filled with his presence a house already filled with another spirit, an antagonist spirit of malevolence? or that he would have even approached the contentious scene? Something quicker and stronger than reasoning—an instinctive conviction—tells us he would not. What is the change, then, which we suppose him to have since undergone—or what the peculiar grounds which lead us to expect—that he should mingle with our strifes and countenance our schisms? He is still the Spirit of peace, and can he approve of our wars? He is still the Spirit of love, and can he dwell amidst the elements of anger and hostility?"

The Divided Church Made One—John Harris

CHAPTER 28

DOES RELIGIOUS DIVISION PLEASE GOD?

The teaching of the church of the Lord that one church is sufficient to save the world has long irked the religious world, but in the light of God's word they have been forced to acknowledge the truth that God provided but one church through which the world was to be saved.

"Whether we like it or not there is a decaying significance in denominationalism. We are not doing the cause of Protestantism much good by having two hundred and fifty-six different denominations and sects."

It is Dr. Charles Clayton Morrison's conclusion from his study of the question, "Can Protestantism Win America?" that it is increasingly clear that Protestantism can not win America with its secularized and competitive churches."*

Many religious leaders admit that the divided churches of Christendom are failing to meet the spiritual needs of people today. Many say they derive no benefit from religious services, that they fail to receive from their church the spiritual strength they need. They look to the religious institution with which they are identified for spiritual guidance, but fail to find it. They wait for a message from the teachings of the Savior of men, but fail to receive it.

For this reason there are twenty-five thousand deserted church buildings in America. The churches that met in them died a spiritual death because they lost the message of the Master.

The church in the days of the apostles existed for the purpose of spreading the gospel, making Christians, building character, teaching what Christ taught, and caring for the distressed. Churches of today have become amusement halls. Preachers are side-stepping the issues that confront them, lulling their listeners into false security by watering down the gospel.

Preachers ought to proclaim the religion which Christ gave to the world, for soft, easy, inoffensive preaching will not save the world. Less and less have they lifted their voices against sin, less and less have they pointed out the need for reformation of life upon the part of their members. The gospel of Christ is kept in

---
* *Pulpit Digest.*

the background, and a lot of pretty phrases and empty talk about love, and humanity, and brotherhood, are handed out to people who are literally starving for the gospel of Christ. Today, people "join" this church or that church for social, political, or business reasons. Where is the expression, "join the church," found in the Bible? It is not there. The teaching of God's word is that the Lord adds one to his church by obedience to the gospel.

In generations past, preachers proclaimed that Christian character was necessary for fellowship. Preachers have preached that which is not the truth of the gospel and have led men to think it was from God's word. The failure of that invented gospel to convert, to reform and to save has been charged up to the true gospel which has been forgotten and cast aside.

Never was the gospel of Christ more needed, never was there a more glorious opportunity for the denominations of Christendom to come back to the Bible than now. This is the day of their opportunity, but never was the religious world less alive to their opportunity, than it is at present.

The common conclusion among religious people seems to be that whatever the laws of the land tolerate is all right for those who profess to be Christians, and that whatever is not forbidden in so many words is allowed. Fairs, festivals, and entertainments, enter into church activities. People forget that the Lord did not establish his church to entertain, but to teach principles of truth, to save souls, and to encourage men and women to live righteous lives.

The churches of the Lord regard the strife, the alienation, and division which exists among professed Christians as displeasing to the Lord. They believe it comes from rejecting the counsel of God's word and following after the commandments of men.

The remedy for these things lies in a return to the teachings of the Lord, the guidance of the Scriptures, and a whole-hearted acceptance of Jesus Christ as head over all things to the church.

Preachers are largely responsible for the division that exists in the religious world, and yet they say they advocate the unity of all of God's people and are working for it. One thing alone will bring about that unity: "If any man speak let him speak as the oracles o God." If all of the religious world would do this it would bring about a revision of the vocabulary of the religious world. It would eliminate such terms as "getting religion," for religion is something you do, and not something you get. To speak as God's word would eliminate the use of the word "Reverend" as a title for ministers. Where do we read that any apostle or evangelist of the New Testament ever called himself by that title? This was a name of God. "Holy and reverend is thy name."

The only message that can possibly meet the needs of the religious world is a plea for a complete return to the teaching of the Lord. Throughout the epistles addressed to the churches of the Lord, they were warned against division, and exhorted to be of the same mind and judgment. Paul taught there is but one body, and shows that the one body is the church. How altogether different is the condition that prevails at the present time. We have in this fair land about two hundred and fifty separate denominations. Get this picture—two hundred and fifty distinct denominations existing for the purpose of teaching the Christianity of Christ. People are called upon to believe that all of these denominations compose the church of the Lord, and that all are necessary for the proclamation of the religion of Christ. Is Christianity less effective at the present than when first established, that we need two hundred and fifty ways to convert men, the thing that was accomplished through ONE Church in the gospel age?

No one is so unwise as to contend that there are two hundred and fifty different kinds of Christianity. If Christ established one church, who established the others?

Was the Christ so weak as a teacher, that men must create two hundred and fifty different churches to tell what he taught in the ONE church he built?

To contend that these denominations are necessary for the promulgation of the gospel, is just another way of saying that we are wiser than the Savior who gave us one kind of Christianity, taught in one church, as revealed in one Bible. All religious people profess to be guided by the one Bible, to believe in one God, and in one Christ. Does this Bible create and perpetuate all of these religious organizations, churches, and denominations, that separate and divide people who want to serve God?

Any student of the Scriptures knows that the Savior prayed for the unity of his followers, saying, "Neither pray I for these alone, but for them also which shall believe on me through their word, that they may be one."[1] Christ never authorized the divided and warring factions of the religious world. They are foreign in principle to the unity for which Christ prayed and which the apostles taught. Concerning unity, Paul said, "Now I beseech you, brethren, by the name of our Lord Jesus Christ, that ye all speak the same thing, and that there be no divisions among you, but that ye be perfectly joined together in the same mind and in the same judgment."[2]

1. John 17: 20.
2. 1 Cor. 1: 10.

Since God's word thus teaches unity to religious people, if unity does not prevail, it necessarily follows that someone has failed to follow God's word.

All churches of the religious world cannot be right, differing as they do in doctrine, practice, and worship. Thoughtful men of all religious faiths are now awake to the evils of division. They know it divides their forces, squanders their resources, promotes infidelity, and pleases Satan. The unity of all religious people would do much to bring the world into subjection to the Savior of men. Efforts are being made among the denominations to unite certain groups that are similar in faith and practice, and the leaders in this work are commended by the daily newspapers and religious magazines. But this is not something new. The churches of Christ have always advocated the unity of all believers and their teaching efforts have called attention to the need for unity.

The subject of unity brings up this question, "Is it possible for all religious people to stand together?" Certainly it is possible. The church was united in the beginning. There is but one divine institution revealed in the New Testament. Unity is just as important and necessary today as it was when the church was first established. The church in the beginning was guided by the apostles' doctrine. As the gospel was carried to other communities and believers were added to the Lord, they, too, became subject to the same guidance. Just as long as they were guided by what the apostles taught, they all spoke the same thing and there was no division among them.

When Paul learned of discord among the disciples at Corinth, he rebuked them for it with these words, "And I, brethren, could not speak unto you as unto spiritual, but as unto carnal, even as unto babes in Christ, I have fed you with milk and not with meat, for hitherto ye were not able to bear it, neither yet now are ye able. For ye are yet carnal: for whereas there is among you envying, and strife, and divisions, are ye not carnal and walk as men?"[3]

Paul thus shows that strife and division among God's people are wrong. In calling the attention of the Ephesians to the one body, Paul said, "And hath put all things under his feet, and gave him to be the head over all things to the church, which is his body, the fulness of him that filleth all in all."[4]

In that one body unity prevailed. All who obeyed the commands of the One Christ were brought into the one body. No one could be in the body and not be in the church for the simple reason that the one body and the one church were the same.

---

3. 1 Cor. 3 : 1-3.
4. Eph. 1 : 22.

The New Testament shows that all the early disciples were members of the same church, taught and believed the same doctrine, and were of the same mind and judgment. So long as they were guided by the apostles' doctrine, all spoke the same thing and there were no divisions among them. This unity prevailed until after the death of all of the apostles.

Is it out of harmony to plead for the same unity today? This question is often asked, "Who then divided the church that the apostles left united?" The teachings of the inspired apostles were recognized as the source of authority in the beginning. The apostles imparted this teaching by letter and by word of mouth, under the guidance of the Holy Spirit. Even after the death of the apostles, the church continued to recognize their authority as revealed in the epistles.

From the beginning at Jerusalem, the church grew and expanded until it covered the Roman world. Its growth was due to the spirit of unity that prevailed among the followers of Christ. But with the beginning of the next century the mystery of iniquity began to work. Men denied that Christ intended for his apostles to be the source of authority. Aspiring men began to set forth their opinions upon certain subjects in opposition to the elders and the evangelists who contended that the writings of the inspired men were the only divine source of authority.

The speculations of men upon the nature of Christ, resulted in a council being convened at Nice in 325 A.D., by Constantine. This council composed of three hundred and eighteen uninspired men, formed a creed which became the pattern for others which followed.

This council marks the beginning of the apostasy that ushered in the Dark Ages, during which human laws were substituted for divine laws, and the word of God was forgotten.

A hierarchy developed which was dominated by a man on the banks of the Tiber, in the city of Rome. This ecclesiastical kingdom corrupted the truth of God's word, and so persecuted the true church of the Lord that it was forced to flee into the wilderness.

For a thousand years the knowledge of the truth was lost to mankind, then Martin Luther tried to restore the word to the world. He took a long step out of apostasy, but failed to restore the purity of the church established by the Lord. Other reformers followed, each endeavoring to restore some part of the teaching of the New Testament, but overlooking the necessity of restoring all that the apostles taught. Around each of these reformers a group of people rallied and from them a religious denomination developed which was ruled by a human creed.

Thus the Reformation prepared the foundation for the divided and confused condition that prevails in the world today. Neglecting to return to the teaching of the apostles, men formed creeds, divided into groups, assumed names and forms of worship, unauthorized by the word of God. No Bible scholar contends that these different groups, wearing different names, accepting doctrines that differ with all others, are produced by the one book, given by one God, through his one Son.

In order to bring about unity among religious people some have suggested that all groups come together and each surrender some point of doctrine and thus they would stand united.

Doubtless this would produce a creed loose enough and elastic enough to accommodate all faiths, but such a procedure would lack the unity that is taught in the New Testament. No church manual, creed, confession of faith, prayer book, or church discipline, could possibly form an acceptable guide or standard, for they represent only the opinions of men upon religious subjects, and they have always produced division instead of creating unity. Because they are human productions, no combination of them would satisfy all people, but all who want to be Christ's followers could accept what he has said through the apostles. The apostles' doctrine, as revealed in the New Testament, formed the basis of unity for the church of the Lord. No one was ever required to believe more than the apostles taught. On their teaching the church stood united with ONE God, the Father above all; with ONE Lord, Jesus Christ; with ONE Spirit which gave us the ONE Book which teaches ONE baptism, by which we become identified with the ONE body, where we have ONE hope, eternal life with our Lord. What more does the church need today? Upon these things the church can stand united.

Chapter 29

A SECOND APOSTASY

Attention has been called to the growth and rapid progress of the church in the apostolic age. Cities of commercial importance, centers of political prominence, and communities of paganism heard the gospel of Christ. This system of religion had no attraction for the vulgar since it was uncompromising in its opposition to paganism, demanding of those who were converted to it, purity of life and character. From all quarters it encountered bitter opposition, yet at last it exerted an influence upon the thoughts and actions of all citizens of the Roman world.

We read that believers were the more added to the Lord and the number of disciples multiplied in Jerusalem greatly, and a great company of priests were obedient to the faith.

The persecutions which attended the growth of the church served as wind to scatter the seed of the kingdom, for in less than forty years after Jesus was crucified, Christianity had penetrated to every province of the then known world. Such is the picture of the church of the first century when the gospel was in all the world, and bearing fruit. But before the death of the last apostle the great apostasy which corrupted the church had begun its work. Churches became heretical, the clergy began to develop, false teachers perverted the gospel of Christ, the study of God's word was neglected, and the time subsequently came when a human creed was formed to tell the people what to believe. With the formation of that creed, other heresies developed which led the church into the period of time we know as the Dark Ages, where it remained for twelve hundred sixty years. Thus was the light of God's word extinguished, and in the place of the church established by Christ, we see the rise of an ecclesiastical system, altogether different from the church of the first century, which eventually developed into a hierarchy dominated by the Pope of Rome.

When the Reformation ended, the effort was made to lead the church out of the mists of Romanism and denominationalism, and once more the church flourished in its simplicity and purity.

The plea to speak only as God's word directed, led multitudes to Christ. Here was the basis of the unity for which our Savior prayed. "That they may all be one as thou Father art in me, and I in thee."

Within the church a desire to be like the denominations around them began to develop. Alexander Campbell was much opposed to the formation of any institution that encroached upon the work of the church. In speaking of the church of the Lord and the work and worship of the assembly, he said,

> "The order of their assemblies was uniformly the same. It did not vary with moons and season. It did not change as dress or fluctuate as the manners of the times. They had no monthly concerts for prayer; no solemn convocations, no great fasts, no preparation, nor thanksgiving days. Their churches were not fractured into misionary societies, Bible societies, education societies; nor did they dream of organizing such in the world. In their church capacity alone they moved. They neither transformed themselves into any other kind of associations, nor did they fracture and sever themselves into divers societies. They viewed the church of Jesus Christ as the scheme of heaven to ameliorate the world; as members of it they considered themselves bound to do all they could for the glory of God and the good of men. They dared not transfer to a missionary society, or Bible society, or education society, a cent or a prayer, lest in so doing they should rob the church of its glory and exalt the inventions of men above the wisdom of God. In their church capacity alone they moved. The church they considered 'the pillar and ground of the truth'; they viewed it as the temple of the Holy Spirit; as the house of the living God. They considered if they did all they could in this capacity, they had nothing left for any other object of a religious nature. In this capacity, wide as its sphere extended, they exhibited the truth in word and deed. Their good works, which accompanied salvation, were the labors of love, in ministering to the necessities of saints, to the poor of the brotherhood. They did good to all men, but especially to the household of faith. They practiced that pure and undefiled religion, which, in overt acts consists in 'taking care of orphans and widows in their affliction, and in keeping one's self unspotted by (the vices of) the world.' "*

Though Alexander Campbell was opposed to the establishment of any institution which conflicted with the work of the church, he later advocated the establishment of such institutions to safeguard the gospel and perpetuate the principles of the restoration.

1840 A.D. BETHANY COLLEGE FOUNDED

Alexander Campbell founded Bethany College and became its first president, a position he retained until he died. In a very short time after his death the college became the kind of an institution he had opposed in earlier years. Young men were trained to become professional proclaimers of the gospel. This was the beginning of

---

* *The Christian Baptist—Campbell.* Volume I, Number 1, Pages 6, 7.

the apostasy which produced the clergy, the one man pastor system, the missionary society, the use of instrumental music in worship, and divided the church of the Lord. Alexander Campbell's estimate of the clergy is revealed in these words—

> "Besides this there is another fact to which we would advert, viz., that when there is a voluntary association of any number of disciples of Christ, met in any one place to attend to the duties and privileges of a church, should they call anyone of their own number, who possesses the qualifications belonging to the bishop or overseer, laid down by the Holy Spirit in the written word: and should they appoint him to office, as the Holy Spirit has taught them in the same written word—then it may be said to such a person, 'Take heed to yourself and to the flock over which the Holy Spirit has made you overseer.'
>
> But this bishop of whom we have now spoken, is neither priest, ambassador, minister of religion, clergyman, nor a reverend divine; but simply one that has the oversight of one voluntary society, who, when he leaves that society, has no office in any other, in consequence of his being an officer in that. His discharge of the work of a bishop is limited by, and confined to, the particular congregation which appointed him to office. If he should travel abroad and visit another congregation, even of the same views with that of which he was or is bishop, he is then no bishop; he is then in the capacity of an unofficial disciple. To suppose the contrary is to constitute different orders of men, or to divide the church into common classes of clergy and laity, than which nothing is more essentially opposite to the genius and spirit of christianity.
>
> We have seen some bishops, ignorant of the nature of the office, acting very much out of character, placing themselves in the bishop's office, in a church which they might occasionally visit, and assuming to act officially in an assembly over which they had no bishopric. In the meantime, we conclude that one of those means used to exalt the clergy to dominion over the faith, over the consciences, and over the persons of men, by teaching the people to consider them as specially called and moved by the Holy Spirit, and sent to assume the office of ambasadors of Christ, or ministers of the Christian religion, is a scheme unwarranted by God, founded on pride, ignorance, ambition, and impiety; and as such ought to be opposed and exposed by all them that love our Lord Jesus Christ in sincerity."*

Alexander Campbell acknowledged the truth of Mosheim's statement that the catechetical school established at Alexandria, Egypt, and presided over by Pantaenus, Alexandrinus, Origen, and other early Christians, became the grave of primitive Christianity.

> "Having in the preceding number introduced the opinions and speculations of the philosophical religionists, before and at the Christian era, we will now give our readers an account of the corruption of the Christian religion by those opinions and philosophical religious teachers. This we shall do in the words of one who

---

* *The Christian Baptist*, Volume I, Page 21.

can not be much suspected for an extraordinary attachment to primitive Christianity. Mosheim, from the mass of evidence upon this subject to which he had access, satisfactorily shows that the first 'Theological seminary,' established at Alexandria in Egypt, in the second century, was the grave of primitive Christianity. Yes, it appears that the first school instituted for preparing Christian doctors was the fountain, the streams whereof polluted the great mass of Christian professors, and completed the establishment of a paganized Christianity in the room of the religion of the New Testament. . ."[*]

Relative to the establishment of Bethany College, the editor of a religious magazine, published in Tennessee, said,

"We think the most fatal mistake of Alexander Campbell's life, and one that has done much and we fear will do much more to undo his life's work, was the establishment of a school to train and educate young preachers.

We believe the whole principle of taking young men with undeveloped characters and unfixed habits and educating them for preachers, or for any other specific work in the church, is hurtful in the extreme. It has a tendency to make merely professionals of them. They are educated for preachers. They often lose their first ardor and then think they are entitled to a living out of their profession and look to it more as a means of making a livelihood than of doing good."

As the clergy developed, churches which once strongly opposed any departure from the New Testament plan of work gradually adopted the practice of securing a preacher to labor with them continuously.

Thus the elders were relieved of their responsibility of supplying the spiritual needs of the flock and the church drifted farther and farther away from the pattern revealed in the New Testament.

This practice has come down to the present time, but those who endorse it search in vain for the example in the New Testament of a congregation hiring an evangelist to assume the work that should be done by the elders.

Moses E. Lard, a pioneer preacher of the church said,

"The modern office of pastor is an office not known in the New Testament, hence the limit of power which may be claimed to belong to it is not therein laid down. Consequently it is extremely difficult to say when the person who fills the office is usurping power which does not belong to him. Indeed this can not be done. He is clearly a lawless one; and may, if he sees fit, go to great lengths, and do great mischief before he can be checked.

To me, I am free to say, the points of resemblance between pastor, priest and pope are more than the mere circumstance that each word begins with a "p." From pastor to priest is only a short step, from priest to pope only a long one; still the step has been

[*] *The Christian Baptist,* Volume I, Pages 61, 62.

taken; and for one, I am afraid to run risks; at least, I think it is safest not to run them. Let us see to it that the ancient practice is our model, and the ancient Scriptures our sole guide in this and all other matters. That our churches need the most constant care I well know, and also that without it even the best of them must decline; but let us create no imaginary office, no imaginary officer, in order to meet the case. Better is no church with the word of God unbroken than is the best of so-called churches reared on its ruins."

Little wonder that James A. Harding said of this innovation,

"The Pastor is not a necessity. He is a fungus growth upon the church, the body of Christians, dwarfing its growth, preventing the development of its members; and until the church gets rid of him it will never prosper as it should."

"There is no use denying the fact that the 'pastor system' exists among the churches of Christ today. It is a growing evil. It constitutes a major menace to the cause of Christ. If it continues to develop as rapidly during the next quarter of a century as it has during the last one, the greater part of the church is going to be corrupted by it."*

The pastor system in operation among some of the congregations caused many of the outstanding evangelists to speak against it in no uncertain terms. A prominent evangelist who gave a lecture before the student body of a large college at which a great number of evangelists were also present said,

"It will not be seriously denied that there is an arrangement in operation in the church of Christ which bears a suspicious similarity to the pastor system of the denominations. It is idle to deny this. Elders have in many instances employed an evangelist to feed the flock and take the oversight thereof, to the utter neglect of the work themselves. It is not surprising that, where this is done, the elders are, too often, regarded as but mere figureheads, without authority and influence in the congregation.

The elders are the pastors of the flock and not the evangelists; and it is their duty to care for it and tend it. Evangelists are to carry the glad tidings of salvation to the lost, and preach the gospel in regions where it is not known. These facts are so obvious and so well known among us, we attempt no defense of them here.

Yet there is a disposition on the part of many congregations to ignore this and thus to create a new office in the church by transforming the evangelist into a pastor with duties, powers, and responsibilities which belong to the elders alone, requiring him to spend his entire time engaged in this work, and in some instances, absolutely forbidding him to extend his labors beyond the limits of the congregation he serves.

We cannot but regard this situation as an evil and alarming tendency of the times. It is naturally to be expected that the preachers, recognizing the situation and the responsibility of carrying on the work, themselves, seize authority which the Lord has never given them. Not infrequently do we hear men speak of

---

* L. L. Brigance in *Gospel Advocate* July 24, 1941.

'My elders,' 'taking charge of the church,' etc., etc., expressions which indicate that the preachers are becoming the masters of the churches, instead of their servants. Able brethren throughout the brotherhood are becoming more and more alarmed and fearful of the arrangement now in operation among us. It is time that the elders assert their authority, no longer shirk the responsibility that is theirs, and begin to do the work the Lord expects them to do, thus releasing the preachers to carry the gospel to the lost.

We know of nothing that will serve to create more respect of the elderships and restore to them the authority and prestige that is rightfully theirs, than this. We believe that the pernicious and church destroying doctrine of majority-rule is the outgrowth of the incipient pastor-system now in operation among us. Other evils will surely result if a halt is not soon called.''

Since the evangelists are heralds to carry the message of salvation to places where the gospel has not been made known, they should fulfill the responsibility God has placed upon them and allow the elders to do the work that God ordained for them to do, feeding the flock of God, taking the oversight and ruling with watchful care and diligence.

It is time to end this departure from the divine plan and get back to the word of God and to the pattern revealed in the New Testament.

The plea that every congregation needed a located minister, a pastor for each assembly was the first step in the second apostasy. The apostles of our Lord under the guidance of the Holy Spirit taught that each congregation of believers should have its own elders and deacons, and these men were the only permanent officials of the local church.

True, the New Testament reveals that congregations received instruction from the evangelists and apostles, but they did not become an integral part of the local assembly.

Isaac Errett, who did much to lead the churches into a second apostasy, made the effort to justify the pastor by saying he was justifiable as a necessity and was not to be accepted as a finality, but when once the churches had adopted this plan they refused to go back to the practice of the church edifying itself.

1849 A.D. THE MISSIONARY SOCIETY ORGANIZED

The Christian Missionary Society, first known as the General Missionary Convention, was organized in this year at Cincinnati, Ohio, with a president, vice-presidents, managers, membership terms, and church delegates. Alexander Campbell became the first president of the society, an organization which he had opposed in the beginning of the restoration movement.

The establishment of The Christian Missionary Society produced a storm of protest against such an ecclesiastical organization. The strongest objection to the society was based upon the contention that it was not authorized by the scriptures and was therefore an unscriptural organization. Life directors, members, and delegates, were appointed upon the basis of their contribution to the society.

Even before the society became a reality, Jacob Creath, Jr., began to write against it in the *Christian Age,* of which David S. Burnet was the editor. Most of his articles were rejected, and later the columns of the paper were closed against him. David S. Burnet was a strong advocate of the society and became its second president. After Benjamin Franklin began to publish *The Proclamation and The Reformer* in 1850, Creath was able to secure a hearing through the columns of the publication, though Franklin was a friend to the society.

Jacob Creath affirmed that no scriptural authority could be found for such an institution. He pointed out that the missionary society was largely the production of young men, while older brethren were opposed to it. In the early part of 1851, a Brother Field asked Brother Franklin to give a "thus saith the Lord" for the missionary society. He called upon Brother Franklin to harmonize human societies with what Brother Campbell had said against them in the early issues of *The Christian Baptist.* He believed, in view of the statements contained therein, that Alexander Campbell and Walter Scott had given up everything for which they had contended in the beginning, thus creating a need for a new reformation. The opposition of Alexander Campbell to the formation of societies of any kind to do the work of the church is a matter of record.

> "It was this view of the position and doings of the clergy th. led Mr. Campbell to condemn Sunday schools, missionary, education, and even Bible societies, as then conducted, because he thought them perverted to sectarian purposes.
>
> In Sunday schools the denominational catechism was then diligently taught, and the effort was made to imbue the minds of the children with partisan theology. Missionary societies then labored to propagate the tenets of the party to which each belonged, and even Bible societies seemed to him to be made a means of creating offices and salaries for a few clerical managers, who exercised entire control."

"I do not oppose, intentionally, at least," said he, "the scriptural plan of converting the world. . . . My opponents do represent me as opposing the means of converting the world, not wishing to discriminate, in my case at least, between a person opposing the abuses of a good cause and the cause itself."

Of Bible societies he remarks "In the multiplication of copies of the scriptures I do rejoice, although I do conceive even the best of all good works is managed in a way not at all comporting with the precepts of the volume itself. And shall we not oppose the abuses of any principle because of the excellency of the principle itself?"

His chief objection, then, to the instrumentalities employed for missionary and other religious purposes was that, in the hands of the clergy, they were perverted to denominational aggrandizement and to the perpetuation of the yoke, which they had imposed upon the people. His view, on the other hand, was that God's revelation was complete, and that it was able, as it affirms of itself, "To make the man of God perfect and thoroughly furnished to every good work." He taught, furthermore, that the church of Jesus Christ, formed and organized according to this work, with its elders and deacons, was appointed to be "the pillar and ground" or support "of the truth," and that such a society is "the highest tribunal on earth to which an individual Christian can appeal."

"The Lord Jesus Christ," said he, "is the absolute Monarch on whose shoulders is the government, and in whose hands are the reins. That his will, published in the New Testament, is the sole law of the church; and that every society or assembly meeting once every week in one place according to this law, or the commandments of this King, requires no other head, king, lawgiver, ruler, or lord than this Mighty One; no other law, rule, formula, canon or decree than his written word; no judicatory, court or tribunal, other than the judgment seat of Christ." Again, he says: "I am taught from the Record itself to describe a church of Christ in the following words: It is a society of disciples professing to believe the one grand fact, the Messiahship of Jesus, voluntarily submitting to his authority and guidance, having all of them in their baptism expressed their faith in him and allegiance to him, and statedly meeting together in one place to walk in all his commandments and ordinances. This society, with its bishop or bishops, and its deacon or deacons, as the case may require, is perfectly independent of any tribunal on earth called ecclesiastical. It knows nothing of superior or inferior church judicatories, and acknowledges no laws, no canons, or government, other than that of the Monarch of the universe and His laws. This Church, having now committed unto it the oracles of God, is adequate to all the purposes of illumination and reformation which entered into the design of its founder." Such being his view of the position occupied by a church of Christ, he found in this an additional argument against such missionary and other societies as acted independently of church control.

"Every Christian," said he, "who understands the nature and design, the excellence and glory, of the institution called the church of Jesus Christ, will lament to see its glory transferred to a human corporation. The church is robbed of its character by every institution, merely human, that would ape its excellence and substitute itself in its place."

"Believing that the primitive church never transferred any of its duties to other associations, but fulfilled them always in its own character, that Christ might be glorified, he was jealous of every separate organization formed to accomplish any of the purposes for which the church was established."*

Benjamin Franklin withdrew his endorsement of the missionary society about twenty years after its organization. Though he at one time had been the corresponding secretary for the Missionary society he became opposed to it as an unscriptural institution. This became the conviction of many of the evangelists and congregations. Some of the congregations took the matter up directly with Brother Campbell, among which was the congregation at Connellsville, Pennsylvania.

This congregation was not far from Bethany, Virginia, and is thought to have been established by the Campbells or by some of their fellow laborers in the work of the Lord.

"The Church of Christ at Connellsville, Pennsylvania, having received from the 'Christian Missionary Society' a circular, enclosing its constitution, held a meeting to take into consideration the propriety of becoming an auxiliary society; and after an impartial investigation of the Scriptures in reference to this subject, the following resolutions were unanimously adopted:

1st. That we deem it the duty of every Christian to do all within his power for the advancement of the cause of Christ, by holding forth the word of life to lost and ruined man

2nd. That we consider the church of Jesus Christ, in virtue of the commission given her by our blessed Lord, the only Scriptural organization on earth for conversion of sinners and sanctification of believers.

3rd. That we, as members of the body of Christ, are desirous of contributing, according to our ability, for the promulgation of the gospel in foreign lands; but,

4th. That, conscientiously, we can neither aid nor sanction any society, for this or other purposes, apart from the church, much less one which would exclude from its membership many of our brethren, and all of the apostles, if now upon the earth, because silver and gold they had none.

5th. That we consider the introduction of all such societies a dangerous precedent—a departure from the principles for which we have always contended as sanctioning the chapter of expediency—the evil and pernicious effects of which the past history of the church fully proves.

* *Memoirs of Alexander Campbell*—Richardson. Volume 2, Chapter 2, Pages 57, 58, 59.

6th. That we consider them necessarily heretical and schismatical, as much so as human creeds and confessions of faith, when made the bonds of union and communion.

7th. That for missions, both foreign and domestic, we approve of a plan similar to that adopted by the brethren of Tennessee, for evangelizing in that state.

8th. That we consider it the duty of all churches to co-operate in home missions, and that we are willing and ready to unite with those of Western Pennsylvania, in sustaining evangelists to proclaim the gospel in destitute places.

9th. That we highly approve of a new and pure translation of the Holy Scriptures, both for home and foreign use.

10th. That a copy of these resolutions be sent, for publication to the 'Millennial Harbinger,' 'Christian Age,' 'Christian Magazine,' and 'The Proclamation and Reformer.'

The above resolutions are not the off-spring of an overheated imagination, nor the result of wild enthusiasm, neither are they dictated by a spirit of covetousness. We have no desire to appear peculiar; no disposition to divide or distract the body of Christ; no longings for rule or pre-eminence; but they are the result of mature deliberation, calm, dispassionate reflection, and a thorough investigation of the word of God; are dictated by a spirit of love, and a determination to be guided by the Holy Scriptures though they should fail to furnish us with a king like those of the surrounding nations, and to sanction nothing for which we can not find a 'thus saith the Lord.'

We know that many of our good brethren are contending for these measures which we condemn, as earnestly, as zealously, and as conscientiously, as ever Saul of Tarsus persecuted the church of God; for, as the object for which these societies are instituted is a good one, there are many warm hearted and zealous Christians who look only at the end, and rush forward, without pausing to consider the means taken to accomplish it.

We would not, however, impute to them any other than the purest and best motives, and we hope they will attribute the same to us, and not condemn the course we have taken, without giving it that earnest attention and impartial investigation which the vast importance of the subject demands.

That the church of Jesus Christ is, in its constitution and design, essentially missionary, we conceive to be an axiomatic truth.

Not *a* missionary society, but emphatically and pre-eminently *the* missionary society, the only one authorized by Jesus Christ or sanctioned by the apostles. Her president is Jesus Christ; her constitution the Holy Scriptures."*

1869 A.D. INSTRUMENTAL MUSIC INTRODUCED INTO THE WORSHIP OF THE CHURCH OF CHRIST, ST. LOUIS, MO.

Over the solemn protest of the elders of the congregation and many of the older members, mechanical music was introduced into the worship of the church. Those who opposed the use of the organ

---

* *"Millennial Harbinger,"* Volume 7, Number 5, May 1850.

were locked out of the building and compelled to seek other quarters for services. Those who retained the building took the name Christian Church, and thus was the united body of Christ rent asunder.

This event was probably the result of the kind of preaching that was done in that period of time. Because most of the pioneer preachers of that age stressed obedience to the gospel and paid but little attention to matters of faith and practice, those who were converted by their teaching knew but little about church government and discipline.

Their knowledge of what constituted acceptable worship was woefully lacking also. Those who had given up denominationalism and accepted the gospel of Christ began to want the church of the Lord to be like the churches from which they came. This brought a request for the use of mechanical music in the services prior to the Bible study. When this was refused by the elders, those who had opposed any departure from the divine plan, were excluded from the building and forced to seek for a place of worship elsewhere.

This was just another step in the second apostasy which brought division and discord in the church of the Lord. The introduction of mechanical music into the worship was in direct opposition to the teaching of Alexander Campbell. His biographer, in speaking of his attitude toward the use of musical instruments said,

> "Similarly, he loved to see the utmost simplicity in the order and worship of the house of God. He delighted in the public reading of the Scriptures, the plain and earnest exhortations of the brotherhood, and in solemn psalms and hymns of praise.
>
> He had no relish for anything formal or artificial, such as repetitions in fugue tunes or the establishment of singing choirs. As to the use of musical instruments in worship, he was utterly opposed to it, and took occasion at a later period to remark in regard to it, that it was well adapted to churches 'founded on the Jewish pattern of things' and practicing infant sprinkling.
>
> 'That all persons' said he, 'who have no spiritual discernment, taste or relish for spiritual meditations, consolations and sympathies of renewed hearts, should call for such aid is but natural. Pure water from the flinty rock has no attractions for the mere toper or wine-bibber. A little alcohol or genuine Cognac brandy or good Madeira is essential to the beverage to make it truly refreshing.
>
> So to those who have no real devotion or spirituality in them, and whose animal nature flags under the oppression of church service, I think that instrumental music would be not only a desideratum, but an essential prerequisite to fire up their souls to even animal devotion. But I presume to all spiritually minded Christians such aids would be as a cow-bell in a concert."
>
> *Millennial Harbinger*, Series IV, Volume 1. Page 581.*

* *Memoirs of Alexander Campbell*—Richardson. Volume 2, Chapter 10, Page 366.

It is the firm conviction of those who are identified with the church of the Lord that the New Testament does not authorize the use of mechanical music in the worship of God. When the church of the first century came together it was for the purpose of observing the Lord's Supper.

Mosheim states that as late as the beginning of the fourth century the worship still consisted of hymns, prayers, the reading of the Scriptures, and the observance of the Lord's Supper. The church historians, Eusebius, Mosheim, Neander, and Fisher, referring to this period, make no mention of instrumental music in connection with the services of the church. As apostasy developed, men became dissatisfied with the simplicity of the divine plan and began to change the worship to satisfy their own desires.

These changes in the pattern of the worship were at first gradual, for apostasy is always of slow growth.

True, there are isolated instances of the use of a harp or flute in the worship, but not until we approach a much later period of time do we find mechanical music in general use in religious services.

At the present time instrumental music is used in many places in religious services.

The question naturally arises, when and by whom was it introduced? The organ is said to have been first introduced into church music by Pope Vitalian I in 666.

Later instrumental music was excluded by Gregory VII, in 1074, and for one hundred fifty years after that time instrumental music was not used in the churches of Rome.

Thomas Aquinas, one of the wisest men produced by the Church of Rome, said,

"Our church does not use musical instruments as harps and psalteries, to praise God withal that she may not seem to Judaize."

It is true that mention is made of the use of musical instruments in connection with the Jewish system of worship, which was of course abolished when Christ was nailed to the cross, but when we come to the New Testament they are not spoken of as being used in the worship of God. The only conclusion is that they were left out because the Lord did not want them in the worship. Under the inspiration óf the Holy Spirit the apostles indicated the procedure to be followed in praising God. "Let the word of Christ dwell in you richly in all wisdom, teaching and admonishing one another in psalms and hymns and spiritual songs, singing with grace in your hearts to the Lord."[1] "Speaking to yourselves in psalms and

---

1. Col. 3 : 16.

hymns and spiritual songs, singing and making melody in your hearts to the the Lord."[2] The use of instrumental music is therefore opposed, simply because God has not authorized its use in connection with worship, either by command or example.

It is sometimes asserted that the Lord did not forbid its use, yet the very fact that the Lord specified the kind of music or melody that was to be produced—"making melody in your heart to the Lord," would exclude all other kinds of music.

No one can use mechanical music in the worship and walk by faith, for faith comes by hearing God's word. "So then faith cometh by hearing, and hearing by the word of God."[3]

When first mechanical music was introduced into the church of Christ, one of the strongest opponents to its use was Brother J. B. Briney.

> "It was a glorious day for the cause of truth when the pious and venerable Thomas Campbell conceived and set forth the principle contained in the following language:
> 'Where the Scriptures speak, we speak; where the Scriptures are silent, we are silent.'
> This declaration contains the germ and pith of the present Reformation. It was the guiding star of such men as the Campbells, Scott, Stone and Creath, in their march back to apostolic ground. It was the watchword of those noble, grand old veterans, as, weak in numbers, but strong in faith, they bared their bosoms to the darts of popery and rushed forward to rescue the ordinance of Jesus Christ from oblivion's embrace.
> This was the banner that gave them possession of many a hotly contested field, and led them on to glorious victory.
> Under it they fought, under it they conquered, and, dying they bequeathed it to us, that under it, at least, we might hold what they had gained. So long as we adhere to this principle we may march forward with heads erect and banners streaming. But the moment we abandon this we will be at sea, without compass or rudder, and our ship will be driven before the merciless blasts of the head winds of sectarianism in the direction of the port of Rome; and in this state of ease we may well haul down our colors and seek recognition in 'courts ecclesiastic.' We will need the sympathy of such courts then. It is no matter of astonishment that, when the foregoing principle was enunciated, such a thoughtful man as Andrew Monroe should make the following statement: 'If we adopt that as a basis, then there is an end of infant baptism.'
> I beg leave to make the following respectful suggestion to Bro. J. S. Lamar: If we adhere to that as a basis, then there is an end to instrumental music in the worship. But we must adhere to that, or the Reformation is a failure.
> This brings us to the main point had in view in the preceding essays. That singing as worship is a divine appointment is abundantly clear from the following Scriptures:

---

2. Eph. 5 : 19.
3. Rom. 10 : 17.

'What is it then? I will pray with the spirit and I will pray with the understanding also. I will sing with the Spirit, and I will sing with the understanding also' (I Corinthians 14: 15).

'And be not drunk with wine wherein is excess; but be filled with the spirit; speaking to yourselves in psalms and hymns, and spiritual songs, singing and making melody in your hearts to the Lord' (Ephesians 5: 19).

'By him, therefore, let us offer up the sacrifice of praise to God continually, that is, the fruit of our lips, giving thanks to His name' (Hebrews 13: 15).

Singing is worship only as it consists in prayer and praise. It is not the sound simply, the mere music, that renders it acceptable to God, but the sentiments of devotion.

From the first of the above quotations we learn that in these sentiments of prayer and praise the spirit and the understanding unite. In the third quotation these sentiments are called the 'sacrifice of praise,' and are defined to be the 'fruit of our lips." It follows, then, with the clearness of a sunbeam, that the instruments to be used in offering this sacrifice are the vocal organs, with which God has endowed His creature, man.

Here, then, is a divine ordinance consisting in the offering of prayer and praise to the Lord with our lips, this latter term being used generically to denote all the vocal organs.

Now, I affirm that an 'instrumental accompaniment' is an addition to the ordinance, and affects its character, and is, therefore, an infringement of the divine prerogative.

That singing as worship is a divine ordinance will not be questioned in the face of the Scriptures cited above. That the instrumental accompaniment is an addition, is simply certain from the historical facts in the case, it having been born five hundred years out of time. Therefore, whatever men may think of its expediency, it affects the character of the divine appointment, and can not be tolerated for a moment.

There is no room here for expediency or man's wisdom. It is not the prerogative of expediency to say in what an ordinance shall consist. Inspiration has ordained that the sacrifice of praise shall be offered with the human voice.

Then let expediency neither add nor substract. Expediency may regulate my voice; that is, it may determine whether I shall sing with a bass, tenor or alto voice; but beyond this and the like, it must not go. It must not say with what I shall praise, for it would be determining in what an ordinance shall consist, which, as we have already seen, must not be allowed.

From the foregoing, it seems to follow, both logically and Scripturally, that the 'instrumental accompaniment' nullifies the ordinance.

Now at this somebody may get 'scared, feel his hair standing on end, start to run, find somebody else sitting by the camp fires nodding,' etc. Be it so. I could only wish that this fright were real. I should think that a man might well afford to become frightened when he sees himself tampering with an ordinance of the Almighty. But when I see a man affecting fright to try to excite mirth at the expense of a brother who is earnestly contending for the faith, my heart sinks within me.

The 'accompaniment' is expedient, we are told. Expedient, forsooth! 'Infant baptism is expedient,' say Stewart and Beecher. Now, the New Testament Scriptures are just as silent upon the 'accompaniment' as upon infant baptism. If, therefore, expediency may introduce that, why not this?

But in what respect is the accompaniment expedient? If it is expedient, it is because it gives some good result which would not be obtained without it. But if this be true, the Savior either failed in His wisdom or His benevolence, for he never ordained the 'accompaniment.' Expediency, stay thy impious hand! That the instrument in the worship gives a good result which would not otherwise be realized, is an assumption which never has and never will be proved. And just here is the point at which the argument for the instrument must forever break down.

Am I told that it is expedient because 'it attracts the world'? I beg leave to state that the worship of the Lord's House was not ordained for the world. Is the church of the Lord Jesus Christ to be brought down to the standard of the world? Is this the program of expediency? If the caprice of the world is to be regarded in these matters, the very same emergency that demands the organ will demand the very best skill in its use and, therefore, the beer-bloated Dutchman from the theatre of Saturday night will be in demand in the sanctuary of God on the Lord's day.

We are told that the organ need not affect the worship of the individual; that those who are opposed to the instrument may worship in spite of it. This I might do. I might worship, but it would only be in the silent breathings of my spirit. I can not engage in singing as an act of worship where there is an 'instrumental accompaniment,' for this would nullify the ordinance. Now some one may say that in this I am so straight that I lean back a little. Be it so. If I lean back it is but to rest upon the Word of God and resting upon this I dread not the fall. Call to mind the illustration of the supper. The bread and the wine are on the table. But the congregation from consideration of 'propriety and expediency' have determined to add water. Do you observe the Lord's Supper when you sit down with those brethren and partake of the bread and wine, though you reject the water? You do not. Neither do I worship God when I sit down and sing with brethren who add an 'accompaniment.' Yet once more."*

The arguments have never been overthrown though the author of them later became identified with the Christian Church. Those who endorse the use of instrumental music in religious services admit that they hold on to something that is not authorized by God's word and which is not necessary to properly worship the Father.

There are only two kinds of music in the world, so far as the human family is concerned, vocal music and mechanical music. If the Lord had not revealed unto us the kind of music he desired in worship, any kind would have been acceptable. But God was spe-

---

* J. B. Briney in the *Apostolic Times* June 10, 1869, Page 69.

cific in this matter. He revealed the kind of music he wanted. He specified vocal music. "Speaking to yourselves in psalms and hymns and spiritual songs, singing and making melody in your heart to the Lord."[4] This excludes all other kinds of music than that which is here allowed.

The assertion is sometimes made that the word "psallo," which is translated "sing," meant to pluck or pull a bow string, to cause to vibrate. This is true. But the instrument to be plucked, to be caused to vibrate, must be learned from the context and not from the word itself. So when the Holy Spirit inspired the Apostle Paul to use the word "psallo," he added the instrument with which the psallo-ing is to be done and said, "Singing with grace *in your hearts* to the Lord." When the King James translation of the Scriptures was made, forty-seven of the wisest scholars of the seventeenth century agreed that the word "psallo" should be translated sing.

The Revised Version was translated in 1901 by one hundred and one of the wisest scholars of that period of time. They, too, translated the word "psallo" to sing. The question is often asked by those who favor the use of mechanical music in the worship of God, "Where did God say not to use instrumental music in the worship?" The questions may well be asked, "Where did God tell Noah not to use hickory wood in making the ark?"

Where did God tell Moses not to kill an ox at the Passover?

When God told Noah the kind of wood to use, all other kinds were excluded. In the same way, when God told Moses to tell the children of Israel to kill a lamb for the Passover, that excluded the use of any other animal. In the same way, when God said "Speaking to yourselves in psalms and hymns and spiritual songs, singing and making melody in your hearts to the Lord," that excludes any other method of making the melody. Let us then learn to be content to accept what God has said in his word without adding to it or taking from it.

> "It was held by the first Christian believers,—as well as by many earnest Church Reformers since their day, in common with our Early Friends,—that in their assemblies for Divine worship, the introduction of regular or artistic singing, far more its accompaniment by any instrumental music, were wholly inadmissible; being inconsistent with the spiritual nature of the New Covenant dispensation. *

1889 A.D. OPPOSITION TO THE CONTINUED GROWTH OF APOSTASY

The introduction of the modern pastor system, the missionary society, instrumental music, and the organized Sunday School, in-

---

4. Eph. 5 : 19.
* *The Early Christian Church*—Kimber. Pages 85-86.

The Sand Creek Meeting-House

dicated the direction in which some of those who once constituted a part of the body of Christ were going. Those who favored these innovations succeeded in convincing some, that because God did not say not to have a missionary society or not to use instrumental music, that there was nothing against it in God's word.

Others were opposed to these changes because they did not indicate a return to New Testament Christianity, but rather a return toward the church of Rome. These innovations were also contrary to the principle which the men of the Restoration had established by the slogan, "We speak where the Bible speaks, and where the Bible is silent we are silent." In an effort to stay the growth of apostasy, brethren from many congregations assembled at Sand Creek church of Christ in Shelby County, Illinois, in August of 1889, and declared that they would refuse from that time forward to fellowship or endorse the congregations which were adopting practices unauthorized by the word of God.

The Address and Declaration setting forth their conviction follows:

"To all those whom it may concern, greetings: You doubtless know that we as disciples of Christ (with scarcely an exception), many long years ago took the position that in matters of doctrine and practice, religiously, that 'where the Bible speaks, we speak, and where the Bible is silent we are silent' and farther, we held that nothing should be taught, received or practiced, religiously, for which we could not produce a 'thus saith the Lord.' And doubtless many of you also know that as long as the above principles were constantly and faithfully observed, that we were a happy and prosperous people. Then we were of one heart and of one soul; we lived in peace and prospered in the things pertaining to the kingdom of God and the name of our Lord Jesus Christ.

Then what was written as doctrine and for practice was taught and observed by the disciples. And, it may not be amiss in this connection to say, that many, yes, very many in the sectarian churches saw the beauty, consistency and wonderful strength and harmony in the plea, as set forth by the disciples for the restoration of apostolic Christianity in spirit and in practice; and so came and united with us in the great and godly work.

It is, perhaps, needless for us to add in this connection, that we, as a people, discarded all man-made laws, rules, disciplines, and confessions of faith, as means of governing the church.

We have always acknowledged and do now acknowledge the all sufficiency of the Holy Scriptures to govern us as individuals, and as congregations. As an apostle has said, 'All scripture is given by inspiration of God; and is profitable for doctrine, for reproof, for correction, for instruction in righteousness, that the man of God may be perfect, thoroughly furnished unto all good works.'

And now please allow us to call attention to some painful facts and considerations. There are those among us who teach and practice things not taught nor found in the New Testament, which have been received by many well meaning disciples; but rejected by the more thoughtful and, in most instances, better informed in the Scriptures, and who have repeatedly protested against this false teaching and these corrupt practices among the disciples. Some of the things of which we hereby complain, and against which we protest, are the unlawful methods resorted to in order to raise or get money for religious purposes, namely, that of the church holding festivals of various kinds, in the house of the Lord or elsewhere, demanding sometimes that each participant shall pay a certain sum as an admittance fee; the select choir to the virtual, if not the real, abandonment of congregational singing; likewise the man-made society for missionary work, and the one-man imported preacher-pastor to take the oversight of the church.

These with many other objectional and unauthorized things are now taught and practiced in many of the congregations, and that to the great grief and mortification of some of the members of said congregations. And now, brethren, you that teach such things, and such like things and those who practice the same, must certainly know that they are not only not in harmony with the gospel, but are in opposition thereto.

You surely will admit that it is safe, and only safe to teach and practice what the divine record enjoins upon the disciples. To this none can reasonably object, and this is exactly what we want and for which we contend. And, now, we say that we beg of you to turn away speedily and at once from such things, and remember that though we are the Lord's freemen yet we are bound by the authority of our Lord Jesus Christ. You know that it is by keeping his commandments and not the commandments of men that we have the assurance of his approval.

Therefore, brethren, without addressing you further in using other arguments and without going further in detailing these unpleasant, and as we see them vicious things, you must allow us in kindness, and in Christian courtesy, and at the same time with firmness to declare that we can not tolerate the things of which we complain; for if we do, then we are (in a measure at least) blameable ourselves.

And let it be distinctly understood, that this 'Address and Declaration' is not made in any spirit of envy or hate, or malice or any such thing. But we are only actuated from the sense of duty to ourselves and to all concerned; for we feel that the time has fully come when something of a more definite character ought to be known and recognized between the church and the world.

Especially is this apparent when we consider the Scriptural teaching on the matters to which we have herein referred—such for instance as the following:

'Be not conformed to the world, but be ye transformed, by the renewing of your mind, that we may prove what is that good, and acceptable and perfect will of God.'

It is, therefore, with the view, if possible, of counteracting the usages and practices that have crept into the churches, that this effort on the part of the congregations hereafter named is made, and, now, in closing up this address and declaration, we state that we are impelled from a sense of duty to say, that all such that are guilty of teaching, or allowing and practicing the many innovations and corruptions to which we have referred, that after being admonished, and having had sufficient time for reflection, if they do not turn away from such abominations, that we can not and will not regard them as brethren.

Signed—P. P. Warren, A. J. Nance, Daniel Baker, Peter Robinson, J. K. P. Rose, James Warren } for the Sand Creek Church

Randolph Miller, Charles Ervin, Wm. Storm, W. K. Baker } for the Liberty Church

Wm. Cazier) for the Ash Grove Church
I. H. Hagen) for the Union Church
Isaac Walters) for the Mode Church

The brethren whose names stand alone in signing this document represented the churches from which they came. Besides these, Elder Colson of Gays, and Elder Hoke of Strickland congregations, signed, but as individuals only, because the congregations whence they came, had not been called together so as to send them formally.

Green Creek congregation, by a letter from Bro. Jesse Baker, endorsed the movement."

"Concerning the foregoing document we wish to make a few statements.

1st. It originated with the churches and is sent forth as the conviction of those churches that are represented by the brethren whose names are subscribed thereto.

2nd. In and for itself this document is only intended to serve as the expression of the churches by which it has been adopted. Besides, its declarations affect the life of the Christian rather than the question of doctrine. While maintaining doctrinal correctness the purpose is to cut off all practical crookedness and worldliness, and thus it will meet the approval of all soberminded people, both religious and ir-religious, wherever found.

3rd. There are churches and individual brethren all over the brotherhood that have for years, no doubt, entertained the same conviction which in this document is expressed.

In the mass meeting last fall in Moberly, Mo. and in the meeting at Richmond, Mo. the year before, the question of drawing a line of demarkation between the churches of Christ and our innovating brethren was discussed.

4th. Ten years ago the subject was agitated in the columns of the Review by a brother who is now connected with the paper. But it was then thought by the brethren generally that some other solution than a formal division could be reached.

5th. But as innovators have made their devices tests of fellowship, having in many instances explicitly or by implication declared non-fellow-ship with those who oppose their devices with persistence—as they have done this, it has become evident that they have abandoned our original position and have gone out from us because they were not of us.

6th. In view of such conduct on the part of innovating disciples called 'Modern Schoolmen,' it is evident that they are the dividers of the brotherhood, and the sooner this is generally acknowledged by the adoption of the sentiments of the brethren who assembled at Sand Creek, in Shelby County, Ill., on the afternoon of August 17, 1889, the safer and better it will be for all concerned.

7th. Let it be distinctly understood that we have from the first agitation of this subject been numbered with those who earnestly endeavored to find some other solution of the problem than a formal separation.

But having learned from personal experience that there is no law human or divine, which innovators hold themselves bound to respect in dealing with those who oppose their devices—having learned this we declare sadly and reluctantly, but firmly, that we endorse the foregoing document as adopted and signed at the Sand Creek meet-ing. The spirit of that document we regard as the best that could be expressed, and we specially remind all those who may be disposed to differ from the decision of the last statement it contains, that it does not propose to disfellowship any till they have been admonished and refuse to turn from their waywardness.

If innovations be sinful, certainly those who persist in advocating them are persistent sinners. 'The time is come that judgment must begin at the house of God' (1 Peter 4: 17).

If this sentence of an inspired apostle be adopted throughout the brotherhood, then the time will soon come that our 'Modern School Brethren' will have fixed upon them the odium of having by division disgraced the best cause on earth and having thereby become a party among parties, a sect among sects, a denomination among denominations. In the meantime the loyal disciples will be-come more firmly than ever established in their original principles in contending for the faith once delivered to the saints, and en-deavoring to establish everywhere the Kingdom of Christ as it was in the beginning. Amen."*

---

* *Octographic Review*—October 11, 1892.

1891 A.D. THE BEGINNING OF INSTITUTIONALISM

Many were led away from the divine plan by the plea that the quickest way of restoring the gospel would be to establish Bible Schools through which to teach the Bible. Brethren overlooked the fact that when God gave us the church, he gave us a perfect means by which to do all the work that should be done.

This fact was acknowledged by pioneer leaders in the church. Tolbert Fanning, the first editor of the Gospel Advocate said,

> "The church of God is the only authoritative theological school on earth; and it is the only one which Christians can consistently encourage. . . . We maintain the important learning is obtained in the church, and if we are correct, each church of the Lord Jesus Christ is a seminary for instructing the members in the various departments of labor they are to perform."*

David Lipscomb, another editor of the same journal said:

> "We think the most fatal mistake of Alexander Campbell's life, and one that has done much and we fear will do much more to undo his life's work, was the establishment of a school to train and educate young preachers.
>
> We believe the whole principle of taking young men with undeveloped characters and unfixed habits and educating them for preachers, or for any other specific work in the church, is hurtful in the extreme. It has a tendency to make merely professionals of them. They are educated for preachers. They often lose their first ardor and then think they are entitled to a living out of their profession and look to it more as a means of making a livelihood than of doing good."†

At a later period, I. M. Barnes, a graduate of Bethany College, who labored much in Alabama, expressed himself in these words:

> "God's order of worship has the men of the ecclesia (not those borrowed from outside the body), to teach in the exercises (1 Corinthians 14). To teach they must study and learn. If they can teach in the ecclesia, they can teach out in the world, at home. Here it is as heaven planned it and set it in order. This order carried out, would do away with many things and there would not be so much necessity of Bible schools.
>
> Bible schools do the work of lazy churches; the pastor does the work of lazy elders; the Sunday School does the work of lazy parents; the missionary society is a lazy, cowardly set of preachers trying to hire a more industrious and more heroic and poorer set to do their work."‡

Less than ten years after the establishment of the Nashville Bible School, a former student of that institution, John E. Dunn, wrote to his teacher, James A. Harding, expressing his concern over the

---

* *Gospel Advocate*—Volume 2, Page 299.
† *Gospel Advocate*—Volume 17, Pages 345, 346.
‡ *The Way*, January, 1900.

tendency of those who graduated from the school to become "modern pastors" instead of evangelists.

"Dear Bro. Harding: A good brother, who is a good friend of yours and mine, writes me that he fears the Bible School is making modern pastors instead of evangelists such as Timothy was. He also states that the practices of the churches of Christ in Nashville is practically the 'modern pastor system.' I thought I saw this evil in nearly every church in Nashville while I was a student of the Bible School.

There was a strong tendency then on the part of the churches not to do without a preacher on Lord's Day, and since then some of the churches, I learn, have secured 'pastors.' It has been my understanding that the church on South Spruce Street, where you worship, which meets in the school chapel, does not favor the 'modern pastor system,' and on the Lord's Day the worship is entirely congregational, and there is no set discourse at the Lord's Day service. Is this true? I know when I was there you would exhort us not to become pastors of churches, and thus hire ourselves out to build up an unscriptural practice. You would say, 'Boys, preach the word, be instant in season, out of season; reprove, rebuke, and exhort with all longsuffering and doctrine; preach it in a school house, in a tent, in the woods, under a tobacco barn, in a courthouse, in a meeting-house, publicly and privately, anywhere and everywhere, to one or many, to the rich, to the poor, and to all alike, regardless of poverty or wealth, sex or color, preach the gospel to every soul you meet, and trust God with an unwavering faith to uphold and support you.'

When you and I were on the train together one time, you said, 'Do not settle down with any church as a pastor, but go into the world and preach the gospel of Jesus Christ wherever God calls you; and if you will trust God I know he will support you'

I have never forgotten this admonition; I knew then it was God's word, and I realize it far more now to be the only true principle of New Testament evangelizing.

I am trying to be true to my God. I think I am safe in saying on an average of once a month I have an offer to become a pastor. The ease and money in it are tempting to the untaught and weak in the faith. I pray God to keep me from falling into the snare. Some of the boys have joined the society ranks and others have become 'modern pastors.'

They were (most of them) good boys and we loved them. Of course we regret to see this; but you told me once you expected some to depart from 'the Faith' of the New Testament. Many of the boys (I think most of them), will be true to God. I try not to be a time-server. I am set to teach and practice as it is written in the old Book. So far God has been rich in his love to me. While I am poor and have to work hard, yet all my wants are supplied, and I shall be satisfied. I know if we are true to God, he will never leave us nor forsake us.

The best of men are sometimes mistaken and surely our good brother is mistaken about the school making pastors; but I believe he is to some extent right in his view of at least some of the churches. You can read these words and dispose of them as you believe best.

John E. Dunn.

James A. Harding, the editor and publisher of The Way, replied to Dunn as follows:

"Dear Brother Dunn: I am as much persuaded as I ever was that the pastor system, that is, the employment of a person to devote his time to one church, to take charge of it, to do the teaching and preaching, and to take the general superintendence of all the work, is one of the most radical departures from the apostolic order and one of the greatest hindrances to the success of the gospel. And so the Bible School teaches. About 125 preachers who have studied in the Nashville Bible School are now in the field preaching. Fewer than a dozen of these I suppose, practice or favor the pastor system; most of them are intensely opposed to it. The Bible School and the church which meets in the Bible School chapel have always opposed it. Those of our students who depart from the Lord's way at this point do it in spite of our example and teaching.

Not a teacher of the Bible School is, or ever was, a pastor (unless to be one of the elders of a congregation is to be a pastor). Not one of them favors the pastor system. The church of God which meets in the chapel of the Bible School is led in its meetings by its elders, who encourage every brother who will, to take part in speaking, in prayer, or in song, as he has ability to do.

There are not many regular meetings of which fewer than four or five brethren take part in speaking, and the more faithfully we practice in this way, the more clearly we see the vast superiority of God's way to man's way in conducting the church.

Nashville has a greater number of congregations that conduct their meetings without "the pastor" than any other city in America, so far as I can learn. There are seven of them. There are three others that deny that they favor the pastor system that seem to me to be going practically in that way.

At the Bible School church three brethren were selected for elders. They determined to do away with the Sunday morning sermon and to have instead several shorter speeches, with the meeting under the direction of the eldership."*

These brethren were convinced that any institution which purposed to do the work the church was to do, had no scriptural right to exist.

O. C. Lambert sounded these words of warning:

"It has been the history of religious schools that they have been hotbeds and nurseries for heresy. Schools in metropolitan cities in the early centuries of Christianity played a dominant part in the development of Catholicism. Nearly all the great church schools of early American history have long ago outgrown their swaddling clothes, have kicked off their religious parentage, have played the prodigal, and are now in the hogpen of atheism. Harvard, Yale, Princeton, Vanderbilt, in fact, practically every private college and university in the land were once church schools established by those who loved the Bible and had religion enough to leave the civilization of Europe to brave the dangers and hardships of the new land of America, that they might read the Bible and practice its teaching in peace.

---

* Printed in The Way, 1900, Page 83.

These schools at the first were manned by God-fearing believers. No others would have been tolerated. Today in any of these schools a professor who dared to defend religion and the Bible would be subject to scorn and probably would be summarily dismissed as a disgrace to a scholarly profession.

Human nature is about the same the world over and the tendency toward departure from true religion has been experienced over and over among us during the last hundred years. Unfortunately, almost all great and powerful things are capable of a bad as well as a good use, and the devil's agents make more effective use of them than the children of light. If a thing has been tried over and over for thousands of years with only one final result, it is not very hopeful that we can achieve a more desirable end.

Since schools have always finally been productive of more evil than good for the cause of Christ, this seems an exhibition of divine wisdom that no such means have been specified in the perfect law of liberty. The Harding Bulletin says that those operating schools could draw safer conclusions on religious questions. If this is true, the Lord is guilty of leaving out the greatest agency for keeping men in the faith. This a believer cannot for a moment accept."*

H. Leo Boles, former college president and editor, saw the trend of such institutions and sounded this warning:

"Moreover, colleges are taking a firmer grasp on the public. 'Our colleges' are getting a larger and firmer grasp on the churches or congregations. Within another generation the membership of all of the churches will be college-trained or under the influence of some college. There will be but a few congregations which do not have a 'full time' preacher, and he will have been trained in some college. The young preachers will go out from the colleges with the stamp and brand of the college that sent them out. It will be fearful if the colleges do not remain loyal to the book of God.

Here we have to point to the examples of warning found in the colleges of the 'Christian Church.' The preacher will overshadow the elders and will have a greater influence in the congregation than do the elders. This is not as it should be, but it is a statement of facts."†

W. W. Otey warned of the danger confronting the brotherhood in the establishment of these schools which infringe on the work of the church. His words of warning follow:

"About one hundred years ago the work of restoring the New Testament church in teaching and practice was in full sway in America. Perhaps with the purest of motives Alexander Campbell established Bethany College, chiefly for the purpose of preparing young men for preaching the gospel.

Other such colleges were soon established. For a time these institutions were true to the word of God, and were an asset in spreading the gospel. In the second generation new men came into control, men who were not satisfied with the gospel and the church as the

---

* *Bible Banner*, July, 1942. Page 10. (Quoted from "A Treatise on The Bible College"—Harvey).

† *Gospel Advocate*—February 21, 1946.

Lord established it. Young men who were preparing to preach were indoctrinated with the new ideas that had taken root in these schools. These preachers went back to the churches and turned about three fourths of the churches into another denomination now known as the Christian Church.

That apostasy was due almost entirely to the influence of unsound teachers in those Bible Colleges. The colleges were corrupted and produced a crop of corrupted preachers, who, in turn corrupted the vast majority of the churches. When that division was completed, the churches of Christ had not a single Bible College, and a very few preachers who had received their education in them. With the clear light before us of the danger of Bible Colleges becoming corrupted in teaching, and so leading into apostasy, we now find ourselves engaged in the same experiment of establishing Bible Colleges to further the interests of the church of the Lord. We are not only willing to admit, but to affirm that every religious school from the first down to the five infants now among the churches of Christ have been sources of unscriptural teaching.

In view of this fact, the most that can be said in their defense is that they are an experiment. If these do not in the coming years become infected with error that will corrupt the churches, the present and future managers will need to prove themselves wiser and stronger than all others who have gone before in establishing such experimental institutions."

The opposition of these brethren to the Bible College was not because they were opposed to education, but because they were opposed to human institutions doing the work of the church. The early church carried on a continuous study of the word. "And the word of God increased and the number of disciples multiplied in Jerusalem greatly: and a great company of the priests were obedient to the faith."[5] "And it came to pass, that a whole year they, assembled themselves with the church and taught much people."[6]

The church is the body of Christ, its purpose is spiritual, and it is qualified to do all work of a spiritual nature that God designed that the church should do, whether it is sounding out the word of the Lord, caring for the distressed, or teaching its members to observe all things commanded by the Lord. The church can train, instruct, and assist anyone in gaining and using a knowldege of God's word.

Cled E. Wallace, who has been both a friend and a critic of the Bible colleges, said:

"The idea that the churches cannot live and grow and carry out the Lord's will without schools is just plain rot. Churches lived and thrived before there were any schools and will continue to do so even if all the schools we now have apostatize and go to the devil."

Brethren have pointed out that the Bible colleges are developing into apostate bodies, usurping the work the church should do and

5. Acts 6:7.
6. Acts 11:26.

taking over the training of teachers and evangelists for the church. Read and meditate upon these timely words from the pen of I. C. Nance, on the subject:

> "And the things which thou hast heard from me among many witnesses, the same commit thou to faithful men, who shall be able to teach others also' (2 Timothy 2: 2).
>
> This statement contains the simple instructions concerning the training of teachers and preachers in the church, yet, today, we in our 'wisdom' have drifted from the simple pattern given in Holy Writ for the church and have adopted the modern idea of 'Theological Training.' Oh, I know that we dare not call 'our' colleges 'theological seminaries' but say what you will, terms cannot hide principle. Practically every denomination has its theological seminaries through which it incubates and trains its preachers. Not to be out-done, 'we' have 'our' schools from which spring 'our' preachers, seasoned in the 'ethics' and policies of those institutions plus a great deal of enthusiasm for their respective 'alma maters.'
>
> I have visited most of 'our' schools and I am not the only one who has observed the 'trend' which would seem to elevate the school above the church in the minds of the students.
>
> College clannishness has also been observed among college preachers. In a city where there are a number of congregations which have a sort of an unnamed (but nevertheless binding) association of churches, the college preachers usually stick together. And when a vacancy occurs in one of these churches, these preachers are usually ready to recommend one of their 'set' for the place because he 'fits' into their 'association.'
>
> It is clear that the church of the New Testament is to train its own teachers and preachers. The church is a teaching institution (Matthew 28: 19, 20). The text I have given (2 Timothy 2: 2), shows that the experienced men of the church (not the college), should do the teaching to 'faithful' men (not college students). The older and experienced women in the church (not the college), are to teach and train the younger women in the church (not the college co-eds—Titus 2: 2-4). It is obvious from these passages that the church is the institution authorized of God to do this teaching. But the college is another institution doing that which the church should do. . . ."*

The Lord's method of training preachers and teachers was for older brethren to teach the younger. This was the Lord's plan in the apostolic days, and it is the Lord's plan now. The best that can be said for the Bible colleges is that they are human institutions designed to do part of the work of the church. Many theories have been advanced in an effort to prove that those who work through the college are rendering glory to God through the church but the irrefragable truth remains that the college is not the church or any part of it.

---

* Copied from *Gospel Broadcast*.

H. M. Phillips called attention to these same truths:

> "Paul was one who suggested for glory to be given to God in the church (Ephesians 3: 21). This would do away with anything being placed over and above the church, or making the church dependent on any of the institutions of man.
>
> Since it is generally agreed that each congregation is a unit of itself, and that no outside interference is to be, it is well, then, not to put too much pressure on it, lest it might be led away by outside influences. Jesus surely gave a church which would be self suf- ficient, for all its needs and perpetuation. Other things may help, and be of use in many ways, but they surely are not essential to the life of the one church the Lord built. Let us glory more in the Lord and the church, and let other things be of less importance."
>
> "Glory in the church, seems to me," says Brother J. L. Hines, "is a fundamental principle taught in the New Testament. If I have read my Bible to profit, God has but one people, through whom glory is to be had."

"The church is a chosen, foreordained, separated citizenry—in the world, but not of the world. The church is not an organization but an organism, born of God, created of God, and a complete body, with head, members, joints, bands, blood and Spirit.

This one body has a definite, specific, planned and divinely ap- pointed work to do, and that is, telling to the whole world, in every generation, the gospel, which is God's power to save. Caring for the poor saints is secondary—not fundamental, nor a means to an end as many of this age are preaching.

Many good people, and not a few brethren, have been switched from the main line to a side-track and are spending much money, mind and bodily energy, and valuable time in building colleges, orphan homes, hospitals and other like institutions which care for bodies only, while the great task of preaching the gospel has been, and is being neglected.

The church is to "continue steadfastly in the apostles' teaching." The church is to abide in the things which it has learned from its infancy, which things are able to make us wise unto salvation through faith which is in Christ Jesus. For the Scripture, which we have learned, is inspired of God and is also profitable for teach- ing, for reproof, for correction, for instruction which is in right- eousness: "that the man of God may be complete, furnished com- pletely unto every good work."[7]

It seems to me that if the church of the first century, starting with not more than three thousand people, and without colleges, printing presses, railroads, costly buildings, and the like, preached the gospel to the whole world, we just simply do not have faith enough in this generation, or we would circle the globe with good

---

7. 1 Tim. 3 : 14-17.

news also. I am sure that God expects the church to lean on Him, believe in Him and trust Him; but today we have so far departed from the ancient path, until we have become lost in the maze of modernistic philosophies and the dogmas of men, the very thing Paul warned against, when he said: "Take heed lest there be anyone that maketh spoil of you through his philosophy and vain deceit after the tradition of men."

Some Things the Church Has Never Been Commissioned to Do:

A. To build houses for the purpose of carrying out its program. The church of the first century built churches; but the church of the twentieth century is building cathedrals, churchhouses, educational plants; and by so doing, burdening the membership with great debts, which must many times be handled by a financing agency.

The church had no church houses until some time in the second century, and they came after the apostasy set to work. I am unalterably opposed to building church houses before the church is strong enough in its locality to do so. There is just too much begging going on in the name of religion.

B. The business of the church is not to establish printing plants for the purpose of printing religious literature. Private citizens may do this work, but the church never. Religious papers have cluttered the brotherhood, many times because someone has a pet hobby which he cannot get published elsewhere. If preachers would spend more time in preaching the gospel from "house to house," I am sure more souls would be saved.

C. The church should never engage in the farming business; but farming is a mighty good occupation for the private citizen.

D. The church should never engage in the business of establishing colleges, which are three-fourths secular. Neither should some citizens enter into agreement to establish schools, then beg the churches to support them, and this is just what is being done among us today.

E. Certainly James said, "Pure religion and undefiled before our God and the Father is this, to visit the fatherless and widows in their affliction, and to keep oneself unspotted from the world."[8]

It seems to me that if "visiting the fatherless and widows in their affliction" is authority for the establishment of orphan homes and old folk's homes it also gives us authority for the building of hospitals as well.

We should remember that it is Christian to feed and clothe those who are in need; but this does not give us the scriptural

---

8. James 1: 27.

right to establish eating and clothing establishments as church institutions.

It is scriptural for any local congregation under its leadership to supply food, clothing, shelter, medicine, and other human needs to those who come within the scope of James, chapter one and verse twenty-seven; but it is not the business of the churches to establish orphan homes, old folks homes, and hospitals, and put them under the supervision of a picked board. When this is done, we have a human institution, a society attached to the churches, which is just as unscriptural and antiscriptural as any missionary society.

Certainly it is scriptural to house the needy, but even this should be done by individuals or churches co-operating with a single congregation whose eldership has the full right of control as is clearly indicated in 1 Corinthians 16: 1, 2 and Acts 11: 29.

Any local church has the right to teach the Bible seven days each week, and that would be a Bible school; but no church has the right to establish a school, three-fourths secular, solicit funds from other churches, put it under a board of directors, pay teachers, and call it 'our college.'"*

The men who established the first Bible college were opposed to preachers becoming a special class as distinguished from the remainder of the student body.

When it was suggested that theological books and helps be introduced into the curriculum, strong opposition was voiced against it. In an editorial in *The Apostolic Times,* Brother James A. Allen said:

"The simple fact that the Nashville Bible School refused to have a preachers' class, but taught that every Christian is a preacher and teacher, and that it taught that for a man to settle down with a church as 'the minister,' at a stipulated salary, is unscriptural and sinful, and that any church who so hires a man has gone digressive, shows how far the 'Christian Colleges' today have gone from the original ground on which Harding, Timmons, and Lipscomb started the Nashville Bible School.

But today, when entering David Lipscomb College, formerly Nashville Bible School, students are classified as 'ministerial,' just as others are classified as 'pre-medical' or 'business administration.' These 'pre-pastor' students are taught how to qualify for, and hold the best and biggest paying positions as 'ministers' of the best and biggest churches. One 'Doctor' on the College Faculty told them: 'You can write your own paycheck. You can be a $200 a month preacher, a $300 a month preacher, or a $500 a month preacher. It is up to you.' "

* The above is copied from *Apostolic Times.*

J. A. Harding, writing of the Nashville Bible School, said:

> "Our object was to educate whomsoever might come unto us; and we determined to teach the Bible to every student of the school no matter what his age, sex, religion, advancement or purpose of life might be. We determined to teach it because we believe it to be the most practical book in the world, the wisest, the best, the most useful. We believe it contains the seed from which all true happiness, usefulness, peace, and prosperity, for this world and the world to come, grow. We believe that every Christian ought to be a preacher and teacher of the religion of Jesus, and that if he finds himself in any place where he cannot teach, and preach in the name of Christ, he ought to get out of it as soon as possible; for, while there, he is cut off from doing the very thing that God has him on the earth to do."*

Our readers will kindly note that the Nashville Bible School had no special classes for preachers and taught that to be "the minister" of a church is sinful.

But today all of the "Christian Colleges" have "special courses for church of Christ ministers," and each faculty member is "the minister" of the richest church he can get. In addition to conducting "special courses for ministers," the faculty members of Christian Colleges set the example, before the school, the church, and the world, of preachers becoming the "ministers" of churches at stipulated salaries. In addition to drawing salaries from "Christian Colleges," as members of the faculty, each faculty member draws a second salary as "The minister" of the biggest and best paying church he can find. An area of a hundred miles or more around the "Christian Colleges" is almost literally combed for pastorates for "ministerial students."

In the Nashville Bible School, started to make it possible for poor boys and girls who could not go to the high-priced colleges, to get an education, every boy and girl had a daily Bible lesson. But the Bible was the only text book used.

> "In The Way, 1900, Page 11, Bro. Harding said: 'In the Nashville Bible School the Bible is the only text book used in biblical work. We teach the Bible.' "

No other text book was used in teaching the Bible but the Bible.

> But today the "Christian Colleges" use the same textbooks, in "special courses for church of Christ ministers," that are used in denominational theological seminaries to prepare denominational clergymen. This explains why so few of the "ministers," if any, ever preach the gospel with the old apostolic ring and why so few, if any, of them ever stress and emphasize what the apostles tell sinners to do to be saved.
>
> Their "ministerial" training does not embrace that kind of preaching. The same textbooks on how to prepare and deliver ser-

---

* *The Way.* 1901, Pages 89, 90.

mons, and on "Pastoral Work," that are used in preacher classes in Methodist, Presbyterian and other theological seminaries, are today used in "Christian Colleges." Are the "Christian Colleges" Theological seminaries? Who can deny it? The remedy is a full and complete separation of the church and the college. It is, for the church to do its own work, and to use all its resources in accomplishing its own great objectives, unhampered and unhindered by an intrusion of the colleges. It is for the colleges to be colleges, secular literary institutions, with no connection whatsoever with the church. Of course Christians, "faithful men," who shall be able to teach others also, in the college business should teach the Bible to their students, just as Christians in other businesses should teach the Bible to all whom they contact. But the schools they start and operate must be purely secular, literary schools, not church schools, or theological seminaries.

The intense and continual discussion of the "Christian College" shows its immense importance. The cause of the discussion is that the colleges are exerting an almost overwhelming influence over the churches, and that they have well-nigh changed the whole face of things in the churches, from what it was when they were endeavoring to practice the simplicity of the apostolic order of things.

A few years ago no church had "the minister" or the ministerial order of things in either its worship or work. Today most of the churches are impotent and helpless without "the minister." All discussion does good. Investigation, examination, discussion never hurts any thing except falsehood. May we all realize the superlative importance of teaching and practicing the things for which the apostles gave the precept or set the example."*

In the early days of the church of the Lord we do not find the located preacher. The evangelists of the New Testament planted a congregation in a locality and remained long enough to develop elders, and then moved on to other places to proclaim the gospel to those who had not heard the message of salvation.

"Must we not say of preachers who from year to year seek and serve the churches paying the highest salary that they have sold themselves to the highest bidder? Is it not a travesty upon the high vocation to which they have been called that they allow themselves to love money and the things that money can buy so much that they will do this? Have they not become such as Paul spoke of when he said, 'Such serve not our Lord Jesus Christ, but their own belly.'

Professionalism has developed among 'us preachers' to an alarming degree. Churches have encouraged this until today we are on the verge of, if not already engulfed in, the denominational arrangement of clergy and laity. Our service to the Lord has become a matter of so much pay, so much work, and no pay, no work. Many are glad to preach when they can make more money at this than something else, and glad to work at something else when it pays them more than preaching. May God deliver us from the day of 'professionalism,' and may men and women once more seek to serve God because of the love they have for him."†

---

* *Apostolic Times*, April, 1953, Page 89.
† *Gospel Broadcast*, September 6, 1945.

Brethren have admitted that this second apostasy has led the church far from the apostolic pattern. They have warned against the tendency to compromise, of the danger of depending upon "the minister," of allowing him to take over the work of the elders, and supplant them in the work that God ordained for elders to do.

"Most of us preach where the eldership is weak or unqualified and the burden of the work is forced upon us gradually or was done by our predecessor and expected of us also. Members are thinking in terms of the 'pastor.' They will pass by an opportunity to relieve the needy or to break to them the bread of life, to tell the preacher he ought to see about such cases. This strengthens the 'pastor' idea in the minds of the brethren. No small wonder that young preachers going out to minister to the congregations in the proclamation of the word think they are going to 'take charge of a church.' What is the difference in our practice and the theory and practice of the denominations?

In New Testament times the elders had 'charge of a church.' At least one elder 'labored in word and doctrine' and was paid for his work because he gave all his time to it. The church grew tremendously. It is time we began seriously to do something about such a sad state of affairs. The preachers are to blame and the churches are to blame; the preacher because he has not taught the congregation the truth on the eldership question, and the church because it has not searched the scriptures to really find out God's plan in the matter.

I believe in 'pastors,' but in pastors of the New Testament pattern. Elders can be developed and begin work in a congregation and function as such through a life-time of usefulness better than the church can announce that they are ready 'to try out preachers.' Which reminds me that the present practice of choosing preachers among us is a disgrace to the cause of Christ in many congregations—too many.

When we begin to practice the Lord's plan of elders 'feeding the flock,' we will take on a new period of growth. The elders will have 'charge of a church,' and the evangelist will be loosed from the 'pastoral duties' to preach the gospel and establish churches where the word has not been preached."*

C. E. Dorris called attention to the fact, that

"In 1873 there was but one church in middle Tennessee that had preaching every Lord's day. For this reason the preachers in Kentucky, who were acquainted with the pastor system, and accustomed to a professional preacher and sermon every Sunday, thought that the condition of the cause in this territory was deplorable, and considered it a great blight upon the churches in this section.

The intelligent, active, live church is that which can conduct its own worship without the aid of a preacher. The church that needs a preacher to keep it alive, whose members can not find interest and spiritual nourishment in the study of the word of God and the simple worship ordained by Him, but must have an eloquent speaker

---

* *Bible Banner*—May, 1940, Page 15.

to tickle their ears every Sunday, and to do their study for them, to worship for them, is a very weak and helpless church. Others added to such a congregation only increase its weakness, just as extra flesh added to a weak, lubberly infant but increases its helplessness.

The true aim of every church should be to become self-sustaining in every department and support the preacher well in the mission field. Every true church ought to, and will educate and train its own members to do all the service of the Lord's house. It can do this only by exercising them, throwing responsibility upon them and training them to do the service needed. Only that church is strong which is able to conduct all the worship and do all the work of the church within itself.

That church is doing well in our estimation, we will say, according to the Bible standard, that is able to live without the preacher, that is able to edify itself, encourage, and exhort one another, do all of the worship of the Lord's house and the work of the church in the world without the help of the preacher. It is only the weak, helpless church that needs, as a babe, a constant nurse.

No church is firmly established until it has a number of its own true, faithful, self trained members, intelligent in the scriptures, who can conduct the worship and do all the work of the Lord of every description in its own community."

J. C. Reed offers as a remedy for

"this apostasy in which we are entangled, BACK TO THE BIBLE. First, let congregational autonomy be fully restored. Cleanse the temple so to speak (I mean take the profit out of religion). Take everything out of the budget of the local church except what the church actually controls (except emergency gifts to benevolent work under some other local congregation, or to an evangelist in a new field). While we are getting back to the Bible, we might take out the budget, too, and give as we have been prospered rather than how we think we will be prospered. Put the whole church to work in telling others as they go everywhere. Be sure that we can find a thus saith the Lord for everything that we preach, teach or practice. Be willing to grow and change as we come to fuller knowledge of the truth. Let us be ready to admit mistakes and correct them. . . ."

The time has come for those who have followed after the doctrines and commandments of men to call a halt, to make a change and get back to the word of God.

"It is a high crime and misdemeanor in any man, professing to have received the Messiah in his proper person, character, and office, to refuse allegiance to him in any thing; and to substitute human inventions and traditions, in lieu of the ordinances and statutes of Prince Immanuel. Indeed, the keeping up of any dogma, practice, or custom, which directly or indirectly supplants the constitution, laws, and usages of the kingdom over which Jesus presides, is directly opposed to his government; and would ultimate in dethroning him in favor of a rival, and in placing upon his throne the author of that dogma, practice, or usage, which supplants the institution of the Savior of the world."

Christianity Restored—Alexander Campbell

CHAPTER 30

THE CHURCH OF THE LORD

The first congregation of the Lord was established in Jerusalem in 33 A.D. In giving this date for the beginning of the church, attention is called to the Scriptures which show the church could not have been established prior to the death of Christ. In the gospel record of Matthew, we are told that Jesus questioned his disciples about the belief of men concerning him. "And they said, Some say that thou art John the Baptist, some Elias; and others, Jeremias, or one of the prophets. He saith unto them, But whom say ye that I am? And Simon Peter answered and said, Thou art the Christ, the Son of the living God. And Jesus answered and said unto him, Blessed art thou, Simon Bar-jona: for flesh and blood hath not revealed it unto thee, but my Father which is in heaven. And I say also unto thee that thou art Peter, and upon this rock I will build my church and the gates of hell shall not prevail against it."[1]

This proves the church had not been established up to that time. In Mark's gospel record we are told that Jesus said these words, "Verily I say unto you, that there be some of them that stand here which shall not taste of death, till they have seen the kingdom of God come with power."[2]

After the crucifixion of Christ and his resurrection he continued with them for forty days, teaching them the things that concerned the kingdom of God. Before he ascended to heaven, he said unto his disciples, "Thus it is written, and thus it behooved Christ to suffer, and to rise from the dead the third day: and that repentance and remission of sins should be preached in his name among all nations, beginning at Jerusalem. And ye are witnesses of these things. And behold I send the promise of my Father upon you: but tarry ye in the city of Jerusalem, until ye be endued with power from on high."[3] The same writer tells us in the book of Acts of Apostles that Christ said, "Ye shall receive power after that the Holy Ghost is come upon you, and ye shall be witnesses unto me both in Jerusalem and in all Judea, and in Samaria, and unto the uttermost parts of the earth."[4]

---

1. Matt. 16 : 14-18.
2. Mark 9 : 1.
3. Luke 24 : 46-49.
4. Acts 1 : 8.

In obedience to his divine command, the apostles waited in the city of Jerusalem for the coming of the Holy Ghost, which came upon the day of Pentecost. Being thus qualified the apostle Peter preached the first gospel sermon, declaring to the assembled multitude the death, the burial, and the resurrection of Christ, and those who heard were convicted of their sin and cried out, "Men and brethren what shall we do? Then Peter said unto them, Repent and be baptized every one of you in the name of Jesus Christ for the remission of your sins and ye shall receive the gift of the Holy Ghost."[5] The concluding verse of that chapter tells us, "And the Lord added to the church daily such as should be saved." From this time on the church of the Lord is in existence.

Jesus told the apostles to preach the gospel to all nations. Wherever the gospel was preached and people obeyed its divine commands they constituted the church of Christ in that community. By the work of the disciples and the evangelists, the church was thus planted in all parts of the Roman Empire.

The church in the city of Jerusalem continued is the apostles' doctrine and fellowship, and in breaking of bread, and in prayers.

Here is a picture of the worship of the church of the Lord. That worship centered about the Lord's Supper. There was no mystical consecration of the bread, but the simple fact of each partaking of the bread which typified his body and of the fruit of the vine which was typical of his shed blood.

The members of the body of Christ supported the work of the church, the care of the distressed, and the preaching of the gospel by giving "not grudgingly or of necessity," but as they were prospered.

The prayers of the church were from the heart. They had no liturgy or ritual to follow. In the worship of the church, the use of songs is as old as the instruction of the apostles, but the use of mechanical music is not. "Let the word of Christ dwell in you richly, in all wisdom, teaching and admonishing one another in psalms, hymns, and spiritual songs, singing with grace in your hearts to the Lord."[6] This was addressed to the Church at Colosse, to the faithful in Christ Jesus.

As ability permitted and opportunity afforded, the members had a part in the teaching and the exhortations. The congregation in each community, with its elders and deacons guided by the apostles' doctrine, conducted its own worship and teaching, without the aid of a one man ministry.

There were no official boards, missionary organizations, synods

---

5. Acts 2 : 38.
6. Col. 3 : 16.

or any other form of ecclesiastical government, created by un-inspired men to make creeds, rules or laws by which the church was to be controlled. This was the household of faith, the building of God, the church of Christ. All subsequent congregations followed this divine pattern for wherever the gospel was proclaimed and obeyed it produced Christians and when these were banded to-gether, they constituted the church in that community. Thus in any place where the gospel is preached, the church is produced.

When Philip preached the gospel in Samaria and the church was planted there it was not Philip's church, but the Lord's church.

When Paul preached the gospel in Corinth and people obeyed the gospel, the church was established, but it was not Paul's church, but the Lord's. When Peter preached the gospel at Caesarea, the household of Cornelius constituted the beginning of the church of the Lord. So when the gospel was preached in its purity, no matter how far removed from Jerusalem in point of time or miles, it always produced the Lord's church, and not a human institution.

Jesus Christ is the head of the church, the chief cornerstone, with the apostles and the prophets constituting the foundation. "Now therefore ye are no more strangers and foreigners, but fellow-citizens with the saints, and of the household of God; and are built upon the foundation of the apostles and prophets, Jesus Christ him-self being the chief corner stone."[7] Just as Christ is the head of the church for all time, so is it also true that the apostles and prophets constitute the foundation for all time. They had no suc-cessors. From the Scriptures, they speak to us today with the same authority they exercised when here upon the earth. The elders or bishops, as they were sometimes called, looked after the spiritual welfare of each local congregation. There was always a plurality of the elders, but they had no jurisdiction over other congregations, nor was one elder exalted above his fellow elders. The deacons of each congregation were entrusted to look after the temporal affairs of the church and to care for those who were in distress.

The evangelists were heralds to proclaim the gospel of Christ to the world. Those who obeyed the gospel were to be fed the sincere milk of the word and taught the principles of Christian living. "And the things that thou hast heard of me among many witnesses, the same commit thou to faithful men who shall be able to teach others also."[8]

A part of the work of an evangelist was setting in order things that were wanting, teaching young converts and developing men so they might be able to take the oversight of the congregation. The

7. Eph. 2 : 19-20.
8. 2 Tim. 2 : 2.

care of the churches, until an eldership was developed, rested upon the evangelist. They labored to develop elders within the congregation, to teach them how to feed the flock, so that they might be able to carry on the work of the church without the aid of an evangelist. The New Testament churches were not dependent upon "the minister" for all were ministers to edify the body. "From whom the whole body fitly joined together and compacted by that which every joint supplieth, according to the effectual working in the measure of every part, maketh increase of the body unto the edifying of itself in love."[9]

Those who entered the church did so by obeying the gospel of Christ, by believing that he was the Son of God, by repenting of their sins, confessing their faith in Christ as God's Son, and being buried with their Lord in baptism.

They then wore the name Christian, signifying that they were followers of Christ.

Thus the church existed in the apostolic age. After the death of the apostles, men began to seek for a position of preeminence in the church and a distinction began to be made among the elders of the churches, which resulted in one elder being selected as a bishop over his fellow elders.

Doctrines were developed which were contrary to the scriptures and these developed an apostate church which competed with and opposed the faithful church.

With the growth and development of this apostate church the church of the Lord was carried away into the wilderness, which simply means that she went under cover, where she remained for twelve hundred sixty years. As this period of time drew to a close, preachers in various denominations became concerned with the difference between the churches with which they were identified and the Bible. The efforts of Luther, Calvin, Zwingli, Knox, and others did not bring about a return to the New Testament. As these facts began to be recognized, men began to plead for a return to the word of God. Among those who saw the necessity of renouncing creeds and returning to the Scriptures for authority in religious affairs were Robert and James Haldane in Scotland, and Robert Sandeman in England. In America, James O'Kelly who had been a preacher of the Methodist Church, contended for the right of congregational government in the church. Abner Jones of the Baptist Church called upon his people to reject the Philadelphia Confession of Faith and return to the Bible. In Kentucky, Barton W. Stone and Robert Marshall began to preach salvation by obedience to the word of

---

9. Eph. 4 : 16.

God. Soon they were aided in their work by Thomas Campbell, his son Alexander Campbell, and Walter Scott.

None of these men were prophets of God, nor were they the founders of the church of Christ, neither did they make laws for the church. Their only work was to proclaim the same gospel that the apostles proclaimed, to teach the same commands that Christ taught, and to wear the same name that the disciples of Christ wore, in the first century.

The church of the Lord today, teaches the same truths that were taught by the apostles, obeys the same commands, and worships God in the same way in which he was worshipped by the Christians in the first century.

For this reason the churches of Christ have no robed choirs, no instrumental music, no formal prayers, no ritualistic worship, and no titled pastors. There was no provision in the simplicity of Christ's church for these things in the beginning, neither are they needed today. It was God's divine plan to leave them out, and we have no authority to put them in the services of the church today.

"Dare any one say, or even think it unphilanthropic or malevolent, to make an effort to rally the broken phalanxes of Zion's King, and to attempt to induce them to turn their arms from one another, against the common foe? With such a one, it were worse than hopeless to reason, or to exchange a single argument. Shall we not rather esteem it to be the most honorable, acceptable and praise-worthy enterprise, that can be dared or undertaken by mortal men on this earthly stage of action? And as God has ever effected the most splendid revolutions by the most humble agents, and by means the most unlikely in the wisdom of human schools; we think it not amiss or incongruous to make an effort, and to put our hands to the work of peace and love."

Christianity Restored—Alexander Campbell

CHAPTER 31

THE PLEA OF THE CHURCHES OF CHRIST TODAY

From the beginning of the Restoration the plea for unity among those who professed to be the people of God was strongly emphasized in the teaching of Stone, Scott, and the Campbells. They preached boldly against the apostasy and the narrowness of the denominations of that time. Their plea was for the people who were held in the bonds of denominationalism, to break away from the doctrines and commandments of men, and come to the teaching of God's word. They did not propose to establish a basis for unity, but to present to all men the basis of unity revealed in the word of God.

They called attention to the fact that in the church of the Lord there were no presbyteries, no conferences, nor assemblies, to legislate for the church. Neither were the people of the Lord controlled by creeds, confessions of faith, church manuals, or prayer books. This prompted them to announce that all human guides would be rejected and that "where the Bible speaks, we will speak and where it is silent, we will be silent." The unity for which they were pleading was not attained by one step. Those who first heard the plea of James O'Kelly to return to God's word, stood aloof from those who accepted the teaching of Barton W. Stone that it was necessary to surrender the Westminster Confession of Faith, and accept only what was taught in the New Testament.

When the Campbells and Scott learned of the preaching of James O'Kelly, Dr. Abner Jones, and Barton W. Stone, they found they were all pleading for the acceptance of the word of God as an all sufficient guide in spiritual affairs. They saw the necessity of their efforts being blended together. They offered no human plan by which the unity of the spirit could be brought about, but appealed to all men to reject all principles that were contrary to the word of God, to renounce the findings of all ecclesiastical councils, and to accept the simple gospel of Christ and thus be added to the one body of Christ.

This remains today the plea of the church of the Lord.

All people should realize that the commands of Jesus Christ are the commands of God. Those commands are revealed in the gospel of Christ. A careful study of the preaching of the gospel as recorded in the book of Acts of Apostles shows that when men heard it, they believed the message that Christ was the Son of God, they repented of their sins, turned from their evil ways, confessed their faith in Christ as God's Son, and were buried in the waters of baptism for the remission of their sins.

The first thing produced by preaching is faith. "Then Philip went down to the city of Samaria and preached Christ unto them. . . . But when they believed Philip preaching the things concerning the kingdom of God, and the name of Jesus Christ, they were baptized, both men and women."[1] Faith is defined in God's word as "the substance of things hoped for, the evidence of things not seen." It is produced by the word of God. "And many other signs truly did Jesus in the presence of his disciples, which are not written in this book: But these are written, that ye might believe that Jesus is the Christ, the Son of God; and that believing ye might have life through his name." It is universally agreed that faith is necessary for salvation. We read that "without faith it is impossible to please God," and since it is essential in pleasing God, then everyone should want to know how to obtain it that they might please him.

You do not have to wade through some philosophical discussion before you can understand faith and how it is obtained. Paul informs us, "So then faith cometh by hearing, and hearing by the word of God."

This establishes the fact that faith is the belief of testimony, the acceptance of what has been said in the word of God. The faith that saves is produced by testimony. What kind of testimony? That which comes from God's word. It directs and commands, and our faith is shown by our obedience.

One may believe that Christ was divine, but that is not enough. Nobody believes in the divinity of Christ more than the demons.

You may believe that you are away from God, that Christ is the way of life, that he warns you of a hell, and offers you heaven, but it will not save your soul if you do NOTHING about it. The popular doctrine that you can just say, "Lord, Lord," and that Christ will save your soul is not based on God's word. The Savior said, "Not every one that saith unto me, Lord, Lord, shall enter into the kingdom of heaven; but he that doeth the will of my Father which is in heaven."

The commands that Christ gave to us must be obeyed, for, "Blessed are they that do his commandments, that they may have right to the tree of life, and may enter in through the gates into

---

1. Acts 8: 5, 12.

the city." It takes obedience to all of the commands of Christ to obtain that eternal life.

In the great commission, as recorded by Mark, Christ said, "Go into all the world and preach the gospel; he that believeth and is baptized shall be saved; but he that believeth not shall be damned." Luke records that Christ said, "Thus it is written, and thus it behooved Christ to suffer and to rise from the dead the third day: And that repentance and remission of sins should be preached in his name among all nations, beginning at Jerusalem." In Matthew's record of the command of the Savior to spread the gospel among all nations, we find it stated in these words: "Go ye therefore, and teach all nations, baptizing them in the name of the Father, and of the Son, and of the Holy Spirit." What is set forth in these commands? That people are to hear the gospel, to believe it, to repent and be baptized, and that obedience to these commands brings remission of sins.

On the day of Penecost the apostles clearly demonstrated that they knew what Christ meant. The preaching began at Jerusalem. Here Peter informed those who came together that they had murdered the Lord of glory. "Therefore let all the house of Israel know that this same Jesus whom ye have crucified is both Lord and Christ." Did they deny it or did they believe it? Certainly, they believed it; but that belief did not save, for we read, "with many other words did he exhort them, saying, Save yourselves from this untoward generation." Believing the preaching of the apostle Peter, they cried out, "Men and brethren, what shall we do? Then Peter said unto them, Repent and be baptized every one of you in the name of Jesus Christ for the remission of sins·and ye shall receive the gift of the Holy Ghost." Repentance is a turning from sin, brought about by godly sorrow, leading to reformation of life. Some people have suggested that repentance must precede faith, but this cannot be, for faith is that which leads to repentance. The goodness of God is revealed in the gospel, that God sent Christ to die for our sins. Paul tells us, "The goodness of God leadeth thee to repentance." The Apostle Peter said, "The Lord is not slack concerning his promise, as some men count slackness; but is longsuffering to us-ward, not willing that any should perish, but that all should come to repentance."

The faith, or the belief that Christ is the Son of God, must be strong enough to cause one to accept him as the author of eternal salvation, and to so acknowledge him before men. To confess Christ before men shows that one purposes to surrender the old life and henceforth to live for Jesus.

Obedience to Christ is an orderly process and confession is one of the steps of that divine plan.

Jesus said, "Whosoever therefore shall confess me before men, him will I confess also before my Father which is in heaven." Paul, in the epistle to the church in Rome, said, "With the heart man believeth unto righteousness and with the mouth confession is made unto salvation."

Obedience to these commands puts us in condition to be baptized into Christ. The importance of this command is often ridiculed by those who forget that the Savior said, "He that believeth and is baptized shall be saved." Many are placing their hope for salvation upon their belief in Christ as the Son of God, calling attention to the fact that "God so loved the world, that he gave his only begotten Son, that whosoever believeth in him should not perish, but have everlasting life." Others affirm, "The Bible says, 'Believe on the Lord Jesus Christ and thou shalt be saved,'—and there is nothing there about baptism." True, but the same Book tells us in another place; "Repent and be baptized," and there is nothing there about believing. This shows that we must take all of the teaching in the scriptures upon any subject to get the complete will of God. Baptism is the step by which we get into Christ. During the early days of the church there was no question about the purpose of baptism, or how it was performed, or the element necessary for the administration of the ordinance.

Paul shows the purpose of baptism by saying, "For as many of you as have been baptized into Christ have put on Christ." The same apostle shows that baptism is a burial, for in writing to the church at Colosse he said, "Buried with him in baptism, wherein also ye are risen with him through the faith of the operation of God, who hath raised him from the dead."

Baptism was performed in water—not with water. Today the religious world practices sprinkling, pouring, and immersion, and calls all of these acts baptism. In writing to the church at Ephesus, Paul said, "There is one Lord, one faith, one baptism." If there is only one baptism then only one of the above ways can be right. Jesus used the word "baptizo" when he referred to the command which he bound upon the human family.

This word was not translated by the translators of the King James Version of the Scriptures but was Anglicized by dropping the letter "o" and adding the letter "e", for at that time sprinkling was still the practice in the Church of England, having been carried over from the Roman Catholic Church, which bound it upon the religious world, by the finding of the Council of Ravenna. Christ alone had the right to command what was necessary to bring one into relationship with Him. This right was not transferred to any man or any group of men. When we substitute commands that have been made by men for those given by Christ, we dishonor the Son of God. Here is the thing that produces division. The world is divided, not over what God or Christ has commanded, but over what men say will do just as well. All Bible scholars, familiar with the Greek language, readily admit that the original form of baptism was immersion. Every person who has studied the Greek language knows that the word used by the Savior and the apostles meant to dip or to immerse. It is so defined in Greek lexicons. All that is claimed by religious teachers in substituting sprinkling or pouring for immersion is that these will do just as well. They thus admit that they are substitutes for what Christ commanded and for what the apostles taught and practiced.

The churches of the Lord go back beyond the decrees of men and the legislation of church councils to the teaching of the New Testament for their practice on baptism.

Here is safe ground. Here is the ground upon which all religious people could come together and stand united.

We plead for the privilege of restoring to mankind the gospel of Christ, which, when obeyed, adds one to the church of the Lord. As members of the family of God they then wear a new name, a name that was given by divine approval. The prophet Isaiah said that God would give his people "a new name which the mouth of the Lord shall name." He also stated that he would give to those within his house a name that was better than of sons and daughters. "Even unto them will I give in mine house and within my walls a place and a name better than of sons and daughters: I will give them an everlasting name, that shall not be cut off."[2]

This name was "Christian," for we read, "The disciples were called Christians first at Antioch." This was a new name, given by the mouth of the Lord, given to those within God's house, which is the church.

Peter said, "If any man suffer as a Christian"—not if any man suffer as a Methodist, as a Presbyterian, as a Lutheran, as a Baptist—but as a Christian, "let him not be ashamed; but let him glorify God on this behalf." The church of the Lord pleads for people to obey the gospel of Christ, then the Lord will add you to his body and you can then wear His name. In the apostolic age there was only one church in a city, not a multiplicity of religious organizations, with contradictory doctrines, all claiming to be a part of the body of Christ. The denominational bodies did not exist in the days of the apostles of the Lord. They have been pro-

2. Isaiah 56 : 5.

duced by human doctrines, and are responsible for the discord and strife that exists among people who ought to be one.

The churches of men, wearing human names, names that describe some particular doctrine, some form of church government, some principle for which they stand, compete with the church established by our Lord, through the apostles.

Men had no more right to produce these churches than they have to write another Bible. Many people do not know that the denominations developed from the church of Rome, which came into being as the result of apostasy, departing from the word of God. Many people do not know there was just one church established by Christ. They have not considered the importance of measuring the church with which they are identified with the word of God.

Complete obedience to the word of God will bring unity. It is the safe rule of faith and practice. It is the only creed that never needs to be revised.

When the gospel was restored to mankind, the religious world was subject to human creeds. All of them are the product of human wisdom. Not only do they contradict the Bible but they also contradict each other. They believe that it is necessary to form a creed, which is a statement of their convictions upon doctrinal subjects.

Creeds create and perpetuate division among religious people. The church of the Lord did not need them in the beginning, neither does it need them now.

We plead with all religious people to surrender their creeds because they are unscriptural.

They exist without divine authority and cause people to look to them for guidance, rather than to God's word. Peter admonished the Lord's people to speak as God's word speaks, and Paul clearly indicated that all spiritual needs are fully supplied in the inspired Scriptures. "If any man speak, let him speak as the oracles of God; if any man minister let him do it as of the ability which God giveth: . . ."[3] "All scripture is given by inspiration of God, and is profitable for doctrine, for reproof, for correction, for instruction in righteousness: that the man of God may be perfect, throughly furnished unto all good works."[4]

Creeds can never become the basis of the unity which is taught in God's word, because they exclude all who will not subscribe to their dogmas.

The argument is sometimes made that creeds only interpret the Bible for us, but the interpretations men have placed upon the Bible in their creeds are not correct, else there would not be such a wide

3. 1 Peter 4:11.
4. 2 Timothy 3:16, 17.

difference in their conclusions. The church of the Lord pleads for all people to surrender their creeds and take their stand upon the word of God alone. The church of the Lord was sometimes referred to as the church of God, and sometimes it was called the temple of God.

When Paul addressed his letter to the church in the city of Rome he spoke of the congregations he had visited as "churches of Christ." While this name was not given as an official name, it does show the ownership of the church, and the term by which it can be identified.

Never was the name of an apostle called upon the church, never was a religious practice used as a name for the church, never was a New Testament ordinance used to designate the church established by Christ. The scriptures do not justify such a practice. What accounts for such practices? The only answer that can be given is that someone has left the word of God. The churches of the Lord plead with all people to reject all teachings and practices in religious matters for which they can find no authority in the word of God.

The unity for which the churches of Christ plead prevailed in the churches planted by the apostles. All believed the gospel of Christ, obeyed the same commands, and worshipped in the same way. Their only creed was the apostles' doctrine, which proclaimed Jesus Christ and Him crucified. On the first day of the week they came together to observe the Lord's Supper, to worship God, to exhort each other to faithfulness, to give of their means for the support of the needy, and the spread of the gospel.

Each congregation was a complete unit with its elders to teach, admonish, and rule. There were no synods, conferences or councils over the church, through which uninspired men legislated for the church. The New Testament reveals the pattern of the church, its worship, and its unity for us today. The churches of Christ plead for unity among those who want to serve the Lord. The absurdity of partyism and division is fully recognized by the religious world today. The so-called Protestant churches are searching for a foundation for unity. The churches of the Lord have the basis for unity for all people who want to serve the Lord.

That basis is the New Testament. The churches of the Lord have no new doctrines. They have no new creed or articles of faith. They have no desire to establish a new religion. They seek only to perpetuate the one church of the New Testament. They plead with all religious people to renounce everything which they hold as matters of faith and practice which originated with men, and to come back to the simple faith and worship of the church of the New Testament.

Upon its teachings all people can unite. For this we plead and for this we pray.

BIBLIOGRAPHY

History of The Christian Church—*Van De Water*
History of The Baptists—*Armitage*
History of The Christian Church—*Blackburn*
History of The Presbyterian Church—*Hays*
History of The Cumberland Presbyterian Church—*McDonnold*
History of The Church of Scotland—*Heatherington*
History of Methodism—*Stevens*
History of The Christian Church—*Fisher*
History of Christianity—*Abbott*
History of The American Episcopal Church—*McConnell*
History of The Church of Scotland—*Knox*
History of The Christian Church—*Moncrief*
History of The Crusades—*Proctor*
History of The Mass—*O'Brien*
History of The Catholic Church—*Noethen*
History of The Popes—*Ranke*
Analysis of Church History—*Pinnock*
Live Religious Issues—*Kendrick*
Life of Elder John Smith—*Williams*
Baptist Succession—*Ray*
The Israel of The Alps—*Mastun*
Ecclesiastical History of England—*Bede*
Churches and Sects—*Gorrie*
Handbook of all Denominations—*Phelan*
History of The Reformation—*Howitt*
Church History Handbook—*Vedder*
Church History of The Second and Third Centuries—*Jeremie*
Ten Epochs of Church History—*Vincent*
Era of The Protestant Reformation—*Seebohm*
English Church History—*Lane*
History of The Catholic Church—*Gustavus*
Landmarks of Church History—*Cowan*
The Dark Ages—*Graebner*
The Period of The Reformation—*Hausser*
History of The Friends in America—*Thomas*
John Wesley and His Doctrine—*McDonald*
History of The Christian Religion and Church—*Neander*
History of The Reformation—*D'Aubigné*
Life of B. W. Stone—*Ware*
Doctrine and Practice of Primitive Baptists—*Radcliff*
Church History of The First Three Centuries—*Baur*
Text-book of Church History—*Kurtz*

Ecclesiastical History—*Eusebius*
Ancient History—*Rollins*
Decline and Fall of The Roman Empire—*Gibbon*
Handbook of Ancient Rome—*Pennell*
History of All Religions—*Schmucker*
Facts about Luther—*O'Hare*
Beacon Lights of History—*Lord*
History of England—*Harding*
Genesis of New England Churches—*Bacon*
The Massacre of St. Bartholomew—*White*
History of England—*Goodrich*
The Episcopal Church in America—*Hodges*
The Reformation—*Lindsay*
Works of Elder B. W. Stone—*Mathes*
Ecclesiastical History—*Mosheim*
History of The Puritans—*Neal*
Institutes of The Christian Religion—*Calvin*
Manual of Universal Church History—*Alzog*
The Book of Books—*Evans*
Church History—*Cheetham*
The Renaissance and Reformation—*Hulme*
General History—*Myers*
Alexander Campbell—*Grafton*
Thomas Campbell—*Hanna*
History of The English Church—*Gairdner*
History of Methodism—*Daniels*
The Christian Baptist—*Campbell*
A Protestant Dictionary—*Ferm*
The Reformation of The Sixteenth Century—*Bainton*
History of The Waldenses—*Strong*
Life of Wicliffe—*Gilpin*
History of Reformatory Movements—*Rowe*
Universal History—*Parsons*
The English Reformation and Puritanism—*Hulbert*
Manual of Church History—*Newman*
The Early Days of Christianity—*Grant*
History of France—*Marriott*
The Story of The Church—*Jacobs*
Life of Luther—*Winkworth*
History For Ready Reference—*Larned*

INDEX

INDEX